LYLE'S ADMINISTRATION OF THE COLLEGE LIBRARY

fifth edition

by

Caroline M. Coughlin
and
Alice Gertzog

The Scarecrow Press, Inc.
Lanham, Md., & London

British Library Cataloguing-in-Publication data available

Library of Congress Cataloging-in-Publication Data

Coughlin, Caroline M.
         Lyle's administration of the college library / by Caroline
M. Coughlin and Alice Gertzog. -- 5th ed.
             p. cm.
         Rev. ed. of: The administration of the college library /
Guy R. Lyle. 4th ed. 1974.
         ISBN 0-8108-2552-X (acid-free paper)
            1. Libraries, University and college--Administration.
I. Gertzog, Alice. II. Lyle, Guy Redvers, 1907- Administration
of the college library. III. Title. IV. Title: Administration of the
college library.
         Z675.U5C767 1992
         027.7--dc20   92-6328

TO

Irwin Gertzog

Nora H. Weinberg

William M. Weinberg

TABLE OF CONTENTS

LIST OF FIGURES

PREFACE TO THE FIFTH EDITION

This is the fifth edition of *Lyle's Administration of the College Library*. The fourth edition appeared in 1974 and the first in 1944.

When Alphonse Karr wrote, in 1849 "the more things change, the more they are the same," he could hardly have envisioned the rapid rate of global movement, shift and development occurring almost daily in the last decade of the twentieth century. Yet his aphorism is no less true today than when he framed it, particularly as it applies to libraries. Librarians do what they have always done. They organize information.

Still, comparing this fifth edition with Lyle's first exploration into the world of college library administration almost a half a century ago, reveals how substantially library practices have changed in the intervening period. New technology, electronic publishing, systems approaches, planning techniques, network development, increased understanding of environmental, societal and political forces, and user behavior and information needs account for the major differences between the first edition and the fifth.

Lyle set out to write a simple, logical and self-contained introduction to "all aspects of library administration as they applied to college libraries." Our aim is the same. Lyle hoped that his book would be helpful to library school students and librarians new to their positions in academic libraries. We wish for no less. We have tried also to emulate Lyle's middle-ground approach to the subject—neither purely philosophical nor totally experiential; a broad view with a practical component. Lyle's success was legendary. Indeed, an informal survey we administered when writing this text revealed that many library school classes were still using the 1974 edition as a primary text—in 1990!

The authors are very grateful to Guy R. Lyle for his permission to produce a new edition. His remarkable accomplishment served as model, challenge and motivating force for us throughout the process of creating this work.

The structure of the current edition, while bearing a strong resemblance to Lyle's, now reflects an increased contextual and system framework. New chapters on Technology, the Library Director, a Campus Inventory, and Bibliographic Instruction have been added, and Lyle's chapters on The Educational Function and Encouraging the Reading Habit have been integrated into other parts of the book. When library practices are unchanged, Lyle's words still remain as he wrote them.

Bill Eshelman, Past President of Scarecrow Press, is partially responsible for this edition, first by agreeing to publish it, and second by lending support and encouragement. He shoulders no blame for its defects, which are ours entirely.

Permission to reprint the *Standards for College Libraries* was granted by the American Library Association.

In the preparation of chapters, the staff of the Drew University and Allegheny College Libraries lent invaluable support and assistance. Particular thanks are due to Jean Schoenthaler, Alice Copeland, Pam Snelson, Evelyn Meyer, Jan Wanggaard, Eleanor Rawitz, Stacy Mosesman, Bruce Lancaster and Josepha Cook of Drew University and Helen McCullough,

Cynthia Burton and Don Vrabel of Allegheny College. Valerie Weinberg and Barbara Kwasnik counseled us about the Cataloging chapter; Andrew Ford, Provost of Allegheny College, increased our understanding of factors to be considered in inventorying a college campus; Mary Jo Lynch served as a resource about college library statistics; Judy Weinberg translated sketches into usable graphics; The Oberlin Group of College Library Directors shared their experience with us in an informative questionnaire and in personal contacts. Tom Limoncelli, Dottie Friedman and Ellen Falduto assisted us with preparation of the manuscript. We are grateful to them all.

Will and Nora Weinberg and Irwin Gertzog, while patiently awaiting completion of the project, supplied support, meals, comfort and distraction. To them we dedicate this book with our sincerest thanks.

Chapter 1

CONTEXTS OF THE AMERICAN COLLEGE LIBRARY

College librarians, to quote the old Chinese curse, are certainly living in interesting times. They face a fluid and uncertain environment shaped primarily by technological advances and demographic changes as well as by diminished resources and new demands on their profession. Developments in software, equipment and materials occur at a dizzying pace. Keeping up is difficult.

Librarians are commanded to be aggressive, to assume a greater teaching role, to be collegial, to guard against producing a generation of information *have-nots*, to be more accountable, to manage with fewer dollars and to offer new services. At the same time, librarians are also expected to protect and purvey traditional humanistic values, to bear responsibility for preserving cultural artifacts, to create information-literate students, and champion reading as the essential skill of an educated person.

Some librarians contend that technology only provides new and speedier ways to do what libraries have always done. Others maintain that technology has so changed the nature of information that even the basic processes now differ. Both arguments have merit. People still ask questions. Librarians still help them to find answers. But new words have entered the vocabulary. For instance, we are as likely to talk about "access" as we are about "acquisition." The traditional description of roles played by a library—to acquire, organize and disseminate information—now require far broader definitions of acquisition and dissemination than once characterized the concepts. Moreover, new responsibilities have been promoted by technology. The emergence of the wired campus, which enables students as well as faculty to interface directly with the library, without a human mediator, mandates that librarians must find ways to intervene in the information process. They must teach their constituencies about the nature, use and evaluation of information. It is no longer sufficient to introduce students to the library as part of a first-year orientation program. The task, rather, is to make users information-literate, no matter how or where they gain access to it.

William Moffett considers a college to be a mostly undergraduate institution with less than 4,000 students and with libraries containing no more than one million volumes.[1] That definition describes most of the libraries for which the information contained in this volume will be useful, however distinctions applied on the basis of size of student population are of lesser importance. Though college libraries share the umbrella term "academic" with those in universities, they exhibit as many differences from university libraries as they do similarities. For instance, college libraries are often seen as the last refuge of "generalists" while university libraries provide comfortable environments for "specialists." College librarians like to consider themselves Renaissance people; those in universities strive for depth and disciplinary comprehensiveness.

Colleges focus on teaching first and place research second. Nonetheless they differ in their missions. Some are oriented toward the liberal arts, others toward vocational training. Some boast that their curriculum contains no courses of "practice"; others brag that their curriculum prepares students for a job. Neither assertion accurately describes any college. All courses can be placed on a continuum as more or less practical in orientation. College libraries, too, can be seen as existing on a continuum with collections ranging from extensive and deep in elite, private liberal arts institutions to minimal, albeit occasionally excellent collections in newer schools, or ones with less money, or ones where the stress is less on library usage and more on text learning. No matter the nature of the institution or the library, its fundamental activities and concerns remain similar. Methods may differ in particular libraries but the major functions are basically alike and successful techniques do not vary greatly from one library to another.

ENVIRONMENTS

The purpose of this book is to describe the work involved in administering a college library. All college libraries are products of and are influenced by

—— factors external to the campus
—— the social structure of the college
—— the internal configuration of the library
—— the nature of the relationships between these elements and how they interact.

Successful administration of a contemporary college library requires, therefore, an understanding not only of how to run the library, but of the larger context in which the library functions. Academic library service, its provision and use, occurs in, is affected by, and affects what happens in its immediate and greater environment.

Prior to the 1970s, academic librarians assumed that their libraries occupied a relatively stable place in their relatively stable institutions in a slowly changing library world. Accordingly, they concentrated most of their efforts on improving the efficiency of internal functions and tended to ignore how forces outside their institutions affected them. They were also inclined to downplay the importance of campus political and social relationships. The 1980s produced a sea change in attitudes toward knowledge and information, and in the delivery of library services. These changes, coupled with the accelerated pace of social ferment, technological development and the application of systems theories to social organizations, ended forever any notion that libraries were independent of their environments. The myth of the self-sufficient college library had been shattered.

Five environments can be considered to surround a college library. Figure 1 represents the way in which a college library is embedded within them.

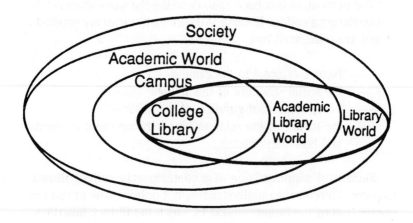

Figure 1
Contexts of a College Library

Each of these environments is described below, and is accompanied by an example that illustrates how one event or occurrence may produce a ripple effect and the way in which influence may be exerted or experienced. They are:

The *Society* which encompasses social, economic, political and cultural trends. Among these may be public attitudes towards education and society's assessments of the importance of information.

The baby boomlet of 1984 will affect the number and quality of students who will attend college in 2002, and this, in turn, will have an impact on the demand for library services.

The *Academic World* which includes, among other elements, the current state of knowledge, research agendas, faculty supply and demand, curriculum priorities, pedagogical and governance trends, and financial support.

The curriculum reform movement of the late 1980s has major importance for collection development decisions.

The *Library World*, which is comprised of the sectors of practice, scholarship, and those agencies which serve the profession, as, for instance, the library associations and the organs of communication, the library periodicals.

The degree to which the profession is currently successful in promoting librarianship as a challenging and rewarding career will influence a college library's ability to recruit a capable staff in the immediate future.

The *Academic Library World*, which includes methods and practices, both new and traditional, for the provision of efficient and effective college and university library service.

The development of bibliographic instruction methods which utilize a problem solving/decision-making approach will change the manner in which College Library X introduces students to in-house library research.

The *College Community*, the most direct context in which a library operates, includes the faculty, students and administration. It has a social structure produced by, among other factors, its history, traditions, geography, cultural climate, resources, size, and academic quality and orientation.

Lack of success in recruiting a sufficient number of tuition-paying students by the administration of College X may result in reduced resources being made available to the library.

SYSTEMS THEORY

Daily, librarians, and indeed college faculty and administrators concerned with the library, are faced with myriad questions about the extent to which the library is meeting its purpose or potential. Mere facts do not supply answers. Knowing, for instance, that more than 50% of all college students use the library only 4 hours or less a week says little about whether that is an adequate or insufficient amount.[2] Studying the issue in context may help. In recent years, systems theory has been widely applied to help describe and explain the workings of libraries. This approach is useful because it assumes that the elements and structures of the institution should be thought of as parts of a whole and as they affect one another rather as distinct entities to be examined separately. Some generalizations about systems theory follow:

1. Systems are composed of interrelated parts and elements;

2. They are not merely the sum of parts, but a totality and should be viewed holistically;

3. Systems are relatively *open* or *closed* based on the extent to which they exchange information, energy, or material with their environments;

4. They are more or less bounded and separated from their environments;

5. Systems are characterized by *inputs* and *throughputs* as well as by *outputs* which in turn provide feedback and appear as future *inputs*;

6. They are comprised of subsystems and are part of suprasystems;

7. Systems generally achieve something. In other words, they are organized for a particular purpose.[3]

Libraries are relatively *open* systems that depend on their environment for inputs and for feedback. They both draw from and contribute to their environments in order to meet social expectations. A system model (Figure 2), based on one devised by Joanne Euster,[4] utilizes a two environment approach to describe the dynamics of an academic library.

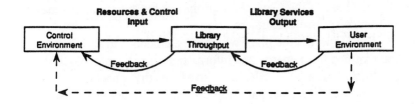

Figure 2
Campus Environments: A Systems Model

The *Control* environment provides the input—the resources and controls on which the library depends for survival—and evaluates the goals, methods and outputs. Inputs are generally considered to be money, services, personnel and information.

Among the controls are the degree of autonomy granted the library. This includes its ability to define or alter its mission, goals, and scope of activities, and its freedom to devise methods to meet its goals and conduct its program.

The *User* environment refers to all segments of the college community which receive the services of the library—the outputs—including students, faculty, administration and those in the wider library community and in the local geographic community who are served by the college library. Outputs may be considered in terms of measurable activities and operations, including circulation, in-house library use, assistance in the use of the library and answers to reference questions. Alternately, outputs may refer to changes in library patrons as a result of library use.[5]

Feedback in this model is delivered directly to the Library from its User Environment and from the Library to its Control Environment. Feedback from the User Environment flows weakly to the Control Environment. User and Control Environments in an academic community share personnel who play different roles in each setting. Administrators, for instance, are members of the Control Environment but function, at times, as library service consumers.

The *Library* is the place where the elements and activities are transformed from energy and information (inputs) into exportable products (outputs). Elements used in the process are the collection and its surrogate, the catalog. The activities usually involved in the conversion are:

Technical Processes—acquisitions, cataloging, classification and collection maintenance

Public Services—circulation, reference services, readers advisory services

Administration—planning, organizing, motivating and controlling.[6]

Figure 3 illustrates the internal process of converting energy and information (inputs) into usable library products (outputs).

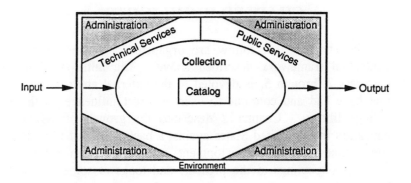

Figure 3
The Library System

Of these activities, some are more boundary-spanning, that is, they are located closer to the system's borders than others. Cataloging, for instance, has traditionally been relatively remote from the library's clientele, although it has open boundaries with book dealers, jobbers, and bibliographic networks, among others in the library world. Public services, on the other hand, directly mediate with library users, and library administrators continually confer and negotiate with the control environment. Technological developments have resulted in the need for far greater numbers of public service librarians, people who must deal directly with members of their campus environments, and for many fewer catalogers.

Libraries, like other organizations, react to the environment in two ways. First, they adapt the library to it. Second, they change the environment so that internal adaptation becomes unnecessary. A library wishing to enhance its input, for instance, must change the value of its output either through improved internal processes or through manipulation of the environment's perception of its value.

CHAPTER HIGHLIGHTS

The chapters that follow are organized according to the contextual framework described above. The initial section, Chapters 2 through 5, is devoted to the external environments that have had and continue to exert a direct influence on the college library. Chapter 2 describes the growth of higher education in the United States against a background of historic events that bear on its development, traces curriculum reform from its beginnings to the present, and looks at some of the problems in contemporary society and their potential impact on higher education. Chapter 3 explores the history and current condition of academic libraries and librarianship within the framework of their relationship to higher education and their connections to the library world. Chapters 4, 5 and 6 deal with the campus context. Chapter 4 highlights elements which, when joined, describe a unique college. Utilizing an inventory format, dozens of questions are posed about such aspects of campus life as the nature of the student body, the faculty, the administration, trustees, and the curriculum. Chapter 5 describes the legal basis of a college and its governance, as well its informal political culture. Chapter 6 places the college library within the organizational context of the institution, as well as describing how the library structures itself internally in order to operate. Organizing principles and practices—traditional and new, formal and informal—are presented.

Beginning with Chapter 7 attention is turned to substantive library matters. Chapter 7 traces the growth of technology as it has been applied to college libraries, explains the uses and parts of an integrated library system and describes what is involved in acquiring one. Chapters 8 and 9 are devoted to the development of the knowledge base, the collection.   Chapter 8 describes the collection development process from selection to acquisition and considers the arguments about who should select what kinds of materials, from which sources and in what quantities.   The acquisition of specialized materials such as periodicals, governments documents, audio-visuals and rare books is the focus of Chapter 9.

Chapter 10, Cataloging and Classification, looks at how the materials, once acquired are organized for use, the mechanisms developed to give access to them, and how the process has changed since the introduction of bibliographic utilities and Online public access catalogs. (OPACs)

Chapters 11 through 14 describe how the college library disseminates its product.   Chapter 11 focuses on reference activities within a college context, explaining their importance to both students and faculty as these groups attempt to meet institutional expectations in fulfilling assignments and performing scholarly research and presents a number of key ethical access issues.   The concept of "information literacy" as a new focus of bibliographic instruction is described in Chapter 12, as are the structures and methods that have been associated with library instruction.   All are presented within the context of current learning theories.   Chapter 13 discusses current circulation practices, including who may borrow which materials and for what length of time.   Questions are raised about the place of reserves in the library and interlibrary loan procedures are considered.   Chapter 14 describes the interpretation and outreach efforts that a college library must make in order to educate users to its mission, to continue to meet its obligation to further reading and literacy, and to seek political and financial support from constituents both on-campus and off.

Chapters 15 through 18 deal with planning, organizing, motivating and controlling, the administrative tasks.   In Chapter 15 the Director's role as leader is explored.   The value orientations of directors, how they interact with faculty and staff, and the processes to be followed in selecting and evaluating them are also discussed.   Chapter 16 describes those matters associated with human resource management, including job classification, recruitment, salaries, working conditions, continuing education, motivation, mentoring and similar concerns. Chapter 17 analyzes student assistants, giving this large group of staff members particular attention. Chapter 18 is devoted to the budget and matters of business and finance. Varying approaches to budget development are presented as are alternate methods of raising funds. Chapter 19 looks at the college library building, explains how to assess its current utility and its potential to provide quality library service, describes how to prepare for a new building, hire a consultant and an architect, and write a building program.

The final Chapter, 20, is devoted to evaluation. The important question of how to assess library goodness or value is addressed and mechanisms that permit librarians to learn how well the library is meeting its goals and objectives and servicing the needs of its community are explained.

SUMMARY

Academic libraries are deeply embedded in a variety of environments, all of which influence the services they provide. Understanding academic libraries as open systems with environmental inputs, boundary-spanning activities, outputs, and feedback mechanisms furnishes librarians with a framework in which to examine what they do and with whom they do it. Ultimately, this understanding permits them to exercise greater flexibility and more control over their circumstances. Systems theory will give an integrated overview, but it is not the only method of analysis used by directors, and it must always be combined with intimate knowledge of an institution's particular framework.

NOTES AND SUGGESTED READINGS

Notes

1. William Moffett, "Reflections of a College Librarian," *College and Research Libraries* 45 (May 1984): 338.

2. Patricia Breivik and Robert Wedgeworth, eds. *Libraries and the Search for Academic Excellence*. (Metuchen, NJ: Scarecrow Press, 1988), 7.

3. Freemont E. Kast and James Rosenzweig, "General Systems Theory," in *Management Strategies for Libraries*, ed. Beverly Lynch (New York: Neal-Schuman, 1985), 132.

4. Joanne Euster, *Activities and Effectiveness of the Academic Library Director* (Westport, CT: Greenwood Press, 1987), 36.

5. Maurice Marchant, "The Library as Open System," in *Management Strategies for Libraries*, ed. Beverly Lynch (New York: Neal-Schuman, 1985), 154-6.

6. *Ibid.*, 153

Suggested Readings

Lynch, Beverly, ed. *The Academic Library in Transition: Planning for the 1990's*. New York: Neal-Schuman, 1989.

Lynch, Mary Jo, ed. *Academic Libraries: Research Perspectives*. Chicago: American Library Association, 1990.

McCabe, Gerard, ed. *Operations Handbook for the Small Academic Library*. Westport, CT: Greenwood Press, 1989.

McCabe, Gerard, ' ed. *The Smaller Academic Library*. Westport, CT: Greenwood Press, 1988.

Miller, William and D. Stephen Rockwood, eds. *College Librarianship*. Metuchen, NJ: Scarecrow Press, 1981.

Moran, Barbara. *Academic Libraries: The Changing Knowledge Centers of Colleges and Universities*. Washington, DC: Association for the Study of Higher Education, 1985.

Richardson, John, Jr. and Jinnie Davis, eds. *Academic Librarianship, Past, Present and Future*. A Festschrift in Honor of David Kaser. Littleton, CO: Libraries Unlimited, 1989.

Veaner, Allen. *Academic Librarianship in a Transformational Age: Program, Politics and Personnel*. Boston: G. K. Hall, 1989.

Chapter 2

EVOLUTION OF HIGHER EDUCATION IN THE UNITED STATES

Higher education in the United States today, as in the past, is an outgrowth of social trends and national needs and policies. Just as college libraries reflect the changing priorities of their parent institutions, colleges themselves mirror values extant in the society at a particular time. While the times prepare the way for change, no social movement or organization is successful without strong leaders who help to shape and further it. Higher education today is a product of the earlier efforts of many distinguished pioneers. Charles W. Eliot of Harvard, Mary Lyons of Mt. Holyoke, Senator Samuel Morrill of Vermont, Daniel Coit Gilman of Johns Hopkins, George Washington Carver of Tuskeegee and Robert Hutchins of the University of Chicago were all significant contributors to the rich mosaic of higher education. Their names respectively are associated with the growth of elective curricula, making higher education available to women, establishing research as a priority of education, sponsoring legislation to establish land grant colleges, providing educational opportunities to former slaves, and developing methodologies to improve undergraduate education.

COLONIAL COLLEGES

The roots of American higher education lie in the colonial period when numerous colleges were formed primarily to train young men for the ministry. The first college, Harvard, was established in 1636 by the Puritans. William and Mary followed in 1693. Other early institutions included Yale, The College of New Jersey (later Princeton), Kings College (now Columbia), Queens College (Rutgers), Brown (formerly the College of Rhode Island), The University of Pennsylvania and Dartmouth. With the exception of Columbia and the University of Pennsylvania, all had a religious affiliation. In addition, all were patterned after the English college; that is, they provided a classical education. The task of the early colleges was to educate Christian gentlemen. Their classical curriculum consisted of a formal, almost ritual, series of exercises designed to form the whole man. Classical education was predicated on two important assumptions:

1. Human history and thought are cumulative and progressive. Homer's language, for instance, is simpler than Shakespeare's because it dates from an earlier time.

2. The material of education—what is studied—is less important than its effect in improving the student's mind. The highest function of education is to lay the foundations for further learning.

As a result, the curriculum of a classical college followed a specific historical path, what has been called "a ritualized progression from the Greek historians through the wilderness of mathematics and the natural sciences to reach the abode of the moral philosophers."[1] Memorization and examination were the principal learning devices. Lectures were repeated year after year, particularly as enrollments increased and books were in short supply. The curriculum allowed for no divergent views, but presented, rather, a unified picture of a world without contradiction. Moreover, the quality of a teacher was gauged more by his fealty to religion and the depth of his conviction than by his scholarship. Indeed, scholarship was rejected as an inappropriate undertaking for faculty; they were expected to have learned everything there was to know by the time they began to teach; further education would only have been redundant.

All of the colonial colleges considered themselves private, and responsible for their own policy formation, even those that accepted public funds. But they were not self-governing, as their English counterparts had been. Boards of Governors or Overseers-magistrates, clergy and others—established policy. Presidents, more often than not, handled all disciplinary problems and carried a major teaching load.

In the process of developing a supply of educated Protestant ministers, each of the nine early colleges assumed a position of leadership in the geographic area surrounding it and in the nation. As the country expanded, these institutions supplied men who were instrumental to national growth and development. Other educational institutions, the emerging professions, various social movements, state and federal governments and, of course, organized religion profited from the dedication of those who had been classically trained in the early colonial colleges.

In the first fifty years of the post-colonial period, the United States quadrupled its population. The settling of the interior brought with it an increasing demand for additional ministers and resulted in the rapid establishment of colleges by religious denominations in the new communities. State universities, too, were organized. Georgia had one in 1785 and North Carolina in 1789. By 1830, nine states had public academic institutions, and the more than 50 colleges were educating about 5,000 male students.

MIDDLE YEARS

The years spanning the crucial Civil War period were marked by diversification, population growth, urbanization and industrialization. During this time, new institutions of higher education mushroomed throughout the nation. Innovative models of colleges, different from the men's four-year liberal arts institutions, arose as attempts were made to service particular clienteles. Women's colleges were one early variation, ushered in with the establishment of Mount Holyoke in 1836. Oberlin became the first co-educational, multiracial college in the nation when it admitted women and Blacks in the late 1830s. Fisk was chartered in 1866; and Howard and Morehouse started a year later; all three Black colleges organized primarily to educate newly emancipated slaves. Other colleges focused on the technical and scientific needs of the United States. The Morrill Acts of 1862 and 1890 gave states Federal lands on which to establish colleges offering programs in agriculture, engineering and home economics. These institutions were called "land-grant" colleges and were dedicated to training people to do the kind of applied research that would advance practical knowledge. Agricultural experimental stations were one example of services developed by these institutions and reflect the thrust toward applied research.

Graduate education made its appearance in the last part of the nineteenth century. Yale had awarded the first Ph.D. degree in 1861, but it did not offer *significant* graduate training until the 20th century. Harvard's first attempts at graduate education were also failures, although Eliot of Harvard in 1869 began slowly to implement an elective system where students could choose at least some of their own courses. Increasingly, however, America had come to believe in Social Darwinism, that the world was becoming better as a natural process and that education was a key to gaining fitness and insuring survival. It was a time that some have characterized as the "Age of Energy," both mechanical and personal.[2]

With the founding of Johns Hopkins in 1876, an institution based on the German model of learning and research, the university era in the United States began. Daniel Coit Gilman, Hopkins' President, changed the face of American education by advocating that its ultimate purpose was to create knowledge that stood on the cutting edge of our understanding. In addition to revising the curriculum, Gilman produced a new breed of professor—one who would be a scholar—and introduced new methods of teaching. Rather than rely on lectures and memorization, students were encouraged to participate in discussion and to engage in independent thought. The seminar approach, highly influenced by laboratory sciences, became the principal method for training graduate students. Faculty no longer thought of themselves only as teachers, but as chemists, historians and economists. Their audience was composed both of students in the classroom and peers reached through journals, books and learned society meetings.

The new orientation was accompanied by a cognizance of how poorly prepared students were to meet the increased challenges of higher education. In 1885, with the formation of the New England Association of Colleges and Secondary Schools, whose purpose was to accredit college preparatory schools, the critics' call for more rigorous standards was answered. While standards were emerging, a parallel development found faculty members beginning to bemoan their lack of autonomy in teaching. Academic freedom, until that time, had signified a student's rights to choose elective courses. Faculty members were routinely and arbitrarily dismissed for expressing unpopular views. Organizations composed of faculty from more than a single institution began to form as these scholars recognized coincident interests. In 1915 the American

Association of University Professors (AAUP) was established. Originally only an elite group, it gradually came to include all levels of faculty. Among its aims was the promotion of professional rights, especially academic freedom.

The nine early colleges all became research universities, but they also retained a commitment to provide superior educational experiences for undergraduates. Most have remained private and have attracted substantial support from alumni and friends, as well as from federal and state granting agencies.

Not all 19th-century colleges developed into universities or research institutions. Many opted to become "colleges" in the 20th-century sense emphasizing baccalaureate rather than advanced degrees. Women's colleges continued to be established. While some offered liberal arts courses, others stressed more practical subjects such as home economics. Women who aspired to graduate schools had to search hard and far for institutions that would accept them. Fellowships were generally available only to men and not every subject was deemed appropriate for women.

Additional Black colleges were founded, many of them state-supported. Often poorly funded and forced to remain segregated, they worked against formidable odds, struggling to survive and to provide their students with an adequate education and sufficient training to enable them to function as teachers, preachers and health workers. Religious denominations accounted for the growth of numerous institutions of higher learning. The United Methodist Church sponsored the development of countless universities and colleges as did the Roman Catholic Church.

By 1900 there existed special colleges for Baptists and Catholics, for men and women, for whites and blacks, for rich and not-so-rich, for Northerners and Southerners, for small towns and big cities, for adolescents and adults, for engineers and teachers.[3]

Public colleges, as distinct from public universities, commonly had their origins in teacher training institutions. As the need for educated workers increased, the teaching profession matured and developed greater expectations concerning the qualifications of its members. State legislatures, responding to pressures to supply teachers, created new colleges or authorized the purchase and upgrading of existing ones. Many of these institutions had programs that were less than four years in duration and students were often admitted without having completed four years of high school. Gradually, colleges founded to train teachers broadened their offerings and became alternate paths to higher education. In time, states created systems of public colleges and adopted standards to assure that quality education was being offered. Community colleges emerged as local conduits to four-year institutions. Two-year schools generally taught basic liberal arts courses, ones that formed the non-specialized core of a bachelor's degree. Other two-year schools began to offer applied terminal degrees in subjects such as fire-fighting or nursing.

Each state designs its higher education system differently. Implicit in each, however, is a set of shared definitions and assumptions that describe what constitutes the appropriate amount of study, credit and curriculum required to earn a particular degree. These agreements are, in effect, the glue that binds American higher education. The credit system makes possible "stopping out" and transferring. In two year colleges—Junior or Community—the programs lead to an Associate degree. The completion of four years of undergraduate education, either at a college or a university, produces a Bachelor of Arts or a Bachelor of Science degree. A Baccalaureate degree constitutes the main prerequisite for admission to most graduate and professional programs. One or two years of study beyond the Bachelor's generally results in a Master's Degree. Universities offer Doctor of Philosophy or professional degrees. By and large agreements about what constitutes appropriate study for various degrees were made in the early part of the twentieth century with the emergence of professional associations. The formation of a system of institutional accreditation and a parallel system designed to define various specializations and professions was inaugurated through joint efforts of professional associations and state agencies to insure quality control.

CONTEMPORARY COLLEGES

With the end of World War II and the provision of educational benefits to returning soldiers, the nation's institutions of learning began a time of significant expansion. The period from 1955 to 1974 witnessed breathtaking growth in higher education. The number of students enrolled in post-secondary institutions students burgeoned from 2.5 million in 1955 to 8.8 million in 1974. The percentage of 18-year-olds attending college grew from 17.8 in 1955 to 33.5 in 1974. Black student enrollment increased eightfold and the proportion of women students rose from 1/3 to 1/2 of all enrollments. Academic institutions, assisted by a variety of federal and state financing sources embarked on ambitious building programs and constructed more dormitories, classrooms and libraries in that period than had been put up in the previous 200 years. The number of community colleges increased from 400 to 973, and the number of students in these schools grew from 325,000 to 3.4 million.[4]

Distinctions between and among colleges became less apparent. Separation of college students by gender and race, in particular, seemed to be making a rapid disappearance. The decision to admit women to previously all-male institutions in the 1960s and 1970s resulted in a decrease of almost two-thirds in the number of women's colleges. Active recruitment of minority students to predominantly white institutions seriously changed these colleges and also had an impact on Black colleges, particularly those located in the South.

Many of the early denominational colleges no longer stress their religious underpinnings. They now offer programs quite similar to those available at non-denominational colleges and universities. Other institutions continue to maintain links to the denomination, some tenuous, some firm. Earlham College, for instance, follows the tenets of Quakerism in the way campus decisions are reached. The curriculum at Yeshiva University reflects its ties to Judaism. Colleges sponsored by fundamentalist Protestant sects are likely to hew very closely to denominational precepts and to base their curricula, social activities and modes of dress on religious doctrine. At other schools, a particular sectarian ethos may be more ambiguous, but may remain part of the fabric of the college.

By the 1980s, higher education was experiencing serious problems, including budget shortfalls, reduced numbers of available students, criticism of its curriculum, violation of ethical standards, racism, accusations about inflated emphasis on athletics, and finally, disapproval of the way in which money was handled. These problems continue into the '90s, with financial concerns and substantially diminished applicant pools among the most serious.

A composite picture of higher education today would reveal 3,434 institutions attended by 12,544,000 students with half of the institutions funded by state or local governments and the rest privately.[5]

The two-year college is the most prevalent type in America, followed by colleges offering bachelors and/or first professional degrees. In 1986 the Office of Education listed 731 four year colleges in the United States. About three-quarters of these colleges are privately controlled, many of them church-related, and about one-quarter publicly controlled. Significantly, the public colleges account for more than half the enrollment.[6]

SOCIAL FORCES

Higher education today mirrors the flux of the world in which it is trying to operate. In addition to the remarkable geopolitical events of the past few years, there are other trends that influence the course of academic life. We have become, perforce, a "learning society," in which rapid change requires a lifetime of learning in order to survive. Among the major social forces affecting higher education are:[7]

1. *An Aging Population.* In 1983 there were more Americans over the age of 65 than there were teenagers. The oldest baby boomers, those born between 1946 and 1964, are now in their forties. There has been a commensurately dramatic drop in birthrates. In 1960 there were 23.7 births per thousand population; by 1975 this had fallen to 14.6 per thousand. Although we are in the middle of a new baby boomlet, there will be a dramatic decrease in the number of young adults between the ages of 18 and 26 in the next decade. Demographic projections are now an important variable in planning on most college campuses.

2. *An Increase in Racial and Ethnic Diversity.* Birth rates among Blacks and Hispanics remain at higher levels and immigration is largely from Asia and Latin America. Demographers predict that by 2010 one of three persons in the United States will be Black, Hispanic or Asian-American. A new emphasis on diversity has resulted in multi-ethnic, multi-racial campuses, and institutions are often unprepared for the demands placed on them by new students with such diverse backgrounds.

3. *Shift to a Service Oriented Global Economy.* The economy of the United States is affected by the economy of other countries. The percentage of people involved in farming and manufacturing is decreasing, while the proportion of the population involved in managerial and professional enterprises is increasing. New educational skills are required for those whose jobs have been superannuated by technology and who face the prospect of accepting non-skilled entry-level service industry jobs. Knowledge of other cultures and languages becomes important for economic as well as cultural reasons. Colleges are

expected to contribute to the production and development of skills that provide economic remedies to societal problems and global opportunities.

4. *A Proliferation of Information.* What was once an industrial society is now an information society. People have easier access to more information than ever before. The amount of information is said to double every seven years. But availability of information does not guarantee better knowledge or ideas. "Information is no more than it has ever been; discrete bundles of facts, sometimes useful, sometimes trivial and never the substance of thought. We must not be tempted to believe that the more information we have, the higher the quality of our thinking and problem-solving will be."[8]

5. *A Continuing High Illiteracy Rate.* Twenty-five million Americans cannot read road signs; 35 million more cannot read well enough to function in the society. A learning society presupposes literacy. Without the tools to learn, the information society described above becomes inaccessible.

6. *Changing Assumptions About the Course of Human Development.* Most members of contemporary society currently assume that the scientific method is the only valid approach to knowledge. They believe that the universe is a mechanical system composed of elementary material building blocks; that life in society is a competitive struggle for existence; and that material progress for everyone can be achieved through technological and economic growth. Students of society, however, recognize a gradual paradigm shift away from these assumptions. The futurist Alvin Toffler, for instance, contends that there is a fast spreading recognition that moral, aesthetic, political and environmental degradation will inhibit society no matter how much material or technological progress it has made.

The societal forces listed above have serious consequences for higher education, and, of course, ultimately for academic libraries. To fulfill the needs of a "learning society," colleges and universities have been and are being asked to become lifelong institutions, to serve older and part-time students with credit and non-credit offerings, to serve multicultural populations, to serve business and to serve local communities. The population shifts have resulted in similar changes in student enrollments. The pool of 18 to 24-year-olds is declining. In 1983 there were 12.5 million, but the number is expected to be only 11.8 million in 1992. Demographers project that 49% of students in institutions of higher education in 1992 will be 25 years or older.[9] Of that number 55% will be women. Among minority groups, young people constitute an even greater percentage of the population, yet presently smaller proportions earn high school degrees.

These population shifts have resulted in changes in the way in which higher education is administered and offered. Three-quarters of older students study part-time and often only in the evening. Multiculturalism has become a reality on most college campuses and educational leaders see their mission as three-fold: to socialize minority students to their institutions and to the majority culture; to socialize white students to the sometimes unfamiliar norms of their minority academic peers; and to socialize both groups to non Western thinking and values.

Competition among private colleges and universities to fill their classes has been heightened by the changing population, by decreased federal support in aid of students, and by increasing tuition costs at private colleges, a factor which has caused many potential students to opt for public schools. Some fear that competition for students may lead to faddish behavior and "a jumble of programs patched together to pander to every taste."[10]

CURRICULUM

Curriculum reform has swept the nation as critics become increasingly vocal in their condemnation of what is currently being offered to incoming students. Simultaneously there are competing cries for more relevant education, pleas for colleges to return to "the canon" or a new facsimile of it, demands for educators to produce students who can "read and write" and calls for multicultural approaches to learning. Most colleges have recognized the need for remediation and have accepted some responsibility for supplying it. A number of recruiting strategies have surfaced. Co-curricular areas of college life have been stressed in admissions literature. Some colleges have lowered their admissions standards in order to "have a class," that is, to insure that an adequate number of students matriculate to keep the institution solvent. Other colleges have shifted from a liberal arts orientation toward one with more vocational content. Some have even adopted vocational or occupational majors. Adults generally enroll in courses for job-related reasons and some colleges try to attract this clientele by altering their curriculum.

A curriculum, according to Phyllis Keller, "is ultimately more than a cluster of courses arranged in an institutionally accepted pattern. It is the statement of a faculty, a college a generation, as to what they believe to be the character and goals of a college education."[11] Curriculum was hardly a question in the colonial colleges. As described above, it followed the English model and consisted of a prescribed set of courses. When Charles William Eliot became President of Harvard in 1869, he instituted a system of electives whereby students could choose the courses they would take. This innovation, he thought, would allow for individual differences, give students a measure of free choice, offer variety in intellectual opportunities and facilitate their gaining depth in one area.

At the time that Eliot introduced electives, students entering Harvard had sufficient preparation to succeed at that institution. Unfortunately, many of the nation's schools that copied Harvard's elective approach recruited students not nearly so well grounded in academic subjects. Gradually the entrance requirements at Harvard were also lowered as the school endeavored to attract "the brightest boys," those who showed the greatest promise, but who might not have received the classical education provided to students who attended elite preparatory schools. Harvard faculty began to complain that the elective system did not lead to intellectual competency. Teaching staffs in other institutions also lamented the poor preparation of their undergraduates.

Abbott Lawrence Lowell, who acceded to the Presidency of Harvard in 1909, replaced Eliot's curriculum with one that required six full-year courses chosen from three fields outside the major. He also instituted a series of concentration requirements. This approach found favor, not only among many of Harvard's faculty, but in the nation's other colleges as well. In the early and mid-20th century the concentration-distribution-elective structure became the norm. The intention was to provide a heterogenous student body with common learning and shared intellectual purpose.

Even greater emphasis was put on common knowledge in the general studies curricula attempted at Columbia and Chicago. Columbia retained a few electives, but aimed to provide a comprehensive overview of the main features and significant ideas of western civilization. Chicago's experiment was more radical. No electives or majors were permitted. The curriculum was wholly prescribed and embodied a series of interdisciplinary courses in humanities, social sciences and natural sciences.

The reformers promoting general education programs insisted that:

1. students be made aware of ideas that shaped the society in which they lived;
2. A common intellectual culture be transmitted.

Harvard's interpretation of general education was that it should have a substantive focus on *heritage-* study of the past to enrich and clarify the meaning of the present—and *change*—understanding that the scientific method of thought demands data testing before conclusions are reached and that conclusions must be tentative.

Harvard, Columbia and Chicago built into the general education curricula their belief that there were bodies of essential knowledge—information and ideas—that every student should acquire.

In the late 1970s, Harvard, like most schools in the nation, found itself with sets of courses masquerading as curricula. Demands for "relevancy" in the 1960s and early 1970s had led to a dilution of common materials. Students shared little in the way of a common college experience, and narrow treatments of discrete subjects had replaced an agreed-upon program of learning. After a difficult process of negotiation, Harvard adopted a *core* curriculum, one which has been widely copied, albeit adapted to the unique needs of individual campuses across the nation. In many ways a return to general education, the new curriculum stresses the major modes of disciplinary thought, rather than specific bodies of literature. Educators have concluded that "it is as important to set a standard of intellectual range for all students as it is to require that they concentrate on a particular subject that engages their interests."[12] They have defined this objective in terms of a set of essential skills and ways of thinking—as starting points for discovering, organizing and understanding the knowledge they would want or need to acquire later. The products emerging from curriculum reform vary from campus to campus. In elite schools, the research-college model, with its more abstract emphasis on process, exploration and discovery will prevail. Learning and knowledge will continue to constitute the "profit" of higher education. In schools where students are less well prepared, remediation and basic skills will occupy much of the first- and second-year experience. Vocational training, preparation for a job or an occupation may monopolize the time of juniors or seniors in undergraduate institutions with a practical interpretation of what constitutes a core.

COLLEGE STUDENTS TODAY

College students today are characterized as poorly prepared, less altruistic, more concerned about self, more anxious about the future. They are less likely to be attending college because of an interest in gaining a general education than for the purpose of acquiring skills which will permit them to be greater wage earners. Today's undergraduates are more middle of the road socially than their predecessors of a decade or two ago, support conservative positions on law and order and are deeply concerned about the environment.[13] In addition, numbers of students lack basic skills in reading, writing and computation, resulting in a discontinuity between high school and college. The competing career concerns of faculty have caused them to divide their loyalties between teaching and scholarship, too often favoring the latter at the expense of students.[14] To some, the quality of campus life seems to be deteriorating and a sense of common purpose disappearing. Faculty and administrators participate less frequently in college life outside the classroom. In a recent survey of college presidents, alcohol abuse, racial tensions, dilapidated student unions and the diverse needs of commuter students were identified as major concerns.[15]

KEEPING UP WITH HIGHER EDUCATION

Knowing how to locate information about higher education serves a dual purposes for academic librarians. It permits them, first, to gain and maintain an understanding of their environment, and second, the opportunity to share their particular skills and expertise with their communities. Professionals in any field have an obligation to become intimate with the environment in which they function. Accepting a position in higher education establishes a relationship between an academic librarian and academia which carries with it the duty to understand and participate in that world. Faculty and administrators in colleges regularly make informed judgments about their needs and often base these judgments, at least to some extent, on institutional realities at comparable schools and on trends in higher education.

Higher education is replete with specialized associations established to consider and act on matters of mutual concern.[16] Most private colleges, for instance, join the Association of American Colleges; land grant institutions may choose to identify as members of the National Association of State Universities and Land Grant Colleges. These organizations serve their members through programs of professional development. They help teachers and administrators focus on standards of excellence, and they provide forums for exchanging ideas. They also serve as agencies for lobbying national or state governments about legislation favorable to their members.

Colleges and universities share their concerns in higher education literature as well as through academic organizations. Journals, newspapers and newsletters inform constituents of current happenings, trends and ideas. Three publications that address the range of academic issues and that are general in their approach and appeal are *The Chronicle of Higher Education*, *Academe*, and *Change*. *The Chronicle*, as it is commonly called, is an independent newspaper published weekly since 1966. Its columns describe current happenings in institutions of higher learning, report on surveys it and other agencies have undertaken, and publish statistics about enrollments, tuition, state aid, faculty salaries, and student attitudes. *The Chronicle* is also a primary source of information about professional vacancies for faculty, administrators and librarians.

Academe is published by the American Association of University Professors. It focuses attention on the concerns of faculty, argues for a greater voice for them in the development of sound educational, personnel and governance policies in all types of colleges and universities. Among its annual reports, the one describing the economic status of the profession is widely used by administrators and faculty to strengthen their relative positions. *Change*, sponsored by the American Council on

Education seeks, as its title implies, to encourage the development of new pedagogical approaches in higher education. While the theme of each issue may vary, the concern for reform and innovation is always present.

Establishing a routing system among librarians for these and similar journals and newspapers encourages members of the library profession to broaden their understanding of higher education, and to make connections between their work and the concerns of faculty and administrators on their campuses. Librarians should also involve themselves in these organizations or consider writing for these journals; communicating with one's peers is part of the process of influencing change in higher education.

In addition to the three general publications, many specialized journals serve the interests of other campus offices—personnel, financial aid, physical plant, research on higher education, for example. A useful guide to the literature of higher education is Lois Buttlar's *Education: A Guide to Reference and Information Sources*.[17]

Statistical information about higher education is available in a variety of sources. National norms may be interesting. Far more useful to administrators and librarians is information about both comparable and goal colleges. Higher education is a status-based hierarchy with a few well-known elite institutions, a larger group with "modest" reputations and a large group virtually unknown outside their geographic regions. Colleges identify as peers those schools which compete with them for students, which share similar goals and missions, which are roughly the same size, and which are controlled in the same manner (public or private), to name a few variables. Colleges also identify as model or goal institutions those schools that are somewhat more successful in student recruitment and endowment. In most cases, the college administration decides these groupings. Once peer and model institutions have been identified, data about them are used for decision making, long-range planning and budget allocations.

Among the best sources for ferreting out statistical information about higher education are:

The Chronicle of Higher Education, which reports on all major studies, often summarizing key findings and data; its annual, *Almanac of Higher Education* is a compilation of the Chronicle's most important data.

The College Handbook, an annual publication of the College Board, contains up-to-date enrollment figures.

American Universities and Colleges, published by the American Council on Education gives institutional profiles, the Council's *Fact Book* summaries a broad array of data.

Digest of Educational Statistics, from the U.S. Department of Education's National Center for Educational Statistics, is another compendium of statistics about all facets of education, including higher education.

A Classification of Institutions of Higher Education, published in 1987 by the Carnegie Foundation for the Advancement of Teaching, reports on groupings of schools with shared characteristics.

SUMMARY

The citizens of the United States, from colonial times to the present have evidenced a strong interest in providing education, first to young, elite, white males and later to all citizens. Originally established to train preachers and teachers, colleges broadened their goals as the industrial society began to require the services of trained employees. When the English method of education with its emphasis on rote learning was replaced by a German model stressing original inquiry at the forefront of knowledge, new importance began to attach to scholarly and research materials. An egalitarian approach to education followed World War II when returning GI's swelled the ranks of college students. Contemporary higher education is composed of a diverse group of institutions—private, public, secular, nonsecular, two-year, four-year, comprehensive and research-oriented.

Societal forces today—an aging population, minority groups with limited access to higher educational opportunities and a post industrial economy in need of highly skilled employees—all influence developments of new programs and curricular offerings at colleges.

Compared with previous generations, many college students today are poorly prepared to undertake a rigorous program of study. In addition, they differ from their predecessors of three decades ago in their lack of concern for the society and in their growing interest in the environment.

According to Vartan Gregorian, President of Brown University, four years of undergraduate education will no longer provide a sufficient education. "The three scourges...[of education] will be mental gridlock in the form of undigested information, cultural anorexia in the form of self-inflicted ignorance and national amnesia toward our heritage."[18]

NOTES AND SUGGESTED READINGS

Notes

1.   Orvin Lee Shiflett, *Origins of American Academic Librarianship* (Norwood, NJ: Ablex, 1981), 46.

2.   *Ibid.*, 57.

3.   Christopher Jencks and David Reisman, The Academic Revolution (Chicago: University of Chicago Press, 1977), 2-3.

4. Jerold W. Apps, *Higher Education in a Learning Society* (San Francisco: Jossey Bass, 1988), 33-34.

5. American Council on Education. *Fact Book on Higher Education*, 1989-90 (New York: American Council on Education, 1989), 100-134.

6. *Ibid.*, 134.

7. Apps, 19-27.

8. *Ibid.*, 24.

9. *Ibid.*, 29.

10. *Ibid.*, 10

11. Phyllis Keller, *Getting At the Core* (Boston: Harvard University Press, 1982), IX.

12. *Ibid.*, 132

13. Alexander Astin and others, The American Freshman: National Norms for 1988, Cooperative Institutional Research Program, UCLA (New York: American Council on Education, 1988). Commonly called Astin Report.

14. Ernest L. Boyer, *College, The Undergraduate Experience in America* (New York: Harper & Row, 1987), 2.

15. *Chronicle of Higher Education*, 2 May 1990, 1.

16. For information about how librarians can participate, see "Tip Sheet for Involvement in Non-Library Association," *College and Research Libraries News* 51 (July/August 1990): 632.

17. Lois Buttlar. *Education: A Guide to the Reference and Information Sources* (Littleton, CO: Libraries Unlimited, 1989).

18. "Periscope," *Newsweek*, 8 January 1990, unnumbered page.

Suggested Readings

Apps, Jerold. *Higher Education in a Learning Society*. San Francisco: Jossey-Bass, 1988.

Bloom, Allan. *The Closing of the American Mind*. New York: Simon and Schuster, 1987.

Bok, Derek. *Higher Learning*. Cambridge, MA: Harvard University Press, 1986.

Boyer, Ernest L. *College, the Undergraduate Experience in America*. New York: Harper and Row, 1987.

Breivik, Patricia Senn and E. Gordon Gee. *Information Literacy: Revolution in the Library*. New York: American Council on Education, Macmillan, 1989.

Chamberlain, Mariam K., ed. *Women in Academe: Progress and Prospects*. New York: Russell Sage Foundation, 1988.

Jencks, Christopher and Reisman, David. *The Academic Revolution*. Chicago: University of Chicago Press, 1977.

Libraries and the Learning Society: Papers in Response to a Nation at Risk. Chicago: American Library Association. 1984.

"The Multicultural Campus," *Academe* 76 (November/December 1990): 10-33.

A Nation at Risk: The Imperative for Educational Reform. Washington, DC: The National Commission on Excellence in Education, 1983.

Oleson, Alexandra and John Voss, eds. *The Organization of Knowledge in Modern America, 1860-1920.* Baltimore, MD: Johns Hopkins University Press, 1979.

Rudolph, Frederick. *The American College and University: A History.* New York: Knopf. 1962.

Veysey, Laurence. *The Emergence of the American University.* Chicago: University of Chicago Press, 1977.

Chapter 3

GROWTH OF ACADEMIC LIBRARIANSHIP

Beginning with the colonial period, the fortunes of academic libraries have been intimately and inextricably bound to the institutions of which they are a part. Changes in the landscape of higher education found strong echoes in academic library development. Curricula, in particular, have played a crucial role in determining how libraries have been viewed and utilized. Happenstance, however, and individual effort are always factors and college libraries in similar institutions have matured and fared differently. The academic library profession evolved slowly, its growth paralleling the increasing importance assigned to books and libraries in the educational process as the nation sought, first, to educate its elite, white, young men, and later to train all of its people.

EARLY PERIOD

Reading was not an essential occupation of students in colonial colleges. Rather, they learned by means of lectures, memorization and recitation. Libraries, similarly, had marginal utility in the educational process. But libraries were important to colonial colleges because their holdings contributed to the institution's wealth and prestige. Indeed, the worth of a college was often measured by the value of its library collection. Books were not only considered artifacts of education, but represented tangible evidence that the community's elite supported the institution. Colonial college libraries were almost always the product of gifts. Donors were courted and rewarded; it is no coincidence that Harvard, Brown and Yale were named for library-conscious benefactors. Without the contribution of private collections, college library holdings would have been negligible.

Books in early college libraries were generally old and often rare. An analysis of John Harvard's donated collection of 250 titles revealed that 65% were entered under Latin titles, and that there were -eight classes of books: theology (65% of the collection), classics, professional (law and medicine), history (a few volumes), philosophy (logic and ethics), poetry (a slight taste), essays, and foreign language (a Spanish-English dictionary).[1]

Scholars who study the early college libraries have concluded that they were designed to keep readers and books apart. Access was a major problem. Consider the situation described in a Harvard report of 1859:

> Just beyond Mr. Sibley's office, there is a spacious and handsome hall, about twenty roomy and comfortable alcoves, all well lighted, ventilated and warmed, furnished with many convenient tables and desks, but

showing in many places an advertisement in large type, conspicuously posted up, announcing that 'No person is allowed to enter.' Without obtaining the special leave from the Librarian, a student may not even seat himself at one of the tables in order to read or write, though most of them are unoccupied nine-tenths of the time. ...The students' privileges in the body of the building are limited to a permission to walk up and down the long hall in the center, consult the alcove lists and admire the President's busts.[2]

A few randomly selected examples suggest that the problems of access continued for most of the nineteenth century.

In the 1840s Amherst not only kept its books covered with white netting, but opened the library only one hour per week. For fifty years after 1856, the University of Michigan steadfastly refused to loan books to students. In 1878, Columbia University lent books only to those who had the permission of the President. The Library of the University of North Carolina for two decades was located in a bedroom in the President's residence.[3]

With a few notable exceptions, the growth of academic libraries during the period from 1780 to 1830 was a product of luck rather than rational planning. Harvard was one of the few to embark on a policy of systematic collection development, particularly when Joshua Green Cogswell held the position of librarian. The University of Virginia, too, under the tutelage of Thomas Jefferson, tried to create a new kind of utilitarian university library. Regrettably, the effort languished after his death.

The lack of good college libraries produced what came to be known as "society libraries." Student-owned and -operated, their capital derived from self-imposed taxes, these libraries contained books which appealed to the popular reading tastes of undergraduates. Materials which could be used in debates, an important collegiate activity of the period, were also collected and made available. College libraries included scholarly books, major works of reference, rare editions and esoteric material. Society libraries, on the other hand, contained recent books, modern poetry and essays, biography, and even some fiction. By 1829, society libraries could boast more than half as many volumes as those owned by college libraries. In fact, many college libraries—the ones at Dartmouth, Middlebury, Amherst and Union, for instance—owned fewer books than did their student-controlled counterparts.[4]

Gradually society libraries merged with those of their parent institutions. Far more generous use and acquisition policies had been associated with society libraries than with college libraries. Students accustomed to daily access to the society library expected no less when they gave up their private collections. In addition, they now demanded that the library select materials of interest to them rather than simply purchase or accept blocks of rare books without regard to their potential use.

Real change came to college libraries after the Civil War. While a new, small denominational college struggling to survive its first ten years might still view books as artifacts and the curriculum as a set of experiences related to memorization and the acceptance of faith, other visions for the role of a college and its library emerged. Teachers and advanced students of Biblical Exegesis, for instance, began to recognize that mastery of certain scriptural passages might necessitate comparing the translation in several texts. When Johns Hopkins instituted its German-based curriculum emphasizing scientific inquiry, libraries were launched into a new and crucial position on the university campuses.

In college after college acceptance that specialization is appropriate to education, adoption of the elective system for students, availability of more sophisticated courses, all influenced the pressures on college libraries to enlarge. Increasing faculty involvement in and commitment to generating knowledge, and acknowledgment that research was a major function of a university "contributed to the emerging consensus that the library constituted the very 'heart' of any self-respecting academic institution."[5] Scholarly communication brought with it new journals and further fueled the library's role as a repository of the latest scientific thought. Some of the surplus wealth developed from commercial and industrial development that had found its way into the treasuries of colleges and universities was channeled into libraries. Institutions established as a result of the Morrill Acts, in particular, benefited from the largesse of this new source of support and their libraries became some of the best in the country. By the turn of the century, it is fair to say that the library was believed to be central to the mission of a university. College libraries acceded to that position early in the 20th century.

EMERGENCE OF A PROFESSION

The office of librarian was one of the first to be differentiated after the presidency in the academic hierarchy of the classical college, but his duties were primarily custodial. He was responsible for carrying the key to the room and seeing to it that it was tightly locked except during the periods of the week when students were permitted to use the books. As the library grew, faculty members continued to serve as librarian, but now they were often joined by a newly graduated bookish male student to help them with the technical work—ordering and organizing—and to keep the library open for a few additional hours each week. Library work was the province of men until the latter part of the nineteenth century when a few women were permitted to work as library clerks or as assistant librarians.

Librarianship, including academic librarianship, emerged as a new specialization in the 1870s. The American Library Association was formed in 1876 and led by respected librarians—Melvil Dewey of Columbia and Justin Winsor of Harvard—who called attention to professional concerns and helped to shape an agenda for the field. Establishment of library schools further aided in affirming the identification of librarianship as a profession. Widespread adoption of the Decimal Classification system formulated by Dewey in 1875 led to better organization which, in turn, made libraries more serviceable. Now, however, the services of a librarian trained in the mysteries and intricacies of the system were required to classify and catalog materials appropriately.

At the same time that librarianship was emerging as a profession, college faculty, their attention increasingly occupied in instruction and research, were no longer willing to allocate a portion of their time to running the library, which now demanded the services of a full-time person who could be expected to possess technical and specialized knowledge. The older, more elite institutions began to hire graduates of the newly established professional library schools. While persons who might also do some teaching were considered more desirable, the library, rather than the classroom, was their primary work site. In this way, the new librarians differed from their "scholar librarian" predecessors, such notables as William Warner Bishop, Andrew Keogh, and Theodore Koch. Some librarians continued to teach, but most now concentrated on the library.

The new breed of librarian attended to, sometimes with missionary zeal, standardizing the procedures of cataloging, developing efficient systems for handling circulation, and improving the methods of ordering, exchanging and shelving books. Spurred on by the public library movement, they adopted a philosophy that placed use and service to all over custodianship and protection. They were intent on making more books accessible on open shelves and breaking down the traditional barriers created by viewing the library as a museum, aloof and dignified. Reference services were extended and improved, orientation on the use of the library became widely available, general reading was encouraged through the establishment of browsing rooms, dormitory libraries, weekly book talks and student library prize awards. In short, library efficiency was improved on most campuses and a high standard of service was set by the leaders of the new profession. Participation in scholarly activities, however, occurred less frequently.

The move away from teaching and scholarly pursuits for librarians, unfortunately, brought them lower status in the eyes of the academic community. A lessened orientation toward participation in scholarly research, coupled with the now prominent distinction between their administrative responsibilities and classroom teaching resulted in library work being viewed as something of lesser importance and certainly carrying diminished educational prestige. The movement of women into the field of librarianship also gave rise among male faculty to skepticism about the profession's academic legitimacy. The proper role of the librarian—manager, scholar, merchant, salesperson—began to capture the attention of librarians in their literature and at their professional meetings. The difficulty of combining all of these roles created an identity problem which still prevails. In short, the modern period of academic librarianship had begun.

TWENTIETH CENTURY

By the start of the twentieth century, academic libraries were growing at dizzying speed, their collections doubling in size every sixteen years. New service patterns were in evidence including longer hours, better trained staffs, and more efficient methods of operation. Larger collections required greater organization and arrangement, and the adoption of more appropriate classification systems often necessitated recataloging whole collections. Buildings were planned and erected specifically for library purposes, not merely as museums to house artifacts. The library was integrated into the college's academic program. New teaching methods, the seminar approach in particular, generated student research and greater use of library materials. Gradually, faculty began to involve themselves in selection and collection development, motivated by pedagogical reasons as well as by self-interest.

Since their creation in the late nineteenth century, regional accrediting associations had always included libraries as one element to be evaluated on any college campus. But now standards were being developed to measure the quality of the library, its building and collections. Prior to 1934, all of the standards were rigid and quantitative in nature, calling for academic libraries, no matter their individual differences, to contain X number of books, periodicals, and pamphlets. Despite the categorical nature of the standards, they were extremely useful to librarians who could utilize them as leverage with administrators to improve inadequate libraries full of inappropriate materials—older books of little interest to faculty or students and housed in cramped quarters. With published standards in hand, librarians were able to argue that poor libraries were an impediment to the educational process and to buttress their contentions by pointing to dictated quantities.

College presidents had always accepted the responsibility for securing outside funding for their libraries. In 1790 the task might have been to obtain a treasured book for the collection from a potential donor; in 1890, the obligation may have been to find a contributor who would help to fund a free-standing library building. In the Depression era of the 1930s, the object was to win foundation support to provide a collection of materials to satisfy the current and next generation of college students.

During the period from 1929 to 1940, several foundations—the most notable of which was the Carnegie Corporation of New York—instituted studies of various types of college libraries with a view toward making grants to selected institutions. Foundation representatives examined more than a thousand libraries, conferred with college presidents, faculty and librarians on such problems as the library budget, book and periodical holdings, and staff. According to Louis Round Wilson, these studies exposed the library as a teaching instrument in a way it had never before been seen, and revealed to presidents of colleges the adequacy or inadequacy of their libraries as instruments of instruction.[6] Not only did some college libraries profit materially from the Carnegie Corporation following these studies, but as a result of the reports, many others found new prestige accruing to them simply as a result of the attention that had been focused on academic libraries.[7] Another important by-product of the reports was the publication in book form of the findings, including lists of recommended titles and standards for adequate library service, both of which influenced and stimulated institutions that had not received grants to better themselves.

Second in importance only to the Carnegie Corporation grants was the financial assistance given by the General Education Board to library schools for the training of librarians, to various metropolitan areas to establish union catalogs and bibliographical centers, and to individual colleges and universities for book purchases, surveys of libraries, buildings and equipment, and special library projects. The grants of the General Education Board were most influential in stimulating the development of library facilities as a part of the general college program, and especially in assisting library development in the South.[8] College libraries also benefited from the gifts of the Rockefeller Foundation for underwriting scholarly publications, bibliographic tools, and contributions to college endowments. The contributions of all three major foundations helped to set a pattern of library giving for smaller foundations.

Another important element in the growth and development of college libraries during this period was the multitude of newly formed Friends of the Library organizations. Libraries in the older, better funded strong liberal arts institutions still had to depend to some extent upon individual gifts, donations, bequests and memorials. Some of the finest special collections in the nation's college libraries today had their source in rich private libraries donated or bequeathed to the institution by the owner. Librarians soon realized that even more important than the original gifts were donations and endowments to perpetuate them, and, to this end, substantial energy was spent in cultivating good relationships between donors and the library. To foster a spirit of community, a number of colleges established Friends organizations in the 1930s—the chief purpose of which was to preach the gospel of more and better books for the library. Not all were successful, by any means, but those that were generally drew their leadership from alumni and members of the faculty. These Friends organizations served their college libraries both directly and indirectly. They bestowed books, or contributed endowments for specific purposes. In addition, they influenced others to donate, placed their librarians in contact with potential donors, and advised them of exceptional bargains in book purchases.

Developments in large public libraries, too, contributed to the strengthening of college libraries during this period. One product of the Depression had been an enlarged educational and social role for public libraries. Their burgeoning clientele borrowed and read increasingly sophisticated material and demanded more intensive reference assistance. College students, used to the services provided by public libraries, expected to find equally well-served libraries on their campuses. Large public libraries now offered thousands of books on open shelves, reading and study rooms for subject specialists, exhibition galleries for prints and drawings, discussion groups, film and record loans, and readers' advisory services. They led the way, too, in proposing divisional organization, in introducing audio-visual services, and in the use of labor-saving devices.

Publishing burgeoned and unprecedented numbers of books were rolling off the presses. Curriculum reform, as described in Chapter 2, led to methods of teaching which could no longer be satisfied by single textbooks. At first the major impact on the library was constant pressure to duplicate required materials. Later, honors and general reading courses, tutorial plans, and other curricular innovations contributed to a different kind of library use and resulted in a demand for new types of material. These two library developments—the substitution of assigned library readings in place of textbooks, and the introduction of independent study and research—introduced major changes in the way in which college libraries provided service. The adoption of the reserve reading program brought out of the stacks many books which had previously merely gathered dust. The consequences for libraries of honors theses and student research was somewhat less noticeable because at first faculty rarely exploited the library's role in connection with these programs. Nevertheless the broad and deep use which resulted from some student research encouraged numbers of faculty and librarians to push for more active participation by the library in the general scheme of college education.

The Depression of the late 1920s and 1930s had seriously effected college and university libraries, just, it seemed, as they were coming into their own. For some libraries, this meant delaying their building programs. Budgets and staffs were slashed. Some help had come in the form of federal aid obtained through the Works Project Administration (WPA), which provided assistance in binding, cataloging, indexing and building repairs in some publicly funded institutions. Most libraries fell behind in collection development, reference services and new construction. Ironically, the Depression produced a number of salutary effects, according to Michael Harris, the most important of which was that it caused librarians to "pause and reflect on their nature and purpose in the general education scene"[9] and stimulated attempts to find alternate ways of extending service despite their straightened budgets. Overcrowding, for instance, which could not be met with new buildings, generated experimentation with new forms of storage including a variety of microforms. The lack of sufficient materials gave rise to interlibrary loan and cooperative acquisitions programs which, while limited, achieved some measure of success.

POST-WORLD WAR II LIBRARIES

When World War II ended, the majority of colleges, and their libraries, were in dire financial straits. Fortuitously, demands by veterans for higher education, coupled with federal legislation which became known as the GI Bill to fund it not only solved the capital problem, but fueled an era of rapid expansion of services, faculties and, indeed, colleges themselves. Academic libraries shared in the boom, augmenting and strengthening their collections and services. Despite the use of new storage techniques, and the widespread transfer of newspapers to microfilm, library stacks were once again at capacity. Collections now were estimated to double every ten years. By the 1950s most colleges had erected totally new structures or put additions on existing ones.

College librarians were called upon to supply not only substantial quantities of traditional library materials, but also to make available a variety of the newer instructional aids to meet the needs of new types of students who were streaming into all kinds of institutions of higher education. In some instances, particularly at the junior college level, the library was no longer thought of as the place which housed books and journals, but rather as an instruction materials center with responsibility for the whole range of books and mechanical teaching aids. The role of libraries as active participants in the educational process itself was enhanced by these new responsibilities. More and better library services also required enlarged staffs. Librarians were in short supply, their ranks decimated by the Depression and World War II. It was necessary to recruit thousands of new workers to the field.

The impetus to increase service further accelerated with the launching of Sputnik, the first Russian space vehicle, in 1957. The Higher Education Acts (HEA) of 1963 and 1965 provided funds for college library resources, for training librarians and for research into the fields of library science. The five years of federal aid for academic library buildings from 1967 to 1971 have been characterized as "the greatest flowering of academic library experience this county has ever known."[10] HEA guidelines were specific about the importance of equalizing educational opportunities for disadvantaged students, particularly in urban areas. A number of previously substandard institutions were able to reach parity as a result of HEA funds. Federal grants were also available for purposes of experimentation and research in academic librarianship. A revision of the Federal Depository Law made it possible for a great many smaller academic libraries to choose by series and groups of publications what they needed from the vast output of U.S. government publications and to become selective depositories under this act. Regional depositories were created, thereby reducing the pressure on libraries to collect everything and allowing them to become more flexible about the maintenance of documents collections in perpetuity. Today the well established federal role stresses research, development of new technologies and recruitment.[11]

Foundation support continued, as well. Ford, U.S. Steel and other corporate foundations made grants to building, book and special bibliographical projects. In 1956, the Ford Foundation established the Council on Library Resources (CLR) with the purpose of assisting in "the solution of problems of libraries generally, but more especially of the problems of research libraries by conducting or supporting research, demonstrating new techniques and methods, and disseminating the results..."[12] The Council made important grants for the development of technology, for studies in academic library management, for fellowship programs that would help mid-career librarians widen their experience, to support network-based systems, book preservation research, improvement of library equipment, and numerous Library of Congress projects. Later, the National Endowment for the Humanities (NEH) encouraged libraries to apply for challenge grant funds. Successful college library applicants built buildings, developed and preserved special collections and organized some new services with monies from these sources.

Many college libraries never profited from the immediate post-war boom or foundation support and continued to work under inadequate conditions with insufficient resources. Black colleges, small church-supported institutions—particularly those in the South and in rural areas—had meager collections and small staffs. As they had in the past, standards became helpful to these underfunded, unequipped libraries. Accrediting associations' clout increased, and they began to withhold accreditation. In 1934, the North Central Association had adopted the principle of measuring a college in terms of its program, rather than by absolute and unwavering quantitative measures. The library segment, assigned to Douglas Waples of the University of Chicago Library School, had produced basic qualitative and quantitative criteria for measuring the relative educational value of college libraries. These more realistic standards were then used by libraries to point out the deficiencies of their buildings, collections, staffs and equipment.

Since they were first adopted, standards have undergone frequent revisions. Today's standards represent the aggregate experience of the profession, rather than the wisdom or experience of individual experts.[13] The most recent, *Standards for College Libraries* were adopted by the Association of College & Research Libraries in 1986. A copy of them appears as the Appendix of this book.

In the recession period of the 1970s college libraries began to suffer reductions in federal and grant support. Retrenchment plans were created and sometimes instituted. New librarians, just recently in short supply, suddenly found themselves without the prospect of employment. College libraries, now large and complex, and without sufficient staff to take care of the enormous increase in routine work, looked eagerly for ways to increase productivity. Technology and increased cooperation in the face of the heavy demand and the "information explosion" promised to provide a partial answer and, indeed, resulted in major changes in the way college libraries operate in the 1990s. Emphasis has shifted to "access" from "acquisition," and networking and automation have become part of every librarian's vocabulary. In the 1960s, OCLC, formerly the Ohio College Library Center, now the Online Cooperative Library Center, was established to provide a computerized cooperative cataloging and union catalog service to a small group of regional libraries. By the 1970s it had greatly expanded its program and spawned similar bibliographic networks throughout the country. Today, it contains more than 21 million records, and can count among its members 11,000 libraries. Other cooperative projects included RLIN (Research Libraries Network), designed to serve research libraries with shared cataloging, interlibrary loan, serials control and acquisitions assistance. New materials delivery services, both electronic and manual, made their appearance. On-line data bases became widely available, as did off-line electronic data bases in CD-ROM format. Colleges began to boast of being "wired campuses" and library buildings were altered to make them "smart," that is amenable to sophisticated technology. In addition, new methods of library instruction were developed as librarians sought to increase their participation in the teaching mission of the institution.

By the 1990s the college library had achieved a position of strength in the educational program and commanded greater respect than ever before from the faculty. The cumulative effect of sustained individual library efforts, the example of successful integration of the library into the teaching program in the smaller progressive colleges, and the support of accrediting associations and foundations all helped to give credence to the significance of the college library's role in facilitating teaching and learning.

What lies ahead? How can college libraries maintain and improve the variety of services they now offer? Surely, the answer lies in cooperation between college administrators, faculty and librarians about the role, function, and operation of the library. The library can only improve if administrators, whose task it is to insure continued financial support, and faculty, who bear primary responsibility for its use, see the need to strengthen the library. It is incumbent on librarians to continue to lead their constituents through the labyrinth of information and to reaffirm the principle that knowledge, not data, is the goal of education. In addition, they must continue to maintain their stewardship over the materials of cultural heritage and scholarly research so that future generations may have also access to their contents.

PROFESSIONAL INVOLVEMENT

Librarians should involve themselves in enterprises beyond the immediate boundaries of their particular jobs, participate in the work of professional associations and, when appropriate, contribute to the literature of the field. Most librarians, like workers in other professions, devote only a fraction of their energy to diagnosis, planning, innovation, deliberate change and growth. Day-to-day considerations demand that the major proportion of available effort be spent in carrying out routine, goal-directed operations and maintaining existing relationships within the system. There is always another library instruction course that can be offered, or a new library handbook to be tackled. Participation in professional life, however, not only expands the individual, but insures the well-being of the profession.

Professional associations that function well furnish bonds through which the community coheres and mediate relationships between practitioners and the profession, as well as between practitioners and the outside world. They speak for the profession and provide avenues of communication. In more tangible terms, professional associations try to safeguard the welfare of their members, improve working conditions, press for advancement opportunities and work toward legally enforced standards of professional competence.[14] In addition, they can influence the quality of personnel the profession recruits.

The American Library Association (ALA) is an umbrella organization for librarians whose purpose is to advance the goals of libraries and librarians. Membership is voluntary. Within ALA, the largest division, the Association of College and Research Libraries (ACRL), is composed mostly of librarians serving in institutions of higher education. Formed in 1889, ACRL has a roster of more than 10,000 members. In addition to sponsoring meetings where matters of interest to librarianship and libraries are discussed, ACRL runs regional training sessions and workshops, and has an extensive publishing program. Among its important publications are the book reviewing journal *Choice* and the monthly publication, *College and Research Libraries*, a peer-reviewed journal that publishes research findings as well as essays on topics important to academic librarians. ACRL also publishes *College & Research Library News*, a monthly newsletter that reports on association matters and activities or projects undertaken by academic libraries. Other functions of ACRL are to encourage research and publication, to develop and publish standards, guidelines and manuals on various aspects of college libraries, conduct training sessions for librarians, and work with ALA's legislative office and other organizations devoted to higher education to lobby for legislation that will benefit academic libraries.

The other publication of general interest to college and university librarians is the *Journal of Academic Librarianship* which also bases its acceptance of articles on peer review and includes reports of research as well as symposia on controversial academic library questions.

Librarians involved in a particular phase or specialization of academic librarianship normally ally themselves with others who perform similar functions, joining, for instance, the Reference & Adult Services Division, the Library Administration and Management Association, the Library and Information Technology Association, and the Association for Library Collections and Technical Services. All of the major components of ALA have their own publications. In addition, there are periodicals generated outside of ALA devoted to these specializations, the most important of which are described or referred to in appropriate chapters throughout this book.

The majority of academic librarians earn that designation by virtue of having completed a Master's Degree in Librarianship in an ALA-accredited library program. Library education has, since its inception at Columbia University in 1887, been the subject of endless debate about whether it is appropriately designated as professional education or graduate (scholarly) education. The matter is complex and most institutions waffle, providing both a smattering of theoretical background and sufficient library skills to make graduates feel somewhat competent. In recent years, there has been increased emphasis on understanding research and research methods, partially in response to academic librarians' calls for faculty status. This view of the academic librarian as researcher/practitioner is controversial and has not been fully embraced. Those who advocate full faculty status for academic librarians find it consistent with the role they envision for librarians. Others, who distinguish between faculty as researchers and librarians as practitioners, feel that the emphasis on research and writing places librarians in an untenable position, with work schedules already too full, and discretionary time essentially nonexistent.

Even for those who make the distinction between practice and research, professional ethics oblige librarians to keep current in the field, through self and formal continuing education, and to add their individual contributions to the collective power of the professional community.

In the nineteenth and early twentieth centuries, academic librarians serving as directors of academic libraries generally had earned a doctorate in one of the classical disciplines. Although the MLS degree is considered a terminal degree, there is a trend toward academic librarians having second master's degrees and, to a lesser extent, doctor of philosophy degrees. While many college librarians hold second master's degrees and a substantial number of directors have doctorates in librarianship, management or education, a subject doctorate is much less common among contemporary library managers.[15] The question of whether to earn a second Master's Degree (in addition to the library degree) in a subject discipline or in an information-related specialty is often posed, and receives no uniform response. Both courses have value. Study beyond the Bachelor's Degree in a physical or natural science certainly leads to increased marketability, as does advanced study in any other area with fewer than the desired number of qualified candidates for available positions.

Academic librarians are currently accorded higher status in the profession than librarians from public and school libraries.[16] This may be attributable to the greater number of academic librarians with advanced degrees, a higher percentage of male librarians in academic librarianship or simply status by association with the prestige of an academic institution. Until recently there has been a tendency in the profession to assume that bigger is better—perhaps richer, more complex—and to hold directors of university libraries in higher esteem than those who head libraries in colleges. As a result, a tilt to the very large institutions is apparent in the assistance offered to the profession by federal agencies and foundations, in unequal access to grant funds, and in the preparation of graduates by library schools. These attitudes have undergone a gradual change, although to some extent they still prevail. Librarians at smaller academic institutions, however, can claim special rewards. They have unparalleled opportunities to work with the whole student, to build excellent carefully selected collections, to influence programs of instruction, and often, a chance to participate in the life of the entire community.

SUMMARY

The history of academic librarianship reflects the history of higher education, but also demonstrates how librarians carved out their own identities as conservators and creative promoters of the records of culture by developing methods to acquire, organize and disseminate information. The efforts of previous generations of academic librarians to insure professionalism by forming associations, establishing library schools and devising standards are validated by the several thousand people who call themselves academic librarians and who work together to define and deliver quality services to colleges.

Academic libraries profited from the new importance attributed to scholarship in the late 19th century when they were promoted from mere appendage to "heart of the institution." By the 1990s college libraries had achieved a position of strength in the educational program. Libraries will continue to command respect if they lead their constituents through the labyrinth of information and maintain their guardianship over the materials of cultural heritage and scholarly research so that future generations may have also access to their contents.

NOTES AND SUGGESTED READINGS

Notes

1. Louis Shores, *Origins of the American College Library 1638-1800* (Nashville, TN: George Peabody College, 1934), 57.

2. Orvin Lee Shiflett, *Origins of American Academic Librarianship* (Norwood, NJ: Ablex, 1981), 33.

3. David Kaser, "Collection Building in American Universities" in *University Library History*, ed. James Thompson (New York: K. G. Saur, 1980), 39-40.

4. *Ibid.*, 38.

5. Michael Harris, *History of Libraries in the Western World* (Metuchen, NJ: Scarecrow Press, 1984), 233.

6. Louis R. Wilson, "The Use of the Library in Instruction," in *Proceedings of the Institute for Administrative Offices of Higher Institutions, 1941*, ed. John D. Russell (Chicago: University of Chicago Press, 1942), 115-27.

7. Thomas R. Barcus, *Carnegie Corporation & College Libraries 1938-1943* (New York: Carnegie Corporation of New York, 1943); William Warner Bishop, *Carnegie Corporation & College Libraries 1929-1938* (New York: Carnegie Corporation of New York, 1938).

8. ALA College and University Postwar Planning Committee, *College and University Libraries and Librarianship* (Chicago: American Library Association, 1946), 69-72.

9. Harris, 237.

10. Guy R. Lyle, *The Administration of the College Library*, 4th ed. (New York: H. W. Wilson, 1974), 7.

11. ACRL Task Force on WHCLIS, "Position Paper on Academic Libraries," *College and Research Libraries News* 51 (September 1990): 713-15.

12. Lyle, 7.

13. David Kaser, "Standards for College Libraries," *Library Trends* 31 (Summer 1982): 9.

14. Anthony Abbott, *System of Professions* (Chicago: University of Chicago Press, 1988), 35.

15. Jean-Pierre V. W. Herubel, "The Ph.D. Librarian: A Personal Perspective," *College and Research Libraries* News 51 (July/August 1990): 626-628.

16. Pauline Wilson, *Stereotype and Status: Librarians in the United States* (Westport, CT: Greenwood Press, 1982).

Suggested Readings

Hamlin, Arthur T. *The University Library in the United States: Its Origins and Development.* Philadelphia: University of Pennsylvania Press, 1981.

Harris, Michael. *History of Libraries in the Western World.* Metuchen, NJ: Scarecrow Press, 1984.

Holley, Edward. "Academic Libraries in 1876." *College and Research Libraries* 36 (January 1976): 15-47.

Houser, Lloyd and Alvin Schrader. *The Search for a Scientific Profession.* Metuchen, NJ: Scarecrow Press, 1978.

Johnson, Richard D., ed. *Libraries for Teaching, Libraries for Research: Essays for a Century.* Chicago: American Library Association, 1976.

Molz, Redmond Kathleen. *Library Planning and Policy Making: The Legacy of the Public and Private Sectors.* Metuchen, NJ: Scarecrow Press, 1990.

Radford, Neil. *The Carnegie Corporation and the Development of American College Libraries.* Chicago: American Library Association, 1984.

Shiflett, Orvin L. *Origins of American Academic Librarianship.* Norwood, NJ: Ablex, 1981.

Shores, Louis. *Origins of the American College Library 1638-1800.* Nashville, TN: George Peabody College, 1934.

Wilson, Pauline. *Stereotype and Status: Librarians in the United States*. Westport, CT: Greenwood Press, 1982.

Chapter 4

CAMPUS CONTEXT

All colleges are products of the same general components. The generic college has students, a faculty, an administration, trustees, alumni, a physical plant, history, traditions, and a library although no two colleges combine components in equal proportions. The particular mixture, however, is what determines the institution's character and renders it unique. The elements themselves, examined separately, reveal information essential to all participants in campus life who aspire to understand the campus culture and the library's place within it, including, of course, the library director and staff. The library professional contemplating employment with a college who makes a decision based solely on the library, without considering its environment as well, is indeed short-sighted.

CAMPUS INVENTORY

A prospective employee undertaking an inventory of a college would require answers to a variety of questions about the institution. The ones raised here represent a broad range of college life.[1] What the answers may imply about a college are often subject to varying interpretation. For instance, a low faculty turnover rate can mean a stagnant environment or one that provides a highly satisfying milieu for scholar-teachers. Other data would be required before even a tentative conclusion could be reached about the relationship between faculty turnover rates and faculty productivity and morale.

Most of the items below have importance in a very direct way for the library. Using information generated by responses to the questions, the library's constituents can be described and their needs identified. The book collection and the nature of the bibliographic instruction program, for example, should reflect the educational background, achievement and goals of both students and faculty. The library's funding will be, to a large extent, a product of the college's financial condition and approach to learning and teaching.

Data required to provide adequate responses to most of the questions can be found in published sources including the guides to four-year colleges used by high school seniors. Documents located in the campus institutional research office offer more details. Not all questions are of equal importance, especially to a new employee, but those that are more significant have been marked with an asterisk. Librarians seeking directorships probably require at least general answers to most of the matters raised. A careful mix of reading on and between the lines of published documents, interviews and observations will reveal the necessary information. The college catalog, often considered a contract between students and the institution, is a rich source of material about many of the inventory items.

Virtually all of the questions produce measurable data which can be compared with numbers produced by like institutions. Care must be taken, however, to assure that the figures are genuinely comparable and based on similar inputs. Statistics of this kind are relatively easy to manipulate, and, unfortunately, many institutions knowingly, or inadvertently, engage in deceptions based on incomplete or misleading data. For instance, colleges wishing to underplay a student attrition rate may present the numbers in terms of the previous year's graduates compared with the number of the current entering class and devise a percentage from that. No indication, however, is given of what constitutes that graduating class—for instance how many have taken six or seven years to complete their studies, or whether incoming class sizes are comparable.

Two difficulties become apparent while attempting to develop items for an inventory. The first is determining when to stop asking questions, and the second is deciding whether the really important questions have been included. A twelve-category scheme has been devised to accommodate the inventory questions. The first category places the college in its proximate physical environment. The second category considers the physical plant and the third covers those factors that apply to the institution as a whole. In the next five categories are questions relating to groups in the college community—faculty, students, administration, alumni and trustees.[2] The next two segments relate to the curriculum and campus life. The penultimate category deals with services which the institution provides and the final segment poses four questions about the library.

SITING

Where a college is located can, to some extent, predict and explain who attends that institution. It can also help to determine the kind of campus social life that will exist as well as whether a wide-ranging public events program will be necessary or desirable. Geographically isolated colleges that attract a diverse non-local student body may have a greater need to build community among campus constituents, to offer a more fully developed social life, and to attach great importance to importing outside speakers and cultural entertainment. The reverse may be true in each instance for urban colleges.

Questions about the location of a college might include:

1. Where is the college located in terms of urban, suburban, or rural environment? How big is the community?

*2. Is it a residential or commuter college?

3. Where is the college located within that environment? Residential area? Industrial area? Depressed area?

4. Is there transportation in and out of the campus and the community?

5. What is the community's socio-economic status?

6. What are the community's resources?

7. How proximate is the college to other academic institutions?

8. What is the town-gown relationship?

*9. What is the economy of the area and what is the economic forecast of the region for the next decade?

*10. Where is the library located on the campus?

PHYSICAL PLANT

Good housing, academic buildings and equipment facilitate a college's ability to provide a quality education. For instance, the proportion of students housed on campus, off campus, and in fraternities may reflect attitudes toward social interaction among students. Some of the important questions related to this category are:

1. How many buildings of each kind (classrooms, offices, dormitories, etc.) are there and what are their age and condition?

2. Are there sufficient buildings to meet campus needs? For instance, are there adequate numbers of classrooms, etc.? How many students live on campus? in Fraternities? Off campus?

3. Is there a building program in force?

4. What new buildings are most needed or desired?

5. What is the nature of the campus security program?

6. What is the condition of the grounds and outdoor facilities?

7. What are the recreational facilities?

8. What percentage of the campus is accessible to the handicapped?

*9. What is the age, condition and projected capacity of the library?

10. Is there a campus based computer network?

ETHOS

Under this rubric are contained questions that relate to the institution as a whole, that is, its traditions, history, aims and goals, plans, funding, affiliations and other college-wide considerations. Recently, some colleges have identified themselves as "research colleges," while others consider they are "liberal arts colleges." An additional set of college is oriented toward vocational or occupational training. The first group contends that the best education is produced through research—both faculty and student. The second maintains that the educated student is a product of the process by which they are introduced to the important works of human thought and are trained to deal with them critically. Those in the third group feel that they must be instrumental in producing marketable students.

1. Is the institution public or private?

2. What is its history? How old is it? Are there famous graduates? What have been the trends over time? What are its unique traditions?

3. What are its affiliations? Is it associated with a religious denomination? If so, does the affiliation translate into policy? What are its professional memberships?

4. Is it accredited? Regionally? In academic disciplines?

5. Does it have clearly stated objectives and goals?

6. Does it have a long-range plan which mirrors these objectives?

7. What is its endowment? What is its wealth related to comparable institutions?

8. What is its budget? What values are implicit in how the budget is apportioned? Does its budget indicate a stable and healthy economic situation?

9. What is its tuition? What percentage of its budget is represented by tuition?

10. How successful is it in attracting foundation support?

*11. Which institutions does it consider either comparable and/or model colleges?

12. What are some recent changes that faculty, students and administrators consider significant?

FACULTY

The nature of the faculty, its role, recruitment, evaluation and treatment are crucial factors in determining the well-being of an institution. Education at the traditional liberal arts college was controlled by its faculty. All policy decisions related to students and curriculum, even peripheral ones, were made by them. In recent years, many campuses have experienced a large growth in the administrative sectors of their institutions and a new definition and separation of responsibilities may lead to contention and division between faculty and administrators. Among the questions which might be posed under this heading are:

1. How many faculty are there? What is the student-faculty ratio? Has there been growth or shrinkage in the size of the faculty?

2. What is the gender, race and nationality of the faculty? What is the male-female ratio? Are there minority group members?

3. How many Ph.D.'s are on the faculty? Where were they earned? What were the dissertation topics?

4. Which undergraduate institutions did faculty attend?

5. How old is the faculty? How many are close to retirement? How many at the beginning of their academic careers?

6. How long have they been at the college?

7. What is the turnover rate among faculty? Does this vary by departments? To what institutions are faculty going when they leave?

8. What is the tenure experience? How many are tenured? How many are eligible for tenure ? What percentage is granted tenure?

9. What is the distribution of faculty within ranks?

10. What is the distribution of faculty by departments?

11. What is the publishing history and behavior of the faculty?

12. Is there institutional support for research? For other forms of faculty growth and development?

13. What is the sabbatical policy?

14. How successful are faculty in gaining outside funding for their research?

15. What are average faculty salaries by rank and what does the benefits package contain?

16. Are the faculty represented by unions?

17. What is the extent of participation in AAUP?

18. How are new faculty recruited?

19. What is the distribution of teaching loads within the college?

20. What is the workload including academic advising, community service?

21. How are faculty evaluated? Are selection, promotion, and tenure considerations clear and uniformly applied?

*22. What criteria weigh most heavily in evaluation of faculty?

23. Is there a commitment to academic freedom?

24. Is there a policy on parental leave?

25. Is salary information public? Are there salary ranges?

*26. Are librarians considered faculty? Do they teach or serve as advisors to students?

STUDENTS

A college's ability to attract and retain a student body is vital to its existence. The nature of the student body predicts, to some extent, the kinds of teaching the faculty will offer, the kinds of programs that will be devised for students, and the experiences they may encounter during their college careers. The questions posed below represent an abbreviated list, those we consider most important. A substantially more developed list of items that relate to college students, specifically to incoming students, as well as the normative answers can be found in *The American Freshman: National Norms,* issued annually by the Cooperative Institutional Research Program of the American Council on Education, the so-called Astin Reports.[3] Participating colleges contribute data from which national norms are established. The information is used by colleges to compare themselves nationally with like institutions, and to track in-house changes over time.

1. How many students are there? What are the student-faculty, student-advisor ratios?

2. Where are the students from geographically? What is the urban-rural breakdown? How many international students are there?

3. What is the gender and racial breakdown? How willing is the college to invest in groups traditionally barred from higher education?

4. From what socio-economic groups does the college draw? What, for instance, are the occupations and earnings of their parents? What is the family's educational background?

5. Where did students receive their secondary education? What is the breakdown among private vs. public or parochial high schools?

6. What are their religions and religious orientations?

*7. What are their SAT or ACT scores? (This figure should not be an average, but the full range for both verbal and quantitative results.)

8. What rank did students hold in their high school classes?

9. What percentage of students who apply are accepted? What percentage of those accepted are enrolled?

10. What is the degree of institutional commitment to support students who require financial aid? Is admission "need blind"?

11. How many students require remediation?

12. What is the attrition-retention rate and the cohort survival rate?

13. What percentage of the student body is part-time? How many older students are there?

*14. What percentage of students do honors work?

15. What issues concern students as revealed in the student newspaper or in senior exit surveys?

16. What percentage of students work part-time while attending school? How many work on campus?

ADMINISTRATION

On many college campuses there are strong divisions between the administration and the faculty. Students also find themselves in conflict with administrators. Without far-sighted administrators, whose vision encompasses the entire institution, its mission and role, the campus cannot function optimally. Among the questions which might be posed about the administration are:

1. What is the size of the administration? How big is it in relation to the faculty and the student body?

2. What are the main administrative offices? How do the offices relate to one another?

3. What is the gender and racial breakdown of the administrative staff?

4. What is the President's academic and professional background?

5. What kinds of academic and professional backgrounds do other key administrators have, including the library director? How have they been educated?

6. How are they recruited? Is there promotion from within?

7. What are the salary ranges? How do they compare with faculty compensation?

8. What is the turnover rate?

9. What is the management style of the college at present?

*10.   What is the faculty and student role in governance?

ALUMNI

The successful undergraduate institution commands great loyalty from those who have completed its program. Alumni may play an important role in the life of the institution financially and in recruitment, as well as in other ways. Answers to the following questions would help to indicate the degree of involvement of alumni in the college.

1.   How many alumni are there? Of those, how many can be considered active and how many inactive?

2.   What does the college know about them?

3.   What percentage have higher degrees?

4.   What are their current occupations?

5.   How many contribute to the annual fund or to special funds?

6.   How many return to the campus or attend local alumni meetings?

TRUSTEES

The governing board of a college is expected to oversee the institution and to hold it accountable. The major duties of the Board are to appoint a chief executive officer, develop policies, and make sure the institution is fiscally sound. A more detailed description of the board's responsibilities appears in Chapter 5, in which governance is explained. The questions posed here are directed more toward board membership than they are toward legal responsibility.

1. How many Board members are there?

2. What are their backgrounds, ages and current occupations?

3. How many are alumni?

4. How long have they served on the Board? What is the turnover?

5. Does the Board have a relationship with the National Association of Governing Boards?

6. To what extent do (and must) Board Members contribute financially to the College?

7. What, if any, interaction is there between Board members and faculty and/or students?

CURRICULUM AND ACADEMIC PROGRAMS

Curriculum reform is a fact of life at most American four-year colleges today. Unhappiness with the education of students, both at the secondary and college level, has led to major curriculum overhaul, and reinstatement in one form or another of distributional requirements that include the skills that faculty and administrators wish students to possess at graduation. The lack of consensus about what the new curriculum should look like has led in many institutions to a Chinese menu approach—one from group A and two from group B—which dissatisfies major segments of the faculty and confuses students. It is somewhat difficult, therefore, to pose the appropriate curriculum questions. Those which follow are sufficiently general to be germane to most colleges today. Consideration of various pedagogical approaches to education, and their impact on the library, is saved for later chapters.

1. Is there a relationship between the stated goals of the curriculum and the courses offered?

2. When was the curriculum last evaluated and what major changes resulted from the evaluation?

3. How do departments compare with each other in size of faculty and number of students served? Class sizes?

*4. What are the popular majors?

5. How many new courses are introduced each year?

6. Have there been new majors and minors adopted recently?

7. What are the requirements for graduation?

8. Is there a summer school?

*9. Are there special programs such as study abroad, independent projects, senior theses, internships, interdisciplinary studies?

10. How do librarians learn about new curricular efforts?

CAMPUS LIFE

Campus life is lived both in and out of the classroom. A variety of activities and experiences are offered on most college campuses to enrich and enliven the institution. In this category appear such important educational and extracurricular programs as speakers, public performances, and athletic participation. Among the questions that might be asked are:

1. How extensive is the public events and speaker-visitor program? How often are students exposed to well-known professionals in all walks of life?

2. To what extent are students offered the opportunity to participate in cultural events such as plays, musical performances, and art shows? What percentage participate?

3. What writing and broadcasting outlets are available to students?

4. How important are inter-collegiate sports? How many students participate? Is there an even-handed approach to men's and women's athletics?

5. Is there a well-developed intramural program? How many students participate?

6. Is there a student government? How many students participate? What is its role in the extra-curricular life of the campus? Does it have financial resources?

7. Are there fraternities and sororities? What is their role on the campus? What percentage of students participate?

8. What relationships do campus organizations have with external ones?

9. What opportunities exist for interaction between faculty and students outside the classroom?

10. Are there service opportunities for students in the geographic community in which the college is housed?

SERVICES

Most colleges provide a variety of services for the campus. Some of these are directed solely or mainly at students. Others can be utilized by the college community as a whole. Technology and a new understanding of the importance of psychological and career services have resulted in a mushrooming of personnel whose job it is to offer these services. Among the questions to ask here are:

1. Does the college have a career-development or placement office? Who does it serve?

2. Is there a psychological counseling office? Is it available only for students? Does it include drug and alcohol counseling, as well?

3. Are there health services? Who may use them?

4. How accessible are computers and computer-training? For whom?

5. Is there day-care for children of employees and for children of students?

6. How developed is the student advising program?

7. What is contained in the orientation programs for students, for faculty and for administrative employees?

8. Does the bookstore carry trade books as well as textbooks and convenience items?

9. Are there any support groups or services available to particular audiences such as women, minorities,

homosexuals, students needing tutoring, or those from other countries?

LIBRARY

A potential college library employee would have scores of questions concerning the library. Other new college employees, faculty and administrators, should be interested in some aspects of the library. Some questions have been posed about the library under appropriate headings. However, a few additional matters seem essential to consider.

1. What are the strong collections of the library?

2. What are the library's evident needs?

3. What is the nature of the library instruction program?

4. How involved are librarians on campus? Do they participate in the institution's governance, curriculum decisions, extracurricular affairs, and social life?

5. What is the pattern of staff turnover and promotion in the library?

6. What are the recurring compliments/complaints received by the library staff?

One could gather the information provided by the answers to the questions above, analyze it, and still not have a real grasp of a particular college. Obviously, the institution is more than the sum of all of these parts. Another series of considerations whose answers are less tangible, and more subjective, is described in the following chapter, where attention is turned to governance and politics.

A substantial group of extremely important questions regarding 'outcomes' of the college experience are left both unasked and unanswered, and yet should not be ignored. The extent, for instance, to which the institution has enabled students to make moral choices is surely among the important questions one could pose about a college. The degree to which students are able to gather and evaluate information is another mark of the success or failure of an institution. The librarian has an important role to play in developing these skills, one which will be discussed in later chapters as the role of the library in the educational process is explored.

SUMMARY

Learning a college is a complex process, one that can sometimes engage the energies of an intelligent seeker for a lifetime. Snapshot views resulting from inventories taken in a moment of time serve as indicators of the strengths or weaknesses of a school. Data gathered from this kind of 'institutional scanning' should be compared with information about similar schools and balanced against general demographic and economic indicators. While all colleges have similar components—faculty, students, administrators, alumni, trustees, curricula, physical plants, and of course libraries—their individuality lies in how they have traditionally provided for these elements and how they are meshed.

NOTES AND SUGGESTED READINGS

Notes

1. Middle States Association of Colleges and Schools, Commission on Higher Education, "Characteristics of Excellence in Higher Education" (Philadelphia: Middle States Association, 1988); Regional accreditation standards are often organized around goals and major program areas and can be used to

examine a campus. Ernest Boyer, *College: The Undergraduate Experience in America* (New York: Harper and Row, 1987) is a recent report of the Carnegie Foundation for the Advancement of Teaching which can serve as an overview of campus life.

2. The assumption here is that the campus is a community composed of administrators, faculty, students, alumni, and trustees all playing their roles toward the fulfillment of a goal—to create an educational institution. Some models of colleges are student-centered, presupposing that the college exists only to educate students with all energy directed to that purpose. Others are faculty-centered—driven by the concept that faculty are the core of the institution. Yet others are organized around the notion of an administrative hierarchy. These approaches, while not necessarily mutually exclusive, each provide a somewhat different orientation toward college work and life.

3. Alexander Astin and others, *The American Freshman: National Norms for 1988*, Cooperative Institutional Research Program, UCLA (New York: American Council on Education, 1988). Commonly called Astin Report.

Suggested Readings

American Council on Education. *American Universities and Colleges*. 13th ed. New York: Walter de Gruyter, 1987.

American Council on Education. *Fact Book on Higher Education 1989-90*. New York: American Council on Education, 1989.

Boyer, Ernest L. "Foreword." *A Classification of Institutions of Higher Education*. New York: Carnegie Foundation for the Advancement of Teaching, 1987.

Chaffee, Ellen Earle and William G. Tierney. *Collegiate Culture and Leadership Strategies*. New York: American Council on Education, 1988.

Clark, Burton. *The Distinctive College*. Chicago: Aldine, 1970.

Fiske, Edward. *Fiske Guide to Colleges*. New York: Times Books, 1989.

Mayhew, Lewis B. *Surviving the Eighties*. San Francisco: Jossey-Bass, 1979.

Wolotkiewicz, Rita J. *College Administrator's Handbook*. Boston: Allyn and Bacon, 1980.

Chapter 5

LEGAL STATUS, GOVERNANCE AND POLITICS

Legal status refers to the characteristics of a college specified by charter and to its statutory placement within the world of other organized groups. *Governance* is the codified arrangement whereby a given college systematically assigns to its various constituents responsibilities and rights. Typically, the status of certain groups is linked to the particulars of the legal status of the institution. *Politics* is the process by which individuals and constituencies seek to influence decisions about the distribution of resources. The administrative structure within which a system manages its operations is discussed in Chapter 6. The mechanisms described in this chapter, however, are those that determine how successful constituents of the system will be in their competition for recognition and scarce resources.

LEGAL STATUS OF THE COLLEGE

Most, if not all, colleges—whether liberal arts or land grant, junior or teachers—are invested by society with a corporate character. All corporate forms of organization are dependent on their legal status. In the United States, individual state governments maintain more direct control over matters pertaining to the public welfare than does the national government. Corporations, for instance, owe their existence to the states, not to the federal government. Colleges are established in a similar fashion. They are either chartered by special acts of the state legislature or incorporated by the educational or corporation laws of the state. The charter has been defined as a "special enactment by the legislature of the state authorizing the establishment of the institution and defining its powers and privileges," whereas articles of incorporation "consist of an agreement by the founders of the institution, drawn up under the provisions of a general statute."[1] The difference between the two methods of establishment lies in the specificity with which the institution is described. A charter granted by the state legislature applies to one institution only. With articles of incorporation, the legislative action is general and the institution to be established is covered by provisions which were made for other, similar institutions.[2]

Early college charters had the force of a contract and enabled colleges to manage their own affairs. Since 1850, however, when the United States Supreme Court guaranteed the inviolability of the Dartmouth College charter against legislative nullification, states have usually reserved the right to amend or repeal the charter or articles of incorporation of colleges established under general laws of incorporation.

Most colleges and universities established before the educational reform movements of the late nineteenth and early twentieth centuries have their origins in charters. As a result, these institutions may have unique rights or opportunities for development. The charter for Drew University, for instance, issued by the State of New Jersey in 1866, was a permissive document. In time it was invoked by the Board of Trustees to support the establishment, first, of a Seminary, and subsequently, of a College of Liberal Arts and a Graduate School. Should Drew decide at some later time to add other professional schools it could do so based on the general nature of its charter.

Articles of incorporation granted to privately supported colleges and public institutions founded after 1900 were likely to be more specific and limiting. They were commonly given permission to develop an undergraduate program, If they decided to offer a Master's degree, they had to return to the legislature for a revision of their articles of incorporation. In recent years, state departments of higher education have developed policies to avoid excessive duplication of programs, to set minimum standards that must be met before colleges can be incorporated, and to define characteristics that allow an institution be called a "college" or a "university," although definitions can vary across state borders. These state agencies, as well as the Association of Governing Boards of Universities and Colleges, also concern themselves with the role of college trustees.

From the standpoint of legal control, the first and most important distinction between colleges is their origin in either the public or private sector. Public colleges are controlled by a government agency—the state, county or municipal government. The degree of control depends on the nature of the articles of incorporation. Private colleges are generally incorporated as non-profit charitable organizations and are controlled by a private corporation whose composition and authority are laid down in the college charter. Both types of colleges are exempt from property taxes and exercise certain other powers and rights. These powers are usually vested, under the legislative act or charter which created colleges, in a board of trustees. The Board owns property, enters into contracts, accepts responsibility for the acts of its officers and employees, and provides the institution with its continuity.

In private colleges the number of trustees, their mode of selection and terms of office are usually mandated in the college charter. Ordinarily the board is self-perpetuating; that is, the trustees themselves select new members as vacancies occur. Denominational colleges usually have representation from the sponsoring church, and many boards, both public and private, have alumni as members. Less typical, and indeed somewhat controversial, is the practice of having a faculty member from the institution, a student, or a representative from a union under contract with the college serve on the board. A few boards of public colleges are elected by the public, but more often they are selected by the governor and confirmed by the state legislature. Terms of office vary from life-time appointments to a maximum of two successive terms.

State colleges are frequently governed by the state board of education and may not have separate groups of trustees concerned with specific campuses. By and large the members of the boards which control public and private colleges are drawn from the ranks of prominent members of the business community, lawyers, alumni, professional people, foundation executives, educators, civic leaders, and long-time supporters of the college. In the recent past, a good deal of effort has been exerted toward changing the gender and racial profiles of typical college boards by adding women and minority persons to them. At the same time, colleges have increased their expectations about participation of trustees in the life of the community. Such expectations include support for capital campaign contributions at a significant level and support for one or more aspects of campus life through involvement on a trustee committee. Trustees are also expected to be well-informed about the college and able to generate approval and understanding for the mission of the institution in the wider community.

When overseeing college operations, trustees have the authority to draft and put into effect regulations that affect governance, and to define their relations with the college. Generally, such rules are called bylaws and are looked upon as vehicles for implementing the more general grants of authority found in the charter or articles of incorporation. The bylaws contain such information as the official title and address of the college, aims, officers, and members of the board and their selection, powers and duties, meetings, and standing committees. Frequently the bylaws and the charter are printed together and distributed to board members, college officers and other interested persons. In the absence of bylaws, or in addition to them, there may be official regulations in which the operating responsibility and authority, and procedures for continuing review are clearly defined. A framework for such a document is suggested in the "Statement on Government of Colleges and Universities" issued jointly by the American Association of University Professors, the American Council on Education, and the Association of Governing Boards of Universities and Colleges.[3]

LEGAL STATUS OF THE LIBRARY

The legal status of the college library is determined, if it is formalized at all, by the charter or articles of incorporation, the bylaws, and the institutional handbook, by whatever name it is known. The charter, as the governing document of the college, is the basic source of authority. Beyond an occasional reference to the authority of the board of trustees to purchase books, however, most charters and articles of incorporation have little or nothing to say specifically about the library.

Statements of varying length and complexity on the library appear in the bylaws of some, but by no means all, colleges. The topics covered will generally include the authority of the director of the library as an officer of the college, a general statement of the duties of the library director, a brief statement about the nature of library resources, and perhaps some mention about the methods of appointment of the library director and the professional staff.

GOVERNANCE

In addition to bylaws, most colleges issue a handbook that lists the rules and regulations governing appointment, promotion and retention of faculty. It also describes the standing committees of the faculty and faculty participation in the governance of the college. These provisions are linked to the bylaws. But, while bylaws are the specific province of the board of trustees, the contents of the faculty handbooks are subject to change by the faculty, with the consent of the president and the board of trustees.

What constitutes faculty on a college campus has become a matter of great concern to librarians, many of whom feel that, as professional librarians, they are entitled to faculty status. The troublesome issue of faculty status has generated heated debate among academic librarians, who sometimes even disagree on the meaning of the term.

Faculty status is generally accorded to college and university classroom teachers and brings with it both a structure of rankings and a combination of privileges and responsibilities. Four faculty ranks are commonly assigned to resident faculty at most institutions. They are Full, Associate and Assistant Professor, and at the lowest rung, Instructor. Salary levels for faculty are based on rank as well as on years of service, and quality of work performance. Those holding any of the three professor titles usually have earned a Ph.D. degree, while instructors may be in the process of obtaining one. In most institutions, Full and Associate Professors are tenured, while those in the other ranks are not. To be awarded tenure is to be granted a permanent position. Continuous faculty employment may be abrogated when financial exigencies necessitate college-wide retrenchment or when a faculty member is found guilty of an act of "moral turpitude," or is proved to be no longer performing duties in a satisfactory manner.

In most institutions, judgments about tenurability are made by or before the seventh year of a faculty member's presence on the campus, and follow one or two contract renewals. The probationary time can vary, however, and some institutions have adopted "clock-stopping" mechanisms for delaying the determination. Decisions regarding tenure are always made by the president of the institution with approval by the trustees. These decisions, however, are generally based on peer review and a series of recommendations first by a faculty member's department, second, by a school-wide committee, usually elected by the faculty; and third, by the dean or vice-president/provost. Criteria for granting tenure include quality of teaching, quality of scholarship and quality of service to the institution and community, with the first two carrying the most weight. Most colleges have formal procedures for appealing decisions on tenure and non-renewal of contracts. The system of tenure was adopted as and remains a protection of intellectual freedom inside and outside of the classroom. Faculty and administrators often lose sight of this original purpose and regard tenure as job security.

Among the privileges associated with faculty status is access to sabbatical and other leaves. The term sabbatical has its origins in the practice of allowing land to remain fallow every seven years in order that it may renew itself. Each institution frames its own sabbatical policy, but commonly faculty members with tenure may anticipate a paid leave of absence for at least one semester every seventh year. Grants, fellowships and research funds are more accessible to those with faculty status than they are to other members of the academic community. Other characteristics of faculty status include: active involvement in campus governance and curricular affairs; voting memberships in permanent committees of the faculty; and participation in the faculty councils and senates of an institution.

Academic status, a term adopted by some institutions to describe those who are not primarily classroom teachers, but who are involved in the educational program, usually carries some, but not all, faculty privileges. However, faculty rank, tenure, and readier access to sabbaticals and research development money may or may not be part of the package. Traditions and practices vary among colleges, as do definitions of faculty rank, faculty status and full faculty status. Rank often means the use of titles, but not full privileges, while status means titles are not used. Full usually means equal to teaching faculty in all respects.

FACULTY STATUS FOR LIBRARIANS

Good arguments have been mounted on both sides of the status for librarians debate. Outspoken advocates have been known to shift positions over time. Former opponents of tenure for librarians have become advocates. Still others recommend a middle course, accepting some elements of faculty and/or academic status for librarians while rejecting others. In 1974 the Association of College and Research Libraries and the American Association of University Professors issued a joint statement asserting that the correct status for all librarians working in colleges and universities is full faculty status. A number who endorsed the statement have since recanted or withdrawn their support. A revision of that policy has recently been issued.[4]

Those who favor faculty status for librarians maintain that it insures they will be recognized as equal partners in the academic community and as members of the instructional and research staffs of the institution. Different titles, salaries, schedules, and methods of selection and evaluation cause librarians to be regarded as something different and inevitably as inferior to teaching faculty. The contribution that librarians make to the educational process is, after all, intellectual in nature. It is the product of considerable formal education, includes training at the graduate level, and culminates in a terminal degree. Librarians perform a teaching and research role by instructing students formally and informally, as well as by advising faculty in scholarly pursuits. In addition, faculty status permits librarians to become, themselves, productive scholars because they would have access to grants and sabbatical leaves.

Among the other dividends of faculty status for librarians is the emergence of a collegial model of library governance, one which permits participative management and peer participation in personnel decisions. Hiring becomes a search committee effort, and promotion and tenure are based on criteria accepted by faculty both inside and outside the library. Further, aligning with the faculty, particularly if they are unionized, gives librarians bargaining leverage. Finally, in the same way that tenure insures individual professors the right to speak out on matters they consider important, tenure for librarians helps to protect librarians against capricious decisions, enables them to criticize the administration with impunity, and permits them to exercise purely professional judgments when purchasing materials they believe are appropriate to the collection.

Arguments mounted by opponents of faculty status are often based on the premise that librarianship is a different profession from that practiced by classroom teachers and, should therefore be measured by a different yardstick. Opponents see the goals of teaching faculty as presenting in systematic fashion a coherent viewpoint on a given portion of reality. They view librarians as bringing order from chaos and making various bodies of truth available in a useful fashion. Librarians, they contend, should be librarians, not ersatz professors, and should be rewarded on the basis of an independent, self-reliant position. They should be judged by standards which relate to what they do, not to what someone else does. Tenure, they point out, is generally granted on the basis of teaching, research, professional activity, service to the community and general usefulness, often in that order. Librarians considered for tenure must either have these priorities reordered, or else be granted status based on different, perhaps lesser performance when it comes to research, or reorder their own priorities and work schedules. Many who question faculty status have witnessed the extraordinary pressures on librarians aspiring to tenure under circumstances requiring them to maintain full library schedules, and to publish and teach in the classroom. The opponents of faculty status also question the motives of those who support it, suggesting that prestige and social benefits may be the primary reasons for its being sought.

Traditionally, library directors at colleges were the only library staff members to hold full faculty status or even a partial form of faculty rank. Other librarians had no formal access to participation in the academic life of an institution. More recently, however, some colleges that grant faculty status to librarians are loathe to include directors, whom they consider administrators. In yet other institutions, library directors hold positions as chairs of library departments and on that basis are included among the ranks of faculty. Newer colleges with collective bargaining agreements, colleges with a strong history of participative management, publicly supported colleges, and a bare majority of the quality liberal arts colleges have a governance approach that seems to favor the inclusion of librarians in the faculty, albeit with some reservations. While practices vary, the full integration of all librarians in the teaching faculty is relatively rare, even when they share nomenclature and are awarded tenure. Distinctions between faculty and librarians are found in the way in which promotion criteria are articulated and implemented, in relative financial rewards, in granting of leaves and in providing opportunities for research and education support. In a recent survey of 59 college library directors by Kathleen Moretto Spenser, 23 indicated that their librarians have faculty status, 20 maintained that their status was comparable to faculty, but only 8 directors reported that tenure was available to librarians.[5]

ROLE OF THE COLLEGE ADMINISTRATION

More essential even than status considerations, perhaps, is the need to articulate and codify the positions of librarians in the bylaws or in the faculty handbook. It would seem self-evident that the library—involving as it does considerable responsibility for funds and personnel—should have a clearly expressed code of policy or governance. In fact, because libraries are so infrequently mentioned in an institution's official documents, control and governance are largely determined by tradition, precedent and personalities. Unfortunately, the tradition of the library in the college history is often not an exalted one, and librarians are seldom regarded as influential policy makers. More typically they are looked at as quiet and able administrators, in charge of worthy and necessary domains, but not among the principal campus policy makers. Robert Munn's comment, made in 1968, is still apt: "Librarians are not normally part of either the administrative inner circle itself or the select group of faculty oligarchies and entrepreneurs whose views carry great weight. They are thus excluded from the real decision-making process in the institution."[6] Among the real dangers in depending entirely on unwritten customs for library governance are confusion and disagreement. Informal agreements on library policies, moreover, do not necessarily remain effective when there is a change in either the college administration or the library directorship. A clear-cut statement that describes the relationship of the library and librarians to the other parts of the college community and provides for appropriately shared responsibility and activity among them will serve to prevent misunderstanding.

The college administration's unique, as well as most obvious, role is to define the director's authority and responsibility and to identify the library director in the web of organization and services of the institution. Among the matters which need formal codification, or at least guidelines are the flow of authority from the president to the library director, the control of funds for the purchase of library materials, the establishment and administration of departmental libraries, the control of the location of library materials, the selection of the staff, and other similar concerns. Because library directors must deal with and exert pressure on a variety of constituencies—deans, departmental chairpersons, faculty, students, administrators—they must have some recourse to formal documents that clarify issues of governance. Every library director should keep a file in which records of substantive discussions or policy changes in any of these areas are kept. The file can document for an incumbent director why certain practices are in force. Without such a record, library directors and administrators, both old and new, must rely on oral histories which may be either inaccurate or ambiguous. Custom and trust are terribly important on a college campus, but it is well to also have some documentation.

POLITICS

Unlike their 19th-century predecessors, few directors today report directly to the president of the college. The majority do, however, report to the chief academic officer—the dean of the college, the provost or the academic vice president. Library directors with reporting relationships at this level have some regular opportunities to participate in institutional policy decision-making. If the director holds the rank of dean, and meets with other Deans, the potential for influence is even greater. Most library directors, unfortunately, do not meet formally with the person to whom they report more than once or twice a year. When meetings are set, it is more often than not during times of budget review or budget development. In optimal situations, however, meetings are far more frequent. The dean at Swarthmore College meets with the director of the library on a weekly basis, to insure, he says, that the director knows that he, the dean, considers the library central to the task of the college. While few librarians report directly to the president, access to that office is not difficult on most college campuses.

In addition, many directors see presidents socially, as well. One college library director invites the president and his wife to dinner once a semester to create an informal environment in which views about the college and the library's role in it can be exchanged. Other library directors seek informal campus opportunities to nurture their relationships with faculty and administrators. Serving on a search committee, participating in an accreditation self-study, or playing a role in a long-range or strategic planning effort all help to identify the library director or staff member as part of the academic community. Visibility in the informal and formal life of the college is important. The process of gathering support for the library is ongoing and requires strong political and inter-personal skills. Librarians are not successful, nor are their libraries good, simply because the books are ordered and shelved expeditiously. Librarians are successful, in part, because they have opened channels of communication with their constituents and developed mutual respect and understanding with them.

Membership in standing committees of the faculty presents yet another opportunity for participation in policy-making by librarians. Most college have faculty committees—both appointed and elected by the teaching staff—to advise the president on policy and practical matters, to consider curriculum, to decide on cases of reappointment, promotion, and tenure, to evaluate faculty requests for research funds, to plan public events, and to award honorary degrees, among other tasks. These committees vary in importance from campus to campus. It is not difficult, however, to identify at any given college which committees are prestigious and include faculty who are well-respected and considered influential. Elected committees tend to be more highly regarded than appointed ones; those that deal with items of concern to the president, those that accept responsibility for the conditions of employment of their peers, and those that consider curricular, budget, and planning matters are generally important.

While librarians who hold faculty status may sit on these bodies, too often they are overlooked when committee assignments are made. Particularly shortsighted is the non-appointment of librarians, even in an ex officio capacity, to the committees responsible for curriculum decisions. Ignoring the library when considering new courses for adoption carries the danger that the library holdings may be insufficient to support the subjects being offered. Despite their exclusion from committees, librarians should be aware of the pecking order—the relative status of serving on one or another of the committees. Courting support for the library from faculty members whose opinion is respected by their colleagues is not unseemly behavior. Individuals are thought of as leaders when they have something to say which resonates with the opinions of those who become followers. This is equally true on a college campus. Library directors are well advised to listen carefully to those faculty members who are elected to the important standing committees, who are chosen by the administration to ad hoc, long-range planning committees or appointed to committees to search for high-level administrators.

Building a core of library supporters among the faculty is facilitated by the enlightened self-interest of those professors who are particularly interested in having resources available for their own work as scholars. Publicizing new library resources to the faculty therefore becomes an important means to recruit library supporters. Faculty in departments with strong majors whose students use library materials are seen as particularly valuable allies. A recent informal study of library directors revealed that although support for the library was found most often among History and English faculty, no generalizations about the degree of support from other disciplines could be made.[7] On one campus, the library's strongest friends might be found in the chemistry department and on another, among the political scientists. In any given year there are also a few vocal student leaders who gain power by virtue of their ability to sway the opinions of other students. They, too, should be identified and kept informed about the library.

LIBRARY COMMITTEE

The one faculty committee on which the library director is assured membership is, of course, the library committee. Virtually all colleges have, as part of their permanent faculty committee structure, one which considers the role, function and operation of the library. With proper members, the library committee can play an invaluable liaison role on the campus. While some librarians are emphatic in their praise of library committees, others are frankly skeptical about their value. The division in opinion stems from the fact that, like almost everything else on a college campus, the library committee is a product of its environment. The degree to which it is thought important or influential will determine who is willing to serve on it. On one campus it may be composed of influential and interested faculty members. On others, it may be seen as a way to meet a community service commitment without having to do much work. The size and composition of library committees will vary from campus to campus. They may be large or small depending on whether they are designed to represent departments or divisions. Members of the committee are selected in one of three ways: appointment by the president, appointment by the chief academic officer, or, most commonly, appointment by the faculty—either directly or through a faculty committee on committees. Combinations of these methods are found in some colleges.

Members serve from one to five years, though there are occasional instances in which the term of office appears to be indefinite. A plan that ensures continuity without sterility provides for rotating membership on the committee, with one or two new professors replacing long serving ones each year. Student representation on the committee can give both the library director and the committee a better understanding of how students view the library—hours, regulations, undergraduate collections—than they can obtain from other sources.

Library committees are almost always *advisory* and not administrative. Their function is to consider matters of general library policy, how best to develop library resources, and the most effective means by which the library program can be integrated with other academic activities of the college. While their clout is limited by their "advisory" capacity, members' advice and recommendations on policy questions as well as on matters of administration can be invaluable. The professional staff may set library policy, but undergirding collegial politics and practice is the assumption that others have a need to review the implications of that policy. That is the function of the library committee. If the library committee is seen as a rubber stamp for the actions of the director, it is unlikely to be effective either in advising on library matters or in interpreting them to the faculty. Some directors find it exceedingly difficult to refrain from dominating committee deliberations. For this reason, among others, a librarian should not serve as chair of the library committee. Some have suggested, perhaps facetiously, that the librarian act as secretary to the committee, thereby making excessive participation more difficult. No matter who takes the minutes, however, they should be carefully kept and widely distributed. Routinely routing copies to the president, dean, provost and chief business officer insures access to any information about recommendations, resolutions or other actions which have been considered by the Library Committee.

The liaison role is one of the most important functions of the library committee. On the one hand, the library serves the entire college, and its actions effect the entire community; on the other, the library is a tight, complex agency whose inner workings are largely unknown to those who use it. Library administrators utilize the library committee to keep them fully informed about new educational policies, new courses, new instructors, and new plans for campus development. They also depend on the committee to act as their interpreter to the wider community, to explain how it operates and why it follows particular procedures. The committee's Janus-like relationship to the community and the library can help to prevent misunderstandings and to keep the library from being isolated. Historians, mathematicians and professors of English, all taking their turn serving on a library committee, gaining familiarity with the library's management and utilization, learning why it makes certain decisions, constitute a knowledgeable corps of faculty members in position to inform their colleagues about the library. Often these former members become the library's strongest supporters as they serve on other committees which affect the library.

The success of the library committee is determined by the attitudes toward it of the director and of the faculty members who serve on it. The committee members must be genuinely interested in the development of the library as a whole and not merely in their departmental relationships with it. The director must have faith in the usefulness of the Library Committee, must be willing to share information with it, and must have the patience to let the committee work its way through library matters. The agenda items may be crucial to the interest which faculty members sustain in the committee. If they are called upon to discuss inconsequential details, they are unlikely to show much enthusiasm. Neither, however, will their interest be peaked by endless discussions of unrealistic five-year plans that will never reach fulfillment.

The distinction between policy determination and administrative matters is best ignored by the library committee. Its central mission is to improve the library's effectiveness in the educational program of a college and to collaborate on the development of policies and practices to meet these goals. Some of the chief topics which appear on library committee agendas are: budgets, automation, allocation of book funds to departments, policies and practices of bibliographic instruction, library resources, campus satisfaction with the library, duplication of reserve materials, policies on purchase of audiovisual materials, periodicals, gift policies, staffing practices, enlarging, remodeling or constructing a new building, circulation rules and regulations, departmental collections and staff status.

SUMMARY

Each college has a defined legal status. Description of the role and responsibilities of the library director and of other librarians may be sparse in the college bylaws, but some official publications such as the faculty handbook or the college personnel policy manual document their positions and duties. Tradition most often governs the important relationships between the library and its constituents. Important interpretations of policy or practices, however, should be noted and kept on file to prevent misunderstanding and to educate a new president or dean. In addition to the formal structures, librarians should develop informal communication networks of support and information which can be utilized both routinely and in times of emergency changes on the campus.

NOTES AND SUGGESTED READINGS

Notes

1. Floyd W. Reeves and others, *The Liberal Arts College* (Chicago: University of Chicago Press, 1932), 62.

2. *Ibid.*, 62.

3. American Association of University Professors, *Bulletin* 52 (Winter 1966): 375-379.

4. ACRL, "Guidelines for Academic Status for College and University Libraries," *College and Research Libraries News* 51 (March 1990): 245-6.

5.   Kathleen Moretto Spenser, *Unpublished Survey* (September 5, 1989).

6.   Robert Munn, "The Bottomless Pit," *College and Research Libraries News* 21 (January 1968):   51.   See also Dennis P.   Carrigan, "The Political Economies of the Academic Library," *College and Research Libraries* 49 (July 1988):   325-331.

7. Caroline Coughlin and Alice Gertzog, *Unpublished survey of 60 Directors of Liberal Arts College Libraries* (October 1989).

Suggested Readings

Association of College and Research Libraries. Academic Status Committee. *Academic Status: Statements and Resources*. Chicago: American Library Association, 1988.

Association of College and Research Libraries. "Standards for Faculty Status for College and University Librarians: a draft revision." *College and Research Library News* 51 (May 1990): 402-4.

Biggs, Mary.   "Sources of Tension and Conflict Between Librarians and Faculty." *Journal of Higher Education* 52 (1981): 182-201.

Carnegie Commission on Higher Education. *Governance of Higher Education. A Report and Recommendations*. New York: McGraw Hill, 1973.

The Control of the Campus. Washington, DC: The Carnegie Foundation for the Advancement of Teaching, 1982.

Hardesty, Larry and David Kaser. *What Do Academic Administrators Think about the Library?* A Final Report to the Council on Library Resources, April 1990.

Holley, Edward G. "Defining the Academic Librarian." *College and Research Libraries* 46 (November 1985): 462-468.

Knowles, Asa A., ed. *International Encyclopedia of Higher Education* San Francisco: Jossey-Bass, 1977, v. 5. "Governance and Control of Higher Education."

Ladenson, Alex. *Library Law and Legislation in the United States*. Metuchen, NJ: Scarecrow Press, 1982.

Oberg, Larry R. and others. "Faculty Perceptions of Librarians at Albion College: Status, Role, Contribution and Contacts." *College and Research Libraries* 50 (March 1989): 215-210.

Peterson, Marvin, ed. *Key Resources on Higher Education Governance, Management, and Leadership*. San Francisco: Jossey-Bass, 1987.

Tucker, Allan and R. A. Bryan. *The Academic Dean: Dove, Dragon and Diplomat*. New York: Macmillan, 1987.

Werrell, Emily and Laura Sullivan. "Faculty Status for Academic Librarians: A Review of the Literature." *College and Research Libraries* 48 (March 1987): 96-103.

Chapter 6

ORGANIZATION OF THE LIBRARY

In the early history of American colleges, administrative organization was hardly needed. There was a faculty and from its ranks one person was selected as president. The faculty was small and the president the only officer with executive authority. As the college grew, the first positions to be differentiated from that of the president were those of librarian and registrar. Both were chosen from the faculty, and the librarian generally held that post on a part-time basis. Since all records of the institution, including student courses and grades, were kept by the registrar, his office became the natural center for institutional planning. Gradually, as the college increased in size and complexity, these record-keeping duties were divorced from planning and a new academic executive position was created with the title of dean. Generally speaking, the academic duties of the dean and the executive tasks carried out as deputy to the president described only part of that position's functions. The dean almost always also fulfilled responsibilities relating to the personal problems of students.

ORGANIZATION OF THE COLLEGE

As college student bodies became larger, a further division of labor occurred. New administrative offices were created to oversee such problems as health care, business management and the physical plant. Each officer of these new departments reported directly to the president, until, finally, the number of people with direct access was greater than time available. The president could no longer provide adequate time for the kind of consultation necessary for effective academic administration. Administrative overload, then precipitated the creation of new reporting relationships. What finally evolved was a pyramidal structure, one now followed by virtually every college in the country. Variations abound, of course, depending on the nature of the institution and its size. In recent years, the pressure on college presidents, particularly in private institutions, to raise funds has resulted in the designation of someone other than the president to serve as the college's chief academic officer. Often this is the vice president for academic affairs, the provst, or the dean of the college, although other titles are sometimes used. While structures may vary from institutions to institution, college organizations generally resemble that in Figure 4.

Nomenclature, too, may vary. The provost/dean of the faculty is as likely to be called vice president-academic affairs, or vice president-instruction. The treasurer may be the chief financial officer. The head of development may be called institutional development, and so on. It is customary practice for the library director to report to a provost or academic vice president, but this, too, differs by institution and the director may report directly to the president. The implications of reporting relationships particularly as they relate to librarians, were considered in the previous chapter in conjunction with the discussion of governance and politics.

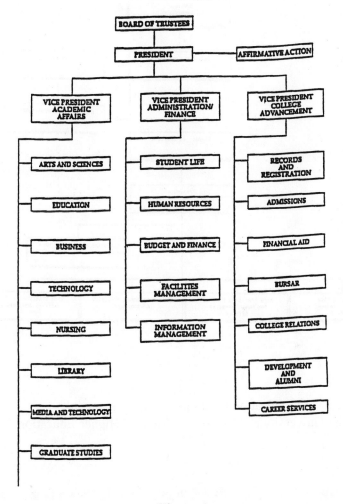

Figure 4
Organizational Structure of Trenton State College Trenton, N.J.

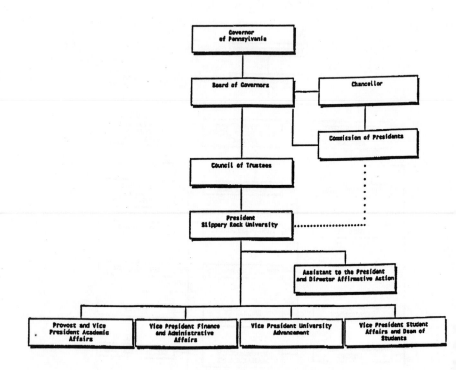

Figure 5
Organization of Slippery Rock University:
The University and the State System of Higher Education

Figures 4 and 5 represent organizational structures of two public institutions. They describe the administrative structure of many public colleges in the United States today. A dotted line represents a staff or advisory relationship; a solid one, the chain of command relationship. In each of these figures, the board of

of command relationship. In each of these figures, the board of trustees is the ultimate authority, although in the case of Figure 5 there is a State Commissioner of Higher Education in the employ of state government who also exercises authority over the institution. The president is accountable to the trustees, while the library director reports to the chief academic officer of the institution.

New structures in university libraries suggest that a direct relationship between library directors and presidents may once again be instituted. At Columbia University, the positions of Library Director and Director of Computing Services have been combined. A single person, a librarian with the rank of Vice-President has been named to oversee both operations and report to the president. Similar arrangements are emerging on a few college campuses including St. John's University in Collegeville, Minnesota.

The library director as administrator must be intimately acquainted with the pattern of administrative organization on the campus in order to deal effectively with the management team. The director usually works closely with: the campus personnel director to recruit and reward library staff; the head of the physical plant to repair and maintain library facilities; the dean to insure coordination of the library and academic programs; the director of financial aid to arrange for work-study student assistants; the business manager to monitor and reconcile the library's finances, and the development office to attract gifts.

THE LIBRARY AS AN ORGANIZATION

All organizations exhibit some similar characteristics. Before discussing how college libraries have been structured, how they are currently configured and how they may be organized in the future, it would be well to look at the traditional hallmarks of an organization as they relate to libraries. The following description is borrowed from Richard Hall:

> An organization is a collectivity with a relatively identifiable boundary, a normative order, authority ranks, communications systems. This collectivity exists on a relatively continuous basis in an environment and engages in activities that are usually related to a goal or set of goals.[1]

College libraries, as we have said, exist within a parent body. Like the administrative arm of the larger institutions, they are generally organized as hierarchies and have levels of authority and responsibility. Their aims and goals should be reflected in their organizational structure, which, in turn, should serve as the vehicle by which choices are made about how operations and staff will be arranged, coordinated and integrated. Structural arrangements should never be immutable, but rather should be available to be manipulated as required to help achieve new or changed goals and objectives. Two of the most important duties of a library director are to clarify for the staff and for the college the library's role, and to select appropriate means to carry it out.

Each of the library's constituencies may have different expectations for it. Faculty members may believe that the library's chief function is to further their research and, therefore, deem collection development to be the library's most important activity. College administrators, on the other hand, may stress managerial concerns, and concentrate on the library's ability to acquire, organize and disseminate information efficiently and effectively. And, finally, students may assume that the library's preeminent role is to assist them in locating and securing materials, particularly those placed on reserve by their instructors or perhaps to be there as a study hall twenty-four hours a day.

Obviously, all of these expectations are legitimate and must be satisfied, at least to some extent, by the library. The degree of importance attached to each group's interests by the library director, together with existing institutional norms and traditions, will shape the organizational structure of the library.

FORMULATING GOALS AND OBJECTIVES

Formulating goals and objectives for the library is an important task, one which should be accomplished regularly, at least every three years. They should be crafted with the active participation of students, faculty and administrators and library staff. A library director may serve as the primary drafter and then ask the library committees, both staff and faculty, to assist in the shaping of the finished document, or work may begin at the department level in the library and move upwards and out. Goals and objectives not only help to determine staff structure, but serve to explain to the campus what the library is trying to achieve. There are additional, very important, reasons for formulating goals and objectives.

1.   The act of articulating goals and objectives is, in itself, a *consciousness-raising* experience. If, after their formulation, they are banished to a closet shelf to gather dust, the exercise will still have been worth the effort, given the heightened understanding of the library and its role in the educational process they have provided.

2.   Goals and objectives can be used to rationalize staffing patterns. Individual roles and activity groups can be compared with the objectives to insure that harmony exists among them.

3.   A publicly available list of goals acts as a contract with the college community. If it has been negotiated with interested parties, it can serve to reconcile the vested interests of all of the library's constituencies.

4.   The list has importance as a public relations document. Any college library faces heavy competition for college dollars. Obtaining funds for a department on a college campus may involve engaging in the intellectual equivalent of warfare, a battle in which each participant tries to make the best case and

gain adequate leverage. A formulated set of objectives helps to solidify and explain the centrality of the library to the college's mission.

The first set of objectives is often formulated as part of a planning process. Any number of guidebooks are available which provide directions on how to do it, almost in cookbook fashion.[2] The specific procedure followed is always modified to meet the needs of a particular institution.

The planning process generally begins with a statement of the mission of the library (or the college). It is followed by a community survey including an environmental scan and demographic analysis. Depending on time and staff constraints, some or all the information generated by responses to the questions posed in Chapter 4, Campus Context, would be included. The next step is to articulate the goals of the library, as related to the goals of the colleges. Based on these goals, objectives are formulated. Objectives differ from goals in that they are less general and always measurable. For instance, while one of the goals of a college library might be to "create information-literate students," the objective might read, "College X will offer twelve bibliographic instruction courses to 300 students during the Fall semester of the academic year, 1992." It should be noted that "Missions," "Goals," "Aims" and "Objectives" do not always share the same meaning in library literature. "Goals" and "Objectives" are sometimes used interchangeably. So, too, are "Goals" and "Aims." The final step in the planning process is evaluation. During this time, an assessment is made of how well the library has met its objectives. Since the process is circular, it begins again. The mission is reaffirmed, any changes in the community are noted, the goals are reconsidered to see if they still reflect accurately what the library seeks to accomplish and the objectives are reformed or changed as needed.

The following Statement of Goals and Objectives (Figure 6) was prepared by the Upjohn Library at Kalamazoo College and contains the concerns common to most college libraries:

**Upjohn Library, Kalamazoo College
Statement of Goals and Objectives**

Mission

The mission of the Upjohn Library is to provide services and resources to meet the present and future scholarly and informational needs of the Kalamazoo College community, and in so far as possible, to share these resources with the broader scholarly community.

Continuing Goals

1.   To provide a collection of information resources which meet most of the curricular, informational and research needs of the College community.

2.   To organize and control the collection for maximum utilization.

3.   To maintain the collection in usable physical condition and conserve the material for future generations of users.

4.   To organize, monitor, and evaluate library services and procedures to assure the effective and efficient utilization of funds available now and in the future.

5.   To provide bibliographic aids and assistance in identifying, locating, and using information resources, including those not available in the Kalamazoo College collection, but which are needed to support the instructional and research programs of the College.

6.   To provide facilities and equipment for the storage and use of information resources.

7.   To maintain and further develop a highly capable library staff through systematic programs of career development and effective utilization of individual talents to fulfill the library's mission and support its objectives.

8.   To maintain effective administration planning services.

9.   To maintain a close and meaningful working relationship with administrative and academic departments, academic planning groups, and the user communities, to assure effective development of library services consistent with objectives and programs of the College, and to advise the College as to requirements and costs of these resources.

10.   To promote the use of the library and information resources.

11.   To continually investigate opportunities to increase services and access to collections beyond the College through cooperative programs with other libraries, library organizations, and information retrieval systems.

12.   To maintain constant exploration of professional and technological developments with a constant view to applicability for Kalamazoo College.

13.   To insure continued development and utilization of those collections of a specialized pre-eminent nature which are distinctive to Kalamazoo College and which are of recognized and national interest.

Figure 6
Statement of Goals and Objectives Upjohn Library,
Kalamozoo College, Kalamazoo, MI.[3]

A timeline chart from Occidental Colleges (Figure 7) illustrates the relationship between goals, objectives and schedules.

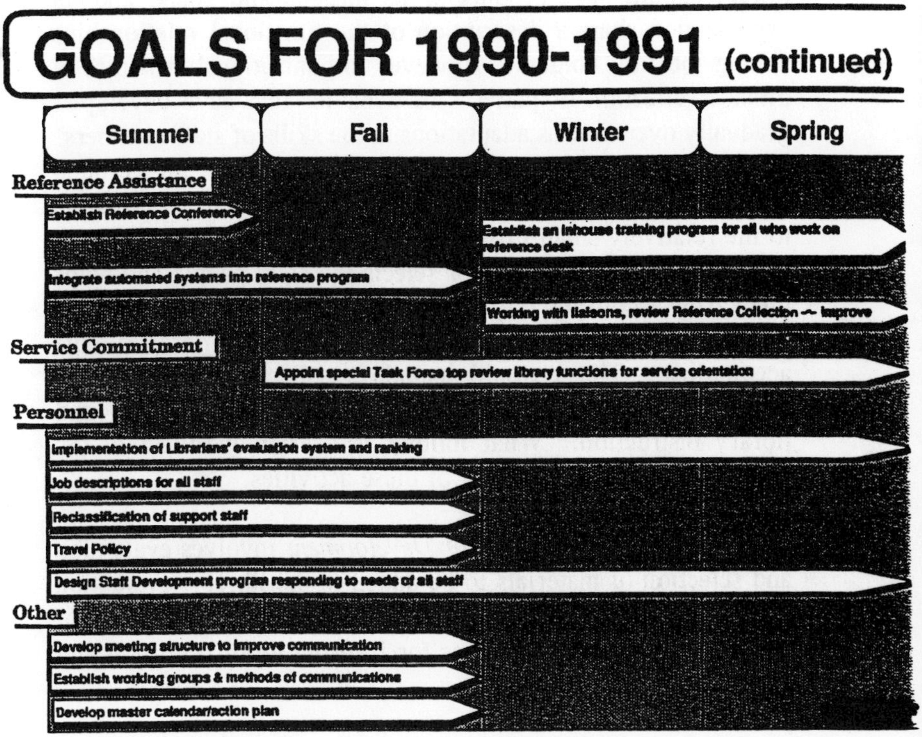

GOALS FOR 1990-1991 (continued)

Summer	Fall	Winter	Spring

Reference Assistance

Establish Reference Conference

Establish an inhouse training program for all who work on reference desk

Integrate automated systems into reference program

Working with liaisons, review Reference Collection ~ improve

Service Commitment

Appoint special Task Force top review library functions for service orientation

Personnel

Implementation of Librarians' evaluation system and ranking

Job descriptions for all staff

Reclassification of support staff

Travel Policy

Design Staff Development program responding to needs of all staff

Other

Develop meeting structure to improve communication

Establish working groups & methods of communications

Develop master calendar/action plan

Figure 7
Goals for 1990-91, Mary Norton Clapp Library,
Occidental College, Los Angeles, CA

ORGANIZATIONAL STRUCTURE

As mentioned earlier, the organizational structure of the library should be a product of its mission and goals, and its organization chart a description of the functional relationships among job title holders. However, organizational structure is often a reflection of patterns of behavior that have developed gradually over time as adaptations to the skills of staff members. Individual strengths and weaknesses account for crucial differences in an organization's success, particularly in relation to the relatively small groups represented by the college library staff. The wise administrator selects the right people and helps them grow according to their individual talents and interests. On the other hand, there are activities that all college libraries must accomplish. These would include: collection management, acquisitions, cataloging, circulation, reference services and library instruction. What follows is a brief overview of the major tasks involved in each of these activities.

Collection Management or Development involves evaluation and selection of materials to be added to the library, evaluation and weeding of materials no longer useful, preservation of library holdings and strategies for insuring rational growth and curriculum support.

Acquisitions includes ordering materials, monitoring deliveries, and approving payments. Among the duties are searching files for ownership; collecting bibliographic information; selecting suppliers; ordering and checking deliveries; initiating claims for unreceived materials.

Cataloging entails recording, describing, and indexing the holdings of a library. The number and kind of access points for retrieving each item are determined and established, and the quality control of all bibliographic records monitored.

Circulation encompasses activities revolving around the flow of library materials; that is, managing the removal and return of items to and from their shelf locations.

Reference Services involves helping users locate, retrieve and otherwise gain access to information.

Library Instruction refers to teaching students how to use the library and its materials.

Special Collections, Archives and Audio-Visual Services may be called out separately in larger libraries.

Special Collections includes those materials deemed rare by virtue of their great age, subject focus, printing history or, in a more practical approach, particularly high price.

Archives refers to the historical collection of official and semi-official records of the college. They are organized by issuing agency and housed separately, often under the control of the library.

Audio-Visual Services, also known as Media Services or Instructional Media, encompasses the in-house production and classroom distribution of films, videos and audio materials. The production and distribution function may be separate entities on a given campus and either or both may be under the control of the library.

College libraries today adopt many different organizational structures depending on their size, institutional environment and available space, among other factors. The size of the campus and the distances that library users must traverse in order to reach the library may determine, for instance, the extent to which departmental libraries are desirable. Automation, too, accounts for differing organizational structures among college libraries and also contributes to fluctuating conditions and rapid change. The opportunity for altered arrangements presented by the new technology, as well as discontent with current operating structures, has spawned numerous suggestions for reorganizing academic libraries. A number of proposals for change are considered here, following a description and discussion of how academic libraries are currently organized.

In the small college library there is either no elaborate organization or the library has organized its work around the particular skills of a few staff members. There is very little departmentalization, and duties are assigned to the person who has the time or who performs them best. While organization in a small or medium-sized library often represents adaptation to individual capabilities, the duties assigned to an individual staff member should be closely related, if possible, and that person should be asked to report to only one supervisor. Adaptation in the small library can result in effective service patterns and a well-functioning operation. On the other hand, it can produce a dysfunctional, unbalanced institution, with some staff severely overburdened and others under-utilized.

As the library grows larger and there are more than three or four staff members, the common pattern is consciously to divide areas of responsibility. Six bases on which libraries are organized have been identified.[4] Most college libraries contain examples of each of these bases of organization. They are: 1) function, 2) activity or process, 3) clientele, 4) geography, 5) subject, and 6) form of material. A functional arrangement would be the traditional organization depicted in Figure 8.

Activity or process as a basis of organization may be illustrated by such units as photocopying and book repair. An organization based on form of material would include separate departments for serials, and documents, and collections such as manuscripts, rare books and other materials which require special protection. Department libraries are often formed on the basis of location and/or subject. The form of information, particularly information generated by computers and audio-visually, has resulted in widespread departmentalization. Few

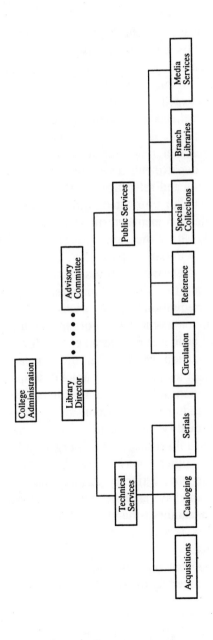

Figure 8
Example of a Typical College Library Organization

college libraries, for instance, are currently without a media department although this too may change with recent attention to content no matter the format. Figure 9 depicts a typical library with a structure that mixes function, format and location.

The organization chart fulfills two important purposes. It provides a structure for job titles and it describes the relationship between them. In this way, the areas of responsibility and authority are delineated. The current organization chart of most college libraries reflects a structure which is hierarchical and crafted along predominantly traditional functional lines. Technical Services, Reference Services and Circulation generally have their own departments (See Figure 8). Some libraries combine circulation and reference services into a single unit and maintain a two-part, or bifurcated, structure composed of public services and collection management services (See Figure 10).

Unfortunately, it is the rare college library director who maintains an up-to-date chart of the library's internal organization, complete with staff assignments. Most charts are created at the request of a new administrator or at the time of a self-study for accreditation and, librarians contend, only capture the reality of a given moment in an organization's development. They cite lack of available time as an excuse for not maintaining a current organization chart. But there is also widespread reluctance to accept a chart as an accurate descriptor of reporting relationships. Dotted and solid lines may indicate ideal advisory, coordinating or authority and responsibility paths, but they do not reveal the quality or frequency of exchanges between individuals who hold titles. Two organization charts that duplicate each other may describe entirely different organizations. In one, a library director may meet frequently with the provost and have an excellent working relationship with that officer. In another, the provost may let a year go by without seeking a formal meeting with the director and the library may suffer.

Organizational structures of college libraries have tended to imitate those of university libraries. Job titles are duplicated and

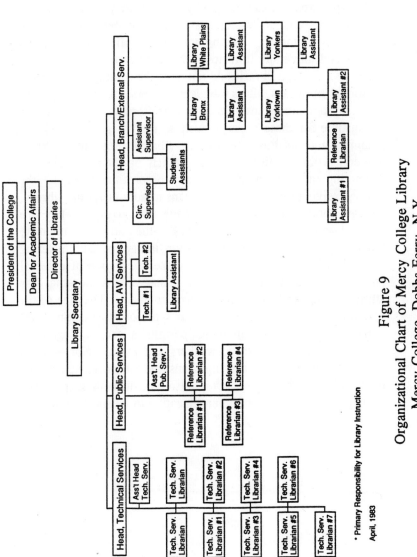

Figure 9
Organizational Chart of Mercy College Library
Mercy College, Dobbs Ferry, N.Y.

* Primary Responsibility for Library Instruction

April, 1983

attempts are made to follow similar internal operations. Critics contend, however, that college libraries should not try to copy university libraries. The objectives and roles of the two differ and the patterns that suit university libraries may be inhibiting to new services and professional staff development in a college library environment.[5] Among the major differences between college and university libraries is the absence of staff specialist positions. College libraries do not have the resources to employ personnel librarians, library budget officers, or even, in many cases, system librarians. In a college library, the director is responsible for these areas as well as for the general tasks of planning and leading the overall library program. While university library directors focus much of their energies on promoting and explaining the library to constituents outside the library, relying on associate librarians to administer the library, college library directors do not have that luxury. They are charged with speaking for the library to the outside community, but they also bear day-to-day responsibility for administering their libraries. It is this dual role—the integration of external and internal responsibilities on a manageable scale—that has attracted librarians to the college environment. The size of the operation also has a bearing on their sense of satisfaction, since work in a smaller organization permits a greater degree of personal interaction with co-workers and users. Not only do college library directors and librarians find the work exciting and personally satisfying, but they also consider their potential influence and impact on higher education to be substantial.

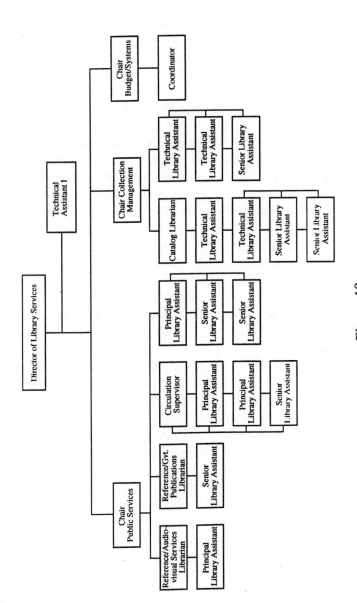

Figure 10
Organizational Chart of Ramapo College of New Jersey Library
Mahwah, N.J.

DEPARTMENTAL AND DIVISIONAL LIBRARIES

One of the most controversial and difficult problems which college librarians have faced has been the library's relationship to certain collections housed in other places on the campus. Early colleges were composed of a single building which served as a dormitory and provided classrooms, offices and a library. As the campus grew from one building to several, it was common for libraries to develop within each one. With further departmentalization, these libraries grew and often became the fiefdoms of the faculty members associated with the subjects they taught. It was not unusual to find numerous small department libraries on a college campus. They were frequently administered and maintained by academic departments. During the last three decades there has been a major push to divest campuses of satellite libraries. The action was predicated on both pedagogical and management concerns. Not surprisingly, the effort to eliminate departmental libraries provoked a storm of protest from faculty and resulted in political crises on many campuses. One library director at a Southern university who disbanded departmental libraries was burned in effigy by faculty and graduate students.

The issues involved in decentralization-centralization, divisionalism and departmentalization are complex and have been subjected to continuing debate. Good arguments for all positions can be offered. With centralization, there is less need to duplicate texts and records. Moreover, material is made available to the entire student body, rather than only to the majors. In this way, overlapping and interdisciplinary documents are not located in a variety of sites. Better organization, coordination and control over materials is possible, and planning for the development and balancing of collections is facilitated. Housing all materials in a main library assures better services to the public by providing: 1) longer hours of access, 2) more agreement on rules governing libraries, and 3) the services of a professional staff to do justice to the collection. In addition, the central library becomes a meeting ground for students and faculty from all disciplines, thus discouraging parochial attitudes among disciplines and departments. Finally, centralizing improves security control over materials and insures that items requiring preservation are given appropriate treatment.

But many faculty prefer libraries in close proximity to where they teach and do their work. This gives them unlimited access to library materials and, often, more awareness of their existence. Research into library use has repeatedly shown that, based on the principle of least effort, use is a function of accessibility which in turn is defined as distance, time and/or familiarity. Departmental libraries may promote library use. In addition, centralized libraries require larger physical plants than may be available. Eliminating departmental libraries may therefore represent a costlier change than many colleges are prepared to undertake. It is often contended that centralized libraries provide more uniform service across disciplines. However, even advocates admit that it is not always as good for particular patron-groups. Many librarians without strong science backgrounds rely on faculty to help students use departmental science collections. With centralization, a subject deficiency on the staff may become more pronounced and critical. While it is true that centralization reduces *library* costs, it is also true that it may increase *user* costs and be more expensive in the long run.

In the 1960s a number of academic libraries began to embrace a divisional system of organization, with humanities, social sciences and science having separate rooms or even buildings. This compromise plan exhibits advantages of both departmental or centralized libraries, although it retains some of the drawbacks of both. A divisional approach characterizes the curriculum of many colleges, and libraries so structured are able to relate most directly to the program of instruction. Librarians who administer humanities collections, for instance, will grow to know their particular clientele, thereby offering better service.

Interdisciplinary problems are reduced by having materials together. On the other hand, divisional libraries are more expensive than functional ones. A larger and more varied staff is required, and finding divisional subject specialists is difficult. This organization may lead to disputes over particular kinds of materials, and area study specialists will have trouble using the collection.

In recent years a number of the leading liberal arts colleges have chosen to build a science division library when the library became overcrowded, rather than expand the main building. This decision may result in gaining an additional twenty years of service for the old building and could save the institution a considerable sum of money. Scientists are more successful in obtaining their own library than members of other disciplines because their need to have materials placed in closer proximity to laboratories seems more compelling. In addition, foundations have been more willing to support requests for science libraries than they have other kinds of applications. Within the past few years Franklin and Marshall and Bowdoin Colleges have followed the lead of Smith, Earlham, Knox, Wellesley, Wesleyan, Swarthmore and Colby and have built or established separate science libraries.

Institutions that decide to support, or tolerate, departmental or divisional libraries should put into place a set of controls to monitor and limit their growth. The first hedge against their proliferation is a statement of policy on departmental collections and libraries, endorsed by the college administration and the faculty, either through the library committee or via departmental chairs. The second defense is to limit the funds available to satellite facilities, and to discourage fund-raising for them by departments. The third, and most important, way to discourage the proliferation of departmental libraries is to provide good service in the main library.

TECHNOLOGY AND ORGANIZATIONAL CHANGE

Ironically, many of the arguments in favor of centralization disappear with the arrival of new methods of document storage and retrieval, and many observers predict a new "decentralization" of libraries. Online systems are "distance-independent." Online public access catalogs and bibliographic data bases are accessible through any computer and are therefore not limited to a particular location. With the addition of electronic mail delivery systems, materials can be brought directly into the office of any faculty member or the dorm room of any student. Staff, too, are less rooted to a particular site. Catalogers need not be in proximity to the catalog to accomplish their work, nor do those who place orders or check in serials. As the campus is increasingly wired, access becomes less limited to place and more dependent on the user's knowledge of how to gain entry and how to evaluate the information once retrieved. Attention will be focused on how best to approach this problem in Chapters 11 and 12, in which Reference Services and Bibliographic Instruction are discussed.

Hugh Atkinson predicted, in 1984, that the organizational pattern of the academic library of the future is likely to be a decentralized one:

> ...one can already see the beginnings of new pressures and new organizational patterns with the advent of high density, optical digital discs, carbon fiber optics, and satellite communications, which provide even more distance independence and the potential for storage of large volumes of material in many remote locations so inexpensively that the very existence of a central store of data can be open to doubt. The rise of good, inexpensive, rapid long-distance electronic document storage transmission may... change the organizational patterns of individual libraries.[6]

College libraries, like other libraries, must be flexible in order to meet the challenges of an environment made uncertain by the new technology. The traditional bifurcated or trifurcated college library structure described above is undergoing careful scrutiny based on the impact of automation, the implication of other technological developments, and increased understanding of how organizations function.[7] Although the functional departmental structure still prevails, it is not unusual to find a systems development or an operations unit either within a technical services department or as an independent group. Gradually, these units may serve as intra-library centralizing forces given their potential to encompass cataloging, circulation and acquisitions.

Automation leads to other organizational changes in libraries. Personnel are added and decreased. The ratio of professional to support staff tends to shift in favor of the latter as day-to-day operations become more routine—tasks of sorting, filing, counting are taken over by computer. New nonprofessional jobs, however, often require increased support staff who have greater skills, experience and training. Automation may deprofessionalize some formerly professional tasks. For instance, many college libraries are forming production-oriented, rapid cataloging units where the tasks are basically clerical, in contrast with traditional cataloging departments where the work is primarily of an intellectual nature. There is some evidence of a gradual shift in personnel resources away from cataloging and acquisitions toward public service activities such as reference, library instruction and aspects of collection development.[8]

The impact of technology on the organization of a reference department may be just the opposite. The use of online reference services may necessitate not only additional staff, but service delivered through formal appointments. New data bases often require a knowledge of the subjects they cover or, at a minimum, their protocols. Not all members of a reference department can perform all searches.

There may also be a change in the decision-making structure of the library.

> The effect of changes now must be taken into account to a larger degree than before automation. Decisions have become more complex and involve greater risk. Organizational decisions that previously were reached at the departmental level, increasingly have become the responsibility of the top administrative level of the library. As a result, the planning process is more important, with each decision requiring thorough preparation and deliberation.[9]

For college libraries this often means the establishment of coordinating committees or task forces that cross department lines. These may be standard or ad hoc groups depending on the nature of the problem at hand.

A recent trend toward combining academic computing centers and libraries into "Scholarly Information Centers" has met with mixed reactions. Those who oppose this union see differences between the library's and the computing center's use of computers as a major stumbling block. The library, they contend, generally provides access to externally generated information, while computer centers are concerned primarily with internally produced data such as records and intra-campus networks. Those who support such a merger see the "Scholarly Information Center" composed of two groups: public or user services, and technical services. Public services would teach patrons to gain access to information (in print or machine-readable form). Technical services would provide support by preparing data for input, and making decisions regarding appropriate purchases of systems, documents, hardware, software and other media.[10]

Although most college libraries are formally organized in a bureaucratic, hierarchic fashion, egalitarian collaboration among departments and a well-developed system of partial participative management exists in most, nonetheless. Teamwork and individual initiative are widely encouraged even in those libraries not following a collegial model of organization. Dickinson's (PA) Library is one of the few college libraries organized on a departmental model. As a department of the College it has an elected Chair drawn from the ranks of the six professional librarians. Term of Office for the Chair is three years and he or she may serve for two terms if reelected. Only the professional staff operate collegially. Non-library professionals and support staff remain in a bureaucratic structure.[11] A number of problems are associated with the collegial model described above, among which are accountability, organizational flexibility and the fact that decision-making is very time-consuming. In addition, communication between collegial and hierarchical structures can be difficult. And finally, many librarians are uninterested in management and are unwilling and sometimes unable to serve as chairs.[12]

SUMMARY

In a college library, the primary aim of the administrative structure is to provide the best possible service to library users. A second aim is to insure efficient and effective operation of the library. Internally, libraries should be arranged with units that perform related tasks placed in close proximity to one another so that work can progress serially. All college libraries, no matter how small, have structures and procedures that can be described graphically in organization and flow charts.

On the other hand, even small college libraries are in danger of rigid compartmentalization when department members forget to relate the goals of their departments to the mission of the library; forget they are part of a whole team rather than exclusively catalogers or reference librarians.

The formal organization of a college library, though important, is secondary to the attitudes and behaviors of the administrator and staff. How employees work with one another, the degree to which they understand and share goals, the extent to which the library director and staff can articulate the organization's goals and mount a plan for their achievement, how well the library director can assure the personal well-being and development of its staff—these are of far greater moment to the achievement of the organization.

NOTES AND SUGGESTED READINGS

Notes

1. Richard R. Hall, *Organizations: Structure and Process* (Englewood Cliffs, NJ: Prentice-Hall, 1972), 14.

2. Guy Beneveniste, *Mastering the Politics of Planning* (San Francisco: Jossey-Bass, 1989); Robert G. Cope, *Opportunities from Strength, Strategic Planning Clarified with Case Examples*, ASHE-ERIC Higher Education Report #5 (Washington, DC: Association for the Study of Higher Education, 1987).

3. Larry Hardesty and others, *Mission Statements for College Libraries*, Clip Note #5 (Chicago: ACRL, 1985), 115.

4. E. A. Wight, "Research in Organization and Administration," *Library Trends* (October 1957): 141-146.

5. Gerard McCabe, "New Patterns for Managing the Small Staff," in *The Smaller Academic Library* ed. Gerard McCabe (Westport, CT: Greenwood Press, 1988), 95.

6. Hugh C. Atkinson, "The Impact of New Technology on Library Organization," *Bowker Annual of Library and Book Trade Information.* 29th edition (New York: Bowker, 1984), 34.

7. Judy Reynolds and Jo Bell Whitlatch, "Academic Library Services: The Literature of Innovation," *College and Research Libraries* 46 (September 1985): 402-417; Peggy Johnson, "Matrix Management. An Organizational Alternative for Libraries," *Journal of Academic Librarianship* 16 (September 1990): 222-229.

8. Charles Martell. *The Client Centered Academic Library* (Westport, CT: Greenwood Press, 1988), 5.

9. Gary Kraske, *The Impact of Automation on the Staff and Organization of a Medium-sized Academic Library.* Eric Document 190 153, 12.

10. Diane Cimbala,"The Scholarly Information Center: An Organizational Model," *College and Research Libraries* 48 (August 1987): 394.

11. Joan Bechtel, "Collegial Management Breeds Success," *American Libraries* 12 (November 1981): 605-7.

12. Nancy Brown, "Managing the Coexistence of Hierarchical and Collegial Governance Structures," *College and Research Libraries* 46 (November 1985): 478.

Suggested Readings

Cline, Hugh F. and Lorraine J. Sinott. *Electronic Library: The Impact of Automation on Academic Libraries.* Lexington, MA: Lexington Books, 1983.

Counihan, Martha. "Establishment of Archives." *College Librarianship*, ed. William Miller and D. Stephen Rockwood. Metuchen, NJ: Scarecrow Press, 1981.

Drucker, Peter "Managing the Public Service Institution." *College and Research Libraries* 37 (January, 1976): 4-14.

Ensor, Pat and others. "Strategic Planning in an Academic Library." *Library Administration and Management* 2 (June 1988): 145-50.

Gorman, Michael. "The Organization of Academic Libraries in the Light of Automation." *Advances in Library Automation and Networking*, Vol 1, ed. Joe Hewitt, 151-168. Greenwich, CT: JAI Press, 1987.

Hall, Richard H. *Organizations: Structures, Processes and Outcomes.* 4th ed. Englewood Cliffs, NJ: Prentice-Hall, 1987.

Lynch, Beverly ed. *Management Strategies for Libraries: A Basic Reader.* New York: Neal Schuman, 1985.

McCabe, Gerard. "Contemporary Trends in Academic Library Administration and Organization." *Issues in Academic Librarianship: Views and Case Studies for the 1980s and 1990s*, ed. Peter Spyers-Duran and Thomas W. Mann, Jr. Westport, CT: Greenwood Press, 1985.

Marchant, Maurice. *Participative Management in Academic Libraries.* Westport, CT: Greenwood Press, 1976.

Martell, Charles R. *Client Centered Academic Library: An Organizational Model.* Westport, CT: Greenwood Press, 1982.

Peters, Thomas J. and Robert H. Waterman, Jr. *In Search of Excellence. Lessons From America's Best Run Companies* New York: Harper and Row, 1982.

Stueart, Robert D. "The Liberal Arts College Library Paradox or Panacea." *College and Research Libraries* 51 (November 1990): 524-529.

See also B. Lynch, McCabe and Veaner cited in *Suggested Readings*, Chapter 1.

Chapter 7

TECHNOLOGY AND INTEGRATED LIBRARY SYSTEMS

Larry Oberg, Library Director of Albion College, recently reported to his faculty and administration

> ...the automation of the catalog and most internal procedures, set to occur in 1990, will affect the relationship that students, faculty and administrators alike have to their library. Traditional ways of doing things will change profoundly, both within the library and without.[1]

Colleges in the process of automating their libraries frequently give their online public access catalogs (OPACs) names, and then shorten them to easy-to-remember acronyms. The act of naming symbolizes the quantum differences in expectation that librarians and users alike have for library service powered by technology. Card catalogs were never named. Not all libraries will experience full-scale technological transformations during the next few years. All, however, will become objects of greatly increased expectations and all are faced by a dizzying and continually expanding array of new technologies applicable to library operations.

Instituting technology requires that a library be clear about its purposes, understand how the parts to be automated mesh and can be integrated in a system, and plan in minute detail the steps that must be taken to implement it.

Leadership and vision coupled with clarity of purpose greatly enhance the possibilities of success in arguing for library technology funding. Building a library vision begins, as do most visions of the future, by observing the prototypes, supplementing this insight with scenarios of future societies and bolstering the vision through dialogue with respected thinkers in librarianship and allied fields. Vannevar Bush's powerful conceptualization of a Memex machine, first articulated in 1945, still drives the design of scholar workstation systems.[2] Today, futurist Paul Saffo studies hypertext and conceptualizes a process he calls "information surfing" that enables people to manage information overload.[3]

Clarity of purpose springs first from a rigorous review of the library's goals and structure, and second from a careful analysis of procedures to determine which areas of library work are most amenable to and/or most need automation or a particular new technology. Setting goals and objectives enables librarians to proceed in an orderly fashion. A goal that stipulates that the library will be on line in five years dictates establishing sequential objectives for each of the intervening years. The historical ability of libraries to develop clear sets of procedures for interlocking tasks stands them in good stead when technologically transforming any area of service.

Only the rare academic library, usually research institutions such as those at the University of Chicago or Northwestern, pioneers the development of a full-scale system. The majority of academic libraries are denied the luxury of investing funds in experimental projects and must accept the role of second- and third-generation implementers of innovation. Each campus will differ in its rate of acceptance of innovation, although each will undoubtedly have one or more programs it proudly claims as innovative. Library technological programs can be understood within the context of the parent institution's attitudes and behavior toward innovation. The speed or delay with which library technology gains acceptance is a function of that mind set. College librarians enhance their positions by allying themselves with campus technological innovations that have applicability to the library. For one college, it may be distance learning; for another, the use of personal computers in the liberal arts curriculum. Still another college may work toward creating a barrier-free campus for its handicapped students. All of these goals can be furthered by one or more library programs. Some may require the library to acquire particular technologies. When forces are joined, the case for funding becomes stronger and easier to make.

One type of technology, the integrated library system, is discussed in this chapter. But neither the particulars of any integrated library system, nor even the functions performed by a standard integrated system, are described in detail. Technology changes too rapidly to make such information useful. The discussion, therefore, is focused on process; that is, on identifying and defining technological needs, on learning what is available to meet those needs, on hiring and using a consultant, on mobilizing support, on planning for implementation, on educating staff and users, and on upgrading systems once they are in place.

THRUST TO AUTOMATE

Following the development of the computer, the impulse to automate gained momentum because technical advances in computer science intersected with societal needs. Among the former, the innovation that had the greatest impact on college libraries was the rapid and widespread use of bibliographic telecommunications networks. Pushing the acceptance of the technology were a need for accountability, financial considerations, rising expectations, and increased interdependency.

Bibliographic utilities, an infrastructure invention of the late '60s, are characterized by a focus on the cooperative development of machine-readable bibliographic data bases.

The first of the major networks, OCLC, was started in 1967. In the early '70s Stanford University's technical processing system, BALLOTS, began to receive widespread use, first by other California libraries and later by members of the Research Libraries Group (RLG) which, in 1978, chose BALLOTS as the basis of its Research Libraries Information Network (RLIN). These two developments meant that the field had constructed two powerful national networks. A third network, Washington Library Network (WLN), has chosen a regional focus for most of its existence, but its attention to issues of quality control influences all network developments.

Interlibrary loan, acquisitions, union lists, bibliographic access, cataloging, reference, circulation, collection development, literature searching, processing, communication among libraries, staff development and management information are just some elements of local library service that have been affected by the presence of networks. These networks, now so vital to libraries could not have developed without impetus and support from other segments of society.

Because the history is so recent, it is hard to distinguish which societal trends among major influences are the most important, but the following must be considered to have played a role.

The notion of accountability came to college campuses in the mid-1970s as administrators began to demand documentation about activities and outcomes based on measurable units that could be compared from year to year. This need to be accountable caused librarians to review their programs and attempt to rationalize them. The ability of computers to generate information about who was using what part of the collection provided librarians who were seeking to tailor their buying habits to fit the uses to which the collection was being put with a reason to automate.

A second precipitant to interest in technology was the renewed need for economic belt-tightening, another development that forced librarians to review their allocations for materials and services. Automation, with its tentative promise of savings in personnel, began to look extremely attractive.

A third factor propelling automation was the increased importance attached to information by a more enlightened clientele, who insisted not only on its availability but on its rapid provision. For this group, effectiveness, not economy, was the issue. The influence of this group in the awarding of government contracts in science information retrieval experiments was considerable.

The final impulse to automate resulted from new developments in networks and other cooperative activities that brought with them requirements for the generation of accurate shareable information. Because computers permitted ease in compiling union catalogs, insured that librarians geographically distant would have access to the same information, and had the further attraction of monitoring cost-sharing among those who chose to participate in the system, computers were readily accepted as viable tools in libraries.[4]

There has been a convergence of goals and means in a relatively short time. Among the technological options currently available to modern libraries are local area telecommunications networks designed to distribute voice messages and data through computers, dial access services to external data bases, computers with capabilities of storing and manipulating ever increasing amounts of data, CD-ROM products, dedicated and dial access terminals with links to national bibliographic utilities, and satellite transmission of data and video images through broad band channels, to mention just a few. Visionaries assure us that low cost, copyright protected, full text retrieval systems, connected to present bibliographical databases, with user friendly information management techniques are imminent. The new systems will allow scholars expeditiously to create, manipulate, store and retrieve their texts and other materials. Shaw and Culkin contend that there is a convergence of thinking among librarians about how various computer-based capabilities can be packaged for end users. The components of these new and greatly enhanced systems will include: 1) traditional automated library systems; 2) public access terminals; 3) online search services; 4) electronic publishing; 5) electronic delivery; 6) micro-based videodisc services; 7) non-bibliographic databases and 8) personal computers and scholar work stations.[5]

AVOIDING TECHNOLOGY'S PITFALLS

Reading the literature of innovation is an exhilarating, intoxicating experience. Claims made about the transforming powers of technology are convincing, particularly in their promises to provide excellent library service. Only knowledgeable and wary consumers recognize how excessive and misleading they may be. At one time, proponents prophesied that the use of instructional media (AV) would radically change all of higher education. Instead, as with most new communication vehicles, instructional media takes its place alongside other technologies and standard print sources as an additional resource, not a substitute for existing ones. The telephone and television are classic examples of technologies that expand our choices, but do not replace the need for printed materials. New technologies offer some possibilities to everyone, although not all can or should be embraced equally. Past experience teaches us that the easier the technology is to use, the more it will be used. Motivation to master a more complicated innovation, however, can be developed when a potential user understands the degree to which its use can simplify, or reduce substantially the time required to complete a task. What can be said with certainty is that each innovation produces unanticipated benefits as well as drawbacks.

All new technologies have a ripple effect on library services. Facsimile transmission, for instance, was originally employed by libraries only in interlibrary loan and acquisitions. The introduction of low-cost facsimile machines for office and home use now gives individuals the capacity to request delivery of materials from the library directly to them and libraries can anticipate heavy demand for this service. Similarly, widespread ownership of video cam recorders and playback equipment has done more to encourage the use of video in the classroom than most other programs that utilize educational media. College libraries are now expected to acquire and make available sizable collections of videos. Personal computers, ubiquitous on college campuses, have become increasingly user-friendly and most are compatible, one with another. Software packages now employ similar protocols and users find it relatively simple to move, for instance, from one word processing package to another. Libraries have profited from the widespread use of personal computers on campuses. Students and faculty are rarely threatened by their appearance in the library, and those who have experienced computers in other contexts learn how to use them with little difficulty.

Ease of use, compatibility with other information products and services, impact of a new technology on the library, and attention to avoiding excessive claims for an innovation are all important guidelines to remember as libraries establish programs that utilize new technologies, install integrated library systems and seek to have them become important parts of the information-into-knowledge cycle.

THE CASE OF OCLC

The Ohio College Library Center, as it was first known in the late 1960s was a brainchild of the Ohio College Association, a group of higher education leaders working together to solve campus problems in mutually beneficial ways. One of the issues it studied was library development. Based on the recommendations of Fred Kilgour of Yale University and Ralph Parker of the University of Missouri, OCLC was established in 1967 to maintain and operate a computerized regional library center that would serve all the academic libraries of Ohio and become, in time, part of any national electronic network for bibliographical communication. Kilgour served as its first president and driving force.

OCLC's first priorities were to develop subsystems for shared cataloging, serials control, technical processes, circulation control subject and title access for users. By 1970 an online catalog card production system became operational and, in 1971, the shared cataloging system was inaugurated. Membership was opened to public libraries in 1972, and service was extended to regional groups outside Ohio. In 1977, it adopted a new governing structure that reflected its national character and changed its name to Online Computer Library Center, retaining its OCLC acronym.[6] As of 1990, OCLC has over 11,000 members world wide and its data base contains more than 20 million records.

In the late 1970s, college libraries were trying first to decide whether to join OCLC and second how to find funds to install a terminal that would link them with the new network. The Kresge Foundation, recognizing OCLC's potential, made grants available to college libraries that wished to affiliate with the fledgling system. In a short period of time most college libraries had enrolled and made the necessary modifications to their procedures. With the decision to join OCLC the libraries had also accepted, sometimes unconsciously, future participation in resource sharing, utilization of telecommunications technology, further library automation activity, quality control and standardization. By embracing OCLC, libraries embarked on a path that led inexorably to yoking computers to library operations. The success of OCLC in college libraries empowered and empowers librarians in two ways: to build on this solid record of achievement as they make their case for further innovation, and to use their experience with OCLC, and their knowledge of its growth, as a bridge to understanding how new technologies will change their programs.

INTEGRATED SYSTEMS

The first attempts to automate library functions occurred soon after World War II when efforts were made to mechanize cataloging and circulation. Shortly thereafter, librarians who recognized the computer's ability to manipulate large data files sought to bring the power of automated bibliographic retrieval to users of libraries. The two goals, one internal, one external in focus, converged, and attention was turned to automating the card catalog to produce an online public access catalog by integrating existing systems for cataloging and circulating materials. Systems for handling acquisitions, managing information, reserves and public access to collections, both monographic and serial, were quickly added to the desiderata lists of pioneers. These efforts reached fruition in the mid 1980s with development of what was termed an "online integrated library system" or integrated library system.[7] The phrase has come to represent a single central data file serving as the source of all record management and display for the library, amenable to change by computer keyed-in corrections, additions and deletions, friendly in its search capabilities and rigorous in its ability to control information.

Librarians first greeted early integrated library systems with skepticism because they were too difficult for patrons to manipulate. As systems developed better user access catalog modules, librarians began to behave more like children in a candy shop—excited and impatient. Today, there are twenty or so companies selling integrated library systems. Some report annual sales of three systems. Others claim to have placed one hundred or more systems during a year and boast customer lists of between one and several hundred. The library computer market is volatile. Companies form and disband with increasing regularity, reacting to the high premium the market places on innovation. In this environment librarians seeking to acquire integrated library systems must proceed with caution.

The first task of a library in search of a system is one of definition—what, for that library, constitutes an integrated library system? The obvious but often forgotten fact is that there are no fully automated systems. Each depends on humans to make them work. Corbin's block diagram (Figure 11) of the process demonstrates the importance of human input.[8] If the college faculty actively uses computers in teaching, if there is a strong academic computer center, if there are other computer specialists available on campus and if there are library staff knowledgeable about the technology and familiar with basic terminology, the library may decide to define its own needs without the services of a consultant. However, if these experts are not present on a campus, librarians who feel less secure in their knowledge will wish to hire a consultant. Either way, it is clear that the important decisions are human decisions.

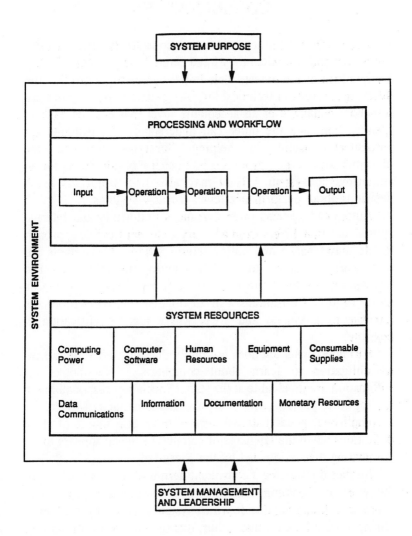

Figure 11
Block Diagram of an Automated System

CONSULTANTS

The work that library automation consultants perform for a library depends on when they have entered the process. If they are involved at the outset, their initial task is to insure that the differing amounts of technical knowledge among participants are somehow equalized at an acceptable level that enables each to speak a language the other can understand. Consultants are particularly useful in helping librarians translate the idiosyncrasies of their processes into general requirements for an automated subsystem. They may also help librarians reach decisions about performance levels for new systems.

Automated systems often demand a uniformity and internal consistency that differs from a library's current flexible approach to file maintenance and policy interpretation. Consultants are particularly valuable to staff attempting to apply specific descriptions of local practices to systems where rules appear more rigid. Consultants can distinguish between protocols intrinsic to a system and areas where local modification is possible.

Hiring a consultant does not imply that the staff relinquishes its obligation to learn about computers. Handbooks on automation are invaluable at the start. Specialists responsible for leading the project will find checklists of activities to be accomplished; generalists will turn to them as a source of clear definitions when the language of computer science appears to be dominating discussions led by the consultant.

Neither does hiring a consultant permit librarians to abdicate the work of becoming familiar with various systems. The consultant should not decide which system is best for the college. Hiring a consultant means, rather, that the library has on its side an expert who can help write or review requests for proposals, negotiate with vendors, explain library needs to computer center personnel, and, in general, guide the library in its expectations and actions.

Even when there is no clear source of funding for a system, it is helpful to begin the process by hiring a consultant to investigate the need for one. Consultants can help the library do the preliminary work of determining the scope of the problem and the opportunities for the future. Establishing a relationship with a consultant also provides the library with a tested source of advice when it is needed.

EDUCATING CAMPUS LEADERS

Once the staff is comfortable with the technical terms, is familiar with the process, and understands the magnitude of the project, the education of campus administrators begins. Librarians usually realize easily the enormous benefits that accrue from using the contents of a single file to perform all library operations. Administrators may have difficulty understanding the beauty and power of this technological advance. Explaining the systems' potential advantages to users in terms of new subject searching capability via keywords rather than fixed terms may have more meaning. Discussing options for the future, such as the integration into a system of index tapes, can be done in a way that makes clear that the option is not available unless the basic system is installed first. Administrators and trustees respond to evidence of good planning. At a minimum, librarians must know the following about systems: how much they will cost and over what period of time, what their capabilities and drawbacks are, how they support the curriculum, and what is happening at comparable schools. A tentative schedule for implementation, one that costs out the related task of barcoding the collection and establishing authority control, is part of the process.

The money may be unavailable for several years, but most colleges will eventually be able to afford a system, especially if its implementation is coordinated with the installation of a campus network or a statewide network for public colleges. The administration may impanel a task force that includes faculty, trustees and the director of the academic computer center, as well as key library staff, to set the implementation process in motion. At this time, visits to libraries that have already acquired integrated systems, while desirable, may not be essential. Asking faculty who use other college libraries to report on their experience with other systems serves two purposes: the library learns more about user requirements and the campus hears one more voice in favor of an integrated system.

CHOICE OF COMPUTER

When most librarians view integrated library systems in ideal terms, their previous experiences with bibliographic utilities, online search services, stand-alone microcomputer-based acquisitions, serials and circulation, and even CD-ROM products and COM catalogs inform the discussion and guide their definitions of requirements for a functional system. A smaller group of researchers, scholars, librarians and computer scientists think in futuristic terms of scholars' work stations complete with full-text retrieval capability, access to all other electronic indexing and bibliographic services, with excellent production capabilities. Despite their different visions, both groups understand that adherence to national standards for cataloging records is vital if future developments are to be encouraged and that room for growth and new functions must be built into any system. There is also increasing demand for the creation of systems that are sufficiently flexible to allow users to search the local catalog or external data bases in their own natural languages.

Librarians often want the online public access catalog (OPAC), acquisitions, serials, circulation, cataloging and reserve modules of an integrated system to perform powerful new routines while still honoring currently existing local practices. It should come as no surprise that conflicting demands make it difficult for vendors of integrated library systems to thrive and prosper in the market. The combination of high expectation for individualized service, low tolerance for standard packages and rapidly changing opportunities to improve a product mix have challenged vendors. Those that have survived have done so because they developed a software program that met the needs of many libraries, and because they have been able to devote enough of the company's resources to research, development and service. Annually, the April issue of *Library Systems Newsletter* carries a report on each of the companies active in the field. The new information about a company's business during the past year is eagerly sought by librarians in the market to purchase systems. Past performance is, to some extent, an indication of a company's present and future behavior. Most libraries cannot risk the dollars made available for a capital investment of between $75,000 and $200,000 for software alone—on promises of system enhancements to come. Only the largest libraries have sufficient bargaining power to effect change in a given system's software, and even they risk having installation delayed or a period of being the Alpha or Beta (early or test) sites with less than full functionality or countless bugs. Colleges with strong systems staffs may find they can agree to serve as a Beta site. Most institutions, however, will be purchasing an as-is product with a tentative schedule of enhancements.

Among the decisions facing librarians who are about to implement an integrated library system is whether they must use a particular computer. Some campuses are IBM environments, others use DEC equipment, still others are mixed computer environments. Decisions about whether or not to allow more than one brand of computer equipment are usually made at the vice-presidential level and involve discount opportunities and availability of personnel to service the machines. If a campus has mandated the use of one or another type of hardware, the library is constrained from making a choice. All integrated library systems are currently available for each of the major types of computers. Even when the librarian is free to choose among brands of hardware, it is still important that the head of the computer center or the appropriate vice president be involved in any decision in order to insure that it will be well supported. Computers should have sufficient capacity to handle projected growth in holdings as well as room to support any external databases that may be loaded onto the system. No computer can be expected to last forever, but the work associated with selecting a new one is sufficiently demanding, time consuming and expensive that it is prudent to plan to use a particular computer for at least five to ten years.

Determining the acceptability to the campus of the hardware utilized by a system is but one criterion used to evaluate its suitability. There are many additional questions that must be answered. Often the task of making these decisions is assigned to a library committee composed of representatives from the acquisitions, cataloging, reference and circulation departments with a designated leader who is the staff member most knowledgeable about library automation. The director acts as overseer, critic, advisor, encourager and enthusiast.[9] The group begins its work by reviewing the literature, visiting some sites, and studying available products at library exhibits. Often this work is done twice, once early in an automation cycle as part of general education, and again at purchase time. An outline of characteristics required by the system is prepared, using, in the absence of a consultant, sample requests for proposals. Staff not directly involved in the project will also need to be educated and informed. Ongoing demonstrations and orientation sessions by the task force will help to allay their fears and rally their support.

When funding goes from possible to probable, the group finds the pace of its work accelerating. A new seriousness of purpose prevails as members realize, first, the extent of the financial investment the college is about to make, and then, that they must live with the final choice for at least five years. Fears surface about picking the wrong system. Comparing the capabilities of various subsystems with a list of functions the committee has deemed necessary helps to winnow the list of potential systems and reduce anxiety. A final comparison of the functions of modules among the remaining candidates should eliminate all but one or two choices.

Toward the end, the process may seem mind blurring, especially when vendors display their latest versions at conferences but can only show earlier ones in operation at installed sites. Knowing which functions are essential to the local library is one way of sorting through and limiting the amount of information that must be digested. If an AV booking module is not required, that function should be ignored. Preparing a set of sample queries and testing them with each system reveals differences among them. Judgments need to be formed about the relative ease of use or elegance of various subsystems offered by vendors. Eventually, after reviewing the products, distinctions between the quality of one vendor's circulation or OPAC module and another's become clear. One vendor will boast a well-developed acquisitions system, another a strong OPAC, and a third, an exceptional reserves module. Reference to the college's priorities will help shape the library's choice among them. For one college, an OPAC with full Boolean search capability makes most sense. For another, the ability to have faculty learn what materials have been ordered and whether they have arrived in the library is more important. The choices are made between products at reasonably similar levels of development. A highly acclaimed system feature in one product will probably become available in a competitor's package in the future. Therefore, unless the feature is crucial to the library it should not sway the decision.

Before signing any contract with a vendor of an integrated library system, libraries need to investigate the company they have selected. A company that can boast a cluster of satisfied users in similar type colleges gives a good indication of how it operates. Visiting sites where the company has installations helps in learning about problems. These can be reviewed with the company under consideration to help avoid misapprehensions and misunderstandings about product performance. The desire to be in a user group with prestigious colleagues is not sufficient reason to select a particular integrated library system. The company must also be solvent and, even in this time of rapid expansion, able to service its present customers in a timely fashion. Checking the financial stability is necessary, as is establishing the rights of the customer in the case of the company's bankruptcy. While the library director may not have been on the technical task force, the director must be involved in any final decision. Criteria for selection must be clear, and perhaps even accorded weights, and must include technical, financial, and service concerns.

INSTALLATION AND AFTERWARDS

Companies and libraries should develop mutually agreed implementation schedules. For instance, the schedule may designate Day 1 to represent the contract signing, and Day 100 as the day on which the library may expect the system to be installed, tested and available to the public. Libraries attempt to target Day 100 to coincide with times when the library's hectic pace is slowed, perhaps by a summer vacation or a semester break. Those modules intended for staff use are installed first to permit them to gain familiarity with the system before they in turn must educate the public to it.

Some companies sell software only. Others supply hardware as well. In either case, additional purchases are necessary to make the system operational. Arrangements must be made with companies that process archival tapes, those that eliminate duplicate records and provide authority control work on tapes; and those that generate customized, or smart barcode labels, and, finally those that sell and install furniture, equipment and supplies. Some flexibility in the schedule may be required. For instance, some of these services are provided by just a few companies, and waiting lists develop.

Two kinds of training with the system and the new technology are necessary, one for staff, the other for users.

Staff training is frequently provided as part of the system's purchase price and companies usually offer additional assistance through customer-support divisions where personnel are available to answer questions.

New technology is more easily introduced on campuses where computer use is widespread or where voice/data networks have been installed. Faculty who are comfortable with electronic mail services, or who use computers in their courses or in their offices, are more likely to feel comfortable with new OPACs. In addition to running training sessions for faculty and students, well-prepared documentation for the first day of public use facilitates the orientation process. Transmitting a clear sense of what the new library system contains avoids having students, and some faculty, expect it to double as a subject index to periodical articles and government documents. Introducing an integrated library system involves educating users about distinctions between the system's current capabilities and what it *may* offer. The future will depend on the availability of additional funding, technological improvements and the ability of the library to demonstrate the system's importance to the teaching and learning mission of the college.

All systems will require change over time. This fact may represent the harshest reality to college librarians new to the world of large-scale technology. It is some, albeit small, consolation that once the initial installation has been completed, subsequent changes loom less formidable and are certainly less costly. Joining an active integrated library system users group insures learning quickly about modifications and additions to the system. To make their investment work, user groups are not loath to exert pressure on companies to induce them to make needed improvements in their basic system, but there are limits to their usefulness, since the companies know the users will not easily migrate to a new system.

Some lines between materials and equipment budgets for college libraries have gradually been effaced as a result of the introduction of the new technologies. It may be reasonable to view software that provides information equivalent to that found in print indexes as "materials" and fund it accordingly. Purchase of the equipment needed to run the software tends to come from the equipment budget. The boundary lines between public and technical services have also begun to disappear and staff can no longer be distinguished as working exclusively in one or the other area. Even small libraries may find themselves hiring a systems librarian. Patterns of library use will certainly be altered when the computer allows text and bibliographic information to be distributed routinely to offices and dormitories. Currently, libraries can gain access to twenty million bibliographical records quickly, but document delivery options are limited by local custom, funding patterns and copyright restrictions. Improvements in optical scanning will permit economical storage of large files, but simpler solutions may emerge as well. Changes in use, in staffing and in budget allocation patterns are only three among many structural alterations that are certain to eventuate from the introduction of technology.

Rapid change can produce stress in staff, in users, in those who make the decisions, and in those who make the financial investment, an investment that could be as high as $3,000,000 in the late 1980s. Planning well, assuring that budgets incorporate funds to upgrade existing technologies as well as to expand into new ones, training staff and offering refresher sessions help to alleviate concerns and lessen the tension. Libraries aim to foster in users the ability to acquire, control and utilize needed information. Technology is a means to achieve these goals, not an end.

SUMMARY

Technology promises libraries powerful new capabilities in all aspects of library work. Integrated systems tie together acquisitions, cataloging, circulation and reference through a single data base containing bibliographic and status information about all library holdings. Before purchasing any new technology, it is necessary to review and revise thoroughly current practices and procedures. Managing technology requires paying attention to planning, to budgeting, to educating users and staff, and to the effects of change. The purchase and installation of an integrated system follows the same kind of process and decision-making involved in acquiring any new technology.

NOTES AND SUGGESTED READINGS

Notes

1. Larry Oberg, "The Changing Role of College Libraries," *College and Research Libraries* News 51 (April 1990): 329.

2. Vannevar Bush, "As We May Think," *Atlantic Monthly* 176 (July 1945): 101-108

3. Paul Saffo, "Electronic Publishing for the Future," Speech at Fourth Annual Oberlin Group Conference (Whittier College, CA: 15 October 1989).

4. Sheila Intner, *Circulation Policy in Academic, Public and School Libraries* (Westport, CT: Greenwood Press, 1987), 9-12.

5. Ward Shaw and Patricia B. Culkin, "Systems That Inform: Emerging Trends in Library Automation and Network Development," *Annual Review of Information Science and Technology*, 22, ed. Martha E. Williams (Amsterdam: Elsevier, 1987), 266-267.

6. Albert F. Maruskin, *OCLC: Its Governance, Function, Financing and Technology* (New York. Marcel Dekker, 1980), 9-17.

7. Walt Crawford, *Patron Access: Issues for Online Catalogs* (Boston, MA: G. K. Hall, 1987), 253.

8. John Corbin, *Managing the Library Automation Project* (Phoenix, AZ: Oryx Press, 1985), 5.

9. *Ibid.*, 53.

Suggested Readings

Beninger, James. *The Control Revolution: Technological and Economic Origins of the Information Society*. Cambridge, MA: Harvard University Press, 1986.

Bigelow, Linda and Alice Calabrese.   "Libraries and Telecommunications Technologies." *College and Research Libraries News* 50 (March 1989): 195-199.

Boss, Richard W. *The Library Manager's Guide to Automation*. 2nd ed.   White Plains, NY: Knowledge Industry Publication, 1984.

Britten, William A.   "BITNET and the Internet: Scholarly Networks for Librarians." *College and Research Libraries News* 51 (February 1990): 103-107.

CAUSE and EDUCOM. "Evaluation Guidelines for Institutional Information Technology Resources" *EDUCOM Bulletin* 23 (Winter 1988):8-10.

Clare, Richard W., III.   "High Technology Bibliography." *Bowker Annual*. *1989-90*. 34th ed. New York: R. R. Bowker, 1989. 490-502.

Fratkin, Susan. "The Future of Information Technology in Higher Education: The Federal Perspective." *Change* 23 (January-February 1991): 46-51.

Kaske, Neal. *Library Program HEA Title II-D: College Library Technology and Cooperation Grants Program. Abstracts and Analyses of Funded Projects 1989.* Washington, DC: Office of Library Programs, Department of Education, 1990.

Library Systems Newsletter 1981-. Chicago: Library Technology Reports, American Library Association.

Lyman, Peter. "The Library of the (Not-So-Distant) Future." *Change* 23 (January-February 1991): 34-41.

Martin, Susan K. "Information Technology and Libraries: Towards the Year 2000." *College and Research Libraries* 50 (July 1989): 397-405.

Matthews, Joseph, ed. *A Reader on Choosing an Automated Library System.* Chicago: American Library Association, 1983.

OCLC and Association of American Colleges. *Integrated Planning for Campus Information Systems: A Series of Conferences for Undergraduate Institutions.* ed. Daphne N. Layton. Dublin, Ohio: OCLC Online Computer Library Center, Inc., 1989.

Reynolds, Dennis. *Library Automation: Issues and Applications.* New York: R. R. Bowker, 1985.

Taylor, Robert S. *Value Added Processes in Information Systems.* Norwood, NJ: Ablex, 1986.

Weiskel, Timothy. "The Electronic Library and the Challenge of Information Planning." *Academe* 75 (July-August 1989): 8-12.

Chapter 8

COLLECTION MANAGEMENT

Academic libraries exist to further the educational mission of the institutions of which they are a part. They fulfill their roles by providing access to information and materials needed by various segments of their communities, particularly access to those materials that support the curriculum and faculty research interests. They supply faculty with scholarly publications so they may keep current in their fields. They make available materials of general and professional interest for the entire college community. Finally, the college library provides access to information well beyond its walls and own collections.

A rational, well-conceived systematic program of collection development, management and acquisition is among the crucial ingredients of a first-rate library. Information is the core around which sound teaching and learning takes place in a college, and the library is where access to information is realized. In system terms, it is the collection, or knowledge base, that is utilized in the process of transforming input to output and outcome.

159

Success or effectiveness of the transformation is influenced by the collection's strengths and weaknesses. The term collection d e v e l o p m e n t — o n e   a s p e c t   o f   c o l l e c t i o n management—encompasses a wide range of activities which, taken together, ensures that a library owns the books, periodicals and other materials required to support the programs of its college. Additional functions involved in collection management include acquisition of materials according to a policy, maintenance and preservation of the collection, housing storage, and deselection and discarding, again within the framework of a policy. A complicated process, at best, these tasks involve the efforts of staff, faculty, students, administrators and representatives of commercial vendors or jobbers.

College library materials collections differ from those in university libraries in a number of important ways. Perhaps the most significant of these is the premium placed by undergraduate libraries on selectivity and by universities on comprehensiveness. Even with the new emphasis among university libraries on cooperation in collection development, the number of titles they hold is still considered the essential figure. On the other hand, while sometimes honored more in the breach, the need for and relevance of each individual title is what should govern decisions about collections in college libraries.

This chapter is based on certain important assumptions. First, we contend that print will continue to be the most common medium for library materials in the next decade. To date, there is little to indicate that the print publishing industry has contracted under the impact of the new technology. The paperless society, if it becomes a reality, will not make its appearance before the end of the century. Instead, books will continue to be published, and more and more information will also be available in multimedia and electronic formats. Although for the foreseeable future extensive collections of print published materials will remain the heart of the academic library, many new formats will supplement books and periodicals. As time goes on, printed sources will constitute a diminished proportion of the total information available for scholarly purposes. Pat Battin has affirmed, "We must provide new structures of access to knowledge in an increasing variety of formats and, at the same time, continue to preserve, manage, and make available scholarly information in the traditional printed formats with appropriate links between all formats."[1] In other words, college libraries cannot abandon the commitment to books, journals and microforms, but must somehow expand the range of media they make available, with or without an expanding budget base.

Collection development librarians are often confronted with dilemmas that require not only expertise, but tact. The Scylla of curriculum and student requirements, for instance, is continually challenged by the Charybdis of faculty needs and the librarian must steer a narrow course to avoid collision with either.

The burgeoning of information, new subject areas, new technology to enhance learning and new demands for other than intuitively devised estimates of what people are doing in the library all add to the complexity of describing the collection development and management process. Metz, among many other researchers and critics of the library scene, contends that librarians make fundamental decisions based on untested assumptions about the materials that different groups of readers come to the library to use.[2] This, in turn, has consequences, for instance, for: 1) decisions about the layout of library buildings; 2) the delegation of responsibility and resources for collection development, and 3) the establishment of departmental libraries. Other difficulties in collection development and management emerge from the shrinkage in library budgets and the mounting costs of books and periodicals.

College library collections are composed of materials for a number of different audiences—with students and faculty as primary recipients and members of the entire college community and the wider geographical community in which the college is housed as secondary users. Broadly, these materials can be classed into five major types which are found in every college library.

1. A basic collection for students' curricular needs
2. Materials to meet faculty research need.
3. A collection of materials of use to administrators to help them with their work.
4. A good reference collection to help identify materials in the library and resources elsewhere.
5. A collection of cultural and recreational materials

The curriculum, faculty interests and size of the acquisitions budget are important factors bearing on the development of the materials collection policy in the college library. They are considered below.

CURRICULUM

Curriculum is the single most important influence on the nature of the materials collection. What is taught at an institution determines in great measure the direction the library collection will take. Indeed, some commentators place such heavy emphasis on the importance of curriculum that they maintain that it describes not only the nature of the college library materials collection, but the nature of the college itself. In other words, the college is what it teaches. The collection, in turn, constitutes a statement of how well the library has understood the educational goals and policies of the host institution.

What a college teaches, however, is limited by the nature of the student body and its abilities. The degree to which students require remediation and the extent to which they are capable of undertaking independent study will affect the curriculum, probably in subject distribution, certainly in the level at which courses are offered.

Among the measurable curriculum factors that most academic librarians consider when formulating a collection development policy are: the number of departments of instruction, courses, major fields, what courses are offered at what level, and, if there is a graduate component, the number of different fields in which a master's degree is offered. How many courses are seminars, whether students write senior essays, and the extent of an honors program, if it exists, also affect the library collection. The differences among disciplines, the proportion of laboratory to literature courses, the amount and degree of opportunity for student investigation including library based research, and the extent of inter-disciplinary studies will all influence the nature of the collection. Less tangible, but equally salient factors guide the interpretation of the policy. These include which professors in which courses regularly require library research; which faculty members use yellowing lecture notes without recourse to the discipline's newer research; departmental expectations about bibliographic depth in student papers; and the degree to which course assignments mirror a particular instructor's narrow research interests.

In addition, monitoring changes in courses and in course enrollments produces valuable information about trends. Any expansion of one department or group of departments in relation to others will need to be reflected in the collection. Has the college decided to strengthen its science offerings? Does the periodical collection support that decision? Are more students interested in the social sciences? Does this include the necessity for access to current numeric files? Within the disciplines, emphases change. Women's Studies, for instance, which used to have a strong sociological orientation, now finds important support materials being published in literature, economics, psychology, political science, history, biology and other fields. As various disciplines alter their focus, the library must understand the implications of these paradigm shifts and acquire information representing the new direction, all the while being alert to the differences between materials that may be merely faddish and those destined to become part of the long-term collection.

The extent to which primary sources may be necessary is another example of how the curriculum shapes the collection. The decision about whether to collect rare books and manuscript materials ideally emerges from curriculum considerations and from whether an institution chooses to call itself a "research college" or a "liberal arts college." If the college offers some graduate work, the library may have to supply original materials. The complete files of newspapers or periodicals, for instance, may be required by a student undertaking a historical study. In the following chapter, consideration is given to collecting special kinds of materials in a college library.

Needless to say, anticipating the future, in addition to serving current needs, is an important dimension of collection development. Judgments made today by an academic institution's senior administrative staff and faculty are instrumental in shaping future demand when they decide whether to phase out old programs or which new ones to establish. Librarians often have difficulty gathering timely information about the directions the institution is taking because they are rarely involved in the deliberations. It is not easy to prepare for curriculum changes if one is not part of the process. At a minimum, ongoing and substantive conversation with key faculty members will give the library collection development officers a modest amount of pertinent information. An effective library committee may serve as the conduit to the library for information regarding curriculum issues.

The curriculum reform movement of the 1980s, despite its stress on general education, did not produce a national curriculum. Colleges still vary even in their basic course offerings. Collection development remains unique within each institution.

FACULTY INTERESTS

Faculty use the college library to keep current in their field, to develop courses, to further their research, to learn about cognate fields, to explore new ones, and for recreational and other reading. The extent to which the college library is prepared to perform all of these roles depends on funding, tradition and predilection.

Characteristics of a college's faculty that influence collection development include its size, how active members are in keeping up with their fields, the number of different disciplines they represent, and the extent to which they engage in scholarly research. A first-rate faculty requires the library to provide them with journals, proceedings, society publications and the like to keep them current with scholarship in their fields. The supply of such material cannot be cut off without risking intellectual famine.

Library literature is strewn with debates about the extent to which a college library can serve the research needs of its faculty. Available funding, of course, plays a major role in decisions about whether to apportion monies for these purposes. But the argument is larger and more substantive than consideration of availability of financial resources. It goes to the core of the unwritten contract between the college and its faculty, and involves the degree of support faculty members may expect as they engage in individual scholarly pursuits. No one disputes the obligation of the library to provide *access* to research materials. The reference collection should and usually does serve as the link for faculty between their needs and the universe of resources available.

The argument lies, rather, in the frequency with which access is translated into acquisition. Some librarians maintain that purchasing esoteric documents required by a single instructor is not the responsibility of most institutions. Students, they contend, are the primary clients, not faculty members. Undergraduate teaching institutions, they say, cannot afford highly specialized research material. If material is purchased to support faculty research, then students will be shortchanged. Others, who might countenance purchase of material for established faculty, argue that to buy for junior members who may be denied tenure is short-sighted.

Here, as in other instances, the librarian must be familiar with the institution and its aims and goals. Does it call itself a "research college" or a "liberal arts institution"? Are its faculty expected to publish in order to achieve tenure or be promoted? If so, to refrain from acquiring materials works against the expectations of the college for its faculty. And in the case of newer faculty appointments, to *not* purchase needed materials may be to jeopardize their careers. Does the administration see the provision of research materials as part of the library's mission? If so, is it prepared to fund what are sometimes extraordinary expenditures? Alternately, does the administration provide research and travel funds and release time for faculty members so that they can visit the libraries where materials they need are housed, thus precluding the necessity of making them available on the premises.

When public librarians congregate informally, they are prone to swap tales about the deviant behavior of library patrons. College librarians, on the other hand, frequently share stories about encounters with faculty members. Often these stories relate to demands on the library to acquire particular materials. One librarian at a smaller, but strong, upwardly mobile college recently described a new junior faculty member, an expert in medieval British law, who is methodically working her way through the comprehensive bibliography on the subject, ordering everything listed. An excellent teacher, this woman's classes are filled and students are responsible for a major paper in the course. When confronted with the extent to which she is ordering materials in this subject, the instructor is able to cloak her own research needs in the guise of curriculum support. Tenure is probably in her cards, but there is more than a remote possibility that she may choose to leave the college and associate herself with a major university where she will not be required to teach general medieval history as well as her specialty. She will leave behind a splendid collection of materials on British medieval law that may never again be exposed to the light of use. Such events occur with sufficient frequency to cause college librarians to hesitate about purchasing specialized research materials in favor of more general ones in a given field.

FINANCIAL CONSIDERATIONS

The 1970s and 1980s were marked by a number of societal events that had major consequences for college libraries. Among them were financial difficulties experienced by academic institutions; diminished federal grant funds; and cutbacks in budgets made in anticipation of a shrinking student population resulting from the end of the baby boom.

Academic libraries were simultaneously faced with prices that far outstripped inflation (books, for instance, rose 33% between 1977 and 1981), smaller increases in college book budgets, the disappearance of grant funds for acquisitions, the end of Title IIA federal support, and an "awesome" leap in journal subscription prices (for the same period, 1977-81, periodicals rose 60%).

At the same time, the print publishing industry experienced no shrinkage—700,000 new book titles are produced around the world annually, as well as millions of less trackable items, among which are pamphlets, newspapers, printed documents, technical reports, videotapes, maps, data tapes and bases. And electronic media burgeoned, placing additional demand on already diminished budgets. Obviously, libraries were buying less material for more money.[3]

These factors—declining budgets, rampant inflation, and increased publishing of all kinds—were and are now responsible for the great financial and managerial collection development problems that libraries are experiencing. Trying both to maintain and expand their holdings and to fulfill their user needs is a daunting task. Expectations have not lessened. Indeed they may have escalated. Administrators expect the library to continue and prevail despite increasingly limited fiscal resources. Faculty expect the library to continue to provide the materials and services they are used to receiving.

FUNDS

Academic libraries spend, on average, 37% of their budgets on acquisitions.[4] Limited financial resources for collection development necessitate difficult choices on how funds are allocated. To some extent it may be considered a zero-sum exercise. The selection of any major expensive set, for instance, may mean the rejection of other needed works or the postponement of their purchase.

A recurring challenge of college librarianship is to allocate equitably the materials budget among competing subject claims. Unfortunately, there is no single agreed-upon method for apportioning funds. Each institution must develop its own approach and guidelines.

In colleges where faculty retain primary responsibility for the materials collection, there is often a fixed allocation of the book budget, although many librarians consider the allocation suggestive rather than constraining. When librarians make the bulk of the selection decisions, there may or may not be a formally allocated budget. Even in the absence of specific dollar allocations, however, librarians by virtue of their decisions establish distribution patterns.

Allocations are generally made in two ways, usually a combination of both:

1. By format (books, periodicals, microforms, etc.). The median allocation among liberal arts college libraries for periodicals alone, exclusive of binding, is 42% of the materials budget.[5]

2. By substantive area (scholarly discipline).

It is likely that in the foreseeable future, format will be a less salient consideration than content in the allocation of materials budgets. Science information, for instance, is currently found most often in periodicals and increasingly in electronic form. Literature, on the other hand, still appears as print on paper in a bound volume.

Responsibility for allocating the materials budget generally rests with librarians, although the advice of the library committee or other faculty and administrators is often sought for both practical and political reasons.

Many colleges now use allocation formulas to distribute their acquisitions budget. These schemes have evolved from simple to sophisticated. The major attraction of the budgeting formula is "rhetorical in that it serves to convince faculty members and departments that their allocations are fair."[6] On the other hand, critics of formula allocations contend that using one provides evidence to skeptical faculty and administrators that librarians have little professional expertise to offer and are willing to trust collection development to generic formulas rather than their own knowledge.

Early budget allocation formulas, many of which are still followed, based new budgets upon past spending. In other words, departments or disciplines were allocated their last year's amount plus an across-the-board percentage increase.

New formulas for allocations call for using a combination of tradition and some or all of the following criteria:

1) Student population overall and in each major; 2) population of research students (those in graduate programs) and faculty involved in research; 3) curricula; 4) new programs; 5) strength of existing collection; 6) circulation (collection use); 7) growth rate of collections; 8) non-curricular reading needs; 9) growth of literature; 10) prices of publications, including inflation rates in various disciplines.[7]

The allocated materials budget should be sufficiently flexible to ensure that special needs—unanticipated contingencies, exceptional opportunities—can be met.

The amount college libraries spend on materials varies from institution to institution and is, once again, influenced by history, tradition, and the current context. Unfortunately, librarians who bear responsibility for developing the collection rarely have time to assess what might be the correct amount of money to spend. Rather, they tend to focus on the best way to spend the money allotted to them, a task made ever more demanding as electronic media generate new and different information products.

Time constraints notwithstanding, it is important that librarians each year request increased funding for needed materials, utilizing data from peer institutions, standards, publishing industry sources and recent college history. Caution is necessary when using these data to mount arguments for increased funding. Peer comparisons may have a shock effect and ACRL standards can illuminate weaknesses in a collection. Neither, however, substitutes for linking a request for additional funds to institutional priorities and new programs. Faculty must be led to conclude that the library has realistic expectations and is a good provider and manager of currently available resources. Immediate improvements to the materials budget rarely result from such applications, but the argument must continually be made.

COLLECTION SIZE

Numbers of volumes—the mere size of a collection—exercise a remarkable influence over all college administrators, faculty members, publishers and politicians. Librarians are not exempt from the charms of this popular fallacy. Size is emphasized in their annual reports, where the total dimension of the collection is highlighted and any increase in materials stock is pointed to with pride. The Office of Education and professional associations gather and report statistics. Yet, as every sensible person knows, the value of a college library is determined by its quality, not its size.

Everyone agrees that libraries should be "good," but affixing criteria to "goodness" is almost impossible. Size has been assumed to be one measure of a "good" collection. Certainly it is true that if enough of what is available is purchased, some of it is bound to be valuable. On the other hand, this approach produces an awful lot of "bad," as well.[8]

Nevertheless, size is seen as a symbol of strength by so many people that it must be confronted and explained. Quantities are easily understood by lay persons. When evaluating budget requests, numbers suggest objectivity. Robert Hayes has observed that "when questions of allocation of limited resources among competing institutions arise, quantitative criteria provide a means of avoiding a morass of politics and special interests."[9]

Collection development is an inexact science. It has long been recognized that a finite limit on the size of a collection may be desirable, but no agreement on that upper limit or how it is to be determined has been reached. Librarians are loath to admit that they have arrived at an optimal size, primarily because administrators too often misunderstand the concept, and use the admission to cut funding. Also, no method of assessing the adequacy of a collection has yet found consensus in the profession. Formulas are arbitrary devices. Nothing substitutes for informed decisions.

Accrediting agencies, not library organizations, began the push toward calling out a minimum size for college libraries. The first college library normative standards promulgated by librarians were produced in 1959. The influential Clapp-Jordan Formula was published in 1965.[10] It called for determining whether an academic library collection is large enough to support the teaching program by taking into account seven factors: (1) the student body—size and characteristics; (2) faculty—size and involvement in research; (3) curriculum—number of departments, courses, etc.; (4) methods of instruction; (5) availability of good study places; (6) proximity to other libraries;

and (7) intellectual climate of the college. Because of the difficulty of measuring some of these factors objectively, only the first three were used by the compilers.

The 1975 Standards for College Libraries included a formula that described the minimal size a college libraries could be and still meet standards. This was revised in 1984, and in 1986 enlarged to permit adding together print volumes, bibliographic unit equivalents for AV material, and a number of items borrowed or obtained through resource sharing agreements.

The formula is a cumulative one, and includes:

1. Basic collection of 85,000 volumes; Additional volumes for
2. each FTE faculty member 100 volumes
3. each FTE student 15 volumes
4. each undergraduate major or minor field 350 volumes
5. each master's field 6,000 volumes
6. each 6th year specialist degree 6,000 volumes
7. each doctoral field 25,000 volumes

Based on this collection size, then a college with 1,900 students, 175 faculty members, 20 major or minor fields and one master's degree should have a minimum of 137,000 volumes or volume equivalents.

Quantitative standards, in recent decades, describe "normal behavior" and arise from the possible.[11] Although some well-established liberal arts colleges have strong collections, many others do not meet ACRL standards. Standards provide these poorly supplied colleges with goals to aim for and with tangible numbers to give to administrators in their quest for institutional support.

College libraries should not attempt to be small versions of university libraries. Financially, they do not have the resources to even try. Evan Farber suggests that college librarians must, rather, build a "A collection of cultural and recreational materials to expand student's horizons."[12]

Farber advocates no-growth or steady-state college libraries. What he means is that using formulas, or other means, a library should reach its optimum size and remain there by continuous weeding of little used materials and purchase of relevant items. Collection development requires "hard analysis of the individual title in its relation to some conceptualization of the book collection."[13] The selector of a fixed-size library must continually evaluate the collection. Daniel Gore argues that the answer is not more books, but "fewer books better used."[14] He suggests that little-used materials should be quickly removed and materials for which there is greater demand be generously duplicated. When first presented, Gore's arguments were seen as visionary and provocative. Yet the goal now for most college libraries is to establish a currently useful collection. On the other hand, while slower growth rates characterize most college libraries, Richard Werking found that few directors currently believe they are facing a no-growth library situation.[15]

CORE COLLECTION

Much attention has been given to the degree to which we ought to supply "core materials" or a "core collection." By "core" we generally mean "important material." Unfortunately, or perhaps fortunately, for college libraries, the core remains undefined and most college librarians doubt that it exists. A real core, asserts Ross Atkinson, would have a periphery—a boundary—separating it from the remainder of the universe of publications.[16]

Opening day collections and other lists are useful in identifying important materials for college libraries. However, standard catalogs and lists of "best books," for instance, or *Choice's Opening Day Collection* cannot adequately respond to patterns of use and patron need as effectively as faculty members' selections or librarians' knowledge of actual patron use. In addition, such lists are out-of-date on the day they are published.

It used to be assumed that although the collections will vary from one institution to another depending upon local needs, core holdings, if compared would overlap significantly. Studies, however, have revealed less commonality than assumed in college library collections. Nugent found 40% title overlap across the holdings of six New England state university libraries.[17] The proportion of unique titles held by academic libraries has been found to range from 50 to 86%.[18]

Those who support the establishment across college borders of a "core collection" argue that it will bring uniformity and a commonality to libraries and, in turn, would have a salutary effect on the budget. If there were agreement on this core, each library could begin its budgeting by allocating necessary funding for the core collection. Based on a defined core, all academic libraries, but especially smaller ones, would be able to communicate their budget needs more accurately and forcefully to their parent institutions. Accreditation might also utilize core holdings as one of its assessment items.[19]

Those who see a core as impractical argue that, like a core of knowledge—a canon, in curriculum terms—a core library collection is suspect. Who will determine it? Does it represent an orthodoxy which may screen out more radical ideas? Core collections, in reality, go out of date from the day they are constructed. Value changes over time. Materials can only be judged within the context in which they are used. Context, too, changes over time. In addition, those who view the core as unrealistic maintain that use is dependent on the makeup of patron populations and that campus populations are so varied that the demand for heavily used materials at one institution may be negligible at another.

Library use studies have consistently demonstrated that only a small part of most collections find their way into the hands of users. Trueswell concluded that 80% of the circulation is satisfied by 20% of the stocked items and that 99% of circulation demand is satisfied by 60% of a collection.[20] Larry Hardesty found that 80% of need was satisfied by 30% of the collection.[21] In addition, McPherson reported that 50% of total library circulation occurred in 20% of the Dewey Decimal classification and 69% in 34%.[22]

Findings from a controversial study undertaken at the University of Pittsburgh revealed that 10% of the monographs accounted for 50% of use, 27% for 82%, 46% for 96%, and, finally, 60% accounted for 100%. Therefore, the researchers concluded, 40% of the monographs in those collections never circulated and perhaps never should have been purchased. The Pittsburgh study was attacked for its attention only to circulating materials. The authors were accused of ignoring the "browsing" behavior of users—in other words, materials readers examined and replaced on the shelves. Those who found the study compelling insisted that what patrons took home was far more important than what they looked at but did not find important enough to borrow.[23] Even those who conceded that the results were probably valid argued that although much of the material purchased would never be used, the nature of scholarship made it impossible to predict which selections would sit on the shelf and which would find use by patrons.

Unfortunately, the needs of library users are little understood. Library use is difficult to measure. Many library activities leave scant if any material record for analysis. Most library studies are based on circulation records, an inaccurate description of collection use.

Coupled with this difficulty has been the reluctance of some librarians to do much analysis, fearing that the results might somehow be detrimental to the broader humanistic goals of the library and of the college. Paul Metz, for instance, contends that: "To base library policies on use data alone would be to abrogate a serious professional responsibility." But, he continues, "To base policies on value judgments alone, or on value judgments and untested assumptions about use is also irresponsible and invites a very inefficient deployment of resources, to the detriment of important institutional goals."[24]

Recent studies about the use of academic libraries indicate that:

1. overall use is lower than we think, or like to think
2. in-house use and external circulation are correlated
3. use is highly concentrated over a small number of titles and previous use is generally the best single predictor of subsequent use
4. interest in materials is subject to a process (generally asymptotic) of obsolescence
5. foreign-language materials are significantly underutilized in proportion to holdings.[25]

COOPERATIVE COLLECTION DEVELOPMENT AND RESOURCE SHARING

No library has ever been self-sufficient. The myth of a self-sufficient or "comprehensive" collection that meets all or most of the needs of its patrons has been punctured by a series of collection overlap and interlibrary loan pattern studies that indicate there is a surprising amount of unique material distributed among American libraries, even in small colleges. This knowledge, coupled with financial, space, and staff considerations, argues strongly for some cooperative collection development and shared storage, preservation and cataloging. Technology has made cooperative resource sharing and collection development substantially more feasible today than it would have been even a decade ago.

The most common resource-sharing programs are shared holdings through interlibrary loan and shared acquisitions through agreements among libraries to accept responsibility for collecting materials in specific substantive areas.

Preconditions exist that must be met before libraries can successfully participate in a cooperative collection development program. Among them are on-line bibliographic access to member holdings, rapid delivery of materials, formal agreements on shared responsibility for collection development and a long-range time frame.[26] In addition, they must have the following information about their own collections in order to make informed judgments about apportioning collection responsibilities. They must know

1. the number of holdings, median age, and availability of titles in each subject area;
2. the subject distribution and age of items circulated and used in-house;
3. the subject distribution of previous years' acquisitions;
4. the subject distribution of previous years' interlibrary loan and back-up reference activity.[27]

Despite the new emphasis on access rather than acquisition, libraries will nonetheless be responsible for providing locally the materials required to meet the routine needs of their users. College libraries will continue to devote a large portion of their resources to their own collection development because each institution will remain the primary source of materials to meet undergraduate requirements. Networks today, and for the near future at least, do not enable colleges to place the cost of providing instructional material elsewhere.

Writing in *Library Journal*, Richard DeGennaro warns that:

We must husband [our] existing resources and increase them in the future. It would be a tragedy if those who fund our libraries were to misunderstand the purpose of resource sharing and use it as a rationale for further reducing library appropriations. Resource sharing will permit us to do more with less by pooling our resources, but only if we keep the pool replenished.[28]

The decisions about what to collect locally and what to relinquish to another institution or a system are not easily made. The following considerations should dictate policy:

1. College libraries should supply items which are most frequently in demand by students and faculty and provide *access* to other resources and information that cannot be provided on site.

2. Resource development at the local level should be designed to respond to what users need to meet their recurring educational, recreational and intellectual needs. This results in high use collections geared to primary clientele.[29]

Designing organizational structures that support decision-making for substantive cooperation without limiting individual library autonomy is complex and difficult. The system, or the group of cooperating libraries, is responsible for planning, describing and defining areas of cooperation, but all members participate in its realization.

The college librarian who enters into a cooperative agreement would do well to insure that the following conditions, described by Billy Bozone, are operant:

1. A governing authority, that is, a mechanism to insure continuous interaction, task forces to create frameworks, constant promotion of system among faculty and other constituents;

2. Assured equitable funding for activities, planning, training;

3. A network base linking members which provides online access to reliable information and collections;

4. An effective information delivery program to supplement interlibrary loan;

5. Collection development policies based on parity, common vocabulary and descriptors, collection strengths and collecting missions; and,

6. Agreement on what cooperative collection development will include. Cooperative selection, deselection, shared purchasing, preservation, serials, uniform methodologies for use and user studies, collection evaluations and verification and overview studies are all possible. Cooperative acquisitions need not be limited by form and format.[30]

There are drawbacks to cooperative collection development. All cooperative endeavors take longer than anticipated. Completing the necessary paper work is time-consuming and expensive. For instance, cooperation cannot begin until libraries are able to communicate with one another about their collections on an item-by-item and categorical basis. Another drawback is that scholars prefer not to depend on resource sharing. They find it less convenient, slow, cumbersome and uncertain. Periodicals are a great problem. Faculty want them retained and great diplomacy (as well as evidence) is required to convince them that the materials are easily and quickly accessible through telefacsimile, electronic mail or inter-campus delivery.

Other Factors in Building Collections

We have referred often to how necessary it is to relate the educational aims and goals of the college to collection development. Most colleges consider as important parts of their mission the provision of a strong extra-curricular program and the development of skills which will permit students to lead productive and satisfying lives after college. Based on this aspect of the college experience, the college and the library will have to decide to what extent extra-curricular reading should be supplied. We believe that encouragement of general reading is an important dimension of the library role. Reading for its own sake is an essential attribute of culture. In a technological society, reading perpetuates the humane tradition.

Unfortunately, books of current general interest have a low budget priority when funds are limited. Finding money to purchase a sufficient quantity of new books is difficult. Too often, the general interest materials are snapped up as soon as they appear and are seldom to be found on the shelves while they are relatively new. In truth, library staff members often account for much of the first wave of new book borrowing. Proximity, after all, has some advantages.

What kinds of non-curricular related reading a college should supply is another matter of debate within the profession. Some suggest that there be no pandering to popular taste. Only books of "quality" should find their way to the new book shelves. Others argue that while intellectual content is somewhat important, what really counts is the degree to which students develop a taste for reading. Good contemporary novels, short stories, biographies, autobiographies, film criticism, popular science essays are among the types of material which traditionally appeal to undergraduates.

Other factors have an impact on collection policies, as well. The proximity of the college to other library collections, the present strengths and weaknesses of the college library collection, and the extent to which the college cooperates with other institutions in sharing library resources all have relevance for collection building. Another group whose interests should be safe-guarded are those readers who wish to pursue interests that are unrelated to the curriculum.

In addition, the specialized information needs of administrators should be met, to some extent, by the college library. The personnel manager of a college once told us that he had no right to expect the library to provide professional materials for him since it existed to serve students. He seemed startled when we explored with him the notion of the library as a participant in the life of the entire college community and explained the range of options he had for service from the library including access to materials.

The extent to which a college library considers the needs of the wider geographic community in its collection development policies is governed partially by the nature of that community, its relative isolation, the strength of other libraries within the community, the activity of other institutions in collecting local history, and the historic relationship between the college community and its environment. Decisions, for instance, about the extent to which the college library will serve local high school students will influence collection development decisions.

PARTICIPANTS IN THE SELECTION PROCESS

It seems obvious that in order to develop a sound college library collection, there must be a working combination of administrators, faculty and librarians. Broadly speaking, no member of the college community should be excluded from the process of collection development. The *Standards for College Libraries* suggests that, "Although the scope and content of the collection is ultimately the responsibility of the library staff ...[one should develop] clear selection policies in cooperation with the teaching faculty" and encourage faculty to select new titles.[31]

Historically, there has been a persistent and largely unchallenged tenet of college library acquisitions policy that teaching faculty would have the dominant voice in the materials selection process. College librarians of the past not only accepted the faculty's role in library acquisitions, but concurred in the decision to accord them chief responsibility for library book purchases and collection building. Librarians traditionally have allocated the materials budget, wrestling with the difficult decisions involved in appropriating according to equity and need. They considered their major role to be filling the gaps and acquiring basic reference material.

A shift in university collection selection patterns brought about by rapid increases in funding and in emphases on building all-inclusive research-level collections made its appearance in the 1960s. University administrators as well as librarians realized that superior research collections could be created by professional bibliographers on the library's staff and that this course of action would heighten the academic library's ability to respond rapidly and rationally to the manifold new information needs of its users. The librarian's role in selection became a more active one, and at times even dominant. Indeed, Ross Atkinson comments that in the university "the primary responsibility for selection of library materials has passed from faculty users to academy library staff."[32]

In colleges, however, it would seem that the teaching faculty continue to serve as the primary agents of selection in the great majority of institutions. A number of college librarians feel that the time for reconsideration of this policy has not only arrived, but is long-overdue. Most, however, still prefer to depend heavily on faculty recommendations for selection, while insuring for librarians strong participation in the process.

Good reasons exist for faculty making the bulk of library selections; good reasons abound for librarians to play the same role. The following is a summary of arguments for assigning faculty primary responsibility in selecting library materials. Teaching faculty know the literature of their own subject fields best; they can best identify what material they need for research; and they are best prepared to select course related material. Among the arguments mounted against faculty doing the bulk of selection are that they are often uninterested, they tend to be narrow in their selections, often stressing advanced work in their own subject fields and forgetting that the mission of the library is to support undergraduate instruction, not research. In addition, they may be unfamiliar with current materials in their fields. Further, faculty do not recognize gaps and weaknesses in the collection as a whole nor can they observe, as do librarians, what is being used. A real danger exists that gaps will develop when there is no department for a particular subject or if interdisciplinary materials fall into the chasm between them. Finally, an allocation controlled by a department lessens flexibility and the ability to make mid-course corrections as a control against over- and under-spending.

Much of the debate seems to center around whether the selector should be a specialist or a generalist. Many librarians feel that subject knowledge is a necessary, but insufficient prerequisite for selection. Others, more radical, feel that too much expertise can be detrimental to selecting the appropriate materials. In his research, Metz found that specialists and nonspecialists approach literatures differently. "When library policies are set by client groups [faculty], the result may be private virtues which are public vices."[33] His argument supports the position that professional librarians are the best guardians of collections and mediators of competitive and conflicting interests. If academic departments select collections, they may purchase materials that specialists find useful, but that undergraduates cannot utilize.

As with other library issues, who selects depends on the nature of the institution, the interest of the faculty and tradition. Where the faculty has traditionally selected most of the materials, it may be politically perilous to withdraw this prerogative, or even to insist that the library have final say on selections. It can test the fragility of the delicate relationship between librarians and faculty. On the other hand, often a minority of faculty systematically select materials and rely, in making their selections, on materials that do not automatically guarantee the quality of the collection. Building interdependent systems in which faculty are active in recommending titles for purchase based on review sources supplied to them by librarians—*Choice* cards, for instance—may be the best approach to collection development, particularly if it is combined with regular consultation and periodic examination of particular collections.

In institutions where librarians participate heavily in the collection selection process, it is important that they have some level of substantive expertise in topical areas. Unfortunately, reduced college library financial resources may mean that subject specialists on library staffs are less in demand. Without subject expertise, there may be a tendency to rely on blanket orders with commercial vendors. Depending on vendors, in turn, undermines the need for substantively trained libraries.

Who chooses better materials for the library, faculty or library staff? Better, in this context as in so many others referring to libraries, has been defined as amount of "use" of library materials. Research into the question has produced ambiguous or contradictory data. Evans found that titles selected by librarians circulate more frequently than do those chosen by faculty or book jobbers; Bingham replicated Evans' study and found books selected by faculty circulated more frequently than those selected by librarians, except in humanities. Geyer studied community colleges and found no difference.[34]

The student's role in selecting materials for library collection is a lesser one. Nonetheless, suggestions from students should not be overlooked. Student opinion on the readability, for instance, of certain materials is often the final verdict on the degree to which they are used. Although students cannot be expected to select the readings within courses, it should not be forgotten that they are the ultimate consumers.

Librarians can cultivate student interest in collection development by soliciting suggestions for purchase. A suggestion box placed in a prominent library location can stimulate student participation in the process. In addition, students should be represented on the library committee, if there is one.

COLLECTION DEVELOPMENT POLICY

A number of problems involved in the collection development process that require individual institutional solutions have been described. Who selects materials, for what purpose, to what extent, and for whom are matters that should be spelled out in detail in a Collection Development and Management Policy. All college libraries should formulate and write total collection *management* policies. Most librarians agree, in principal at least, that a collection development policy is essential. It should include, as considerations, the college's curriculum, its goals, attention to the quality of documents, level of materials to be collected, use of library materials, and meeting faculty research interests. Along with the collection development statement, the collection management policy should include a retention, discard and weeding policy, and a preservation policy that includes binding, microforming, restoration, housing, storage and housekeeping statements.

Sadly, studies indicate that many college libraries never write policies and few are doing anything formally in collection development. The bleakness of this picture is scarcely relieved by the realization that many institutions have "unwritten" policies that guide them in collection development and management. Without a collection development statement, it is far more difficult to build a library collection effectively and insure that the information needs of the college will be met. In addition, a policy is protection against the unreasonable demands for provision of particular kinds of materials. Ross Atkinson says that "The creation of a unified collection policy is intended to articulate and render consistent criteria which are often already being applied by selectors. The purpose of the policy is to raise those criteria to consciousness, to compare and coordinate them, to adjust them to meet the varied and competing needs of the institution as consistently as possible."[35]

Many librarians are loath to embark on the task of devising a collection development and management policy because it is a time-consuming, demanding endeavor, requiring a great deal of data. Some remain unconvinced of the efficacy of the project or even the process, and conclude that time would be better spent in teaching an extra library instruction course, or checking another subject bibliography. We believe the value of constructing a policy far outweighs the drawbacks in demands on time and resources. It is the only way to ensure that a college library collection is based on selectivity, integration, and direction rather than becoming a product of haphazard miscellaneous growth.

A collection development and management policy includes, in one form or another, the following elements:

1. *Overview.* The collection management policy is framed by the scope, objectives and goals of the library, as is any policy. These are to be clearly articulated at the outset. Preliminary material also describes the community; identifies clientele; states the parameters of the collection; describes in detail the types of programs or patron needs that are to be met by the collection; includes a section of general limitations and priorities that will determine how the collection will be developed; and discusses in detail the library's participation in cooperative collection development programs.

2. *Scope of Collection* describes in detail the subject areas and formats collected. The policy should set out priorities and levels of collecting intensity. The Research Libraries Group (RLG) Conspectus has designed a six-step numeric system to aid institutions in assessing current collection strength and decision-making about desirable collecting levels. They are:

0. out of scope, not collected
1. minimal
2. basic information
3. instructional support
4. research
5. comprehensive[36]

Collection development policies should specify the level of comprehensiveness to be attained in each area, based on the instructional and research needs of the user communities. Most college collections will have materials through category 3, instructional support, although in certain cases research levels may be desirable. The quality of the student body will influence collecting levels, since in a strong undergraduate college with honors work, the level of collecting will be higher and include some research material. Collection development statements often limit collection areas by substantive topic, historical period, geographical area or language of publication.

3. *Collection Responsibility.* There should be a clear statement about who is responsible for selection, for deselection, and what guidelines are to be used in the process.

4. *Miscellaneous Issues.* Gifts, Weeding and Discarding, the bases for decisions regarding binding, housing, equipment, microfilming, preservation and/or restoration and/or replacement; and how to handle complaints all require delineation.

5. *Intellectual Freedom.* A statement committing the library to support of academic and intellectual freedom and against censorship should appear in every library collection development policy.

Collection development statements are effective only if they are produced jointly by staff and users—particularly students, faculty and administrators. Among staff members serving on the team to design collection development policies should be preservation officers, reference and circulation librarians, as well as those who bear direct responsibility for selection and acquisition.

The collection development statement serves both as an informational and a public relations document and deserves wide dissemination upon completion or revision. That means placing it in the hands of administrators, making it available to students, and giving copies to new teaching staff as part of their orientation packet. This insures that the community members will receive authoritative information and helps to impress on them that the library has considered these issues.

A few additional points about collection practices and policies merit particular comment:

1. Sufficient flexibility is necessary in selecting books so that funds may be applied to acquire items that are important, regardless of whether or not they are immediately germane to someone's teaching interest. For example, no librarian should have ignored Deconstructionist literary theory even if faculty on the campus were not teaching it. Some materials are acquired because of the intrinsic interest of the author's writings, even if their influence is not agreed upon and even if no one is demanding them at the moment. The principle may be difficult to apply, but it should be kept in mind.

2. Since funds are limited, the matter of duplication is important. If there are departmental libraries or neighboring college libraries which cooperate, either informally or by contract, duplication should be avoided wherever possible, the exception being in course reserves (which are discussed in Chapter 9).

3. Librarians have been indoctrinated for years against the purchase of textbooks, primarily because some faculty order them freely and in multiple copies for their students. Obviously, not ordering texts is a short-sighted policy. In some fields the seminal works are texts. Samuelson's *Economics* can be so described. In addition, textbooks can serve to provide minimal or basic information in subjects which are not covered by the curriculum, or for which introductory material is required.

4. The use of materials funds to cover all types of printed and nonprint material should be clearly defined in the policy statement. The music department may be expected to finance music recordings from its instructional budget for a listening center in the department, but the library may still be responsible for spoken-word recordings and tapes and for a broad selection of music for leisure listening. Who pays for films, videos, slides and other materials needed by departments for their own use should be clearly articulated.

5. Certain kinds of material serve little purpose outside the department or office where they are housed. Laboratory manuals, handbooks and similar materials which are needed for constant use in the laboratory, classroom, or office, and which cannot be made generally accessible to library users, should be charged to instruction funds, even though the library may act as the purchasing agent. The policy should make clear that these materials can not be charged to allocated library funds.

METHODS OF SELECTION

A college library has the opportunity and responsibility to develop a uniquely appropriate collection. It does this through careful selection and weeding.

Material selection, framed against the overall goals of the institution, the size of resources in particular areas, the level and depth of the instructional programs, involves a continuous series of choices made within the context of the collection development policy.

The most important criterion for inclusion of material in a college collection is need. Quality, in this instance, plays a secondary role. But selectivity is more important than comprehensiveness. The critical concept in selection, therefore, is the choice of an individual title as it fits in the collection.

The categories of materials included in a college library may be described in different ways. The following is one system of classification:

Subject collections - standard works in each subfield, current and retrospective. General practice holds faculty chiefly responsible for selecting these materials, in accordance with the collection development policy.

General materials - those which provide current as well as background information that cuts across lines of academic disciplines, including titles that are important in their own right, regardless of the immediate demands of the curriculum. Librarians generally claim responsibility for selecting these materials, systematically searching the major reviewing media for items of interest.

Reference collection - materials for consultation and bibliographic investigation—encyclopedias, dictionaries, atlases, indexes, abstracts, yearbooks, bibliographies. These include both print and electronic media—online data bases, CD-ROMS, among others. Most reference materials are selected by the reference staff.

Special collections - these include rare books, manuscripts, photographs and the like that illustrate the history of the book, reveal examples of man's thought, or exhibit the books as an object of beauty. These materials are, for the most part, donated to a college library. Universities, on the other hand, often seek and pay large sums for such collections.

We know little about the methods faculty use to select library materials. The following, which represents approaches taken by at least some faculty in some institutions, can be recommended as producing salutary results:

1. The primary source used by most selectors—both librarians and faculty—is *Choice*, a monthly book selection periodical designed to evaluate current books of a scholarly or academic nature considered of interest to undergraduate libraries. Many college librarians have found it useful to subscribe to *Choice's* "reviews-on-cards" and to distribute them among appropriate academic departments.

2. Scholarly or technical journals containing reviews can be regarded as a primary source of information about new books. Unfortunately, scholarly reviews are often very late in making their appearance. Faculty sometimes consult the "books received" section of these journals and make selections from the titles based on their knowledge of the author's scholarship and reputation, or on the basis of the subject matter which may be of special interest to the department. The library must provide methods of access to the most important of the review journals in a way that encourages and stimulates their use by faculty.

3. Faculty tend to use publishers' and book dealers' announcements to a greater extent that do librarians, again basing their selections on knowledge of their disciplines. These brochures, then, should find their way into faculty hands as quickly as possible after they are received.

4. Some faculty members prepare "want lists" of retrospective material they need to build up collections in their fields. A subject that has only recently gained academic attention, for instance, or one that has come back into vogue may not have the collection support it requires. Librarians and faculty will need to consult second-hand and out-of-print catalogs to locate materials in these subjects. The preparation of "want lists" should be encouraged both as a way to improve the collection and to further faculty participation in the library.

Librarians supplement faculty choices by looking at the generalized needs of their constituencies. The importance of being well-read and well rounded cannot be over emphasized. It is necessary to insure the health of the collection as well as to enable appropriate communication with faculty members.

Even in institutions where the faculty are prime selectors, the final responsibility to approve and disapprove orders is often left in the hands of the librarian. Turning down a faculty request requires courage and sensitivity. In addition, and of equal or greater importance, the librarian must be able to render an intellectual justification about why an item makes no useful contribution to the collection.

In a college library, most professional staff members are involved in the selection process. Unlike the university library, college libraries simply do not have staff funds, except perhaps in a few instances, to employ subject specialists who devote their time to collection development. By assigning responsibility among the professional staff to "watch over" certain subject areas, the library can guard against omissions, narrow choices and redundancies in the collection. In addition, the staff can assure that current, general works find their way to the shelves in a timely fashion. When exciting new books of imaginative literature appear, the college community should have an opportunity to read them on publication. Professional and scholarly interests must be balanced against matters of more general import. *The New York Times Book Review* and the *Times Literary Supplement* play an equally important role in collection decisions as do *The American Political Science Review* or the *MLA Journal*.

APPROVAL PLANS

An alternate method of selecting current materials for a college library's collection is to use an approval plan. Approval plans are arrangements with book jobbers that call for automatic shipment of new books issued by specified publishers or on specified topics. They can also be drawn up directly with particular publishers.

Approval plans are based on a carefully developed, and frequently reviewed, profile of the library created after extensive discussions with a broad range of faculty members as well as with the library staff. Although materials are automatically shipped, the library reserves the right to reject after examination any book it deems unsuitable and to return it to the publisher for credit. Faculty members in subject disciplines, and librarians responsible for those areas, are expected to examine each individual title and to judge its appropriateness. Approval plans are used most heavily by universities, although a number of colleges that have adopted them contend that they have the potential for stimulating creative faculty-librarian relationships.

Among the major advantages of approval plans is that materials in selected subjects areas are received at the *time of publication*. Pre-selecting titles on the basis of subject allows for rational decision-making and planning input from a broad range of faculty members in all subject areas, and may reduce the impact of a few faculty with vested interests. Some argue that better quality selections emerge because the actual books can be examined. Selectors can make recommendations after inspecting the materials, rather than basing decisions on the opinion of reviewers. Another benefit of selecting in this way is the increased ability to plan allocation of a significant portion of acquisition funds to purchase books at the time when they cost least. Finally, this method requires fewer staff in acquisitions departments because titles need not be searched or have other pre-order in-house preparation.

On the other hand, there are disadvantages to acquiring materials through approval plans. Books may be added without having undergone *careful* review. Important titles may be overlooked if the vendor or publisher does not supply them. It is difficult to insure that faculty or staff will examine the materials as they arrive and there is the potential for a greater lack of involvement by them in the collection development process and therefore even less awareness about new titles being added to the collection. Evans and Argyres found that approval plans, even when carefully monitored, add more unusual materials to the collection than do either library or faculty selections.[37]

Approval plans, though related, are not the same as standing order plans by which the library agrees to purchase groups of titles from a publisher or a vendor. Standing Order Plans are generally placed for series, yearbooks, annuals and may be on a "'Til Forbidden" basis; that is, publishers and jobbers continue sending the title until they are notified.

A number of ways to encourage library-faculty cooperation in collection development have been suggested. Among them are:

1. Make known to faculty the method of budget allocation and seek their input on equitable percentages for disciplines or formats.

2. Urge each department to appoint a coordinator of library purchases, whether or not funds are allocated, and request that all orders from departments be channeled through those persons. Coordinators should also represent special needs and problems of their departments to the library, and their opinions should be sought on subscriptions, replacements, and gifts. It would be helpful, additionally, if coordinators could be made to understand the importance of attaching correct bibliographic information to their orders and could be urged to act as liaisons in explaining this to members of their departments.

3. Encourage departments to spend their allocations in a timely fashion in order to insure that the materials flow is even and that serious bottlenecks are avoided. Some institutions, particularly those in the public sector, require that funds be committed by the middle of the academic year in order that they may be spent before the fiscal period ends.

4. Circulate second-hand catalogs to departments where they will be found useful, and warn faculty that they must be returned promptly if the materials they seek are to be secured. Competition for out-of-print titles is so fierce that to order books more than a week or ten days after receipt of a catalog is hardly worthwhile.

5. Explain carefully to the college community the reasons for allocating a substantial portion of the book fund to general purposes. They should be apprised of ways to make suggestions for the use of these funds. In

addition, they should be made aware of any special contingency funds which might be available for major purchases that cannot be met from the departmental allocations.

In summary, good book collections are the product not only of faculty-library cooperation, but also of effective organization. In the academic world, the idea of organizing anything may be greeted with suspicion; yet without it, the selection of materials becomes haphazard and incomplete, and in many cases superficial. A good organization provides for orderly, systematic acquisitions, vigilant attention to new developments, and flexibility.

WHERE AND HOW TO BUY

College libraries buy most of their materials through several, if not all, of the following sources: book jobbers or wholesale dealers, publishers, reprint publishers, out-of-print dealers, local booksellers and subscription agents. For the individual library, one or two of these agents will seem more important than the others, but each has special advantages for certain kinds of purchases.

The best sources of current books for college libraries are book jobbers or wholesalers. A number of benefits accrue from using their services. First, by consolidating all library book orders from various publishers in one order, librarians are able to reduce record keeping and the number of bills to be paid. Second, because they deal in bulk orders, jobbers are able to offer substantial discounts. Third, most jobbers are familiar with library procedures and library needs. As a result, they can anticipate requests and deal with them efficiently as they arise. Fourth, jobbers who have been awarded the major portion of a library's orders can be expected to deal with smaller items on which there is little or no profit, or to make special purchases, such as continuations. And finally, jobbers can facilitate the return of unwanted materials and make adjustments, two occurrences frequent in all acquisition transactions.

It is reasonable for libraries to expect jobbers to have large inventories of titles; to promptly and accurately fill orders, to report regularly on items not in stock, and to give personal service at a reasonable price. Jobbers, on the other hand, can rightfully expect libraries to cooperate by placing orders accurately and in a timely fashion, to order, for instance, all copies of a book that may be needed; to keep paperwork to a minimum—that is to keep the invoice procedure as simple as possible; and to make prompt payment for services.

Librarians occasionally forget that jobbers are in business to make a profit and are therefore influenced in their relations with libraries by the amount of business placed with them. This suggests that a library would be well advised to order heavily from a single book jobber whose discounts and service are known to be good rather than distributing its purchases among a group of jobbers. On the other hand, the library should guard against permitting the discount size to govern the decision about which jobber to select, since service considerations such as turn-around time, receipt time, fill rate and others are of equal or greater moment.

The following considerations surround the two elements of discounts and service:

1. *Discounts*: Discounts will depend on the volume of library business; the efficiency with which library orders are prepared and sent to the jobber; the type of material bought; and continuity in the library/jobber relationship. As a rule libraries can expect a discount of at least 30% on trade books and 10% on short-discount books (reference works, technical books, etc.). A conscientious librarian will check the discounts at frequent intervals to insure that they have not suddenly disappeared or been substantially reduced. Libraries that are able to join forces with a group of

libraries—a regional consortium, for instance, or a county library system—may benefit from substantially larger discounts because of quantity purchasing. Agreements to participate in these cooperative buying groups sometimes carry with them the obligation to remain with the group no matter whom it selects as jobber. Changing jobbers can be both costly and detrimental to service.

2. *Service*: Good service, as we said, is an equal partner with the discount rate in selecting a jobber. Jobbers must be prompt in delivery, have an acceptable fill rate, make suitable transportation arrangements, adjust bills and orders as necessary, and be accurate. Of great importance is the "follow-up" pattern—the accuracy and promptness with which the jobber reports back on "shorts" and out-of-print titles. Faculty frequently complain about the time lag between their ordering a book and its placement in their hands. The time element is a major consideration. A four-week period of delivery may be considered the outside limit for domestic in-print books in the United States. A jobber with a large inventory should be able to meet this time by supplying a substantial portion of a current book order from the shelves.

Bidding

Some libraries, particularly those supported by public funds, may have their choices of jobbers limited by law. They may be required to select a jobber on the basis of competitive bidding. These libraries send out *Requests for Bids* and often must have at least three proposals in hand before decisions can be made on a jobber. Bidding as a method for selecting jobbers has some virtues. It can lower cost and eliminate patronage. On the other hand, having to choose the lowest bidder relegates considerations about quality of service to a subsidiary position. Any librarian experiencing undue delays or poor handling of service queries will testify about the short-sightedness of this approach.

Foreign Acquisitions

When buying foreign books in print, it is probably preferable for college libraries to deal with an importer in this country, particularly one with representatives in the various European centers of distribution, rather than an exporter in a foreign country, although the opposite may be true in the case of large universities and larger college libraries. Dealing with an importer carries fewer risks, and less chance of misunderstanding, and generally results in greater speed and efficiency. On the other hand, importers may be more expensive. Some experienced academic librarians prefer to use a single, well-known dealer, say, in England, who is familiar with academic library procedures in this country and who frequently sends representatives to the United States to discuss library acquisition problems with their clients. If a college library buys extensively in foreign books, then the practice of selecting a dealer in each major country has much to commend it. Jobbers of foreign materials seldom offer discounts from the list price on books, but most import and foreign dealers will search for out-of-print titles.

Publishers

While it is true that on occasion publishers may offer a larger discount than other book agents, generally the best discount is offered by jobbers. In addition, ordering through publishers is often financially unwise in light of the paperwork required to deal regularly with numerous publishers. Particularly in small libraries where minimal staffs struggle continually for time to do the more important jobs demanded of them, ordering books from many agencies is economically unsound.

On certain occasions, and for certain types of material, however, ordering from domestic publishers may prove beneficial:

1. Rush orders, when a book is needed urgently and the jobber reports it not in stock;

2. Orders for materials obtainable only from the publisher. Some publishers do not sell to jobbers or offer such a limited discount to jobbers that they can scarcely afford to carry their books. In these cases, librarians have no recourse but to deal directly with the publisher;

3. Special orders: these include nontrade publications which are offered in very limited editions and which may be sold out if not ordered promptly (society publications, limited editions of poetry, museum publications); first editions of living authors where the library is building a special collection; and books which have been reported out of stock or out of print by the jobber, but which are still listed in current volumes of *Books in Print*. In this last instance, ordering directly from the publisher serves a double purpose in that it frequently secures the books which the jobber has not been able to get and at the same time serves as a check on the reliability of the jobber in reporting shorts.

The case against dealing directly with publishers in foreign countries is doubly strong. British book publishers offer no discount to libraries and only a few European publishers do so; there is therefore no advantage in the matter of discounts. Experience has shown that direct purchases from foreign publishers often bog down in time lost, high transportation costs, annoying formalities, and the uncertainty of remittances.

Local Booksellers

Academic libraries use local booksellers only on rare occasions. Most local bookstores have inventories geared to popular tastes and they are unlikely to be able to meet academic library requirements. In addition, they do not usually offer the depth of discounts available from jobbers, nor the rapid and convenient service generally provided by them.

Remainder sales at local bookstores at which books are offered substantially below their original publication prices should be monitored. Good bargains may be acquired in this way, but they should be chosen with care.

Out-Of-Print Materials and Reprint Buying

Books go out-of-print far more often than they did before the Thor Power Tool Decision of 1980, an IRS ruling that held that "writing-down" the value of inventories to a low level each year was illegal. Producers followed this practice in order to be able to declare a "paper" loss and deduct it from income, thus reducing tax liability. The United States Supreme Court ruled that writing down inventories resulted in taking current deductions for future estimated losses, and disallowed it.

The Thor decision was deemed applicable to publishing companies who had also followed the practice of writing down inventories. As a result, publishers currently make shorter press runs, and are less willing to risk publishing books predicted to be slow sellers. Librarians now must be alert to the fact that this year's imprints may be out-of-print next year. Collection development librarians used to delay acquisition of particular materials, hoping that future budget allocations would be more favorable. This option is no longer viable for many trade publications. The material may simply be unavailable. Materials that publishers have permitted to go out of print can sometimes be procured by scanning out-of-print or second hand catalogs, or by ascertaining its existence as a reprint.

Many libraries have found it useful to construct a "desiderata" or want list composed of materials either requested by faculty and other community members, or identified by library staff. This list becomes the basic tool for searching second-hand markets and reprint lists. As in other ongoing library files, the desiderata or want list requires continuous review in order to insure that it contains no dead wood—titles no longer needed or ones that have recently been reprinted.

Three main approaches to second-hand buying are followed by libraries: asking an antiquarian bookdealer to search for items on a desiderata or want list prepared by the library; selecting from second-hand catalogs, or advertising.

Dealing through an antiquarian bookseller may involve a time-consuming search. The dealer should be given a sufficient period to look for the title and to offer a quote before the list is sent to another dealer. The cost will almost always be higher than prices appearing in a second-hand catalog, but quotes or scarce items are rarely rejected. A number of directories to the antiquarian booktrade enable librarians to locate out-of-print dealers and ascertain their specialties.

Second-hand catalogs can be a rich source for locating out-of-print materials, but searching them requires blocks of time and is often a thankless task. Not all librarians agree that reading second-hand catalogs is worthwhile. On the occasions, however, when works of major utility appear and can be secured, the effort seems more than justified. In fields where scholarship is as much concerned with older materials as it is with contemporary ones, there is no alternative but to consult second-hand catalogs.

For older titles that the library has been unable to secure through other sources, advertising may produce results. A subscription to the *The Library Bookseller* entitles a library to list an unlimited number of book wants at no further cost. Libraries may advertise at a special rate per line in the *Antiquarian Bookman's Weekly*, which also carries a "for sale" listing that often turns up important titles at very reasonable prices.

The reprint boom of the 1960s had great benefit for college library collections. Books that had been long out of print were suddenly once again available. Often, however, because of limited sales, the prices asked were shocking to librarians. On the other hand, today's price will probably appear cheap compared with the one levied next year, and the librarian who chooses to wait may feel penny-wise and pound-foolish. Establishing whether or not a particular title or set has been reprinted is not an easy task. The best sources currently are the annual *Guide to Reprints, Announced Reprints* and the *Bulletin of Reprints*.

Libraries now can have reprints made on demand, in microform or hardcover, for materials which are in the public domain. Both forms are expensive, although microforms generally cost somewhat less than hardcover reprints. But choice of format must be made first on the basis of potential use, and secondly, on cost. A microfilm copy of a reserve book would certainly be less appropriate, for instance, than a hardcover copy no matter the cost.

ESSENTIALS IN ACQUISITIONS WORK

After materials are selected, they must be obtained by the library. This process is generally called acquisitions and refers to the clerical aspects of order and deliveries. Integral parts of the acquisitions process are:

Collecting sufficient bibliographical information to describe an item with precision in an order; identifying an appropriate supplier; preparing and dispatching an order; verifying materials received against order forms; and initiating procedures for payment.[38]

Relationship to Collection Development

The Acquisitions Department coordinates collection development and monitors its operations. Publishers' announcements, reviews, catalogs and other sources useful to those involved in or responsible for collection development are routinely received in the Acquisitions Department and routed to appropriate selectors, as expeditiously as possible.

The Acquisitions Department bears responsibility for insuring that channels for sending orders are made clear to selectors, that proper forms for placing orders are made available to them, and that fund ordering lags caused by faculty inertia or other reasons are brought to the attention of the librarian in charge of the collection. Fund balances are monitored by the Acquisitions Department and sent to departments.

The Acquisitions Department determines whether material recommended for purchase is on order or already in the college library. Duplicates are a major headache for every kind of library. Errors are easy to make, and may not be discovered until after the library has engraved its marks of ownership into the book. Sometimes a book suggested for purchase is actually part of a numbered series; or the corporate author is difficult to identify. Experience in searching and ordering are the best antidotes to these mistakes.

Relationship to the Business Office

In practically all colleges the relationship between the library and the business office is a close and important one. At the very least this relationship will involve presenting library bills approved for payment to the business office, and receiving running reports from the business office of library expenditures and accounts.

The purchase of library materials is a specialized job requiring specialized knowledge of books and other materials and their suppliers. For this reason, the library should be free to select its dealers. Further, since speed is frequently the deciding factor in securing certain materials—second-hand, reserve—librarians should be able to utilize the best source and be authorized to place orders directly rather than through a purchasing office. This may be done by appointing the librarian as deputy to the purchasing agent. Where such an arrangement is in effect, the library must assume the obligation of maintaining complete financial records of the transactions and furnish the business office with periodic statements of total expenditures and encumbrances from the materials funds. Computer acquisition programs can provide immeasurable support to this undertaking.

Organization

Acquisitions are made in one of three ways: by purchase, gift, or exchange. Purchase is, of course, the most important method. The other methods are also useful in collection building. Librarians who have indifferent or negative attitudes towards gifts may run the risk of discouraging legitimate interest in the library. But gifts can present major headaches to librarians. The same judgment should be applied to gifts added to the collection as is given to purchased materials. A gift policy should be clearly described in the Collection Development Policy. It should be sufficiently explicit and flexible to permit the librarian freedom to decide whether to add all or part of a gift to the collection, whether to offer it on exchange, whether it can be given to another part of the library, whether to sell it at a future library booksale or elsewhere, or whether to simply discard it. Every effort should be made to avoid accepting gifts on which the owner imposes restrictions, particularly those that contradict normal library practices. But donors, too, have rights. They have the right to expect to be informed of how the gift will be handled. They have the right to decide whether or not to sign a document indicating that the library may handle the gift as it sees fit. It is inappropriate for librarians to appraise the value of collections they will receive. However, they can give donors advice about how to locate local appraisers. If staff time permits, or the collection appears to be a good one and perhaps destined for the library, potential donors can be advised and or helped to organize their materials prior to an appraisal. Most colleges have duplicate materials that they can exchange with other institutions. The simplest and most common form of exchange involves periodical titles which are listed and exchanged on a piece-for-piece basis. The Duplicate Exchange Union, administered by the Serials Section of the ALA's Association for Library Collections and Technical Services, affords a medium for such exchanges. The Union is composed of small libraries that annually mail to each other one or more lists of duplicate materials received.

The organization of acquisitions work is essentially the same for purchases, exchanges, and gifts. The principles to be kept in mind are:

1.   All acquisition functions should be centralized and cleared through one person. Preferably, this person combines business skills with a thorough knowledge of trade bibliography and the organization of the American book trade.

2.   Records should be limited to those essential to permit appropriate information to be passed on from one stage to the next. The procedures, therefore, should be straight, undeviating and uniform, from verification and checking of orders to the order process itself, until all pertinent information is passed on to the cataloger.

Order Routine

Details of the order routine may differ according to the preferences and size of the collection. The essentials of a good order procedure, however, are the same for all college library acquisitions departments.

1. A request or order is generated by a selector. It arrives with as many of the bibliographical details on it as the orderer has seen fit to supply, and with the name of the selector, the department, and perhaps the initials of the departmental representative, if the order is placed by a faculty member.

2. The bibliographic information is verified, that is, the existence of the particular item is verified, and the bibliographic data corrected or supplemented as need be.

3. The requested item is checked against the library's holdings and its on-order and in-process files to ascertain that it is not already present, about to arrive, or in process of being cataloged and made ready for the shelves. Titles "not yet published" are placed in a "hold file" and are checked regularly against trade bibliographies to insure that they will be ordered as soon as they appear.

4. The information compiled and verified on the order slip is now transferred to an official order form, on the computer or on a fan-fold, multiple-copy order slip. If the latter, one copy is sent to the vendor and other copies are reserved for internal use. One may be placed in the books-on-order file, if it exists, another may be reserved for faculty notification, and so on. At this point the funds have been encumbered.

5. When the materials arrive, they are checked against the order and with the bill. The date and price are added, the cost is charged against the appropriate fund in the accounting records, and discrepancies against encumbrances are reconciled.

6. The materials and appropriate records are forwarded to the catalog department.

Automation of Acquisitions Functions

Acquisitions work requires exquisite attention to detail. Its routines are repetitive and control is difficult to maintain. Fortunately, one of the clearest applications of automation in libraries is acquisitions work. Computers can be used to improve control over funds, increase efficiency, permit multiple access to files, keep better records and generate more accurate reports, speed the production of orders and improve management information.

Before automating the acquisitions function, however, librarians would be well advised to consider whether adequate administrative support for computing exists; whether ongoing funding will be available; how the staff feels about it; whether indeed it will save staff, time, space and money; and what impact there will be on efficiency and service. Assuming a decision to automate the acquisition function, the librarian will then have to balance the advantages of a locally developed system against one provided by an outside source. It would seem short-sighted at this juncture to embark on a computer system for acquisitions which is not integrated with all other library functions.

WEEDING OR DESELECTION

Weeding, or deselection, is an essential, often neglected, aspect of college librarianship. It is an intellectual process requiring the care and attention of professionals—librarians, subject specialists, or bibliophiles. Decisions about what in a collection should be retained and what discarded are of at least equal moment to those made in conjunction with the selection process. Some consider them to be even more important because of the relative finality involved in jettisoning material.

College librarians must exercise great care while weeding in order not to retain too much or discard potentially useful works. In truth, the real problem is convincing librarians to discard anything. A number of reasons account for this reluctance:

1. Librarians fear making an error because it is hard to predict the future.

2. Librarians have difficulty explaining any withdrawal to faculty who tend to inflate the usefulness over time of materials.

3. We still suffer under a bigger-is-better mentality. Larger collections carry more prestige.

4. Weeding is time-consuming and pressures to do it are often only associated with major space considerations. Librarians tend to permit a variation of Parkinson's Law to prevail—collections expand to meet the space available.

5. There is a tendency to feel that it is better to have more books than one needs than to run the risk of having one too few.

6. Weeding is expensive. There are costs in educating the staff and in record changing—deaccessioning, reclassifying, clearing the shelflist, card catalog, union list, and so on.

On the other hand it is expensive not to weed. More materials require more maintenance; they take up needed shelf space and the library is carrying insurance on superfluous materials. More importantly, effectiveness dictates that libraries systematically monitor their holdings to create collections that permit undergraduates and faculty alike to feel confident that the material they find on the shelves is up-to-date and authoritative. A 1938 Personnel Management text may be of value in a university library where scholars are tracing the history of the discipline, but its appearance on the shelves of a college or undergraduate library does major disservice to users, particularly first- and second-year students who may be unsophisticated in their ability to assess the credibility of a particular volume.

There is an extensive literature relating to the criteria for weeding. Judgments are made on the basis of academic discipline, timeliness, physical condition of materials, duplication, reliability (reflecting changing viewpoints), availability elsewhere, coverage in indexes, and so on. In addition, circulation history is considered. A number of studies have demonstrated that past circulation is by far the best predictor of future use.[39] On the other hand, a book may have a value and function in a particular collection even if it has not circulated in twenty years.

The weeding process requires the same degree of participation by faculty as is called for during the selection process. Although library staff members usually cull from the shelves potential materials to be discarded, faculty should examine the titles after they have been earmarked for disposal in order to ascertain whether their utility has, indeed, expired. A collection evaluation schedule, designed to cover the entire collection within a finite period, helps to routinize and normalize the process. If faculty are informed that it is their academic expertise that is required at their convenience,that the task is finite and can be accomplished, they may become more amenable to fulfilling this responsibility.

After materials have been removed from the active collection decisions must be reached on what to do with them. Three choices are available. First, the materials can be stored, either in compact storage within the library, or sent to an off-campus location where little used, older materials are housed, or sent to cooperative storage. Second, an attempt can be made to sell or give away the materials, through a book sale, to a dealer, or by means of a list circulated among other college libraries. The final alternative is to destroy the materials, an unhappy choice, but sometimes the only option.

PRESERVATION

The 1980s saw a rise in interest concerning problems of conservation, preservation and ways to ensure that holdings do not deteriorate. "Library stacks are littered with the powdered or shredded residues of rapidly deteriorating materials. Large portions of collections may be irreparably damaged and lost."[40] There is a new emphasis in research libraries on finding ways to maintain fragile, retrospective collections because the potential loss to future scholars of these materials is now recognized. College librarians, too, have begun to understand the dangers of ignoring deteriorating materials.

Preservation and conservation are complex undertakings that require skill, attention to detail and commitment. Given the volume of materials currently deteriorating, an organized approach to preservation will have the effect of establishing priorities within a collection and minimizing the occasions when instant decisions are required.

Estimates of the numbers of materials requiring preservation range from 20% brittle to 80% acidic.[41] A recent sample of the Carlton College collections, for instance, revealed that of 508,000 books, periodicals, and documents, 100,500 items have brittle paper, and about 200,000 are on acid paper which will become brittle. Loose pages are apparent in 9,500 items; 52,600 have damaged bindings and 67,900 have loose hinges. Leather bindings on 4,500 also are in need of maintenance.[42] Knowing the magnitude of the problem is an important first step toward devising a solution to meet it.

Not all materials require preservation. College libraries do not often own great quantities of unique material. In addition, brittle materials can generally withstand a few uses if they are not in high demand. But libraries hoping to retain their basic collections of heavily used books and periodicals should begin to develop an integrated approach to collection protection. This will include regular vacuuming, greater attention to HVAC (heating, ventilating and air conditioning) issues and the development of proper shelving, binding, and photocopying procedures. The widespread use of copying machines not designed to handle books has been responsible for severe damage to bindings. The newer, book-friendly copiers should inhibit further injury to bindings.

Mass deacidification should also be considered. Until recently, the only process available to libraries was a highly labor intensive procedure which required dismantling a book and treating each page separately. Needless to say the procedure was employed sparingly, primarily on rare books, manuscripts and other materials, and perhaps art reproductions, that could not otherwise be duplicated. Currently, however, numerous deacidification methods are under development that have the potential, with minimal expenditure of between $3.00 and $6.00 per volume, to protect and perhaps even strengthen acid damaged materials. Fortunately, the percentage of materials produced on non-acid free paper is rapidly decreasing.

Materials in poor condition which are deemed insufficiently rare for preservation but which are heavily used can be replaced with reprints on acid-free paper or by sending them to a producing bindery to have high quality reproductions made. The first alternative is the more desirable one, since having a reproduction made is expensive, about $60 per volume. Less frequently used deteriorating volumes are candidates for microprints or, at least, cleaning and encapsulating.

In order to properly survey preservation and conservation needs of a collection, college libraries must do two major studies: They must sample the extent to which the collection is deteriorating; and they must sample their collections for age and use.

Armed with this knowledge, the library can then embark on a long-range program of conservation and preservation. It is an expensive proposition, but bound, in the long run, to save money and the collection.

SUMMARY

Ensuring that the college library has the materials it needs to support the curriculum and, to some extent, faculty research requires formulating a collection development policy, determining how to allocate available monies, establishing procedures for faculty involvement and maintaining a steady flow of orders. College libraries differ from their university counterparts in their attention to the quality of a collection rather than its size. Questions linger about whether librarians or faculty are best situated to make decisions about which materials to acquire. A joint effort invariably results in better collections.

Libraries must also decide, with faculty consultation, which materials should remain and which should withdrawn from the collection. Finally, there must be a program that insures preservation of any rare items and provides for the sound maintenance of the regular collection.

Libraries, at the heart of a college, are sustained and nourished by their collections. For librarians, collections represent their enduring legacy to the institution. For faculty, the collections may be *the* reason for the library.

NOTES AND SUGGESTED READINGS

Notes

1. Pat Battin, quoted in Carolyn Bucknall "Organization of Collection Development and Management in Academic Libraries," *Collection Management* 9 (1989): 20.

2. Paul Metz, *The Landscapes of Literature* (Chicago: American Library Association, 1984). 1.

3. Paul Mosher, "A National Scheme for Collaboration in Collection Development," in *Coordinating Cooperative Collection Development*, ed. Wilson Luquire (New York: Haworth, 1980), 21.

4. Richard Hume Werking, "Collection Growth and Expenditures," *College and Research Libraries* 52 (January 1991): 15.

5. Data concerning serials expenditures as a percentage of materials expenditures for a group of sixty-two liberal arts college libraries, in authors' possession.

6. Jasper Schad, in Ross Atkinson "Old Forms: New Forms: The Challenge of Collection Development," *College and Research Libraries* 50 (January 1989): 512.

7. F. A. Ehikhamenor, "Formula for Allocating Bookfunds," *LIBRI* 33 (June 1983): 150.

8. Elizabeth Futas and David Vidor, "What Constitutes a 'Good' Collection?" *Library Journal* 112 (April 15, 1987): 45.

9. Robert Hayes, "Quality and Quantity in the College Library," Association of American Colleges, *College Library Notes* (Winter 1969): 2.

10. Verner W. Clapp and Robert T. Jordan. "Quantitative Criteria for Adequacy of Academic Library Collections," *College and Research Libraries* 26 (September 1965) 371-380.

11. David Kaser. "Standards for College Libraries," *Library Trends* 31 (Summer 1982) 9.

12. Evan Farber, "Collection Development from a College Perspective: A Response," in *College Librarianship*, ed.

William Miller and D. Stephen Rockwood (Metuchen, NJ: Scarecrow Press, 1981), 127.

13. *Ibid.*

14. Richard Johnson, "The College Library Collection," in *Advances in Librarianship*, v. 14, ed. Wesley Simonton, (Chicago: Academic Press, 1986), 148.

15. Werking, 19.

16. Ross Atkinson, 513.

17. William R. Nugent, "Statistics of Collection Overlap at the Libraries of Six New England State Universities," *Library Resources and Technical Services* 12 (Winter 1968): 43.

18. W. G. Potter, "Studies of Collection Overlap," *Library Research* 4 (1982): 3-21.

19. Ross Atkinson, 517.

20. Richard Trueswell, "Some Behavioral Patterns of Library Users: The 80/20 Rule," *Wilson Library Bulletin* 43 (January 1969): 458-61.

21. Johnson, 148.

22. William McPherson, "Quantifying the Allocation of Monograph Funds," *College and Research Libraries* 44 (March 1983): 116.

23. Summarized in Metz, 4.

24. *Ibid.*, 108.

25. *Ibid.*, 3.

26. Julia Reed-Scott, "Introduction," in Luquire, 5.

27. Karen Krueger "A System Level Coordinated Cooperative Collection Development Model," in Luquire, 57.

28. Richard DeGennaro, "Shifting Gears: Information Technology and the Academic Library," *Library Journal* 109 (15 June, 1984): 1207.

29. Krueger, in Luquire, 50.

30. Billy Bozone, "HILC at Thirty-Four: A View from Within," in Luquire, 217.

31. Association of College and Research Libraries, "Standards for College Libraries," *College and Research Library News* 47 (March 1976): 192.

32. Ross Atkinson, 507.

33. Metz, 108-9.

34. Summarized in Mary Sellen, "Budget Formula Allocations: A Review Essay," *Collection Development* 9 (Winter 1987) 13-24.

35. Ross Atkinson, 507.

36. Nancy Gwinn and Paul Mosher, "Coordinating Collection Development: The RLG Conspectus," *College and Research Libraries* 44 (March 1983): 128-40.

37. Gary Shirk, "Evaluating Approval Plan Vendor Performance," in *Issues in Acquisitions*, ed. Sul H. Lee (Ann Arbor, MI: Pierian Press, 1984), 16.

38. Lorraine Sinnott and Hugh Cline, *Building Library Collections* (New York: D.C. Heath, 1981), 4.

39. Herman H. Fussler and Julian Simon, *Patterns in the Use of Books in Large Research Libraries* (Chicago: University of Chicago Press, 1969).

40. Sinott, 12.

41. William Studer, "Current Trends in Preservation Activities in ARL Libraries, Speech (Chicago: Center for Research Libraries, 5 April, 1991).

42. John Metz, "Summary Report, Conservation Study," unpublished (Carlton, MN: Carlton College, 1989).

Suggested Readings

Acquisitions Management and Collection Development in Libraries. 2d ed. Chicago: American Library Association, 1989.

Bucknall, Carolyn. *Guide for Writing a Bibliographer's Manual*. Chicago: American Library Association, 1987.

Clor, Virginia. *Books for College Libraries: A Core Collection of 50,000 titles*. 3d ed. 6 vols. Chicago: American Library Association, 1988.

Collection Development Policies for College Libraries. (Clipnote #11) Theresa Taborsky and P. Lenkowski, comps. Chicago: American Library Association. 1989.

Gwinn, Nancy and Paul Mosher. "Coordinating Collection Development: The RLG Conspectus." *College and Research Libraries* 44 (March 1983): 128-40.

Katz, Bill, ed. *The Acquisitions Budget*. New York: Haworth Press, 1989.

Kent, Allen and others. *Use of Library Materials*. New York: Marcel Dekker, Inc., 1979.

The Library Preservation Program: Models, Priorities, Possibilities. Chicago: American Library Association, 1985.

Luquire, Wilson, ed. *Coordinating Cooperative Collection Development: A National Perspective*. New York: Haworth Press, 1986.

Magrill, Rose Mary and John Corbin. *Acquisitions Management and Collection Development in Libraries*. 2d ed. Chicago: American Library Association, 1989.

Metz, Paul. *Landscape of Literatures*. Chicago: American Library Association. 1983.

Osburn, Charles B. *Academic Research and Library Resources: Changing Patterns in America*. Westport, CT: Greenwood Press, 1979.

Slote, Stanley. *Weeding Library Collections*. 3d ed. Littleton, CO: Libraries Unlimited, 1989.

Wortman, William. *Collection Management*. Chicago: American Library Association, 1989.

Chapter 9

COLLECTION DEVELOPMENT OF SPECIAL MATERIALS

Content rather than format should govern a library's collection development process, as well as its materials allocation budget. Selection and retention of all materials, no matter how they are delivered to users, rest on similar criteria and standards of evaluation. Yet, acquiring certain "special types" of materials—in this context, non-book—presents difficult problems that require particular consideration. This chapter describes the selection and acquisition of journals, newspapers, maps, films, videos, tapes, slides, microforms and compact discs, and other special collections.

PERIODICALS

In the college library the most important body of serials is the periodical collection. So important are periodicals, in fact, that the reputation of a college library on its own campus often depends upon how satisfied the faculty and student body are with the periodical collection.

What renders periodicals so essential to college students and faculty is that they contain the most up-to-date information. They are the primary source for learning about the latest theories, trends and viewpoints. Students use periodical literature to prepare term papers; faculty consider them the indispensable source for keeping abreast of the most recent research in their fields; they are the principal purveyors of scholarly reviews and research reports. Finally, periodicals serve the general reading needs of the college community, in particular the students. Periodicals delivered through electronic media surpass those in print-on-paper format in their ability to provide even more rapid access to current information. However, the use today of periodicals online is still largely limited to those whose content is bibliographic or numeric.

Periodicals are important in all fields, but some disciplines seem to depend more heavily on them than do others. Science information is more likely to cumulate than materials in the humanities. In science, discovery is built on discovery and scientists begin research where their predecessors left off. As a result, they seek material on the cutting edge of discovery. The literature of humanities can be, and is, read retrospectively and constantly reinterpreted using alternate approaches and theories. Works of literature or philosophy, for instance, remain primary sources. Generally, therefore, scientists are the heaviest consumers of periodical materials, with social scientists next and humanists somewhat less dependent upon them.

Selection

While standards exist for a basic college library collection, no firm recommendation is given regarding the number of periodicals an institution should own. *The Standards for College Libraries* do indicate that "in general it is good practice for a library to own any title that is needed more than six times per year." In addition, the Standards suggest that of the 6500 titles described in Bill Katz's *Magazines for Libraries*, approximately ten per cent may be considered essential to a broad liberal arts program for undergraduates. To this basic number "should be added as many titles as are deemed necessary by the teaching faculty and librarians to provide requisite depth and diversity of holdings."[1] The number of periodicals held by college libraries varies from as few as 600 to as many as 3,000, and depends on size, financing, curriculum and tradition of the individual college.

The appetite for journals among college faculties is voracious, a hunger rendered even more insatiable by the increase in new periodical titles. About 100,000 periodicals are produced annually. Between 1978 and 1987 the number of journals published in science quadrupled.[2] Burgeoning periodical publishing is attributable, in part, to the knowledge explosion and, to some extent, to the demands on faculty to "publish or perish"—to present evidence of scholarly research in order to gain tenure, be promoted, or receive salary raises. This increase in publishing, coupled with price rises that defy understanding and double, sometimes even quadruple the rate of inflation or the consumer price index,[3] make periodical selection and acquisition a complex problem. Laments about spiraling periodical prices frequently appear in the literature of librarianship. A recently reported study of ACRL members revealed that 71% considered rising journal prices to be the number one critical issue facing academic libraries.[4] Herb White, in a column called "The Journal That Ate the Library," claims that librarians bear heavy responsibility for accepting publishers prices and for accepting treatment as purchasing agents rather than as consumers of periodicals. Subscriptions are continued, he says, to publications which are never read. New subscriptions are entered without considering whether they replace older ones. Materials budgets are not rationally planned and allocated, rather, librarians mindlessly begin to transfer dollars from the monographic budget to the serials budget. They permit foreign publishers to increase prices when the exchange rate puts them at a disadvantage, but never demand the same treatment when the imbalance tips in the other direction.[5]

Increasingly, publishers have adopted a dual price system in which individuals are charged substantially less than libraries, sometimes only a third of the price. Publishers base this practice on the assumption that libraries serve the needs of many users, and therefore should pay more. Evans points to an ethical question produced by differential pricing. "Is it ethical for a library to accept a gift from an individual on a regular basis—of a journal which has a high dual rate subscription?"[6]

Unlike book materials, where faculty are generally given substantial responsibility for selection and have a sense of the dollars available by discipline, librarians usually retain the ultimate decision about the size and composition of the periodical collection. Faculty advice and review of periodical titles within their fields of expertise is sought and heeded whenever possible. Final ordering authority rests with the library staff, in order to insure that a balanced collection supporting a diverse curriculum and constituency will be acquired.

Users complain more frequently about periodicals than about any other segment of the library's collection. Many of the criticisms stem from lack of knowledge. Faculty are not aware, for instance, of the actual costs of journals, nor of how their prices have skyrocketed in comparison with other types of materials. Nor do they know the other complexities involved in maintaining periodical collections, among which are space problems, difficulties in retaining complete periodical runs, and the importance of indexing to finding periodical articles.

A number of years ago Turner Cassity, writing about serials, remarked that Bacon's famous epigram is applicable to periodicals and relevant to their selection. Some are born great; some acquire greatness, and some have greatness thrust upon them. He suggested that one can hardly miss the first category—they are obvious selections, the titles Farber stars in his classified list. Changing notions of intellectual chic make it pointless to try to second-guess faculty members on the third category.[7] If they desperately need the *Antioch Review* or *UTNE* they'll ask for it. The chief difficulty in selection evidently arises from the personal and sometimes sharp disagreements among faculty members themselves and between faculty members and librarians as to which journals are significant for the greatest number of potential users. Often the person making the most fuss about the title is not really familiar with it, or may even have hidden motives for seeking its acquisition. A colleague described how a faculty member demanded that the library subscribe to a little-known philosophy journal whose circulation was almost non-existent, whose material was not covered in any index, and which had received unfavorable reviews when its first and second issues were published. Ultimately the librarian learned that the professor had an article accepted for a forthcoming number of the periodical and hoped to insure its presence in the collection. Students also add to the problems when they request popular magazines covering a topic instead of scholarly journals more suited to their academic needs.

Periodicals selection and management is even more problematic for small college libraries than for large universities because of the limitations imposed by staff, and by bibliographic and financial resources. Decisions about what materials to acquire are based on faculty suggestions, use statistics, subject area title assessment and, to some extent coverage in indexes and citation behavior. In managing a serials or periodicals collection, it is essential to know precisely which titles are crucial to the library and those whose presence would scarcely be missed if cancellation becomes necessary. Many librarians find it valuable to circulate lists of periodicals within subject fields, or departments, and request that they be arranged by the relative importance of each title to the discipline. If information about use of periodicals is available, this can be included with the lists to help faculty with their assessments.

Periodicals are judged useful on the basis of: subject relevance, usage, general availability, accessibility (indexing coverage), cost, format, publisher, reputation, and citation frequency. Efforts to systematize and make uniform decision-making about periodicals have led to suggestions that cost/benefit ratios (cost of journal by its use), or even a formula based on the cost of journal divided by relative worth, be employed. Relative worth in this case would be the weighted sum of:

    a. relevance—accessibility, subject relevance, and format/journal reputation
    b. usage
    c. availability[8]

Some aids that may be of assistance to college librarians in making periodical selections are:

1. Sample Issues: Sample copies may be solicited from the agent or publishers and should be examined when one is in doubt about whether to subscribe to a journal. Check the editorial staff, sample the contents, assess the quality of reviews, if any, and try to determine whether the journal fills a need in the college. Submit samples to appropriate faculty members for opinions. Beware, however, about making a selection based solely on information gained from examining a single issue.

2. Reviews of current journals: Professional periodicals, such as *Library Journal* and the *Bulletin of Bibliography,* carry descriptive notes about new journals and include useful bibliographical and order information. *Choice* carries a brief evaluation of new journals as they appear, and may include critical notes by an authority in its introductory bibliographical essay. Sometimes a general reviewing medium, for example the *Times Literary Supplement*, will carry reviews of new periodical titles, and occasionally a bibliographical essay on the journals in a particular field will appear. Citation analysis has increased

attention to the periodical literature of certain disciplines, and a fairly large number of fields have been studied to track citing behavior.

3. Abstracted and Indexed Journals: If journals are included in any of the major abstracts or indexes, their usefulness is greatly enhanced. On the other hand, Farber warns that periodicals should not be limited to indexed ones.[9] Others may have greater utility. New periodicals are slow to be indexed. Foreign popular periodicals, *Paris Match* or *Der Spiegel*, may be of greater value to students of foreign languages than their indexed counterparts.

4. Guide to periodicals: In the last analysis the selection of periodicals is a skill that depends largely upon the experience of well-informed, intellectually curious, and knowledgeable librarians. However, given the number and range of periodicals, no librarian can hope for familiarity with all or even most of them. Farber's *Classified List of Periodicals for the College Library* was the standard reference work in journal selection for the college library, but a 1972 publication date makes it substantially less useful. Fortunately, monthly reviews in *Choice* update the Classified list. Bill Katz's *Magazines for Libraries*, while not limited to colleges, can be used to good advantage.

It should always be kept in mind that the original cost of a journal is only the first expense. The subscription will probably be maintained over a number years, with the compounded costs of processing, binding and storage. Perhaps even more than book selectors, those who choose serials must have wide vision and a sense of the continuity of scholarship. Decisions need to be made in light of what has been done previously, and what effect current choices may have on the future. Faculty members, on the other hand, may make selections based on immediate need and specific purpose, with little attention to long-range consequences. By canceling a particular title, money may be freed to purchase another one. On the other hand, the library may have a long run of that particular journal which is indexed and is used frequently by students in writing papers. To cancel a journal is to end a dialogue midstream. A snap decision to discard a title may mean reducing the usefulness of the reference department's subscription to an expensive indexing service. Often, librarians neglect to inform faculty that, in order to take advantage of a discount, periodicals have been purchased on a multi-year basis and that subscriptions may not expire for as much as three years. In this case, too, the determination to jettison a periodical is costly.

Before deciding to drop a subscription the following factors bear consideration

1. The cost of the journal, including record-keeping, claiming, storage and binding.

2. The convenience of obtaining it elsewhere.

3. Its availability in alternate format.

4. Coverage of the title in indexes and abstracting services and bibliographic databases.

5. Language.

6. Relevance to local needs.

7. Number of useful articles published per year or issue.

8. The amount of use it received.

9. Its ranking by library users.

10. The political consequences of its cancellation.

Periodical access has been one of the motivating forces in the movement toward library cooperation. The widespread use of telefacsimile, commercial document services, better reprographic techniques and rapid interlibrary delivery systems have strengthened the arguments in favor of selective cooperative acquisition of periodicals. For the college library, formal or informal agreements with neighboring institutions about collecting responsibilities do not solve the serials problem, but they help to stretch the serials dollar, as does judicious use of interlibrary loan and document delivery services.

Organization

Procedures for handling serials from point of selection to point of use differ considerably from library to library. A common practice is to order and "check in" the serials in the acquisitions department, or, if there is one, the serials department, and to shelve the current issues in the periodical area or room. Depending on the nature of the serial shelving, many libraries place all unbound issues of the volume preceding the latest one with the current number. Bound volumes are generally shelved alphabetically by title, rather than interfiled in subject fields.

Periodical ordering and recording require substantial attention to detail and extensive record keeping. Information is needed about changes in price and title, source, missing issues, title pages and indexes, and the like. Fortunately, computerized acquisition systems can now provide serials librarians with accurate and detailed information. It is predicted that soon journals will be checked by ISSN (International Standard Serial Number) barcodes.

A complete list of periodical holdings, including location and format, strategically placed throughout the library—in close proximity to periodical indexes, near where abstracting volumes are shelved, and in periodical areas of the collection—facilitates reader access. Subject subsets made available to faculty keep them knowledgeable about holdings. When an integrated library system is installed, a serials module enables holdings to be listed in the public catalog.

Centralized serial ordering and receipt, housed within a single department or in a section of a department, helps to minimize confusion and mistakes caused by the profusion of items and records. It is preferable for one or two staff members to retain major responsibility for serial activities, under the supervision of a librarian. Serials work requires good supervisory skills, imagination, a flair for detail, as well as the ability to avoid being paralyzed by it, and a certain thickness of skin in the face of perpetual criticism.

Purchases of Serials

It has been the general practice to consolidate all serial allocations into a combined central fund from which all current subscriptions are ordered and paid. This practice has been criticized by collection development specialists who contend that content rather than form should govern how materials funds are allocated.[10] Back files of journals are most often paid for from a general fund and there is usually a contingency fund for replacing missing issues and filling in short-run gaps.

In recent years, the number of subscription agents with which a library might place its order has diminished. Increased postage rates, declining dollar values and few discounts by publishers have resulted in the inability of all but the largest subscription agents to compete. As a result, choices for libraries are limited and decisions are no longer based on discounts offered by subscription agencies, but on how great the fee is for the services rendered.

Nevertheless, except for subscriptions that can only be placed directly with the publisher, or that come through institutionally affiliated memberships in societies, institutes and associations, college libraries generally choose to deal through a serials agent rather than attempt to handle each order separately with its publisher. The advantages can be very real. The vendor provides a central order and billing service, picks up back files of the journal for the year in which the subscription is placed, arranges for a common expiration date and automatic renewal unless otherwise notified, and supplies a detailed annual invoice that contains at a minimum the name of the journal, volume, subscription period, explanation if the title is dropped or must be ordered direct, updated additions and deletions, and changes in names. Vendors secure sample copies on request and are responsible for claims of non-receipt against publishers to ensure that missing issues are forwarded before the publisher's stock is exhausted. In addition, good agents are knowledgeable about reduced rates for multi-year subscriptions and, in this way, can save the library money.

Although dealing with vendors seems highly preferable to ordering directly from publishers, librarians should be aware that there are several drawbacks to this approach. Certainly, the service charge imposed by vendors, about 4%, results in a more expensive periodicals bill. The extent to which this is offset by savings in staff time will have to computed by each individual library. In addition, some control over orders is lost. Without a common expiration date, it is far more difficult to start and stop subscriptions midstream. On balance, these minor considerations do not outweigh the benefits of using a vendor.

To fulfill library expectations, subscription agents must exhibit a formidable array of virtues. Fortunately, the larger agents do provide quality service, particularly for standard journals. For the more difficult out-of-the-way material, librarians may be advised to deal directly with the publisher. In addition, very expensive materials might be renewed directly to save the service charge. Caution in this practice is advised, however, given the additional paperwork involved for both the library and the college business office.

There are a number of general rules to follow in placing subscriptions. The library should avoid the immediate closing and beginning of the calendar year in placing subscriptions. New subscriptions generally require several months before taking effect. Special care should be taken to insure the receipt of title pages and indexes, as well as cumulative indexes when they are published. It need hardly be stressed that libraries should not change agents frequently. On the other hand, it is imperative to maintain a check on the quality of service being provided. The promptness with which an agent follows up on missing issues, errors in mailing and billing, and so on, needs to be monitored. In addition, librarians can probe for ways to take advantage of any discounts that may accrue from prompt payment or prepayment of invoices, or by entering subscriptions prior to certain dates.

If a library finds itself subscribing to a substantial number of journals from foreign countries, it may be advisable to select an agent abroad who is thoroughly familiar with both the current and retrospective periodical market, and who is closer to European periodical dealers than it is possible for an American agent to be. The dollar fluctuations make it essential that the librarian and the dealer follow closely the changing financial scene and remain alert to any opportunities to benefit from placing subscriptions at appropriate moments.

The problem of missing issues is acute. Widespread access to copying machines has, to some extent, ameliorated the ravages of theft and mutilation. Nonetheless, issues disappear whether through inadvertence or theft. Vigilance in securing missing issues promptly before they are out of stock is an important task of the serials department. Unfortunately, too often issues are not known to be missing until a reader asks for them, or a volume is being prepared for binding. Substituting microfilm for binding can help to alleviate this problem. When seeking a replacement, some librarians save time by asking for permission to photocopy the periodical in the event that the original is unattainable.

It is advantageous to maintain a list of sources where replacements may be obtained if they are no longer available from the jobber or the publisher. Some dealers specialize in searching for back numbers of journals. The dealer should be given a reasonable time to fill a want list of needed periodical runs before the list is resubmitted to another dealer. For popular titles, libraries often advertise their need for replacement copies in the campus newspaper.

Foreign title claims are the most difficult to make. At least one European jobber is providing check-in services in the country in which the periodical originates. For a set fee, the vendor checks in titles at the agency office and makes claims for issues not sent by the publishers. The serials are packaged, sent air freight to a receiving agent, and forwarded on to the subscribing library. There are, of course, added fees for this service, but there may also be savings because titles may be charged at the issuing country rate rather than the one for North America.

In building a journal collection, filling in older back files is second in importance only to keeping the current journals complete and bound. If a good run of an original becomes available—in a dealer's catalog or elsewhere—it should be purchased. Broken runs are expensive to complete. An available reprint is probably the best source because the quality of paper and binding is generally very good. The cost is higher, but the paperwork involved and resulting clerical costs are lower. Alternatives to filling in files and binding, such as purchasing back files in microforms, are considered later in this chapter.

Gifts and Exchanges

Unless the library finds a donor or group of donors willing to give scholarly titles as soon as they have been read, which can then be used for exchange or collection purposes, the likelihood of its being able to secure any journals of real value to its readers through gifts is rather remote. Faculty members who do contribute their journals to the library after they are through with them must be made aware that recency is of primary importance and that the value of the gift depends heavily on the promptness and regularity with which it is given.

The publications of a few technical and professional associations may be secured as outright gifts. Sometimes, however, gifts of periodicals which represent propagandist organizations are offered. Librarians will want to assess the suitability of these publications for inclusion in the collection, applying the same criteria they have used for other serials.

It is well for the library to review from time to time its periodical holdings to ensure that a reasonable balance is maintained between various political and social attitudes. When topics are controversial, the future of the West Bank or abortion, for instance, users should expect to find journals with differing viewpoints represented.

Demands by individuals or groups for the removal of certain materials should be met with skepticism and resistance. The library's commitment to intellectual and academic freedom, if thoroughly described in the Collection Development Policy, can be used as protection against would-be censors. Librarians are inheritors of a tradition that has not feared to permit independent thought. Any effort on the part of any person or group to confine, hinder or impede the reading and thinking of college students should be given short shrift.

Binding

The importance of serials in a college library's program promotes the question of serials binding to a matter of major concern. The back files of many titles remain in constant demand from year to year. There is no way to consult past issues of a journal conveniently unless it is properly bound or it appears in a non-print on paper form. Good quality binding extends the life of a journal, prevents loss of separate issues, and maximizes its usefulness in the library's collection. The decision about whether to seek a microform version or whether to bind will depend upon the situation and the options.

Binding should be accomplished according to a schedule that tries to control for an even flow of work as well as for the academic calendar. Depending on the time required at a bindery—the norm is anywhere from six weeks to three months—an attempt should be made to send titles away during vacations, breaks and other periods of predictably light use. Care should be taken, for instance, not to send simultaneously to the bindery issues of *Time, Newsweek,* and *US News and World Report* covering the same time period. Nothing frustrates a student more than learning that the material required to complete a paper is "at the bindery" and is not scheduled to reappear until the week after the paper is due.

Binding must take note of a number of different requirements, depending on the type of material and the ways in which it will be used. Rare books often call for special binding and repair. In selecting a binder, librarians seek one who offers a reasonable price, a short binding time—consistent, of course, with good binding practice—the privilege of "rush orders," prompt return for emergency use of volumes in the bindery, rapid pickup and safe delivery, and a good track record among other librarians. In return, the binder can expect that periodical volumes sent to the bindery are complete; that each volume is accompanied by an instruction sheet; and that each shipment includes a list of titles arranged alphabetically by journal. The primary responsibility for collation rests with the binder. Shipments to the binder should be accompanied by specific instructions for placing supplements and supplementary pages, for binding in or leaving out separately paged advertisements and covers, and for the style of binding wanted.

NEWSPAPERS

All college libraries carry newspapers. Their acquisition, use, and retention are determined by curricular needs and geographic considerations, and practices vary widely among institutions.

Selection

How many and which newspapers a college library chooses to own is dependent on a number of factors. The first, of course, is quality. Most college libraries subscribe to the *New York Times* and have a complete run of the newspaper on microfilm. Long considered the newspaper of record, it has a reputation for objectivity and broad coverage. In addition, its excellent index makes the *New York Times* an unsurpassed primary historical source. Other factors in selecting domestic national papers are the reportorial strength of the newspaper, American regional and partisan differences, and, if back files are kept, their probable value and historical significance.

College libraries almost always subscribe to the local newspaper of the community in which the college is located. In addition, they usually carry at least one paper from the nearest metropolitan area. If the student body is recruited from discrete geographic areas, the college library may also receive newspapers from those communities.

Many libraries subscribe to several metropolitan daily newspapers with national coverage. *The Wall Street Journal*, the *Christian Science Monitor* and the *Washington Post* are three papers that enjoy excellent reputations. College libraries often carry weekly newspapers, as well. *The Village Voice*, for instance, is popular with many undergraduates and faculty alike. As emphasis on multicultural and international materials has resulted in many colleges carrying latino newspapers such as *El Diario*, or newspapers from abroad, perhaps *Le Monde* or *The Times* of London. Libraries that carry foreign newspapers need to decide how important it is to receive them in a timely fashion. They may have to choose among options that are either expensive, such as airmail, or less costly, but slower: air freight, for instance, weekly packets, or a microfilm edition.

Organization for Use

Newspapers present special storage problems. Current issues of newspapers are best handled on sloping racks, on vertical newspaper racks, or simply shelved with the current periodicals on flat horizontal shelving. Recent back issues can be stored similarly, or in nearby cupboards. Even when college libraries have original files of a local paper or the college newspaper which it desires to keep, arrangements can be made with commercial firms to film these materials.

Newspapers offer another opportunity for library cooperation. Within geographical regions, libraries can agree to collect backfiles of newspapers and make them available to cooperating institutions.

GOVERNMENT PUBLICATIONS

The usefulness of federal government documents to the college library's program is limited only by staff familiarity with how to gain access to them. Students of political science, economics, education, sociology, physics, chemistry and history, among others, have discovered that documents contain invaluable information. In no other source can users find census and other statistical reports, congressional hearings, reports of investigative commissions, reports of research in which the government is engaged, and official rules, regulations and laws.

Unfortunately, government documents are generally set apart, perceived as a special resource, requiring special skills and expertise in order to use them. Even some well trained, capable reference librarians eschew their use, often in favor of secondary sources, because on their face they seem so difficult to handle.

Some college libraries, even those with very small staffs, have separate government documents departments apart from the general reference area. Others may have a documents librarian located in the reference department. It is not uncommon for "turf" problems to arise in conjunction with the handling and retrieval of documents, or alternately for documents to be ignored in the absence of the person responsible for them.

A number of important factors complicate the widespread use of government documents in a college library and account for their under-utilization.[11] One difficulty stems from the sheer mass and variety of the federal government's output. Librarians unfamiliar with government structure or publishing, with bibliographic tools and with accessing methods can do little to encourage their use. Another difficulty is the way in which publications are distributed. College depository libraries, usually selective depositories, can designate what they with to receive by series and groups through the Superintendent of Documents. Libraries without depository status must follow a more complicated route. They can request to be placed on mailing lists of certain agencies for their series, or place orders through the Superintendent of Documents.

Thirdly, government documents are classified in a manner unfamiliar to library users. Finally, documents are often isolated in relatively inaccessible special collections. Fortunately, new reference tools, in CD-ROM format, provide excellent access to government documents. Librarians report astronomical increases in usage following acquisition of the *Monthly Catalog on CD-ROM*.

College libraries need fewer state publications, and for these they use the extensive bibliographical coverage in the *Checklist of State Documents*, prepared by the Library of Congress. Besides listing documents issued by the various departments, bureaus, and other administrative agencies of state governments, comprising about one-half of the state publishing activity, the *Checklist* includes publications of state-supported societies and institutions. If a college library should need to go beyond the listings in this monthly publication, current checklists issued by most states can be secured on request. College libraries generally make a special effort to collect documents from their own states and usually can report fairly extensive holdings. In addition, college libraries often acquire state manuals or blue books, constitutions, legislative handbooks and selective items from states contiguous or in close proximity to their own. As with federal publications, the range of topics covered is almost universal and much of the information is current and not obtainable elsewhere.

Few college libraries collect municipal documents as systematically as federal or state documents. They are difficult to acquire and usually not in great demand.

United Nations documents and those of its special agencies (WHO, UNESCO, and others) have become increasingly important for students doing work in a variety of fields that are studied globally, such as international relations, world health, ecology and so on.

Selection and Acquisition

Each type of document—federal, state, local, international or foreign—is accompanied by special acquisition problems and considerations. Libraries will have to gauge the potential utility of documents against the costs, in terms of financial outlay, staff time, and headaches, when they make decisions to acquire them.

Even in selective government depositories, librarians must keep an eye open for important depository items not in the series they have selected.

The primary selection tool for government material is the file of the *Monthly Catalog of Government Publications,* which furnishes information about prices, material that may be obtained free and how to order.

Depositories, full and selective, receive their documents free from the federal government in return for the promise that they will be made universally available. The depository system in the past decade has been threatened by the Reagan administration's plan to privatize information produced by the federal government and by the Paperwork Reduction Act passed during the Carter administration. Both programs have the potential to interrupt the flow of information to citizens. Under privatization commercial vendors, not the government, become the creators and distributors of federal information and the price is usually higher. With the pressure of the Paperwork Reduction Act, agencies must make difficult decisions about which publications to eliminate in order to meet tighter guidelines governing quantity of publication allowed per agency.

Currently, federal documents may still be purchased from the Government Printing Office at its sales office in Washington, or at the regional bookstores it operates in Denver, Houston and Atlanta.

The Library of Congress' *Checklist of State Documents* is the primary selection tool for acquiring state information. Within the last decade most states have established depository programs roughly paralleling the federal depository program. Some states have relatively few depositories, others are more liberal in the number of institutions that receive collections.

UNIPUB, Inc. at the United Nations, New York, is the distribution and information center for international documents, including those of the United Nations and some, but not all, of its agencies. The UN publishes its own comprehensive index, but it does not include publications of its affiliates. Like state and federal documents, international documents have profited from inclusion in computerized bibliographic databases. CIS's *Index to International Statistics* (IIS) and *IBID* are among the tools offering collection development assistance and also are available with companion microfiche collections.

Foreign national documents are rarely collected by college libraries. However, most developed countries have government publications programs that rival the ones in the United States. Cherns's *Official Publications: An Overview* offers information on the government publishing programs of the 20 countries with the highest output. The best course for college libraries wishing to acquire foreign documents is to utilize the services of a book dealer in the country of publication.

Space problems have been ameliorated in recent years by the rise in numbers of government documents available on microfiche, but documents in print form are space consumers. To protect against their rapid multiplication in the stacks, a review procedure coupled with selection criteria for removal at set intervals should be instituted and faithfully practiced. Most government document collections are meant to be current. "Selective" status allows libraries to be just that; materials may be deselected after a statutory period of five years, provided proper procedures are followed.

Organization for Use

Most selective depository collections in college libraries are shelved separately as a government document collection instead of being cataloged and classified by the same system used for books in the library. If the library chooses this path, an attempt should be made to locate close at hand printed catalogs and indexes published by the government which are important to selection and reference . Too many library administrators consider government documents merely a nuisance and discriminate against them. For instance, extensive documents collections are often relegated to the library's basement, as far removed as possible from any tools and staff that might provide access to them, an action which insures low usage of the collection.

The decision not to catalog government documents, but to use the Superintendent of Documents classification may be a wise one. It eliminates the expense of cataloging, makes the documents available much more promptly, and eliminates the deaccessioning steps which would be required after the material has been deselected.

Many small libraries, on the other hand, particularly nondepository ones, catalog and classify all government publications. Bound or substantial paperbound documents, if important, are cataloged and classified with the books on the shelves.

PAMPHLETS AND CLIPPINGS

While most college librarians would not doubt the potential usefulness to reference work of a pamphlet collection, few have the time or staff to care for them adequately. As a result, many college libraries no longer collect pamphlets or maintain vertical files. On the other hand, some librarians argue that nothing replaces the function that a pamphlet file fulfills.

The pamphlet and clipping or vertical file collection, as it is frequently called by librarians, is basically a collection of pamphlets and similar material, largely ephemeral, and often time-dated. The vertical file is generally arranged alphabetically by subject. Few librarians, other than the reference staff, are familiar with its contents. It is not surprising, therefore, that faculty and students are generally unaware of its existence or do not realize that it may contain valuable information. In some instances, pamphlets are a leading source of hard to locate information. Street maps of cities find a home there, as do maps from county surveyors and precinct maps furnished by political headquarters. Examples of propaganda pamphlets, presenting a variety of viewpoints, can be suitably housed in a pamphlet file. If a college library decides to maintain a vertical file, its first effort should be to make users aware of it. A subject heading in the catalog, with a "see vertical file" reference, is one important strategy to promote its use.

The hallmarks of a vertical file should be currency and subject access. As a result, materials should be dated on arrival and files frequently weeded. Out-of-date vertical file material is less than useless. If a library cannot attend properly to a vertical file, it has no business keeping one.

Materials for the vertical file generally must be ordered directly from the producer. Information about their availability may be found in the *Vertical File Index*, *Public Affairs Information Service* (PAIS),*Monthly Catalog of United States Government Publications*, and in professional library sources such as *Booklist*, *Library Journal* and *Wilson Library Bulletin*. Much of the material in a pamphlet file will be free or inexpensive, but this does not mean that its acquisition is inexpensive for a library. Bibliographic verification and letter writing are staff intensive, and therefore costly.

Most pamphlets coming to the library may be described as ephemeral, at best. The simplest way to handle pamphlets is to place them in strong expandable folders, under subject headings in a filing cabinet. Some libraries have experimented successfully with placing pamphlet material in Princeton files on regular library shelving in a separate section, making them more accessible and easier to use. A third method of handling pamphlets is to place them in Princeton files on shelves alongside books on similar subjects. Listing the pamphlets by subject, in the public catalog, promotes the likelihood of their eventual use.

MAPS

Maps are a specialized kind of library material. There are problems in selecting them, and they are both difficult and expensive to organize and house. These obstacles are not easily overcome; nevertheless because of the growing importance of maps, they demand more than cursory treatment.

The selection of maps involves five factors: (1) area to be covered; (2) scale of coverage, (3) type of map, (4) craftsmanship, and (5) date.

Sources and Acquisition

The curricular needs of a college library will determine the extent to which it acquires maps and atlases. The recent interest in environmental studies may mandate, for instance, extensive collections of US Geologic Survey maps. Attention to international relations may require the library to gather strong collections of geo-political maps.

Two journals which carry reviews of maps and atlases, cartographic accession lists, and catalogs and lists of publishers are of particular help to college libraries. They are: *Surveying and Mapping*, the quarterly journal of the American Congress on Surveying and Mappings, which has a regular section on new maps of general and topic interest; and the Special Libraries Association's *Geography and Map Division Bulletin*, which reviews selected atlases and maps and contains an extensive listing of new maps. Among cartographic accession lists, several checklists, including the Map Library Acquisitions Bulletin, issued at irregular intervals by Rand McNally and Company, are very valuable.

Local maps, like other local materials, are especially important. The college library should cooperate with the public library in collecting city plans, zoning maps, and city, county, and state maps and atlases.

Organization for Use

Except for the library that possesses an exceptionally large number of maps, in which case a separate room is desirable, the map collection should be housed in the reference area, of which it is an integral part and where it will be most used. Depending upon the type of material on which they are printed, old and rare maps, and sometimes others, should be mounted on muslin and encapsulated.

MICROFORMS

Microform is a generic term used to describe any information storage and communication medium containing images too small to be read with the unaided eye.[12] They are photographically reproduced and include microfilm, microfiche, ultrafiche, micro-opaque, aperture card, microcards and microprint. There are two broad types of microforms: roll and flat.

Roll: Varying lengths of 16 mm or 35mm microfilm wound on a reel or loaded into a cartridge or cassette.

Flat: sheets of film—microfiche, microfilm jackets and aperture cards.

Opaque microcards and microprint include a complete text in microform, but full-size print classification and cataloging information appears at the top of the card. This simplifies their use. There is no question that the cards are easier to consult rapidly than microfilm since one need not look through an entire reel of microfilm to locate the desired chapter or page.

Typically, libraries buy microforms of publications not available in print, to duplicate print-on-paper materials, or in place of them. Microforms are acquired to shore up retrospective collections. Increasingly, however, new materials never before published are appearing in microform. Microform collections on discrete subjects help strengthen areas where materials are scarce; they save expensive storage space especially with back files of less used periodicals; and they preserve information in danger of deterioration. Microforms can be made quickly available with minimal processing thereby conserving precious time.

Microfilm is used extensively to preserve files of newspapers and periodicals. It represents a convenient substitute for bound volumes particularly of newspapers, saves shelf space, is relatively durable, costs less than binding, can be easily used, and is replaceable. A strong argument can be made that substituting microfilm for frequently stolen or mutilated journals will reduce vandalism. Scholars use microfilm to read books and manuscript material housed in libraries throughout the world. One historian of science, for instance, microfilmed at the

Bibliotheque Nationale the notebooks and letters of a 19th century French biologist which he could then translate and work with at his leisure at his own college library.

The most recent newcomer to the microform family is microfiche, which has all the advantages of microfilm plus a format that lends itself readily to direct reference. Its widespread use for the dissemination of government-supported research has no doubt hastened the switch from other microforms to microfiche. All ERIC (Educational Resources Information Center) reports, for example, may be acquired in this form. Certain large microform producers are now publishing "package" libraries on ultramicrofiche, which reduces hundreds of pages to a square inch of film, so that new libraries or libraries developing retrospective research collections can acquire a large body of material, much of which is now out of print. Experienced librarians recognize that no one type of microform is best for all library and reader needs.

There are drawbacks to substituting microforms for print. For one, it is hard to curl up with a microform. The quality of color reproduction may not satisfy art historians. Another is that a frequently consulted periodical in microform may increase the work of staff members asked to assist with loading and reloading it on microform readers. College librarians have complained about the delay in receiving microfilm copy after a periodical volume is complete. Less used journals, likely candidates for film substitution, are often unavailable in this format. Rare books and manuscripts used on microform prevent scholars from understanding the context—the volume in which a manuscript may be bound, the actual size of a document, and any identifying marks that cannot be spotted on film.

Perhaps the greatest drawback, however, to the widespread use of microfilm is the reluctance of students and faculty alike to accept microforms as alternatives to paper as an information source. Users who have a very strong information need may suffer the inconvenience associated with using microforms. In the absence of strong motivation, patrons may simply avoid microform use. Despite patron hostility, studies indicate that use of microfilm does not produce greater fatigue.[13] Subjectively, however, patrons frequently complain that symptoms such as headache and eyestrain result from intensive microfilm use.

Selection and Acquisition

Microforms represent an impressive technical accomplishment. However, embarking on a massive microform acquisition program requires assessing the basic importance of the material to the collection, the extent of duplication with present library holdings, the availability of good reading machines, the extent to which the project has carried out its editorial claims, the quality of the available microform and the price.

In the process of assembling a microform collection college librarians should be conscious of the dangers of overenthusiasm. An overwhelming number of titles are available and the temptation, to say nothing of faculty pressure, to purchase large blocks or sets of important research material may be great. Selection judgments must be exercised carefully. More frequently consulted current work should not be chosen over little-used material. Finally, as has been discussed above, print-on-paper in a bound volume is far more conducive to use and promotes reading and borrowing. There is no denying the savings afforded by microform in expense and space, but satisfactory service cannot be measured in terms of dollars or square feet.

College libraries acquire microforms in three ways: 1) by placing orders directly with publishers; 2) by placing orders with other libraries known to have a needed title either as a master (first generation) negative or in the original format, and to provide major photo duplication services; and 3) by gift. If a library has been unable to locate a book through the antiquarian book market or reprint publishers, it may place an order for a microform copy from one of the major publishers or firms producing microforms. As a general rule they have large negative banks and publish a catalog, but if the title does not appear there the firm may search for a copy for the library and make a photocopy in response to an order. In the second method, the library locates a copy of a book it needs in a large research library and places an order for a photocopy through its photo duplication services department. In some instances the library may already have a large bank of negatives which includes the desired title and from which a positive copy may be made. Acquisition through gift is not a major source, but faculty members who have been assisted by the library in their research frequently turn over microforms purchased personally through departmental or special grant funds. This kind of gift is encouraged when the library, through its interlibrary loan service, has helped the faculty member to identify research resources and has arranged to act as the agent in ordering the microforms.

Organization for Use

Most librarians agree that microforms and reading machines should be centralized at one place in the college library, although some libraries have chosen to shelve microfilm rolls along with bound periodicals. If the microforms are serviced from the loan desk, the reading machines should be placed near it so that a staff member can assist students who are using the machines for the first time. Since they require special equipment for their use, they are less likely to be stolen.

Cataloging microforms is one way of making known their presence in the library. Information regarding holdings should be interfiled in the library's main catalog. Unless college library users find these materials listed there, there is every expectation that they will be overlooked in the search for information. Some libraries also prepare an annotated catalog of their microform holdings for distribution to faculty and students.

Microfilm, microfiche, microprint and microcards are usually grouped separately in the microform area because of the differences in their size and storage requirements. For this reason, a number of libraries place distinguishing symbols above the call number to indicate microform format. Periodicals on microform will generally be placed in alphabetical order by title in the cabinet housing them.

Equipment

In choosing microform reading machines the librarian is advised to consult the *Library Technology Reports* of the American Library Association and the annual *Micrographics Equipment Review.* The annual reports on micropublishing and microforms in *Library Resources and Technical Services* are crammed with useful information about microreproduction. Great care must be exercised in purchasing reading machines and reader-printers, not only because of the high initial cost, but also because maintenance problems can cause serious inconvenience when machines are out of order. The earliest microfilm readers had simple mechanisms and rarely broke down. Technologically sophisticated readers and reader-printers offer quality images but require more frequent repair because their parts are complex, and they are sometimes difficult to obtain.

While microforms save shelf room, they occupy other kinds of library space. As a result, different physical and financial considerations govern their acquisitions, placement and maintenance. Space must be set aside to house the microforms and the machines for reading roll film, fiche or opaques. Reader-printers are mandatory. The machines require maintenance and someone must be designated to take responsibility for replacing bulbs, cleaning lenses and flats, and so on. Microform cabinets are desirable storage containers for film because they are more likely to provide a dust-free environment. Opaques must be kept under pressure to prevent their curling and cracking. Proper conditions of humidity and temperature are important but are reasonably maintained in most air-conditioned libraries today.

OTHER STORAGE TECHNOLOGIES

The pace of technological development, particularly in the storage of materials, is astounding. So rapid is it, in fact, that any discussion or list of new methods is bound to be superannuated before this book reaches a reader's hands.

For instance, fully indexed books on optical disk, with both video and sound, will soon be available. Knowledge navigator systems that help scholars gain entry to knowledge databases distributed around the world will provide global access. Knowledge databases connected to artificially intelligent software will allow students to create complex models of real-world systems.[14]

Laser technology is receiving increasing attention because of its versatility. Laser discs are capable of storing information in analog form as full-motion video with audio, still-frame video or audio only. A Library of Congress (LC) prototype analog disc, for instance, contains 40,000 photographs, posters, architectural drawings, and other pictorial items from LC collections. Exact images of printed text are digitalized and stored on the disc at a resolution of 300 dots per inch. Storage capacity is from 10,000 to 15,000 pages of text per disc. Laser discs are one form of media that may represent a viable alternative to microforms.[15] *Videotex* is a low cost, easy to use, two-way information system, using video display and computer storage.

A number of database producers are now making full text available electronically. Many publishers are experimenting with compact discs (CDs) as a storage and dissemination medium. Software packages for computers that contain complete texts of Shakespeare, The Bible, and encyclopedias are increasingly available in interactive format with random access and voice components.

Unfortunately, there is no single source we can recommend to follow these developments and librarians will have to search all of the professional literature to keep up with advances. Good background references can be found in William Saffady's *Micrographics,* published in 1985, but its usefulness is limited because the field is undergoing such rapid change.

AUDIO-VISUAL MATERIALS

Audio-visual materials, for the purposes of this chapter, means sound recordings, films, videos, slides, photographs and related viewing and listening equipment. Although microforms technically fall under the rubric of audio-visual materials, they have been treated separately because of their strong relationship to print.

Most college libraries have experienced a great rise in the use of audio-visual materials over the past decade, particularly in video and compact disc format. Although films, filmstrips, phonograph records, audiotapes, slides and photograph collections continue to exist in college libraries, their use is fast diminishing as videos and CDs become more evident.

For a long time, academic library media centers consisted primarily of sound recordings for music and language instruction, poetry readings and dramatic performances. As a curriculum resource, they contained filmstrips, slides, and other materials useful in teacher education programs. Some also were responsible for equipment distribution, and offered graphic production services and film libraries. Audio-visual collections in college libraries were slow to grow because many faculty had, indeed still have, pedagogic and philosophic perspectives that inhibit their ability to see audio-visual materials as valid conveyors of information. They tend to consider only print as a legitimate supplement to their lectures. In addition, faculty find audio-visual materials difficult to use and undependable. They cite Murphy's law—anything that can possibly go wrong, will—to explain what happens when they plan to use a film, or a video, at a particular time in the syllabus.

Technological developments have gradually effaced the line between print and non-print. By the mid 1970s collections began to grow and today some college libraries report video holdings of more than 8,500 items and sound collections containing upwards of 35,000 recordings, tapes, cassettes and compact discs. Despite this growth, audio-visual materials are still viewed as "instructional materials," and primarily curricular. In 1986, ACRL published its *Guidelines for AV Services in Academic Libraries*, a tacit acknowledgment of the increased importance of media.[16]

Media are relatively more expensive than print materials. Therefore collection development staff in colleges should be wary of expanding to meet relatively short-term demand. Rather, decisions about what to acquire should be based on the same principles—quality, usefulness, timeliness, demand and so on—that guide the selection of all other college library materials. The tendency to allow format to govern selection decisions is troubling.

Films and Videocassettes

Movies and television are dominating channels of information for most college-age young people. The advantages these media offer to the educational process have long been recognized and exploited. Film can illustrate better than a photograph the process of cell division or a chick hatching; it can recreate the past or create the future; it can enlarge or reduce; it can show processes invisible to the naked eye through microphotography or spectroscopy; it can control time through slow motion or time-lapse single-frame exposures; it can be made to heighten reality by skilled editing or by eliminating distracting information through animation; and, most significantly, it can provide a common experience for a group in a short period of time.

Building a film collection used to be very expensive. But the arrival of videocassettes, large-screens for showing them to groups, and small recorders that permit them to be viewed individually has substantially reduced the cost and increased the capability of college libraries to develop sizable collections. Films cost anywhere from $500 to many thousands of dollars. Videos, on the other hand, run from $12.95 to $99.95 per unit. Most faculty and students show a strong preference for video because it is simpler to use, more accessible, and can be more easily manipulated to start and stop at particular points.

The decision to engage in acquiring an extensive film or video collection depends on the degree to which faculty are willing to employ this medium and integrate it into their classroom teaching. A college with an extensive film program, involving numerous courses and film series outside the classroom, will be more likely to need a library of theatrical performance films and videos. But film usage is certainly not limited to cinematic offerings and film courses. It can be successfully employed in conjunction with any course in which visual materials can add to the learning process.

A few college libraries currently budget extensively for audio-visuals. Others allocate no funds for their purchase, assuming that academic departments will build video collections into their own budgets. Obviously, these latter are recreating departmental libraries and fiefdoms, with video this time rather than books. One librarian reports that departments are loath to share with the library or other departments their video or film holdings.

Selection varies from one institution to another. A number of libraries secure only those films and videos requested by faculty either by title or by a particular subject. Others prepare filmographies from which faculty members may choose, or develop routing patterns to alert instructors to current films or videos which have become available. What seems clear is that purchase of theatrical performance is the most common type of acquisition.

Many libraries support extensive rental service rather than fund the purchase of videos and film for classroom use, because of the expense and the lack of guarantee that the film will be utilized more than once.

A major problem for college collections of theatrical performance films and videos is abiding by copyright legislation for their use. Although off-air taping and actual classroom use within ten days of taping falls under "Fair Use" and is specifically excluded from the copyright dictum about public performance (section 106), the faculty member or student group wishing to reuse the video in other semesters or to launch a film (video) series must abide by copyright law.[17] Film makers say that public performance may also apply to a student watching a film on video within the library. The American Library Association has contended that one person or one family does not constitute public performance and it is likely that a court case may soon test the limits of the law.[18] What this means for the library is that the video that may be purchased commercially for home use at $14.95, for instance, may cost the library $250.00 if it wishes to comply with the law. In addition, substantial effort is required to limit improper use of home taped programs in the classroom on a repeat basis. Some colleges have avoided the problem by purchasing a public performance license covering a great number of theatrical performance videos and films. License costs are based on the number of titles, the number of facilities, the number of students, the number of performances and so on. Blanket coverage for a small college campus in 1989 ran about $4,000.

Selection and Acquisition

Locating and acquiring educational films and videos usually begins with a faculty request and an incomplete citation. There is no central bibliographic source listing videos, and librarians are dependent on distributors' catalogs and junk mail. A new quarterly periodical *Video Rating Guide,* devoted to non-theatrical videos and begun in 1990, has eased the situation to some extent. Many college librarians depend on the Consortium of University Film Centers as the best location source for rental of films. *The Educational Film and Video Locator* provided substantial assistance, but a 1986 publication date begins to limit its value. Among the largest and least expensive collections from which libraries can rent films are those of Kent State, Penn State, Indiana, and Florida State Universities, as well as the Universities of Illinois, Michigan, Arizona and Oregon. Assuming that collections are similar in comprehensiveness and low rental fees, there are obvious advantages in dealing with collections that are in close geographic proximity.

Occasionally instructors want to preview a film that they are unlikely to buy, but may intend to rent for some future classroom use. It would abuse the arrangement with the film producer to preview the film in the usual manner—free of charge; the reasonable solution is to rent the film from the most likely source for the time in the course schedule when it might be used. After a preview, if it meets requirements, it can be used. And if the film does not measure up, then the instructor will know it and the cost of the rental can be considered part of the cost of developing the course. Book selection isn't always free of error, either.

In addition to purchase and rental, the library may have access to films that are loaned without charge by business, industry, governmental sources or specialized associations such as mental health and health associations. Information on their availability is often difficult to obtain and must be diligently sought. Home market videos, however, are handled by jobbers and by video stores and are much easier to locate and obtain.

Library cooperation, at this time, does not seem to extend to films and videos, and few are available through interlibrary loan. Partially, this can be attributed to contractual agreements with producers and distributors. More germane is that some librarians view the risks of loaning films as too great in view of their tendency to be withdrawn precipitately and unpredictably withdrawn from public outlets, and therefore, to become unavailable for replacement in case of loss or damage.

Some college libraries have developed production facilities and, among other endeavors, tape and dub (duplicate) videos from television for off-air viewing, within copyright regulations, broadcast videos on closed circuit channels, produce videos for cooperation with faculty or students and create an A/V archival record of important campus events as well as offer graphics production services at cost to faculty.

Organization for Use

Colleges which own films and videos generally give them full cataloging and classification and include them in the main catalog. Shelving, on the other hand, tends to be discrete and often away from public areas in closed stacks. Paging, therefore, becomes a requirement, adding to the expense of handling them. Theft of videos is a potentially serious problem since VCR's (video cassette players) are widely owned in the population. Many college libraries are reluctant to permit students to borrow videos, given their expense and irreplaceability. One institution requires students to present a note from faculty members in order to use them. This problem will probably ameliorate as prices decrease and availability is greater. Certainly, if college libraries adhere to their stated aims and goals, to provide not only for the curricular needs of their community members but for their extra-curricular ones as well, they cannot continue to discriminate between users according to status on the campus.

Equipment

The media field is changing so quickly that machines are often rendered obsolete before they have been sufficiently used. On the other hand, a video cannot be shown without a VCR, or a film without a projector. Responsibilities for equipment vary from institution to institution. On some campuses, an AV department not connected with the library manages all equipment and is charged with supplying it to classrooms as required. On other campuses, the library's audio-visual department is also responsible for equipment maintenance and delivery. Practices vary because institutions are still experimenting with the best way to provide audio-visual services.

All college libraries have video equipment on which individuals may view films. Many have larger viewing rooms which can serve entire classes. Information about equipment can be found in the *Audio Visual Market Place: a Multimedia Guide, and The Audio-Visual Equipment Directory*, both of which are descriptive but non-evaluative. *Library Technology Reports*, published by the American Library Association, provides useful evaluations of equipment, but unfortunately they are not comprehensive and do not update previously published information. Popular magazines evaluate video players and film projectors, although their reviews often do not assess durability, an important consideration because of the heavy use they may incur in a library.

Music and Recordings

College students today consider music an integral and important part of their daily lives. Portable cassettes with miniature head sets, "boom boxes," portable stereos with good sound quality, and other technological developments enable them to gain access to music—at any place and any time. It is not unusual to find rows of students in a college library wearing headsets, listening to music and studying simultaneously. In fact, some students report that this is their best defense against library noise. Today's college generation has grown up with music, has watched music videos on MTV, listened to records and tapes, and to all music radio. Many are members of what has been called the "rock" culture. While some students prefer classical music, contemporary popular music is certainly more evident.

In the last two decades, college music courses have offered not only traditional music appreciation and theory, but have included electronic music, African rhythms, dulcimer making, and the history of jazz, to mention a few. College libraries must be prepared to supply materials for a wide variety of musical needs, both curricular and recreational. Too many librarians think about music only in terms of curricular uses. Even those who purchase mysteries and science fiction for recreational use in their communities do not consider music in the same light.

Music listening facilities in a library will often depend on constraints of space. Libraries built in the last decade generally control listening spaces through a central area from which music is filtered to the station where it is listened to on headsets. Music rooms of college libraries may contain reference books, periodicals, vertical file materials, perhaps music scores, and infrequently, memorabilia of the music activities of the institution, although this material is probably best handled by including it in the library's special collections. In the absence of a separate music room, music-related information will be integrated into the general collection.

The essential elements of a music area, therefore, can be limited to recordings and listening equipment. Recordings, for these purposes, mean both speech—plays, poetry and speeches—and music. Because they must be used with listening equipment, it seems convenient to house them together in one location.

A major development in recordings that renders them far more suitable for library borrowing has been the development of CDs. Not only do CDs have far greater fidelity, but they are relatively indestructible and college librarians report that they are converting to them as rapidly as possible. Audio cassettes are the second most preferred medium.

Acquisition and Preparation

Certain important acquisitions policies about music must be decided before beginning a collection. First, is the library going to purchase and care for parts for musical performances? This might mean acquiring four parts plus full score for a string quartet, or more than one hundred separate parts plus full score for a Berlioz symphony, or a hundred or more copies of the choral score for the Messiah. Although many libraries accept as gifts, and sometimes acquire by purchase, parts for small ensembles, most experts believe that the music department of the college is the place for music for large groups. The consensus seems to be that purchase, organization, maintenance and repair of music for large performing groups should be left to the groups themselves. The library can offer guidance on organization.

Second, is the library going to build up a reference and or reserve collection of recordings to be used only in house. Although this may be desirable, much depends on available budget, the extent to which this collection may duplicate one that exists in the music department, and the number of available listening facilities in the library.

Third, is the library going to purchase recordings for its circulating collection? Again, of course, budget will influence this decision, as will the nature of the community and its needs. It may be that because of the importance to them of music, students have discovered ways to obtain it, and its provision on a routine or circulating basis is unnecessary or less important. However, exposing students to varieties of music in creative ways fulfills an important mission of the college and the college library, and to shun this undertaking may be short-sighted.

The *New Schwann Record and Tape Guide*, published monthly, is indispensable to locating "in print" information about 25,000 LP records, digital compact discs, cassettes, and 8-track cartridges. Unfortunately there is no single source for ordering music. It is necessary for libraries to be placed on publishers' and dealers' mailing lists and to examine each list as it arrives.

Many excellent recording dealers give good service and discounts; there are good music jobbers too, but ordering is considerably more of a problem here, particularly since much of the best-edited music is published abroad. Perhaps the simplest and most direct way to find out the names of good dealers is to write or call music librarians at one or two larger institutions nearby.

Cataloging both music and recordings can be relatively easy if LC cataloging is followed with no, or almost no, exceptions. The Library of Congress system of "conventional title," which seems complex and confusing to the uninitiated, is really the only method that will bring order out of the chaos caused by publishers' vagaries. Cataloging is available for most of the music and recordings needed for college libraries. Classification serves little purpose where records are concerned. Authorities recommend shelving by accession number if a closed-shelf policy is adopted. With open shelves, either a single alphabet by name of composer or a series of broad categories (such as "classics," "folk songs," etc.) seems to work well.

Just about all the music purchased for library use, except for some song collections, will be paperbound and will require some kind of protective binding. Items that are thick enough to need a regular library binding can be done in the usual way, so long as the bindery understands that the volume must lie flat for the performer. Library supply houses offer binders that are satisfactory for items of only a few pages, provided the library has someone who can do a careful job of attaching pages.

Organizing the Music Area

The contents of the music room will depend largely on the space available. If books on music are shelved elsewhere, the most simple and flexible plan is to use all 12-inch shelving, which can accommodate large scores, compact discs, records and cassettes. Fixed partitions at least six inches high, placed every 12 inches or so, are necessary to keep records upright and prevent warping. All sizes of music can be shelved together, although if the library has an extensive collection of miniature scores they may be shelved separately. A catalog of music holdings should be available in the music room unless an OPACs terminal is available.

Listening rooms are very nice if the library has space and can afford them. Many institutions find them out of reach for one or both of these reasons. For these libraries, a long table or a number of tables with listening capabilities and headsets is a satisfactory solution. If at all possible, the equipment for listening to recordings should be bought locally so that the dealer can be responsible for maintenance. Attention to the following four major requirements for listening equipment may save a great deal of trouble: 1) it must be sturdy; 2) it must be simple to operate with a minimum of controls; 3) it must have good tone quality, and 4) it must be economical in the matter of recording wear and ease of maintenance.

Filmstrips and Slides

The use of filmstrips and slides has diminished as video has become more popular. Some academic libraries, however, still maintain slide collections, particularly in conjunction with the art department, although it has now become common to transfer art slides on to videos. Often the library will house and organize slide collections, while ownership and control may be vested in the academic department where they are used.

SPECIAL COLLECTIONS

There are many types of special collections. Some are defined by subject areas, or by date of publication, others are collections of books, manuscripts, ephemera and photographs that document a particular time, place, or occurrence. Sometimes a special collection is composed of materials brought together in some field of knowledge or discipline that includes rare or unusual material.[19] Often, colleges separate these rare, irreplaceable, fragile, expensive materials, or those with archival value from the main collections and place them in what used to be known, and in some colleges still is, as the "treasure room." Special collections often contain interesting and valuable materials, but in view of the costs and difficulties in handling, do they belong in a college library?

The argument that a college library has no business dealing in special collections does not stand up in face of the fact that every college library will acquire in time, one way or another, materials which, while not necessarily rare or very expensive, present unusual problems of housing and use. For example, a gift collection may bring to the library some very old books in good condition, among which are likely to be a few titles that deserve to be segregated from the open shelves. Older pamphlets and broadsides that have survived after many years may include some items of unique value. First editions of recognized authors are often collected by a college because of the author's association with the college or region or because of the nature of the library's special subject collections. Privately printed books and other examples of fine printing and binding often come as gifts to a college library, and fit appropriately into a special collections area or department. Large portfolios of maps and unbound prints must be protected and specially housed. Literary manuscripts, correspondence, journals and so forth are nearly always of some genuine value. The college's archives—annual catalogs, commencement programs, student publications, college newspapers and magazines, class histories, college annuals, photographs, and correspondence—all require the kind of care that necessitates removing them from the open stacks and housing them in restricted quarters. Most college libraries are unable to bring together material of this type for display and consultation in well-equipped quarters staffed by a librarian who is capable of stimulating their use by faculty and students. Yet all college libraries have a responsibility to organize and preserve uncommon materials. Over twenty years ago, an Amherst College librarian put it this way:

> The object in providing [special collections]...is, very simply, not to put them behind glass or bars, not to make them difficult of access, but to ensure their proper care against the occasion when they will be wanted for instruction, for scholarship, or for display. The open stack, though for long the Library has proudly and jealously maintained it, is a very chancy place where underscorings, marginalia, graffiti, mutilation, and theft unhappily take their toll. To Special Collections go those possessions for which these risks are too great to take.[20]

Since that statement was written, rare book librarians in college libraries have become more active and sought creative uses of their materials. At Smith College, for instance, the rare book librarian encourages faculty to use her quarters as a classroom. A botany class may compare their textbook with the *Herbvarius Latinus*, published in 1484. Students are encouraged to examine books that relate to their curricular needs or to their interests:

> Making rare books available to undergraduates is not considered casual use. Students are asked to know what they are looking for, but the request does not have to be course related. ...Free to look at what interests them. ...They are learning historical perspective and a sensitivity to the past. And they can hold the past, in book form, literally and carefully in their own hands.[21]

There are, of course, good reasons not to have extensive special collections in a college library. Consider these: Special collections are expensive. They require special cataloging, as well as special processing and handling for conservation and preservation. Separate housing, with careful attention to atmosphere control, is mandatory. Retrieval, too, is complicated and special assistance is required. In addition, there are security considerations. The possibility of theft makes open access unthinkable. Increased insurance at higher rates may be required, although irreplaceable material is sometimes considered uninsurable. Manuscripts, in particular, are expensive to handle and store. Encapsulation, acid free cases and paper dividers, special storage cabinets and other equipment may be necessary.

On the other hand, special collections of rare materials offer strong pedagogical backing for the curriculum, expand the horizons of community members, can support the research aims and aspirations of some faculty and add to the prestige of an institution. If the caveats of affordability and good stewardship are heeded, a well thought-out special collections policy can carry strong benefits to the college.

The establishment of the American Library Association Committee on Rare Books, Manuscripts, and Special Collections in 1954 signaled the beginning of an era of notable progress in developing special collections. An ACRL Rare Books Preconference in 1959 had 187 attendees from 97 institutions. By 1977, more than 1800 people attended. College libraries which once provided a locked bookcase or two for rare items now have become increasingly interested in plans and procedures for improving their special collections and making them available to those who most need to use them. Hundreds of college libraries built or expanded in the sixties and early seventies included a special collections room or suite. In others, a section of the stack was partitioned off and set apart for such collections.

Selection and Acquisition

Most rare books and manuscript collections are products of gifts. Often they are collections built up by individuals over long careers, perhaps whole lifetimes. Generally, donors wish to see them preserved, and perhaps enlarged. It should be emphasized that the purpose of special collections in the college library is largely to furnish a body of basic research materials to undergird the college's program in independent study or honors work. Only collections that have the potential to fulfill that objective should be accepted. While the collections are generally strongest in the areas of the humanities and social studies, the opportunity to acquire material in the fields of the natural sciences should not be neglected. The acquisition of such materials comes primarily through the enlightened generosity of alumni and friends of the college and it is to them that the librarian and president of the college must look for donations. It is also of critical importance to the users of the library that special funds be provided by the college or the donor to pay for the cost of cataloging and processing gift collections, preferably as part of the gift. Another important source of special collections and rare books is faculty, particularly those bibliophiles who may have been collecting in certain subject fields for a lifetime.

Gifts of special collections, manuscripts, or rare books can represent a gold mine or a major headache for college libraries and care must be taken to distinguish between these potential outcomes in the face of offers of material. Librarians must judge the degree to which the material supports the curriculum; whether its value justifies the expense and effort of processing; whether there is space available for it; and, finally, whether there may be a more appropriate home for it. Not every unsolicited gift is worth accepting. The college may be committing itself to large outlays of funds when it agrees to accept a collection, or to start one. Money is rarely given for the upkeep of a collection, or for people to staff it. Decisions about whether or not to accept collections should be the responsibility of the library, but in frequent consultation with members of the college community, and most particularly with the President. Refusing a collection is a particularly delicate matter which may have long-range ramifications for the college. The manner in which it is declined is often as important as the decision itself.

A college that owns a special collection may wish to add to it. A rare book, by its very name, is difficult to procure. Depending on how aggressively material is sought, librarians may want to commission booksellers to be on the lookout for certain types of material. However, somebody on the staff must be knowledgeable about prices and values, must continually read catalogs and be prepared to act quickly in the face of a potential purchase.

Organization for Use

Material in special collections requires not only high security but also protection from theft and fire, proper temperature and humidity control, constant vigilance to prevent damage from insects and mildew and thorough instruction for the assistants who are assigned to handle, process and shelve the materials. Librarians report that the cleaning service handling the rest of the college library is often not permitted into the rare book/special collections rooms. The books and manuscripts in special collections should be listed in the main catalog. In many cases this material remains uncataloged on the shelves of libraries where the staff is too small for the exacting and specialized cataloging required, and as a result it is seldom if ever used. When processing the material, care should be taken to leave every evidence of a book's history. Bookplates or marks of ownership should not be removed or go unrecorded; binding should be repaired, not replaced. A library must decide whether it will mark the item with a library stamp. While it deters theft, it nonetheless defaces the book.

Generally those who work with special collections are asked to use the material in the room or suite where it is housed. People consulting rare books almost always require a number of items at one time, and therefore large tables on which to spread out are provided. This contrasts with other college library space demands where the ideal furniture may be a study carrel. Rarely is material from special collections permitted to circulate, except for exhibit or class demonstration purposes. Most librarians prefer that faculty members bring their students to the special collections area where material may be handled by the class. When photocopying is required, the service is performed by a library staff member because of the danger of damage. Rules on the use of special collections should be routinely distributed to each person who wishes to use them. Special collections are high-security materials, to be sure, but librarians should be flexible and exercise common sense in assisting students.

Interlibrary loan access to special collections is generally limited. Materials require special packing and insurance. Even with special care, books come back in very bad shape. Microfilm is certainly an attractive alternative.

SUMMARY

While monograph selections loom larger in college libraries, the selection of several other types of materials is equally important.

Journals have become the primary medium for reporting scholarly and professional research and current practice. Their proliferation and expense make it difficult to satisfy the voracious appetite of faculty for them. Journal budgets are frequently bloated in relation to the rest of the materials budget. Attempts to reduce them by cancelling subscriptions involves a complicated negotiation process. In addition to scholarly journals, the library must also meet increasing demands for popular periodicals as well as local, national and foreign newspapers. U.S. government documents, another important non-book category in college libraries are recognized as important to citizens, but are not necessarily fully integrated into the library's collections and service currently.

Microform copies of back files of journals have eliminated some preservation problems and saved libraries much needed space. Readers still complain, however, about having to use microforms. CD-ROM and other new storage technologies offer great promise in their capability of holding large amounts of data and images. Video is coming into its own in college libraries, but primarily as an instructional resource.

Most college libraries house special collections of materials, particularly rare books and manuscripts. Problems and responsibilities associated with their acquisition and continuing care must be weighed against the relevance of the collection offered to the mission of the college. However, using rare books and manuscripts permits student to hold the past, in book form, in their own hands.

NOTES AND SUGGESTED READINGS

Notes

1.   Association of College and Research Libraries, "Standards for College Libraries, 1986," *College and Research Library News* 47 (March 1986): 192.

2. Gary D. Byrd, "An Economic 'Commons' Tragedy for Research Libraries," *College and Research Library News* 51 (May 1990): 184.

3. *Ibid.*

4.   JoAn Segal, "Give the Members What They Want," *College and Research Library News* 51 (June 1990): 561.

5.   Herbert White, "The Journal that Ate the Library," *Library Journal* 113 (May 15, 1988): 62-63.

6. G. Edward Evans, *Developing Library and Information Center Collections*, 2d ed. (Littleton, CO: Libraries Unlimited, 1987), 202.

7. Turner Cassity, quoted in Guy R. Lyle, *The Administration of the College Library*, 4th ed. (New York: H. Wilson, 1974), 202.

8. Andrew Peters, "Evaluating Periodicals," *College and Research Libraries* 43 (March 1982): 149.

9. Evan Farber, "Collection Development from a College Perspective: A Response," in *College Librarianship*, ed. William Miller and D. Stephen Rockwood (Metuchen, NJ: Scarecrow Press, 1981), 147.

10. Hendrik Edelman. Conversation with author, October 1990.

11. Kathleen Heim and Marilyn Moody, "Government Documents in the College Library." in Miller and Rockwood, 215-216.

12. William Saffady, *Micrographics*, 2d ed. (Littleton, CO: Libraries Unlimited, 1985), 1.

13. *Ibid.*, 147.

14. Ken King, "The Scholar and His Information: A Look at the 1990s," *Library Acquisitions: Practice and Theory* 13 (1989): 209.

15. George Abbott, "Video-Based Information Systems in Academic Library Media Centers," *Library Trends* 34 (Summer 1985): 151-159.

16. Association of College and Research Libraries, "Guidelines for AV Services in Academic Libraries," *College and Research Library News* 47 (May 1986): 333-335.

17. Jerome Miller, *Using Copyrighted Videocassettes in Classrooms, Libraries and Training Centers* (Friday Harbor, WA: Copyright Information Services, 1988).

18. Thomas Galvin and Sally Mason, ed., "Video, Libraries, and the Law: Finding the Balance," *American Libraries* 20 (February 1989): 110-119.

19. T. W. Leonhardt, "The Place of Special Collections in the Acquisitions Budget," *Library Acquisitions Practice and Theory* 6 (1982): 17.

20. *The Robert Frost Library: Special Collections* (Amherst, MA: Amherst College, 1968), 3.

21. R. Mortimer, "Manuscript and Rare Books in an Undergraduate Library," *Wilson LIbrary Bulletin* 58 (October 1983): 107-110.

Suggested Readings

Association of College and Research Libraries. "Guidelines for AV Services in Academic Libraries." *College and Research Libraries News* 47 (May 1986): 333-335

Association of College and Research Libraries. "Standards for Ethical Conduct for Rare Books, Manuscripts and Special Collections in Libraries." *College and Research Libraries News* 48 (March 1987): 134-5.

Elshami, Ahmen. *CD-ROM Technology for Information Managers.* Chicago: American Library Association, 1990.

Heim, Kathleen and Marilyn Moody,"Government Documents in the College Library." In *College Librarianship.* ed. William

Miller and D. Stephen Rockwood. (Metuchen, NJ: Scarecrow Press, 1981).

"Rare Book Librarianship." *Library Trends* 36 (Summer 1987). entire issue.

Saffady, William. *Micrographics*. 2d ed. Littleton, CO: Libraries Unlimited, 1985.

Stagg, Deborah Bolton. "Serials in a Small College Library." *Library Resources and Technical Services* 29 (April/June 1985): 139-44.

Tuttle, Marcia. *Introduction to Serials Management*. Greenwich, CT: JAI Press, 1983.

Chapter 10

CATALOGING AND CLASSIFICATION

For all books, journals and most other types of material added to the library, catalogs provide access to the materials by developing brief descriptions of them. This process is known as cataloging. Staff also determine where each new addition belongs in the library's scheme of book arrangement—this is classification.

While these two basic definitions have not changed over time,[1] much of the routine work done to establish local listings and locations has altered dramatically. The past twenty five years have witnessed a revolution in cataloging methods caused primarily by four interrelated developments:

1. The creation of a standard format for entering cataloging data into a computer. The cataloging standard developed in the late 1960s at the Library of Congress under the leadership of Henriette Avram became known as the MARC

format, MARC being an acronym for Machine-Readable Cataloging. MARC established a standard format for entering and storing descriptive cataloging information into the computer.

2. The adoption of a new cataloging code. AACR II Revised—an acronym for the *Anglo American Cataloguing Rules*. 2nd edition—is the authority for descriptive cataloging. It specifies the form of entry a cataloger will use to establish the bibliographic record for an item, based on the item itself. AACR II replaced AACR I in 1978 but was not implemented nationally until 1981.

3. The development of Cataloging in Publication. The Cataloging in Publication program (CIP) was begun in 1971 and now includes more than 2500 publishers who submit books in galley form or provide pre-publication data to the Library of Congress where catalogers determine the classification number and catalog entries. When the book is published the information appears on the verso of the title page.

4. The cooperative development of telecommunications based bibliographic utilities. Networks such as OCLC, RLIN and WLN are formed by the agreement of member libraries to use a centralized computer system linked through telecommunications lines to terminals at the local site.

BIBLIOGRAPHIC UTILITIES

OCLC, the first of the telecommunications based bibliographic utilities, and by far the largest, was incorporated in July 1967 in Ohio. Part of its success was due to the creation of MARC and the consequent availability of bibliographic records in MARC format from the Library of Congress. The network passed an evolutionary milestone in 1970: an offline catalog card production system became operational. The national database grew rapidly when in 1971 libraries began to participate in the OCLC's shared cataloging program and contribute original cataloging of items not cataloged by Library of Congress. Both libraries outside Ohio and many types of libraries other than college and university libraries soon sought membership. A structure built on regional brokers of OCLC quickly emerged as regional network brokers such as Palinet (Eastern Pennsylvania, New Jersey, Delaware, Maryland), Solinet (Southern States), Nelinet (New England), and Amigos (Southwest) each developed its own identity and set of services.

Cataloging and classification are no longer exclusively a local activity. Original cataloging is done for less than ten per cent of new acquisitions in the majority of college libraries.[2] Materials can be cataloged through participation in OCLC or another utility or by subscribing to a commercial cataloging service that supplies cataloging data on cards, tapes, or in CD ROM format, such as Bibliophile or OCLC's CAT CD450. Bibliophile is an offline product based on current Library of Congress MARC tapes; CAT CD450 also includes cataloging from OCLC member libraries. Both are selective in their listings. Smaller libraries with collections of current, English language material may find the majority of their cataloging needs could be met by offline products such as these.

When cataloging is purchased from a utility such as OCLC or RLIN (Research Libraries Information Network), UTLAS (Canada) or WLN (Washington Library Network) the library checks its item against the utility cataloging and makes necessary adjustments. It may add subject headings, notes or corrections, after which the record is incorporated into the central store of records for the library. This is known as shared cataloging. There is a fee for each phase of the process—viewing the record, inputting a new record, editing, ordering tapes or cards, and also a telecommunications fee. Selecting a cataloging method based on off-line products requires trading off the ability to edit online using a very large database, for reduced costs and access to a smaller database. Increased interest in resource sharing led OCLC to develop *partial* user and *tapeload* membership categories in 1982. The *partial* user category provides a pricing mechanism whereby libraries may use OCLC to search, to determine interlibrary loan locations, to participate in non-cataloging subsystems, and to capture bibliographic information from the database without actually cataloging items through the system. The *tapeload* membership serves the needs of RLIN members who wish to also have their records available in OCLC for interlibrary loan purposes and to increase the availability of shared cataloging options for other libraries.[3]

As college libraries install integrated library systems and modify their local cataloging procedures, many also examine the costs and benefits of full or partial membership in OCLC. For some, maintaining membership in a national utility is becoming a decision based solely on an examination of local costs, rather than a decision based on a belief in resource sharing. Some migrate to partial membership status while maintaining full commitments to resource sharing programs at the state and national level via other mechanisms.

Definitions

Clearly, the presence of these bibliographical utilities and database products has not solved all the organizational problems inherent in maintaining an accurate library catalog. Instead, the range of duties performed by catalogers in college libraries has changed as each college seeks to participate in shared cataloging and the development of other online systems. Janet Swan Hill claims that while the term cataloging may once have been a synonym for descriptive cataloging, its current usage is much broader. She sees it as encompassing the group of activities that falls between acquiring an item and making it ready for patron use, and including construction of library catalogs as well as maintenance of those catalogs and their individual records long after the pieces have left the cataloger's hands.[4] The management issues are broader than they were when more original cataloging was done locally. Barbara Kwasnik describes how cataloging has changed:

> Whereas cataloging used to be somewhat like the performance of a musical composition—that is, there was room for individual style—in form, punctuation, detail—the requirement of shared cataloging is that cataloging be absolutely uniform and standardized. The computer is unforgiving of even slight discrepancies. Thus the cataloger is now less of an interpreter of guidelines for a given set of users, than an interpreter of a mass of rules that are designed for all situations rather than for the individual library.[5]

Catalog department heads must decide which utility to use, when to use it, and which staff member will perform a given task in an interrelated series of tasks. We now speak of records rather than cards and recognize that the creation and maintenance of this central database is at the core of a library's operations in an automated environment. Being at the core has brought catalogers into the circle of decision making about many areas of library operations, most notably in technical services, but not exclusively.

Catalogers are also expected to sharpen their cataloging skills so that the library's participation in networks will be at a quality level consistent with the reputation of the college. For most libraries in the last decade this has meant mastering the two editions of the Anglo-American Cataloging Rules. In addition to working with a copy of the code, it is imperative to have on hand a file of the Library of Congress *Cataloging Services Bulletin* and the Library of Congress *Rule Interpretation Manual*.

For some librarians the past decade has also been the time when the library switched from the Dewey Decimal Classification to the Library of Congress Classification. In still other libraries the desire to have older materials listed in new online catalogs has led to the establishment of large retrospective conversion programs. Catalogers have always done authority work—names, series, uniform titles, and subject headings—but with online systems meticulous authority work is fast replacing other tasks as the number one priority. Good authority control work ensures that only correct records are retrieved. For this reason authority work has moved from a position of near invisibility a decade ago to one recognized as a major cataloging concern at the national level.[6]

DIVISION OF WORK

The division of work in the catalog department has changed with computerization. It is now more likely that support staff will have increased responsibilities for copy cataloging and even shared cataloging—that is, taking a record from a bibliographic utility, support staff will also input local information; and for making any local revisions to the record online. The head of the department in a small college library, perhaps its only professional, will be spending a significant amount of time in instructing new staff and in training long-term staff in new procedures. Cataloging staff are assigned to work with one or more formats—monographs, journals, microforms—and then, if necessary, further subdivision is by subject or language. Each is expected to have a moderate amount of cross-training with at least one other staff member, to know the overall flow of work, and how their duties fit into the larger picture. Typically, there are gradations of difficulty in work assignments, with more complex work assigned on the basis of experience. The librarian in the department will do the difficult original cataloging, supervise revision of work, train new staff, maintain adequate documentation of procedures for manuals and plan and implement new procedures as systems evolve.

Staff

As online cataloging systems have developed, the ratio of professional to support staff has changed and the number of support staff increased. Often they perform complex duties which are not well understood by college personnel departments. Establishing proper job classifications can be difficult. Up-to-date job descriptions help, but job classifiers in the personnel department need to be taught to understand the independent nature of the work, and the extent to which individual judgment is required in maintaining an authoritative catalog for users. The work involved is no less demanding than the work done by junior programmers or senior support staff in the business office, and should be classified at the same level, or perhaps higher, if the job also entails knowing foreign languages or supervising the work of others.

No college library staff should be without a librarian knowledgeable about national standards for cataloging and capable of organizing quality work at the local level. Combining this knowledge with knowledge of the use of computers in libraries is now essential. Large libraries often report that a training period of up to one year is necessary before a new M.L.S. graduate is capable of doing advanced original cataloging work. Unless the director has a background in cataloging, smaller libraries with only one cataloger position may feel the need to hire someone with extensive experience. Adequate course work, enthusiasm for cataloging, experience in a larger library as a copy cataloger and evidence of organizational skills can suffice as suitable background for most libraries. As with all staff, personal qualities such as a concern for good service, accuracy, a tolerance for ambiguity, high energy, and ability to work with others are important. Keeping the user of the catalog in mind may help a director decide among candidates for a cataloging position as the candidate who exhibits the greatest understanding of the needs of the faculty and students is often the person most likely to be able to devise systems and procedures to benefit them.

Types of Catalogs

The majority of college libraries still use a card catalog or computer output microformat catalog, even as they seek funds to migrate to an online public access catalog. All catalogs, when compared to printed books, have the feature of flexibility, as entries can be rearranged, added to, withdrawn, revised and replaced on either a daily or periodic basis. The global change feature of online catalogs, and the elimination of the need to file or edit cards or pull cards are significant improvements over card catalogs. Ease of maintenance is not the only advantage of online catalogs. The opportunity to develop search strategies using key words rather than formally assigned subject headings is a major escalation in the power of catalogs to reveal their contents. While the library will still describe its holdings by national standards such as the *Library of Congress Subject Headings* and organize the material by the ALA *Rules for Filing Catalog Cards*, users can bypass these systems and create their own subject access methods. Recent research on user behavior at catalogs suggests that users experience difficulty with all types of catalogs and so user education is always needed. Users do not distinguish between author entries and author as subject. Nor do they recognize limitations, for instance that the catalog only contains monograph holdings from or to a certain date. Whichever form of catalog is available, quality control over its contents is important, so that users develop trust that it accurately represents the holdings of the library. Frequently, card catalogs are declared closed or frozen as of a certain date. This means that all subsequent changes and corrections are made only to the online catalog. Though not an ideal situation, it is tolerable if users are made aware of library practices regarding the card catalog.

Many libraries also maintain shelf lists, catalogs which are organized by classification order and that list all copies of titles held. The shelf list will control the problem of issuing duplicate call numbers. It also serves as a checklist when barcoding the collection or taking an inventory of holdings. The shelf list can also be used to estimate the size of a collection, to establish growth rates in certain areas, for planning and inventory purposes or to sample the collection for age. Physical shelf lists may be eliminated once the collection is completely entered into the new system and the system is programmed to generate necessary reports; most libraries, however, seem to choose to maintain the manual file at present. Local authority files may be dismantled at an even earlier date, since the national bibliographic utilities now offer access to the Library of Congress Name Authority file on line as an option.

WORK OF THE DEPARTMENT

One catalog librarian describes his work as a database editor, another sees herself as a problem solver concerned with establishing and maintaining the integrity of the library's official records of its holdings. Neither shirks handling detail or making decisions. Both recognize that their work is part of a chain and that one key task of each is to do his or her part in ensuring that the work of the department flows smoothly.

The catalog librarian should build variety into each department member's work. No one can or should sit at a terminal for eight hours, nor can one person solve all problems. The price reduction available by connecting to OCLC at other than prime time causes many libraries to schedule certain types of work in the early morning or evening hours. Work that does not demand online communication with Ohio can be performed at other times, or batched and sent at off hours. Establishing clear routines prevent snarls from developing and flow-charting a process helps clarify paths through which work travels. A sample flow chart (See Figure 12) hints at the number of decisions and people involved[7]. Texts on cataloging are also helpful in clarifying the logic behind certain cataloging principles.[8]

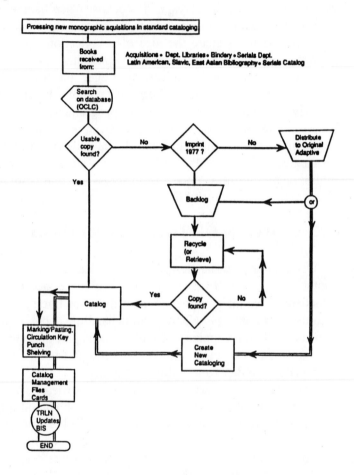

Figure 12
University of North Carolina at Chapel Hill,
Cataloging Flow Chart

RELATIONS WITH OTHER DEPARTMENTS

The catalog department has full responsibility for cataloging books and other materials, but its efforts must be coordinated with the needs and practices of other departments. Copy cataloging has brought the work of the acquisitions and catalog departments closer together. Pre-order bibliographic searching as the basis of copy cataloging helps to speed new books into the hands of users. It is impossible to predict or control when materials ordered will arrive at the library. It is possible, however, to control the smooth flow of materials through departments once they have appeared, by establishing mutually agreed-upon quotas, time frames and procedures to ensure the smooth interaction of the departments. A clear method of tracking orders through their cycle from request by faculty to placement on the shelf is mandatory including cross-training of staff in both acquisitions and cataloging in the use of each other's files. Ideally, data entered into the system at the point of order is used and re-used for each operation. Repetitious inputting, a waste of staff time and a source of error, is thus avoided.

A break in the flow, due to periods of light ordering, permits catalog department members to attend to other matters, perhaps processing gifts or accomplishing some retrospective conversion work. Understandably, tensions between departments occasionally arise at times of heavy receipt of orders, or when cataloging personnel shortages cause backlogs to develop. No tensions should result from unclear procedures. Area heads owe to their staff work plans that establish what work is to be done, when and by whom, and work orientations that minimize divisiveness between departments.

Integrated library systems increase the interaction among cataloging, reference and circulation departments. The principles of file organization embodied in most integrated systems are more familiar to catalogers and catalog department staff. These individuals can serve as interpreters to the rest of the staff, using their knowledge of MARC formats and tagging to help staff unaccustomed to working with computers understand the binary approach to handling information. As reference librarians grapple with the complexities of designing adequate help screens in an OPAC they will need to articulate the logic behind filing rules and subject headings so they can write clear directions. Both departments will find that the ability to change records on a daily basis leads to many more questions being directed to the catalog department about the status of a given item. In turn, the work the catalog department does to ensure that the library's holdings records are accurate will be much more visible. Catalog librarians, already busy people, will find that there is an additional reason to include some time at the reference desk in their weekly routine.

CLASSIFICATION

Studying classification schemes as an intellectual exercise is thought provoking, but classification work as practiced in most college libraries is a matter of deciding between the Dewey Decimal Classification scheme and the Library of Congress classification system. Newer libraries have tended to select the Library of Congress scheme, often because it appears to cover more areas and simplifies copy cataloging routines. Libraries with large collections organized according to the Dewey system will be aware that the staff time involved in modifying Dewey numbers to meet local needs can be significant, but the truth is that both systems call for modifications. A large number of colleges switched from Dewey to the Library of Congress scheme in the 1970s and none have reversed their decision.

Classification today is being viewed more as a location device, or a procedure employed to define local ownership, rather than being championed as *the* method to order the universe into clusters of broad subject areas. The assignment of a classification number is part of the task of creating a call number, which is exclusively the job of the local library, no matter who does the actual descriptive cataloging and subject analysis. The call number identifies the item uniquely in that library. It includes: a) locator code, b) classification number (by topic and form), c) *Cutter number* (to distinguish books in the same class), d) copy number, e) volume number, and f) date.

Subject Headings

The close relationship between classification and the subject headings in the catalog often results in the assignment of both duties to one individual. The *Library of Congress Subject Headings* is the authoritative source for new headings although many consider it too conservative in its assignment of new headings. Its scope is both its virtue and its vice. The challenge becomes to select current headings from the list which best describe a book in the context of the library's collection and the college's educational program, and to decide which headings are no longer appropriate. Commercial vendors will run a copy of the library's tapes against the Library of Congress Authority File and make all corrections as of that date. Once this large scale clean up or de-duplication process is accomplished, updating is done locally as information in the Library of Congress Subject Authority program and Library of Congress Name Authority Files are accessed through OCLC or another utility and reviewed against the downloaded tapes in a local system. The interest in further expediting authority work is intense, and vendors are developing new approaches regularly.

DESCRIPTIVE CATALOGING

Most college libraries now have procedures in place to capitalize on the availability of cataloging in bibliographic utilities. The first step for them is to establish lists of libraries whose cataloging they consider of sufficient quality to be used without major modification. For example, the code DLC indicates cataloging for the item was provided by the Library of Congress. When these initials appear in the record, most libraries accept the cataloging. Some cost-saving procedures now call for temporarily shelving an item for a two-month period if in the first search for records no match is found. When materials receive original cataloging, strict adherence to AACR II rules is necessary. By carefully following accepted practice libraries can achieve the degree of standardization necessary to make shared cataloging trustworthy and beneficial.

Revision

Revision is a fact of life in a catalog department. Only by maintaining the file to keep it current can the library assure users that the holdings listed in the catalog represent all the materials in the active collection. Maintenance routines, whether accomplished manually or online, include filing, noting the number of added copies, or indicating withdrawn volumes, and these tasks are done by support staff. Questions of larger import—for instance, serious inconsistencies in classification, out-of-date subject headings or an inadequate system of cross-references—require resolution by senior staff.

Special treatment and modified routines are necessary when non-print materials, microforms, theses, or other special collections must be cataloged. Special materials constitute only a small part of any collection, but the quality of the cataloging they receive should be no less than the overall quality of monograph cataloging at the college.

Once library materials are cataloged, they are prepared for use by the addition of call number labels, charge out pockets and cards, bookplates and ownership marks, and security tapes if such are used. This work is typically done by trained students and is a final checkpoint for determining accuracy of the information.

Inventory

Some catalog/technical services departments have responsibility for inventory work and for the book repair and binding units. While an acquisitions or circulation department is sometimes charged with this task, inventory work is so strongly related to catalog maintenance that it is usually assigned to the catalog department, or at least involves them heavily. Systematic shelf reading, performed by student staff, is a necessary preliminary step to inventory work and has the added benefit of identifying materials in need of repair.

An inventory may be full, a complete check of all holdings, or partial, a survey, for instance of a heavily used part of the collection. During inventory the shelf list is used to check holdings on the shelf and those in circulation, being repaired or at the bindery. Those materials identified as missing are assessed for current usefulness and are either reordered after a set time and a second rechecking of the shelves, or withdrawn from the collection. High loss rates, of more than five per cent of a collection, should lead the library administration to review present security arrangements.

REPORTS AND STATISTICS

The purpose of gathering statistics is to collect information about work performed and to make decisions about future work. Often certain statistics are kept because they provide libraries with data to use in making comparisons with past years and with other, similar libraries. In the catalog department statistics are kept about the number of titles and volumes cataloged, cards filed, retrospective conversions completed, volumes withdrawn or sent to the bindery, and special types of materials added, such as microforms and musical scores. Staff members keep individual records of their activities which are compiled monthly by the head of the department and forwarded to the director for use in other reports and studies.

One recurring question in academic libraries centers on production levels and costs and asks: How many books does an average cataloger catalog on the average and at what average cost? The majority of studies that have addressed the question produce results that are specific to both place and personnel. A trained cataloger, one without additional assignments such as training support staff, and who deals with current English-language materials with good copy available in OCLC, has an output pattern far greater than that of a new cataloger or one cataloging older, foreign materials. Reports of cataloging output vary widely: the range is from 800 titles a month to less than 100 titles. Average processing costs are estimated to match the cost of the book itself, or, in 1990 dollars to be between $30.00 and $50.00. Local salaries, choices about binding of paperbacks, and decisions about the level of quality in the catalog will cause this figure to fluctuate. Benchmark data, even with these caveats, can be used to determine local costs and levels of productivity.[9] If local situations reveal relatively high costs and low levels of productivity, there may be a serious need to alter procedures. Investigation may reveal that too much is being added locally to the record. What is important is to establish the amount of information necessary to make books easily retrievable by faculty and students.

Studies have looked at the impact of automation in technical services on costs. Northwestern University recently found that after fifteen years of library automation most savings had been absorbed by new costs in other areas. Staff no longer required in technical services had been added to public services departments to meet increased demand for service. Other "savings" were used to pay for service contracts or telecommunications costs of automation. In effect, there were no real savings.[10] Many similar reports from the field indicate that automation increases library use and improves productivity of employees in technical services.[11]

Librarians seek to make the catalog serve its users as a good local index. This involves continually monitoring policies and procedures and weighing the costs and benefits of any change, including the future cost implications of making any short term decisions that do not adhere to national standards. It is precisely these kinds of local decisions made by past generations of catalogers and administrators which created the bulk of today's clean-up work in catalog departments. No catalog will ever be perfect, but it is incumbent upon those who work in this area to balance the needs of accuracy and accountability in a manner that protects the bibliographic record for the future.

SUMMARY

Following the rise of bibliographic utilities such as OCLC and the introduction of the MARC II standard, cataloging has changed from a solitary activity done on the local level to a shared enterprise with significant import for all other operations of the library. While there has always been a close relationship between the catalog department and the acquisitions department, there is now also frequent interaction with the reference and circulation departments as well. Catalogers help these departments understand the principles of file structure and file management. Simultaneously, more and more of the cataloging tasks have shifted to support staff, with librarians responsible for training, planning and supervision. The introduction of local integrated library systems may change the relationship of college libraries to bibliographical utilities in the near future. Gradually libraries have recognized the necessity of strict adherence to maintaining national standards in cataloging, particularly if general resource sharing is ever to graduate from aspiration to achievement.

NOTES AND SUGGESTED READINGS

Notes

1. Michael Carpenter and Elaine Svenonius, *Foundations of Cataloging: A Sourcebook* (Littleton, CO: Libraries Unlimited, 1985), passim.

2. Alice Copeland and Lessie Culmer Nier, Head and Assistant Head, Catalog Department, Drew University Library. Interview by author, 24 April, 1990. As experienced catalogers they agree with the widely shared perception that no more than 10% of college library cataloging is original cataloging and that the figure in some libraries is no more than one per cent.

3. Dennis Reynolds, *Library Automation: Issues and Applications*. (New York: R. R. Bowker, 1985), 350-351.

4. Janet Swan Hill, "The Cataloging Half of Cataloging and Classification, 1986," *Library Resources and Technical Services* 31 (October/December 1987): 321.

5. Dr. Barbara Kwasnik of School of Information Studies, Syracuse University. Letter to authors, June 1990.

6. Hill, "The Cataloging Half," 323.

7. Association of Research Libraries. Office of Management Studies. System and Procedures Exchange Center, *Managing Copy Cataloging in ARL Libraries*, Kit 136 (Washington, DC: Association of Research Libraries, August 1987), 92.

8. Carpenter and Svenonius, *Foundations*; Bohdan Wynar, *Introduction to Cataloging and Classification* 7th ed., ed. by Arlene Taylor (Littleton, CO: Libraries Unlimited, 1980);

Carolyn Frost, *Cataloging Nonbook Material* (Littleton, CO: Libraries Unlimited, 1983).

9. Malcolm Getz, "Analysis and Library Management," in *Academic Libraries Research Strategies* ed. Mary Jo Lynch and Arthur Young. (Chicago: American Library Association, 1990), 196.

10. Karen Horny, "Fifteen Years of Automation: Evolution of Technical Services Staffing," *Library Resources and Technical Services* 31 (January/March 1987): 69-76.

11. Association of Research Libraries, *Managing Copy Cataloging*, 36.

Suggested Readings

Berman, Sanford. *Prejudices and Antipathies: A Tract on the LC Subject Headings Concerning People.* Metuchen, NJ: Scarecrow Press, 1971.

Cargill, Jennifer, ed. "Library Management and Technical Services: The Changing Role of Technical Services in Library Organization." *Journal of Library Administration* 9 (1988).

Chan, Lois Mai. *Library of Congress Subject Headings: Principles and Application.* 2d ed. Littleton, CO: Libraries Unlimited, 1986.

Clack, Doris Hargrett. *Authority Control: Principles, Applications and Instruction.* Chicago: American Library Association, 1990.

Ellison, John W. and Patricia Ann Coty, ed. *Nonbook Media: Collection Management and User Services.* Chicago: American Library Association, 1987.

Foster, Donald L. *Managing the Catalog Department* 3d ed. Metuchen, NJ: Scarecrow Press, 1987.

Gorman, Michael and Paul W. Winkler, ed. *Anglo American Cataloguing Rules.* 2d ed. Chicago: American Library Association, 1988.

Gorman, Michael. *Technical Services: Today and Tomorrow.* Englewood, CO: Libraries Unlimited, 1990.

Hafter, Ruth. *Academic Librarians and Cataloging Networks.* New York: Greenwood Press, 1986.

Svenonius, Elaine. "Bibliographical Control." In *Academic Libraries Research Perspectives*, ed. Mary Jo Lynch and Arthur Young. Chicago: American Library Association, 1990, pp. 38-60.

Svenonius, Elaine, ed. *The Conceptual Foundation of Descriptive Cataloging.* Papers delivered at a conference held at the University of California, Los Angeles, February 14-15, 1987. San Diego: Academic Press, 1989.

Chapter 11

REFERENCE SERVICE

Reference, or information, service consists of the personal assistance provided to users in pursuit of information, either through referral to likely sources of information or in the form of information itself. Reference work, done well, goes to the heart of the teaching-learning process and is the activity center of a college library. In a college library, instruction in how to gain access to library resources is closely linked to the problem of information retrieval. The success of a reference transaction for a college librarian is defined as having provided not only a good answer—one which responds adequately to a stated need—but one which has successfully transferred the skills both to acquire an immediate answer and to locate information in the future.

In this chapter, reference service, that is the retrieval of an information product, is discussed. In the one that follows, approaches to instruction, and how students acquire information and evaluate its utility are considered. Information instruction forms an integral part of every reference encounter. Good reference librarians maintain a constant stream of instructive commentary as they move through the process of identifying and locating materials and/or information. Formal instruction, on the other hand, is more complex, controversial, and requires careful planning. A third chapter in this section deals with the circulation process, getting materials into user's hands after it has been identified.

Technological developments have provided reference librarians with powerful new information locators, among them online bibliographic data bases and CD-ROM products. While these new approaches offer information retrieval capabilities unheard of a decade ago, they also present substantial challenges in developing the skills associated with their use to today's college library users. C. Lee Jones has said

> this era of technical innovation in libraries has become for patrons an age of discontinuity of library services as library practices they have grown accustomed to are rapidly replaced by new ones...it will be the librarians of the present and future who will need to refamiliarize patrons with the library.[1]

If libraries do not play a leading role in providing access to the new information services, then a part of the libraries' purpose will be abnegated and they may have trouble defining their function or demonstrating their worth. If skilled help is not available to use new technological sources, patrons will turn elsewhere. Online databases, for instance, are part of the evolving world of communication and of scholarship. The real problem is that current library practices have not yet changed sufficiently to permit the widespread use of online databases in a manner that truly supports the work of scholars and students.

COLLEGE REFERENCE SERVICE
AND ITS USERS

Reference work is similar in college, university and public libraries; reference librarians in all three answer users' questions, prepare bibliographies and provide telephone reference information. Many of the reference materials consulted are identical; to some extent the users overlap; and the steps followed in defining and answering a question are the same. But there are substantial differences to be recognized. The college library caters to undergraduates rather than to graduate students, researchers, or an undifferentiated "general public." To some extent this relative homogeneity simplifies the problem for college libraries because undergraduates read under fairly strict direction, in contrast with graduate students who are left to their own resources and such help as they can get from librarians. On the other hand it is also true that graduate students can turn to their instructors rather than to reference librarians for subject literature advice in special fields, while undergraduates are much more likely to look to reference librarians as sources of substantive help in their academic pursuits.

New undergraduates, when they arrive on a college campus, are assaulted by a welter of unfamiliar sights and confusing experiences, not the least of which is the college library. Compared with what they have been used to in their high schools, the college library has to be larger, and seems more complex and intimidating despite the best efforts of librarians to make it user-friendly. How freshmen react to their first reference encounter may determine their acceptance of the library as an integral part of the educational process. Should the reference librarian be helpful, friendly and non-patronizing, and should the material be made available painlessly and informally, the student may become a user. On the other hand, an unsuccessful question negotiation or a fruitless search may convince the would-be patron to look elsewhere for information. Selection of an information source is strongly related to accessibility and the perception of accessibility is influenced by experience.

Undergraduate students are not a composite body. They cannot be lumped together with such abstract titles as the "Me Generation" or "Silent Majority." Nor should they be called "The Freshman Class." In all their contacts with the library, students should be viewed as individuals with unique problems, rather than as members of a group about which facile and often inapt generalizations are made. The challenge and responsibility of being a college reference librarian is to insure that first meetings with new students are pleasant and significant, occur fairly soon after the student arrives on campus, and do not represent final encounters.

A further distinction between public and college reference work is the extent to which teaching users how to acquire information is part of the process of answering questions. Patrons at a public library are more likely to demand specific and definite information for immediate use. While college students may occasionally seek the same kind of information, more often their quest is for more general subject material. In this situation, reference librarians draw on different skills to aid students in the solution of their problems. In general, it is the duty of the academic reference librarian to help students learn how to find the material themselves. It is part of the reference function in college libraries to help patrons use their own information-seeking talents.

No elaborate method is needed. Students asking for assistance are given personal tutoring, not sent to the catalog to look under "utopias" or to the third shelf in the back of the reading room where there is a bibliography that might be of use. Newly trained reference librarians are perhaps more familiar with the conventions of question negotiation and problem definition practiced in the reference interview than were their predecessors. The past decade has been characterized by increasing attention to precision in information retrieval—to looking at the relevance and pertinence of answers, to examining the role of intermediaries in the search process, to defining problem statements, and to insuring the appropriateness of the reference interview. These skills, along with an attitude that communicates readiness and a desire to render assistance, will guarantee a successful reference transaction. The process is not easy because it is shaped by ambiguities in human communication as well as by complicated negotiations. In Karen Markey's words, "Question negotiation is an illustration of a complicated interaction between two individuals in which one person tries to describe for another nothing he knows, but rather something he does not know."[2]

Often, in truth, it is reference librarians who help students hone in on topics and narrow the parameters of their searches for information. The reference function is consultative. If a reference librarian is unable to answer a question, the inquiry is turned over to someone on the staff who can. Some questions, of course, are unanswerable. But students should not be left unsatisfied until all the resources of the library and its staff have been tapped. In some of the unobtrusive tests of reference service, answers are judged wrong if the librarian does not conclude the inquiry with the questions, "Are you satisfied? Did you get what you needed?" Incorporating this type of confirmation at the end of each transaction helps to emphasize a commitment to excellence in information assistance.

The total college community—students, faculty, and administrators—is eligible for reference service. Beyond this, if called upon, most college libraries are willing to share their materials and services with scholars outside the college family and with nonacademic users in the community whose needs cannot be met by other local library resources. In working with all of these groups, the purposes are: 1) to provide answers to inquiries requiring specific information, 2) to teach students and others how to use an academic library in connection with their work, 3) to provide bibliographical and other reference assistance, 4) to locate materials for users wherever these materials may be in the library system, 5) to make available material not in the library through interlibrary loan, 6) to organize uncataloged materials for effective reference use, and 7) to build reference collections to support the curriculum and provide knowledge in all relevant areas. These reference department functions are considered below following a brief discussion of the issues of philosophy, organization, staffing and collection development in reference work.

ORGANIZATION

Reference service philosophy has evolved from a conservative to a more liberal approach. Librarians at first saw themselves as custodians, collectors and catalogers, and the reference service they offered was gentle and almost exclusively geared towards inexperienced users. By the turn of the century librarians were recommending the appointment of special assistants for "the work of answering questions," and by 1915, "reference work was ordinarily accepted as necessary service of the individual library and in many cases invested with the prestige of departmental status."[3] Unfortunately, for college libraries this was often merely rhetoric. In 1936, a sample of 302 liberal arts colleges revealed that only about 12 per cent had a designated reference librarian. By 1940, however, a distinguished college president wrote that "all but the smallest colleges have reference librarians whose duties are often described as impressive...but," he continued, "whose actual work consists to a considerable extent in answering routine questions."[4] Reference service was often subsumed under public services, including circulation, and often emphasized collection development.

Reference service began to assume a more significant role in college libraries in the 1960s and 1970s when, following the lead of special libraries, emphasis shifted to a more active service orientation. Reference librarians sought to become members of, or at least participants in, the educational process. Factors leading to this new role were the development and or improvement of reference sources; the trend in better liberal arts colleges toward independent work by students; the effect of regional accrediting agencies and the adoption of bibliographic instruction as an important reference department program.[5] Too often, however, a more active stance describes intention rather than reality. Reference services in college libraries often remain at basic level because students are ignorant about using even simple reference works and librarians do not develop programs that combat this ignorance. The reference staff, small in number to begin with, is kept occupied answering directional questions, building the collection and teaching rudimentary skills. In colleges where students are by tradition expected to work with reference sources and bibliographies and have been at least minimally trained to use basic reference materials, however, reference librarians can be regarded as true friends of scholarship. Colleges able to offer sufficient numbers of reference librarians to insure their continuous availability to students, and a carefully developed library instruction program, can reasonably expect a high level of quality in library-based work done by students.

Most college libraries have separate reference departments, although some have combined reference with circulation, and reference departments often include government documents. Recently, the move toward gathering college library functions into subject-oriented units has provided the possibility of new organizational structures, but few libraries have as yet adopted this approach. A number of larger college libraries have departmental and/or divisional libraries, particularly in the sciences. In these libraries, reference librarians are, or become, subject specialists in the fields served by branches. Librarians in college libraries without subject departmentalization often become *de facto* subject specialists, attracting students and faculty who are aware of their subject expertise. It is not unusual to find one reference librarian characterized as the "online searcher," another as head of government documents, even when there is no separate documents section or department, and a third as one to whom the humanists turn. Libraries that develop staff specialization within a single reference department may serve the dual role of conserving the interests of the general reader and at the same time rendering service to the specialist. Reference librarians who learn the history and bibliography of a discipline through systematic formal or independent study of the literature of the field offer users the advantages of specialization without making necessary the decentralization of the library's reference materials in separate subject collections.

There are good arguments for specialization, but few colleges can afford the kind of specialization which is the rule in university libraries. Too much specialization, too narrow a concentration in a field, can jeopardize the generalist approach to reference that is most effective with undergraduates. What is required is the breadth of knowledge and human understanding to recognize the core of the question and to have a real interest in both the question and in the person posing it. While it is proper and undoubtedly important that reference librarians have special interests, concentration in one field to the exclusion of others could impair their understanding of undergraduates' needs.

The way in which periodicals are handled by college library clientele has some bearing on how reference service is organized. In some colleges the periodicals are ordered, cataloged, and made available in much the same manner as books; that is, through the facilities of the order, catalog, circulation and reference departments. There are college libraries, however, in which all work with serials, including reference, is handled in a separate serials department. The argument for such an arrangement is that serials are a distinct type of publication requiring specially trained persons to handle them. Few libraries currently adopt this approach because it is obviously impossible to classify a reader's needs in advance, and the possible advantages of having a separate serials department staffed by specialists may be offset by the fragmentation of reference services and indexes. On the other hand, serial selection is rarely the ultimate responsibility of the reference department.

In the same way, when online data base searching first appeared in college libraries, there was a tendency to view it as separate from other library functions and to house and administer it apart from the reference department. Librarians have now realized that online data bases are simply another type of reference source and have integrated the use of them into the reference departments along with CD-ROM services and other forms of reference material. Patrons come to the library wanting material about certain subjects; unless an instructor has unimaginatively standardized the process of identifying and obtaining material by stipulating the use of just a few sources, students are not concerned about the form in which material appears—book, microfilm, journal, tape, or CD-ROM. If assistance is required, it is more easily provided at a single reference desk where help is available from all sources regardless of the medium. In this way, patrons do not have to cross boundaries, or explain their problems repeatedly.

New technologies bring with them new kinds of assignments. Reference departments in colleges often have, without additional staff or funding, attempted to launch new services while maintaining existing ones. This situation can lead to stress, and, ultimately, to poor service unless good planning, including job analysis and some reassignment of duties or elimination of tasks also occurs. In many ways, reference librarians have been by-passed by the work-saving elements of the computer revolution. Online catalogs are computer-based reference tools that may improve reference productivity, but OPACs are as much end-user access tools as the card catalogs they are replacing. Online database searching, another computer-based reference activity, has transferred to librarians work that was formerly done by library users; that is, manual searching of printed indexes. Librarians more frequently are serving as intermediaries between technology and users.

The staff manual should clarify the purposes and describe the organization of the reference department. More important in times of change, such as is now being experienced by reference departments, staff manuals require continuous revision as new approaches and new ideas are developed. In large college libraries, reference manuals will emphasize policies regarding interlibrary loan, instruction in library use, and compilation of bibliographies. In smaller college libraries where reference librarians depend more heavily on nonprofessional and student assistants, the manual is more likely to emphasize procedures and routines.

Generalizations regarding the optimal number of reference librarians that should be available in college libraries are difficult to make because functions vary greatly in reference departments, even in similar institutions.[6] Marjorie Murfin suggests that using turnstile figures, coupled with norms of questions asked during particular hours, and taking into consideration whether professional, nonprofessional or student help is available would begin to suggest staffing needs.[7] Even statistics of questions asked are difficult to compare, since they have not been adequately standardized into categories and they are subjectively determined.

The physical organization of the reference department is an important element in providing quality service. The information desk or counter should be centrally located, accessible, and inviting. Studying the behavior of users as they approach the counter or handle reference materials may suggest arrangements of materials and equipment. For instance, few college libraries provide seating in the reference collection area based on the assumption that these materials are for "referral" only. Yet reference books tend to be heavy and cumbersome and difficult to handle. Lack of proximity to seating or counter space militates against their being used efficiently and effectively, and may result in their not being used at all. Counter-height shelving, the placement of some stools for seating, and consultation space for users in one area of the information desk all facilitate use of the reference collection and services.

STAFF: QUALIFICATIONS FOR REFERENCE WORK

To fulfill the duties of reference service in college libraries, librarians need a somewhat formidable array of virtues. A scholarly turn of mind, broad general knowledge, and familiarity with bibliographical resources and the methods of scholarship are essential. A good memory is helpful, although systematic recording of sources and good cross-referencing in the catalog will fortify recall. Knowledge is not enough; reference librarians require sympathetic understanding, patience in dealing with students, and an appreciation of the teaching function in reference work. Imagination is indispensable, intuition useful, and a sense of humor helpful. Lacking these, a reference librarian may lose perspective and overstress unimportant details. Some personality traits or qualities that have been recognized in good reference librarians are confidence, inquisitiveness, a sense of ethics and tenacity. Reference librarians seem able to live with ambiguity and the unexpected.

While the gap between art and science in reference seems to be narrowing, some commentators stress that the artistic and creative nature of leaps of thought are still required in order to link and interpret disparate clues. No set of rules has yet been devised that adequately describes the reference process or satisfactorily teaches new reference librarians how to make the kind of associations necessary to the work. Some doubt that reference service is a codifiable science. The growing importance of information is likely to increase, rather than decrease, the intellectual demands made on reference librarians.

It is exceedingly difficult to pinpoint the qualities of an ideal reference librarian, but relatively easy to point out the weaknesses of a poor one. The most obvious fault of poor reference librarians is lack of appreciation for either the content or the methods of scholarship. They also lack a certain thoroughness and persistence which go with scholarship. They possess only a fair knowledge of bibliographic and library resources. They are abrupt in dealing with students, a trait that stems from lack of sympathy and patience. When asked for assistance, they are too quick to jump to conclusions and fail to get all the facts or to evaluate the ones they have. Because they hold positions where even a slight amount of personal assistance often brings profuse thanks, they have no conception of their own shortcomings, no healthy unease about the quality of their work.

Recent studies of workload and responsibilities of reference-bibliographers at medium-sized academic libraries indicates that the average reference-bibliographer has a 12 month contract, works between 35 and 40 hours weekly, and spends

- 1.7 hours a week on reference
- 7.7 hours on collection development
- 3.1 hours on bibliographic instruction
- 4.3 hours on searching online
- 5.3 hours on publishing
- 3.1 hours on professional reading
- 3.0 hours on in-house library committees
- 2.2 hours on clerical tasks[8]

If reference librarians are also administrators, 11 hours go to general management tasks, usually at the expense of reference service or collection development. Given the changes experienced in many college reference departments over the last decade and the tendency for new services to be added without any being subtracted, a periodic review of assignments and time allocations will benefit most reference departments.

Reference librarians are often reluctant to use non-reference department personnel or other support staff at the reference desk. However, increasing demand for longer library hours and insufficient numbers of reference librarians to cover these hours has led to other staff—librarians, support and student—being more deeply involved than in the past. As early as 1975, Boyer and Theirmer found that two-thirds of a sample of college and university librarians used support staff in reference service, and that support staff accounted for 33% of the hours of reference desk coverage.[9]

Too often, professional reference librarians in colleges spend time doing clerical work, providing simple directional answers to questions, or helping patrons to learn whether the library owns a specific known item. Trial runs have been made in a series of situations, ranging from intensive training of a few select upperclass students to assist at the reference desk of a small college library staffed by one reference librarian, to training of graduate students during a summer session in the reference and bibliographical sources of their special fields and having them serve as part-time reference assistants the following academic year. In some libraries, at Rider College, for instance, each librarian is expected to provide reference service part of the time. In other libraries such job variety is encouraged, but not mandated. From an analysis of the results of these experiments, it would appear that support staff, students and librarians from other areas of the library have little difficulty in handling directional questions and requests about whether a library owns particular items.[10] Adequate staffing levels and professional backup are needed, however, if the service is to perform at optimal levels. The success or accuracy of non-professional staff in handling questions increases when a reference librarian is also present. Students and support staff fare least well when handling subject questions, due, in part, to the complex nature of these kinds of questions and the necessity for interviewing skills.[11]

If it has been the custom to staff reference desks only with trained librarians, the library should now modify that tradition at least to the extent of experimenting with the use of upperclass students and support staff with special library training to serve alongside librarians. Support staff can also be scheduled to work independently for the hours known to be less hectic; students can supplement service at busy hours. One of the joys of academic library work is the pleasure of working with students and seeing their minds develop. With these modifications the reference librarians will be better able to focus on the development of a full program of reference services.

SELECTION OF REFERENCE MATERIALS

Selecting reference materials has been complicated by the appearance of resources in varying forms and by the new emphasis on access. Increases in costs are a significant problem. The new materials, exciting and more powerful in their ability to help supply information, can also be more expensive. Of almost equal difficulty is the pressure to make decisions based on technology which is probably superannuated on the day it is marketed. Altogether, reference librarians are faced with a welter of choices, all of which have far-reaching consequences, both in their ability to provide service and in their cost.

Most reference collections tend to be too large for thorough exploitation by librarians in the service of information delivery. The size and scope of reference collections follow certain general rules. First, the larger the library, the larger the reference collection and the more extensive the types of material for which specialized knowledge and personal assistance are necessary. Second, the nature of reference use is such that collections should be broader in scope than the curriculum, both in subject matter and in approach.

Reference collections like the rest of the collection, should be based on rational policies that have been codified and written down. Unfortunately, a recent study revealed that only 7% of college libraries have written reference selection policies and only 6% have formally articulated their reference collection weeding policies.[12] Older materials in a reference department are a particular danger. Often they are used by unsuspecting patrons who trust that the materials they find on the reference shelves will contain the most recent, up-to-date material.

Weeding the collection of older works is not merely desirable, but essential to the provision of good service. Excluding certain types of material from the reference collection may also help to keep it viable and pertinent.

The library director and the reference staff working together determine the scope of the reference collection and the broad lines of development. Their deliberations form the basis of an annual allocation for reference materials and services. A long-standing tradition in college libraries holds that faculty suggestions can be sought or considered, while the judgments of the reference staff and library directors ultimately decide what will be purchased. Selections are based, first, on curriculum considerations and second on broad, more general concerns. A careful analysis of reference inquiries, particularly those for which information was unavailable, aids in identifying needed materials. There are, for example, questions which recur so frequently that reference librarians are constantly on the lookout for new reference books dealing with them. Subjects in this category include: criticism of an author's work, individual poems, short stories, novels, or plays; critical estimates of artists and musicians and their work; identification of proper names ranging from people to associations; statistics; biography; and current public policy issues. The library cannot have too many sources with which to furnish answers in these areas. The new reference titles do not need to be the best books if they add a group of names, a set of statistics, or an approach which an older and perhaps more scholarly work fails to provide.

The pattern of service on the campus and in the immediate area also has a bearing on the selection of reference materials. If the college library is located in a city where there is a strong public library, it may depend on the city library, for example, for a collection of current telephone directories of the United States. If there are departmental libraries, the specialized reference material in these fields will probably be located with the departmental collection. If there are other college libraries in the area, it should be possible to develop cooperative agreements about specializations.

Online database search service, mediated or not, is now pervasive, normal, and expected. Many entering students who lack an understanding of the scope of printed reference sources in an academic library are familiar with the concept of accessing remote databases. The old argument that online searches are of an add-on or auxiliary nature is no longer defendable.[13] Once considered an expensive extra, online reference is now deemed basic to comprehensive library service. Research indicates that more and more college libraries are considering the availability of an online source in their decisions about whether to purchase a title in paper form,[14] again demonstrating the wide acceptance of the concept of access in place of acquisition in some cases. This is particularly true for institutions where space is short, or where use of certain titles is so limited that ownership is seen as unnecessary. Increased public access to online databases is available through Dialog's Knowledge Index, BRS After Dark, the Source and CompuServe and combine user-friendly search protocol packages called front-ends with databases, to allow PC users ease in searching a variety of online sources.

The development of CD-ROM index products appears to represent a middle ground between online database searching, microform and traditional print indexes and holds great promise for reference and other services in libraries. Digital optical printing on CD-ROM discs has created a powerful new publishing medium in which materials are accessed through special players, controlled by microcomputers. As a result, the same kind of interactive searching available on online databases is available to users in a medium far more conducive to end-user searching.

The major differences between many CD-ROM products and the online bibliographic retrieval systems used for years lies essentially in their comparative economics. Librarians can purchase complete access with a single annual, very costly, subscription fee rather than pay for each individual use.

Therefore every search decreases rather than increases the per-use cost and produces efficiencies of volume not possible with online searching as it is currently practiced. Cost per search, in other words, can be much lower with CD-ROM than with online, although low usage may eventuate in substantially higher cost. The absence of telecommunication connection charges can also offset CD-ROM costs. Librarians who purchase in CD-ROM format buy a superior interface, and may save additional amounts by eliminating the necessity of a mediator to conduct the search.[15] Reference librarians at Allegheny College and Drew University report that mediated online searching decreases substantially with the acquisition of three or four CD-ROM databases and sufficient work stations to house them. In the future libraries may decide that purchasing machine readable tapes of popular indexes and loading them on to the local network is the most cost-effective solution in their situation.

Reference librarians are, in many ways, the pioneers for CD-ROM. Reference desk personnel orient and train patrons in its use. It is anticipated that in the near future many patrons will acquire CD-ROM capabilities in their own work stations, amass their own library of discs and require that CD-ROM discs be available for loan from the library. Other patrons will access specialized reference sources via electronic gateways to other library collections.

In choosing reference materials, librarians check published reviews, study the introductions to new reference books for clues to important titles, and sometimes request books on approval. Reviews and listings appear in Reference and Subscription Book Reviews (*Booklist*), *RSR* (Reference Service Review) and *College and Research Libraries* to name just three of the major sources. CD-ROM's are not yet well reviewed. Evaluating CD-ROM sources and their contents will become more urgent as more extensive publishing of them increases.

In addition to the principal duties associated with reference service, the reference department is responsible for organizing and making available certain types of generally uncataloged materials. These include vertical files, although their use is diminishing, and self-organizing collections such as college catalogs. All reference material should be arranged in a manner which permits readers to help themselves though they should be able to ask for assistance whenever it is needed.

FEE OR FREE

Technological change challenged and continues to challenge and modify the value structures in librarianship. In the early 1970s online database searching created a number of unresolved value issues, including loss of patron confidentiality because of the necessity for mediators to conduct searches, and ownership of information. Perhaps the most important of these issues, involving equality of access to information was the extent to which libraries could or should offer database searching without a fee. As further advances in technologies become available, new dilemmas continue to surface concerning who should pay for them, who might benefit and whether we should adopt them. American librarians generally agree that access to information in a barrier-free manner is an important occupational value and that any inhibiting factor is to be viewed negatively.[16] As a result when online database searching appeared, questions about who would pay for this expensive new service engendered a major debate in the library community.

Those who favored or at least accepted the notion of charging fees offered a number of convincing arguments. They pointed to the add-on nature of online services. Database searching, they contended, was something extra, not something traditionally available in the library. In addition, they pointed to the fact that an online search is patron specific, with the result usable only by a single consumer, rendering it expensive to conduct. They also stressed the need to control the demand for the services; the financial reality of funds not being available from other sources; and the supposed acceptance of fees by library patrons as justification for levying charges.

Librarians opposed to fees suggested that fees have a significant effect on demand for information; that it is possible to offer free searches; that online services will become so integrated into reference departments that fees will be unjustifiable.

The problem was compounded by the new emphasis on access no matter the ownership of an item. When fees are levied for online searches "the result is to discriminate in favor of acquired as opposed to accessed material, and to discriminate in favor of the haves as opposed to the have-nots."[17]

Recently, a number of libraries have reallocated funds from the materials budgets to cover the cost of searching, basing their action on the belief that library budgets should reflect online searching as part of standard reference service. An informal survey conducted in late 1989 revealed that many liberal arts colleges had instituted a no-fee searching policy, some had adopted a policy of passing on charges to departments, and the majority were still charging for online searches.[18] The development of CD-ROM technology has vitiated, to some extent, some of the arguments for fees, since access is offline and negates hourly and connection charges. Even with CD-ROM products, however, some academic libraries are passing costs on to users. One library has installed debit card readers on their CD-ROM work stations, collecting user fees that contribute to paying for the systems.[19]

Other fee-based issues will emerge with new technologies. As access to libraries becomes possible from increasingly remote stations, such questions as who can use online catalogs at dial-up ports will become important. Northwestern University reports that its online number is well known throughout the city of Chicago and entitled patrons will often find the phone lines busy because of heavy use by non-university affiliated users. Eventually they may require a password to gain entry to the catalog from remote locations.[20] In the past, anyone who came to the library could use the catalog, indeed still can. But remote service may be limited to authorized users.

When we have access to electronic texts, will we have to pay for every use of an item, including browsing? Who owns information? The now popular conception of information as a commodity is currently being challenged, based, in part, on the argument that a great deal of information is generated from taxpayer funded government reports. Librarians and producers of information may view these issues differently. Academic librarians cannot expect to develop or receive significant new services without the profession reaching agreement with the publishing industry on the general rights and responsibilities of each party.

We can anticipate the debate to continue to test the values we have traditionally shared as librarians.

WORK WITH STUDENTS

The functions of the reference department in working with students are: (1) to provide answers to specific informational questions, (2) to give personal guidance in the use of the entire library—via the catalog, bibliographies, abstracts and indexes, (3) to consult about term papers, theses, and so on, including methods of finding material and bibliographic form, (4) to give formal instruction in the use of the library, and (5) to supplement individual and class instruction by the preparation and publication of lists, bibliographies, and guides to collections, types of material or ways of locating them. The materials used to carry out these functions are many and varied. They include, in print or electronic form, encyclopedias, dictionaries, handbooks, almanacs, directories, atlases, biographical reference books, indexes, abstracts, national and subject bibliographies, union lists, guides to subject literature, and guides to library resources. The expertise of individuals may also be the source for an answer.

Factual questions stem from class assignments, student activities or individual curiosity. One student comes to the library for the name of the man who invented the quadratic equation, another for a list of one hundred great books, and a third for the caloric and nutritional components of breakfast cereals. Then there are the topical questions, usually in conjunction with a class assignment, which bridge the gap between reserve reading and independent use of the library. For students these investigations represent first explorations among library catalogs and periodical indexes and the questions themselves, which often relate to current issues such as the green house effect, Middle Eastern political strife, and the causes of homelessness in America. Excluding inquiries concerning the location of specific reference books in the library, these factual and topical questions constitute the majority of questions asked by students.

The tests of the library's usefulness in answering either factual or topical reference questions are twofold. One is the ability of the staff to conduct successful interviews in which both members of the transaction understand the nature of the query and what would constitute an appropriate answer. The second is the ability of the staff to insure that students receive the information they want or the knowledge of where it may be obtained as quickly and precisely as possible. It is dangerous to generalize from a few instances, but it would appear that reference librarians err from time-to-time in giving readers more information than they need or want. These librarians suffer from an excess of zeal. In their desire to be helpful, they forget that the purpose of a quick information service is to save readers' time and help them select from among sources the ones that are most pertinent. Between making a display of one's ability to dig out information from any number of sources and referring readers to a single source, even if it is only a clipping, it is usually better to choose the latter—so long as it answers the question. Too much help or too much undigested information dampens the enthusiasm of seekers after knowledge and wastes their time.

Determining the amount of information desired in relation to the anticipated final product is an important activity. One favorite story concerns the young researcher who asked for a history of Judaism. An astute reference librarian, knowing that the college was well-supplied with information on various religions, asked the student, "About how much information do you want?" The answer was memorable and instructive: "About a paragraph." A one-volume encyclopedia was provided, even though entire encyclopedias devoted to the topic were available.

Assistance given to students in connection with term papers, theses, and other class assignments involving wide use of reference materials is among the reference librarian's most challenging tasks. Not only experience, but scholarly background must be brought to bear on the task. As Abraham Barnett said, more than 30 years ago

> The preparation for a library assignment ought to be characterized generally by an attempt to make the student see that in coming to the library he passes from the guidance of one benevolent intellectual authority to that of another—from the professor to the librarian—who is responsible for a distinctive part of his education. This kind of orientation gives a continuity to the experiences of the student, and his life in the library does not become a lacuna in his education.[21]

Often the real challenge in the reference interview process is to help students understand and articulate their research problems, to assist them in posing the questions they will address in their papers. Once this has been accomplished, librarians can steer them in a direction where they will be successful in finding the information to help them respond to their questions.

There is uncertainty among faculty members as to the extent of reference help that librarians should offer students, because they often don't comprehend the functions of reference librarians or because they have failed to consult with them. Professors work under a distinct handicap when reference librarians are not familiar with the purpose of library-related class assignments;

reference librarians are limited in the help they can provide students if faculty do not cooperate in several key ways. Faculty must ascertain that students understand assignments, determine in advance whether the library has sufficient material on the topics assigned, emphasize selection and quality rather than form and quantity in reviewing student bibliographies, and provide students with full and accurate bibliographical references when directing them to sources. Reference librarians, on the other hand, must help students find what they want, not merely steer them toward the catalog. Often it is much easier for reference librarians to answer questions than to tell students how to go about finding the information. Librarians who take this quicker path neglect the opportunity to instruct students, a duty that rests with them no less than with professors. There are no serious differences between reference librarians and faculty concerning the reference function that could not be solved quickly if the instructor came to the library to discuss with the reference librarian the assignments given to students, and the kind of library use expected of them. The non-appearance of faculty members at the library does not excuse librarians from taking responsibility themselves toward understanding student assignments.. A walk across the campus to discuss class assignments with a professor may be invigorating and also produce a salutary effect on the quality of reference service provided to students.

Individual instruction of students in the use of the catalog, CD-ROMs, public access OCLC terminals, and end-user online database searching systems is generally conducted by reference staff members, supplemented by circulation staff. For a large proportion of students, classification symbols, systems of filing, and cross-reference entries simply do not exist. Although it is less cost-effective than a large lecture and frequently catch-as-catch-can, individual guidance in these more esoteric library devices is extremely valuable because it is likely to come at a time when a student has a real need for the information. To supplement personal assistance and class instruction and to assist students in helping themselves, most colleges prepare and publish a handbook or series of guide sheets highlighting general periodical indexes, basic reference books, special materials such as document and pamphlet collections, and information on how to gain access to online data bases. These may also contain brief hints regarding practical procedures in the use of these materials.

Reference work with students requires the full cooperation of all members of the library staff. Reference librarians particularly must acknowledge that sometimes an inquiry can be more satisfactorily answered by another member of the staff. Circulation librarians must recognize that they can often save reference librarians time by handling directly factual or catalog inquiries requiring but a few minutes to answer. Catalogers must insure that new reference books are given a high priority in cataloging and processing. Student employees can remind other students of the usefulness of the library to their work. Library directors may have opportunities to engage faculty in discussions that indirectly promote better use of reference services. Library employees who enroll in college courses can educate their classmates to the availability of reference services.

WORK WITH FACULTY

If the instructor is responsible for initial suggestions, stimulation, and final criticism, librarians can claim special knowledge of bibliography—an essential component of the learning process. The most useful bibliographical tool in the college library is the catalog, assuming that the user is familiar enough with its contents and arrangement to use it intelligently. Between this local index to books and bibliography and the more exhaustive world of bibliographies, guides and reference sources, the opportunities to demonstrate what is available on particular topics are many and varied. Examples of bibliographies are to be found in every good college library, but they are often difficult to discover. For the purpose of undergraduate, or even graduate, student use they may be unwieldy and insufficiently evaluative. From firsthand knowledge of bibliography and students' abilities and needs, librarians can render both teachers and students real service by preparing (and frequently revising) critically annotated subject lists of the library's most useful bibliographies in specific courses or teaching fields. Examples of the kinds that might be frequently requested are: "Art History," "Library Resources in Woman Studies," "The U.S. Congress," and "Sources of Economic Statistics."

Another way in which reference librarians assist faculty is by consulting with them about class assignments, term papers, and library problems, thereby forging a link between reference assistance and instructional requirements. A good illustration of successful cooperation can be seen in the following example: After one semester's experience with over one hundred students seeking the same information on how a law is enacted, the head of the reference department at Drew University Library contacted an eminent member of the political science department and asked him to modify his approach. He agreed, and in subsequent semesters his class received a library instruction session and a brief outline of reference documents to be used in tracing a bill.

Perhaps the most frequent service rendered by reference librarians to faculty members has to do with finding specific information they need for their research or, as is often the case, on a subject that is peripheral to their investigation. In this category fall many of the odd, unusual or out-of-the-way questions that may involve a prolonged search. The new emphasis on access rather than acquisition makes reference librarians even more instrumental to faculty research by identifying access points and locations for information.

Reference librarians interact with faculty in a variety of situations. A number of college libraries, recognizing a more active role for reference librarians or "information officers," as they are sometimes called, have adopted policies to expand the extent of reference staff contact with faculty. These institutions have assigned a single staff member or a group of staff members as liaison to academic departments and administrative offices. Some librarians schedule visits to departments on a regular basis, sometimes allocating as much as six hours weekly to them.[22] Based on the "washroom theory of administration,"[23] reference librarians as information officers make themselves visible in such social settings as art openings, faculty receptions, morning coffee hours and other college forums. They pay periodic visits to faculty in their offices to discuss new research projects, class assignments and other matters equally affecting the library and the classroom. Academic librarians can also engage in SDI (Selective Dissemination of Information). This involves becoming familiar with the work of various faculty members and alerting them to new information in their disciplines. Some college librarians have constructed user-interest profiles of faculty members, thus enabling more effective recognition of information and sources that will be of use, no matter the subject field. As reference librarians accept the role of information advocates for certain or all faculty, they act as a bridge between researchers and both formal and informal sources, and make the information system broader and more human. Librarians and faculty alike benefit from the cross-fertilization between disciplines that ensues.

Recent studies have found that information research habits vary according to subject discipline. In the social sciences, subject matter is generally unstable and constantly changing. Considerable overlap exists between disciplines and there is heavy emphasis on conceptual and statistical information. Social scientists appear to prefer to conduct their own library research, often in the journal literature, using citations, abstracts and indexes, and personal recommendations.

Humanists depend more heavily on monographs and their own linguistic abilities to satisfy their information needs. Research, for them, depends on access to major book collections and good interlibrary loan systems. They, too, are more likely to conduct their own library research, conferring with the librarian during the last stages of their search.

For scientists, personal recommendations and discipline affiliation play a more important role than the use of formal abstracts and indexes in locating references. Science faculty seem happier with library services than do social scientists, due to the compact, "hard" and cumulative nature of their subjects. As a result scientists are more willing to delegate library searches to library staff.[24]

In short, good reference librarians act as information consultants. They point people in the direction of sources that are most appropriate in solving particular information needs; train people in the use of electronic information sources; search sources that are unfamiliar to particular users; assist in the organization of personal electronic information files; keep researchers up-to-date about materials in their fields and about new information sources and services as these become available.

There are, of course, many other reference services offered by college libraries. Reference librarians, tuned into campus curriculum matters may be asked to supply basic bibliographies in particular fields. Volunteering a good source of information to those planning colloquiums or to committees assigned to study new trends, even in the absence of a direct request, is always appropriate. Administrators studying tuition issues may ask for a list of sources on the topic. The Development Office, while generally responsible for its own research into sources of funds, may have biographical questions about potential donors. Sometimes, the line between doing someone else's work and assisting someone to do it is fuzzy and hard to recognize. Again, like so much else on a college campus, context, tradition, and politics are determining factors in the nature and degree of service offered. Considering the source of the question sometimes helps to determine how quickly and completely the information will be provided.

WORK WITH PERSONS OUTSIDE
THE COLLEGE

While college libraries have a primary responsibility to serve their own communities, many individuals, libraries, business firms, and organizations call the college library for reference assistance. Inquiries come in person, by phone and by mail. The extent to which a library chooses or is obligated to serve this diverse clientele depends on many of the same factors which govern other college decisions—the relative size of the library and the community, geographic isolation, other resources in the community, and, once again, tradition. If the college is publicly supported, it may be required by law to serve the wider community. Depository libraries must make government documents widely available.

There are both political and positive reasons for providing reference assistance to community members. The political reason is that good public relations are important, and college presidents take it for granted that librarians will provide any service they can to enhance a favorable image. The positive reason is that reference librarians, like other library professionals, are committed to the basic principle of free access to information and it is difficult for them to refuse assistance or to limit it. So far as they are concerned, reference service to outsiders is just part of the day's work.

No one will dispute that the preeminent responsibility of college reference service is to take care of the needs of faculty, students and administration. Therefore, the important consideration in handling outside questions is how extensively help can be offered to outsiders without detriment to service on the campus. If the reference staff is very good, it may acquire a reputation for excellence and become the target for a great many inquiries. It is difficult to ascertain whether a person who asks a question, particularly by phone, is a member of the college community or an outside user. No librarian likes this task, and where it is attempted it frequently gives a community resident a feeling that the librarians are captious and less than generous in their assistance. Each library will have to ponder for itself the problems of reference service to outsiders. Is the nature of the request trivial or serious? Is the user a member of a consortium that cooperates in the provision of library service? Has the user exhausted other available sources—the high school, the public library? Does the inquirer have a special claim to service? Alumni, for instance, generally have in perpetuity rights to college facilities. The onset of online data base searching has highlighted the problem of how to serve the outside community. A number of libraries have instituted fee-supported search services geared primarily to the business community. If the demand is not too heavy, this may solve the access problem for that particular community. The answers to these and other questions will not be the same in any two institutions.

High school students are perhaps the most controversial outside users of the college library. If allowed unchecked access to the college library, they may create a heavy strain on facilities and resources, which in turn will have a negative impact on the utility of the library for its normal clientele. On the other hand, well-motivated high school students who have exhausted the resources available to them elsewhere should be welcomed by the college library. Adopting a referral procedure in which teachers and public librarians verify the student's legitimate access needs may provide a solution, although perhaps not the ideal one. Another may be to offer group instruction to high school classes in the use of the college's reference material, taking this opportunity to explain the difficulties of granting access to the circulating collection.

The second heaviest group of nonaffiliated users may be local historians, in particular genealogists. If the college is old and has accepted the collection of local history materials as one of its priorities, it is likely that the reference department will be flooded with requests for information from this insatiable group. Policy decisions about the time which may be spent on a genealogical request and the type of efforts the genealogists can undertake on their own should be made and incorporated into the reference manual to prevent unreasonable demands.

PROVISION OF MATERIAL NOT IN THE LIBRARY

All college libraries provide assistance in locating and securing material not available in their shelves. At times, students and faculty members may require information and advice about the location of special collections or nearby libraries with strength in certain subject fields as they plan visits in connection with their research. Interlibrary loan is often assigned to the reference department by virtue of the reference librarian's knowledge of bibliography, research activity in different fields, and the holdings of other libraries. Other popular locations for interlibrary loan are the circulation department or a separate unit.

It is clear that not even the best supplied university library can meet all the research needs of its patrons. Obviously, the college library with fewer materials and smaller funds must depend on the resources of other institutions for research materials. Technology permits everyone to tap into other collections' catalogs and seek information from databases that a library would never dream of owning. Users expect worldwide access on a service level consonant with the best levels of local service. That environmental activist slogan, "Think Globally. Act Locally," also speaks to librarians facing a revolution of rising expectation for more and better access points to collections. Thanks to the extraordinary number of bibliographic records converted to machine-readable form, and the emergence of bibliographic utilities, much of the electronic structure is in place to identify where material is located. Users of services now expect more of the library; that it will own or acquire the resources identified for them in various computerized data bases—a reality leading to newer strains on the interlibrary loan system as well as the collection development program of the library.

Librarians and patrons alike are stymied by the gaps in access service. Our systems of bibliographic access are improving while the systems of document delivery remain the same—slow and cumbersome or swift but not financially feasible. We can determine exactly who owns a desired book or journal by depressing a few keys at a computer terminal in mere seconds, and then we can tell the patron not to expect it for at least two weeks! Managing access opportunities in the future will require becoming more explicit about access options and their service and cost implications.

SUMMARY

Reference work in an active college library offers librarians the opportunity to help shape the research strategies of students and faculty at the time when their need for information is greatest. Reference departments now provide users not only print collections of reference materials, but abstracts and indexes in bibliographic data bases, either online or in CD-ROM format.

Reference sources that utilize new expensive new technology have given rise to questions about user fees that go the heart of librarians' value structures. Offering access to information without financial barriers has been an important tenet of librarianship and the new technology threatens that position.

Managing reference coverage, in the light of new responsibilities for instruction and online searching, has proven challenging, as challenging as the task of correctly interpreting and answering users' questions across many disciplines, each with its own tradition of scholarship.

NOTES AND SUGGESTED READINGS

Notes

1. Quoted in Barbara Moran, "The Unintended Revolution in Academic Libraries: 1939 to 1989 and Beyond," *College and Research Libraries* 50: (January 1989): 36.

2. Karen Markey, "Levels of Formulation in Negotiation of Information Need During the Online Research Interview," *Information Processing and Management* 17 (1981): 223.

3. Samuel Rothstein. *The Development of Reference Services Through Academic Traditions*, ACRL Monographs #14 (Chicago: American Library Association, 1955), 29, 37.

4. Harvie Branscomb. *Teaching with Books* (Chicago: Association of American Colleges, and American Library Association, 1940), 201.

5. Richard Miller, "The Tradition of Reference Service in the Liberal Arts College," in *College Librarianship*, ed. by William Miller and D. Stephen Rockwood (Metuchen, NJ: Scarecrow Press, 1981) 462.

6. Paula D. Watson, "Organization and Management of Reference Services in Academic Research Libraries," *RQ* 24 (Summer 1984): 10.

7. Marjorie Murfin, "National Reference Measurement: What It Can Tell Us about Staffing," *College and Research Libraries News* 44 (September 1983): 321-33.

8. Rebecca Schreiner-Robles and Malcolm Gersmann, "Workload of Reference Bibliographers in Medium Sized Academic Libraries," *RQ* 29 (Fall 1989): 82-91.

9. Laura Boyer and William C. Theimer, Jr., "The Use and Training of Nonprofessional Personnel," *College and Research Libraries* 36 (May 1975): 193-200.

10. Beth Woodward, "The Effectiveness of an Information Desk Staffed by Graduate Students and Professionals," *College and Research Libraries* 50 (July 1989): 455-464.

11. *Ibid.*

12. Mary Biggs and Victor Biggs, "Reference Collection Development in Academic Libraries," *RQ* 27 (Fall 1987): 70.

13. William A. Britten, "Supply Side Searching: An Alternative to Fee-Based Online Services," *Journal of Academic Librarianship* 13 (July 1987): 147.

14. Biggs, 67.

15. Brian Nielsen. "Allocating Costs, Thinking About Values," *Journal of Academic Librarianship* 15 (September 1989): 214.

16. *Ibid.*, 212.

17. Britten, 148.

18. Caroline Coughlin and Alice Gertzog, *Unpublished Survey*, Directors of Selected Liberal Arts Colleges, (February 1990).

19. Nielsen, 214.

20. *Ibid.*, 213.

21. Abraham Barnett, "The Professor and the Librarian...," *Liberal Education* 45 (May 1959): 243-4.

22. Julie Neway, *Information Specialist as Team Player in the Research Process* (Westport, CT: Greenwood Press, 1985), 28.

23. Milczanski, quoted in Neway, 29.

24. Summarized from Neway, 41-60; and Metz, Paul, *Landscape of Literatures* (Chicago: American Library Association, 1984), 108.

Suggested Readings

Hernon, Peter and Charles R. McClure. "Unobtrusive Reference Testing: The 55 Percent Rule." *Library Journal* 111 (April 15, 1986): 37-41.

Katz, Bill and Charles Bunge, eds. *Rothstein on Reference, with Some Help from Friends*. New York: Haworth Press, 1989.

Lee, Sul H., ed. *Access to Scholarly Information: Issues and Strategies*. Ann Arbor, MI: Pierian Press, 1985.

Neway, Julie. *Information Specialist as Team Player in the Research Process*. Westport, CT; Greenwood Press, 1985.

Puccio, J. A. *Serials Reference Work*. Littleton, CO; Libraries Unlimited, 1989.

Rothstein, Samuel. *The Development of Reference Services Through Academic Traditions*. ACRL Monograph #14. Chicago: American Library Association, 1955.

Sieburth, Janice. *Online Search Services in the Academic Library: Planning, Management and Operation.* Chicago: American Library Association. 1988.

Tenopir, Carol. *Issues in Online Database Searching.* Littleton, CO: Libraries Unlimited, 1989.

Whitlatch, Jo Bell. *The Role of the Academic Reference Librarian.* Westport, CT: Greenwood Press, 1990.

Chapter 12

Educating The Library User

Among the newly embraced basic objectives for a college education is to prepare students for life-long learning; that is, to equip them with the skills and tools to become informed about the matters that will have importance in their lives. The knowledge explosion of the last two decades has served to convince educators that understanding process is as important as studying practice, and that students must learn not only bodies of information, but also how to learn. In the so-called "information society" attention is focused on how people acquire information and how they turn it to knowledge once it has been acquired.

Academic librarians, responding to the challenge of providing life-long learning skills, have identified their role as producing information-literate students. *Information literacy* is the current term applied to what earlier had been known as Library Instruction, User Instruction, Library Use Instruction and Bibliographic Instruction. The common denominator linking

327

these approaches is attention to better use of library resources, although conceptually the definition of information literacy, as will be seen later in this chapter, is far deeper and broader. Whatever it is called, it seems apparent that library instruction today is recognized by librarians, at least, as an essential element of most academic library programs and that it has a legitimate role to play in higher education, although the way in which that role can be played best remains debatable.

College librarians who have entered the field in the last decade consider library instruction an integral part of academic library service and find it hard to believe that the movement is a relatively young one.   Yet the field of user education is plagued by doubts and uncertainties and, although most academic librarians are now enthusiastic about it, their excitement is not always shared by faculty, students or administration, partly because these constituencies are often reluctant to accept the concept that the educational function of the library includes teaching information management and use.

While educators continue to debate the definitions of teaching, learning, education and the idea of a university, for purposes of this discussion education will be viewed as the "ability to conceive an idea, to find relevant resources related to that idea, to organize the information available from those resources and to draw rational, supportable conclusions."[1] Unfortunately, students are rarely equipped with either the background or the knowledge to evaluate, compare and select material effectively, or to use it once it is retrieved. It is here that information literacy begins to have an important role.

Librarians, like other professionals, often fall prey to jargon and terminological fads.   As mentioned above, the field of library instruction has worn many titles, with information literacy only the latest of them. Some librarians would argue, and we are among them, that information literacy adds an important dimension to what was previously bibliographic or library instruction.   While bibliographic instruction always focused on how to gain access to information, information literacy includes the ability to evaluate information effectively for a given need. It is based on the contention that in order for students to be prepared for lifelong learning, they must be able to construct information-search strategies, and to locate, evaluate and use information effectively, no matter where or how it is stored. Being able to apply information to whatever tasks are encountered or maximizing the use of information in problem-solving are among the characteristics of information literate people. Critical thinking about information is yet another. Some librarians have eschewed the use of the term information literacy despite having embraced the concepts associated with it. The various terms which have been utilized to describe library instruction are used interchangeably in this chapter.

EMERGENCE OF LIBRARY INSTRUCTION

A great number of factors have contributed to the recent upsurge of interest in library instruction, the appearance of the concept of information literacy and the importance attached to it. Among these are: an assertive stance of librarians toward the dissemination of information; the volume of the knowledge base in all disciplines and the inability of librarians to maintain familiarity with or assume control over it; a changed emphasis on the importance of independent student research; the promises and threats of computer technology, including the availability of powerful new retrieval capabilities, the need for sophisticated skills to utilize them, and the appearance of a generation of students perfectly at ease with computers. Curriculum reform has spurred librarians to argue that the new general education concept provides a natural home for information literacy, particularly in the "learning to learn" scheme where critical thinking, analytical and sophisticated communication skills are fostered. The numerous attacks on education launched during the late 1980s also persuaded librarians to investigate what role they might play in helping to stem the tide of mediocrity of

contemporary students. The result is that many librarians and
some faculty feel that library instruction, properly instituted,
enhances the learning of all students, and in particular,
disadvantaged ones. It may also play an important part in the
training of future teachers, a group especially targeted for
widespread complaint.[2]

Research into library instruction has convinced many fence-
sitters that vast numbers of students, previously untouched by
library service, can profit from carefully constructed library
education. A recent survey revealed that 65% of undergraduates
use the library four hours or less each week and, more
worrisome, that one of four never goes into the library.[3] Under-
use of the library by students is one component of the problem.
Another can be seen in reports from reference librarians about
the degree to which the same questions are posed over and over
again arising from an assignment. Consider the following
situation:

> One hundred students in a political science course ask
> for the addresses of their congressional representative. In
> responses to the first few queries, the reference librarian
> will probably interview the students, ask why the
> information is needed, learn that they are all writing
> about a particular issue. To encourage the spirit of
> inquiry, the first students may be introduced to the
> *Congressional Directory*, to other sources of biographical
> and political information, perhaps *CQ Weekly Reports* or
> *Biography Index*. But five or ten minutes per student,
> multiplied by 100, quickly diminishes the librarian's
> enthusiasm and creative impulse. By mid-way, at most,
> the pages in the *Congressional Directory* are marked and
> simply handed out like books at the reserve desk.[4]

If students are exposed to a group lecture in how to gain
access to the materials, the questions which follow are likely to
be more individual and interesting. Indeed, librarians report that

students who have received library instruction ask many more, and better, questions than those who have not.

Finally, when we discuss future academic libraries, we think of scholars' work stations and access to information from every campus office and dormitory. Librarians, used to approaching students to ask whether they need assistance, will not be on site to assist in the information seeking process. A well-planned program of early intervention, then, becomes not only desirable, but essential. The fledgling information society demands and, indeed, deserves the participation, in innovative ways, of academic librarians.

HISTORY OF LIBRARY INSTRUCTION

Library-based learning has been slowly evolving on most college campuses.[5]

Three distinct periods have been identified as characterizing the history of ideas about Library Instruction: the period from 1870 to 1930, called the Professor of Bibliography Movement; the period from 1930 to 1970, termed the Library College Movement; and finally 1970 to the present which might be labeled the Information Literacy Movement.[6] The context of higher education is as crucial to user instruction as it is important to other developments in academic libraries. The first period, 1870-1930 parallels the rise of graduate programs, land grant institutions and dramatic growth in collections and facilities described in Chapter 2 and 3.

As early as 1840, *Ralph Waldo Emerson* criticized colleges for providing no "professor of books."[7]

But it is *Justin Winsor*, head of the Boston Public Library from 1868 to 1877 and of Harvard University Library from 1877 to 1897 who is usually credited with starting the library instruction movement with his concept of the library as educator and his claim for it as the "central agency in our college methods." The librarian, he contended is indeed a teacher, but not one who hears recitations. Rather, he is one whose "world of books" is the classroom. Winsor viewed the library as a natural rival to the textbook as an approach to teaching.[8]

The University of Rochester's *Otis Robinson* in 1876 maintained that a college librarian was more educator than custodian and described student library use as one in which "curiosity begets inquiry, and inquiry heads to research."[9] Robinson considered independent inquiry in broad scholarship to be essential.

Raymond Davis of the University of Michigan is reputed to have taught the first bibliography course for credit. He instructed students in how to use various resources, highlighting the card catalog, reference works and important books in disciplines such as history, philosophy and literature.

Melvil Dewey, too, believed that "The time *is* when a library is a school and the librarian is in the highest sense a teacher," adding that "The purpose of a college education was to provide tools for further study. The most essential tool of all being the ability to use libraries effectively."[10]

William Warner Bishop, Director of the University of Michigan Library, at the turn of century called for "bibliographic" training which would include the comparative merit of books, characteristics of particular authors, reviewers and publishers and integrate what was already known with what individuals were currently reading.

Charles Shaw in 1928 argued that undergraduates should be taught bibliography just as literature, art, and other subjects.

The years from 1930 to 1970, the second period of library instruction, are marked by cataclysmic changes in institutions of higher learning. Before World War II only a small segment of the population attended college. A new philosophy of education based on merit combined with the GI bill to pave the way for widespread access to higher education and colleges were inundated with students. The launching of Sputnik I provided a rationale for considering higher education essential to national defense. Added funds for libraries went into books and bricks. The need for increased personnel was acknowledged in theory but in practice student-librarian ratios were dramatically enlarged. From 1959 to 1968, for instance, the ratio increased by 23%, from 378 to one, to 446 to one.[11]

The same period saw the emergence of a conceptual framework for library instruction. In 1932, the Carnegie Corporation called for formal instruction in use of library and its bibliographic aids. By 1935, *Louis Shores* proposed his "Library-College," a teaching and learning situation for students that moved most educational experiences from the classroom to the library. As envisioned, the library-college presupposed abolition of regular class attendance in favor of studying in the library, merging all physical facilities into a single library complex, peer instruction of beginning undergraduates by upperclass students, integration of librarians and professors into a single teaching staff and a liberal arts curriculum that focused on techniques of problem solving within a liberal arts curriculum. He saw a true partnership between faculty and librarians.[12]

The library-college concept has been called visionary, idealistic and unnatural. Few academic institutions embraced it. But its influence on library instruction has been widespread and deep. Shores proposed an idea that anticipated developments by three or more decades.

Education in library use during the 1940s and 1950s was characterized by heavy attention to orientation and little to instruction or to students' particular information needs. Instruction tended to mimic the training that librarians had received in library schools.

By the mid 1960s an expanded concept of library instruction, one that utilized learning theory and instructional design, began to develop. It found its origins in the dual recognition by academic reference librarians of how little understanding of library research students brought to the task and the inadequency of their staff resources to fill the information needs of an increased student body on a one-to-one basis.

In 1970, Patricia Knapp of Monteith College, an experimental branch of Wayne State University, developed an exciting program in which the library was to become an equal partner with the faculty in the educational process. Knapp contended that

> Competence in library use, like competence in reading, is clearly not a skill to be acquired once and for all at any one given level in any one given course. It is rather a complex of knowledge, skills and attitudes which must be developed over a period of time through repeated and varied experiences in the use of library resources.[13]

Knapp introduced a well-planned program that had conceptual strength and a strong theoretical structure. She emphasized method orientation, and stressed problem-solving, contrasting this with the approach of most faculty, who she contended were content-oriented. Her assignments, sequentially arranged, included:

- locating call numbers and books for particular courses
- information on particular topics, with a log or diary of steps followed
- writing a bibliographical essay
- locating information on special theories
- annotated bibliography[14]

Library sequences were designed to relate to academic classroom curriculum and to be coherent, intellectually legitimate and practical.

> The significance of the Monteith College Library Experiment was that for the first time the bibliographic structure of a discipline within the curriculum was tied to the library in an intellectual and theoretical framework by using practical library assignments."[15]

For all its importance, the Monteith experiment failed, primarily, according to Knapp, because faculty were unwilling to accept librarians as equal partners. They often, for instance, neglected to invite librarians to planning meetings. Library-faculty relationships in connection with library instruction is explored later in this chapter.

Earlham College, under the direction of Evan Farber, practices, to a large extent, the library-centered idea that Knapp envisioned. The Earlham approach also provides for differing levels of library research, printed bibliographies constructed for class assignments, lecture sessions, small group workshops and careful cooperation between faculty and librarians.

The current period of library instruction or information literacy was a product of the instructional renaissance of the '70s and was facilitated by the changing nature of higher education coupled with a rapid growth of library collections and construction of newer library buildings that gave emphasis to a book-centered educational philosophy.

Bibliographic instruction, as we said, was a "grass roots" movement that emerged from college and university reference departments. Reference librarians, constantly exposed to students who had little understanding, not only of the library but of the process that would provide them access to needed materials began to address the problems. Because they best understood the resources of the library and the user needs, they accepted the role. Unfortunately, few faculty participated, and many were less than enthusiastic.

In the past two decades, academic libraries have evidenced great interest in library instruction. The subject represents what is sometimes known in the library field as a "hot topic." Numerous monographic and periodical publications offer practical and conceptual assistance about its management and delivery. *Research Strategies*, started in 1983, is devoted exclusively to library instruction. In 1977, ACRL founded a Bibliographic Instruction Section (BIS). ALA has a Library Instruction Round Table (LIRT) and there is a Library Orientation Instruction Exchange (LOEX) Center for educational resources located at Eastern Michigan University.

RATIONALE FOR INFORMATION LITERACY INSTRUCTION

Library instruction seems to be here to stay, and its offspring, information literacy, will undoubtedly grow and prosper. There are good reasons for urging its widespread acceptance, but some compelling arguments against its adoption as a basic service are also advanced and should be considered. First, here are some of the important reasons for offering user instruction:

Undergraduates arrive on campus with the experience of a high school or public library. They may be familiar with the *Reader's Guide*, or *Infotrac*, a catalog, probably not an OPAC, and a few other sources. They are now faced with a vast group of specialized tools. Unfortunately the majority will never learn to use them and will continue to depend on references provided by guides to popular periodicals. Some may consult a few new sources, learning their contents haphazardly. Certainly those students cannot be termed information literate or good library users.

Research indicates that large numbers of users do not ask questions even when they have them. This is not because they think they know everything, but because they do not know what librarians do or because they do not want to appear unintelligent.[16] Reference service provides assistance to that relatively small group of students who ask reference questions. Systematic instruction in the use of reference sources and research techniques seems to be the method that will enable librarians to reach the greatest number of students who need it. In addition, instruction helps create users who are more likely to seek out help with their searches for information.

Libraries have championed the cause of free access to information. Access, however, is meaningless if users are ignorant about the quantity and nature of information available, how to gain entry to it and how to use and appraise it once it is acquired. College students are increasingly less able to find their way through the information maze. Control of one's own life is generally accepted as a human need, and by helping students to become more information self-sufficient, Joanne Euster argues, librarians have the opportunity to foster students' personal growth. Those who empower others, she says, are seen as powerful in their own right.[17]

Teaching library use is considered *inappropriate* behavior by a substantial number of academic librarians. They maintain that most librarians are not trained or equipped to be teachers, that they have insufficient subject expertise to compete with faculty members, and that they approach research differently from scholars. Others contend that bibliographic instruction is too expensive, too time-consuming, particularly in light of the shortage of professional staff, and therefore dilutes good reference desk service. One particularly damning criticism is that librarians use library instruction as an excuse to legitimize what they do and to give them a leg up in the struggle to attain faculty status. Indeed, Jesse Shera, for instance, in 1954, called for librarians to forget this silly pretense of playing teacher.[18] Perhaps the most frequently voiced criticism, and the one that has produced the greatest separation between the advocates and the opponents, rests in the argument that is inappropriate for librarians to teach students to find information. The librarian's job, as they see it, is to locate information and to deliver that information, extracted from the source in which it is found, in as complete a digested manner as possible; in other words, to engage in "question answering." Teaching users how to retrieve information themselves, it is felt, falls short of the ideal professional goal of maximum service delivery. Anita Schiller, for instance, questions the validity of the emphasis in library instruction on the patrons' essential obligation to locate their own information. This, she says, restricts librarians' responsibility to pointing the way.[19] Instruction detracts from the reference function. Students introduced to a few sources will stop there.

Those reference librarians who are likely to oppose the widespread commitment to library instruction contend that the services they offer are democratic, available to everyone, not limited to those receiving classroom instruction.

In summary, many librarians believe their function is to build an appropriate collection; to organize it for use and offer assistance when asked. Funds, they say, should be put into developing services designed for individual users. Providing a well-serviced reference desk, printed aids and information sheets is a better use of library resources.

It seems important to add that the number of librarians who make these arguments is diminishing, in part because of the demands associated with the use of information technology, which have resulted in the line between instruction and information being effaced. In addition, recent library school graduates have been socialized to this role. Most librarians realize that teaching a group of students in a classroom situation is far more efficient than teaching them one at a time in the reference room. And finally, there is the suspicion that reference service may be inherently undemocratic since most users do not ask questions and those questions which are asked are often simpler than those which go unasked. As a result reference becomes a service for a few. Library instruction is, therefore, more egalitarian and, further, produces more knowledgeable users and better and more frequent questions. In all these arguments, however, no suggestion is made that library instruction will replace reference service. It is a new, albeit essential, program.

PLANNING AND SETTING OBJECTIVES

A number of important decisions and tasks are associated with organizing to provide library instruction.

Libraries must first define the role their instruction programs are to play, always within the context of the institution in which they are housed. This entails careful planning, setting objectives, and evaluation. Second, the instructional role must be interpreted to funding sources, administrators, faculty, and students. And finally, librarians must gain widespread acceptance of the role.

A library instruction department, with its own staff, may be the best way to provide good service. A separate department, however, is all but impossible in most small colleges in view of their sparse staffs and other financial exigencies. As a result, academic libraries place library instruction in the reference department, where most consider it belongs, in any case. Wherever it is housed, however, library instruction should never be viewed as an appendage, or an add-on service.

Good bibliographic instruction can only grow out of a total plan developed from the realities of the institution in which the library is housed. Goals are shaped by the nature of the institution, subject emphases and major courses, the student profile, an analysis of the library user population, availability of library staff and their specializations, and a survey of library materials and facilities. Goals are limited by financial resources, human resources, lack of skills, lack of credentials, lack of facilities, lack of time and lack of imagination. Above all, goals for library instruction must conform to institutional curriculum objectives, and must define what it is that students should know in this context. Organizations that take these steps, that examine their assumptions and priorities, and that encourage risk-taking in user instruction often achieve goals which otherwise might be unobtainable.

Careful planning involves setting priorities and assuring that certain important outcomes will be reached. In order to achieve this, learner variables, situational constraints, and the personal strengths of instructors must be considered. Realistic objectives based on students' capabilities and relevant to their needs can then be set. Although there is common agreement, based on research findings, that most students lack the basic skills and knowledge to use the library effectively, some college libraries may choose to target certain groups as the first to receive instruction. For instance:

1. Academically less prepared students may warrant special consideration as a result of poor educational preparation, access to English only as a second language, or lack of motivation.

2. Student library workers, particularly if the library is one which chooses to have desks serviced by students, may rank high on the priority list.

3. Faculty. Good reasons abound for targeting faculty for library instruction. Some librarians contend that the most successful student library instruction comes through faculty who have received intensive orientation and instruction from the library staff. In any case,

faculty are crucial to the success of any user instruction program.[20]

Goals and objectives for bibliographic instruction, like goals and objectives for other parts of the library program, must be clearly written, measurable and incorporate relevant learning theory. Once they have been established, existing instruction literature should be investigated to help determine an appropriate evaluation component. A planning document is likely to be in difficulty if both faculty and students have not participated in the planning dialogue. Faculty acceptance is the key to any successful program. Similarly, if the objectives are not influenced by the perceptions of students they probably will not capture their interest and commitment.

User instruction objectives must be limited and realistic, for both pedagogical and political reasons, particularly in the early days of a library instruction program. Unqualified success is the best way to insure continuation of the service. The aims of the library instruction program should never be permitted to expand beyond its capabilities.

A variety of taxonomies and topologies have been applied to the writing of objectives. Bloom's Taxonomy of Educational Objectives,[21] which has been applied to library instruction, progresses through learning levels and can be seen in the following illustration:

Knowledge - Students will learn that Mc is filed as Mac in the catalog.

Comprehension - Students will be able to summarize the filing rule in their own words.

Application - Students will be able to find material in the catalog by an author whose name is McArthur.

Analysis - Students will be able to evaluate filing rules about Mc in other indexes, e.g. *Book Review Index.*

Synthesis - Students can plan search strategies which include reference to particular practices of research materials.

Evaluation - Student will make a judgment about the consistency of an index and therefore its utility.

At a conceptual level, Barbara Kwasnik has projected the attainment of the following skills as goals of information literacy.

1. The acquisition, through experience, of a large body of knowledge within which to integrate new knowledge. Such knowledge includes subject specific knowledge as well as knowledge of processes and methods, such as computing and rhetoric.

2. An ability to organize existing knowledge conceptually, to remember it, to recognize it, and to reorganize it. This is the basis for recognizing and producing relationships, for instance, theories or metaphors.

3. Conceptual flexibility to allow alternative methods of organization, and different and creative avenues of formulating and solving problems. Avoiding a rigid mind set.

4. An ability to analyze a problem into its components, but also to view it in a larger context. An ability to switch from one viewpoint to another.

5. To use the above to define one's information requirements effectively, to choose appropriate problem-solving aids, and to know their limitations. The ability to translate an inchoate information need into the "language" of the system, so

that the system, be it computer, library, or index, can be utilized to advantage.[22]

Sharing the goals with students and faculty is the object of all instruction, although too often it appears that the object is the technical mastery of the objective.

STAFFING THE INSTRUCTION PROGRAM

Perhaps more than any other library activity, staffing a user instruction program is a delicate matter and requires careful review of the strengths and weaknesses of the current staff. The assessment may reveal the need for changes in staffing patterns and staff development programs. It may suggest the advisability, for instance, of recruiting an experienced individual to head the program or of creating a new position, Head of Library Instruction.

Success of the program depends on the strong support of the library director. Yet many library directors are reluctant to give their wholehearted endorsement to the establishment of a comprehensive instruction service. They may see a staff that lacks full educational training, an eroding financial base and a multitude of competing demands for the library dollar. In short, a new labor-intensive service may not be enthusiastically welcomed.

The level of support for an instruction program within the library staff is also important if the undertaking is to succeed. A program of bibliographic instruction has a spillover effect on all other library services. The whole library becomes busier. As use increases commensurate demands on equipment, materials and staff appear. Making available guides and bibliographies multiplies clerical work. More knowledgeable students seek further resources, often through interlibrary loan and on-line data base searches. How prepared are staff to assume this new educational responsibility? Some may resent a user instruction program because they see themselves as librarians, not teachers, and they may feel insecure lecturing to large groups. For them, bibliographic instruction may be a threatening activity. Professional jealousies may emerge between instructional and non-instructional staff. Those not involved may feel that other staff members are attracting more than their share of attention or resources. Utilizing certain reference department members for the instruction program carries the danger of creating an "elite" a group perceived as escaping the demands normally made on library staff, people who are taken away from a reference desk made yet busier by a library instruction program. A library with a mixture of working conditions for professional staff can find itself divided and prone to infighting and resentments.[23]

Some libraries offer instruction opportunities to cataloging and technical process librarians. Katz suggests that "Widening the base of participants also counters the elitism which sometimes finds its way into programs in which only a small group is involved."[24]

Staffing a realistic program, then, means coming to grips with the following considerations:

1. How can limited staff resources be used most effectively?

2. Which staff members will teach? Reference librarians only? Other professionals? Students?

3. Should all librarians participate or just those with specific skills?

4. What skills are needed? How can they be developed?

5. What is the impact of alternate instruction approaches on staffing levels?

What makes a successful instruction librarian? Standardized tests indicate that reference librarians are somewhat more outgoing than other library professionals.[25] It should come as no surprise, therefore, that most instruction librarians find their home in the reference department. Certainly effectiveness is a primary consideration, including the ability to organize and present material in a manner that engages students and stimulates discussion. A suggestion of assertiveness, confidence and a high degree of commitment are essential attributes of a good library-use instructor. Lack of confidence is picked up quickly by students and unfortunately encourages lack of interest in the material being presented.

Only those who wish to participate in library instruction should be required to do so, unless it has been a precondition of employment, since enthusiasm is another key characteristic of the successful library teacher. Bibliographic instructors are sometimes required to offer as many as three or four sessions each day. A great deal of energy and stamina are required, but so, too, is keeping up one's enthusiasm after presenting the same information repeatedly. Political savvy and tact are also crucial elements, given the reluctance of many faculty to support or participate in library instruction.

Some argue that knowledge of subject skills is essential to bibliographical instruction. Others consider training in teaching and learning theory to be more crucial. Both are helpful, although it is unrealistic to require depth in either. Certainly, through continuing education—in-house workshops, tutorials, attendance at courses and conferences—some deficiencies can be modified. Watching and critiquing BI instructors, or being critiqued, is useful, as is analyzing the teaching styles of outstanding professors.

CAMPUS POLITICS AND BIBLIOGRAPHIC INSTRUCTION

While many librarians may be enthusiastic about user instruction, this excitement is often not shared by faculty, students or administrators. Yet support from all of these quarters, and in particular faculty, is crucial to the success of any instruction program. So important is this support, in fact, that the plan of the instruction program completely depends on the level of departmental and administrative cooperation afforded it. Without support, the library may be limited to offering library tours during Freshman Orientation Week as the only component of a library instruction program.

Bibliographic instruction has had to fight its way into the consciousness of academic institutions in order to become a matter of interest and concern. Faculty and administrators are suspicious of librarians' motives for wanting to be involved in the instructional end of the educational process. Often it is simply a matter of turf and roles. Faculty may view library instruction sessions as an encroachment on their turf, particularly when it is presented as producing "information literacy," which faculty may interpret to be solely within their domain. Requests for funds to construct library instruction programs are likely to be met with hostility and remarks such as "That's what faculty are paid to do," and "Librarians aren't teachers." Some faculty who are reluctant to support library instruction may never be won over.

Faculty intransigence is often blamed for lack of success of library instruction proposals and programs. Yet librarians must bear some of the blame, particularly for their inattention to the importance of explaining the goals of library instruction to their constituents. For instance, faculty often understand student research needs quite differently than do librarians. They do not realize that the research training in library skills they have experienced as graduate students does not, nor should it, resemble the kind of research students will undertake at the undergraduate level.[26] Utilizing their interpretation of library instruction, faculty often underestimate the librarian's potential to engage with them actively in the research-instruction process.

The approach to faculty and administrators about library instruction requires careful planning, as well as understanding of and attention to political realities. Institutional inertia produces organizational resistance to change, and library instruction in the form advocated here is new. Adoption of library instruction is facilitated by involvement of librarians in campus policy and governance bodies, and by participation in the planning of new programs. An ideal time to promote bibliographic instruction is when institutions are in the throes of major curricula overhaul or when other institutional change, such as adoption of an open admission policy or competency-based education, is under consideration.

Reaching faculty is not easy. Influential members of the teaching staff may warrant special attention, as may new faculty who can become advocates for library instruction. Ways should be sought to provide incentives to energize faculty. Wheaton College in Norton, Massachusetts, with support from the Charles A. Dana Foundation, has provided special summer seminars and per diem grants to faculty members so that they may become knowledgeable about the library. Together with the librarian, they design course-related experiences that transform students' understanding of libraries and utilize critical thinking skills. A considerable number of faculty are generally unaware of *new* information technologies and resources in any detail. They need to be introduced, for instance, to video disks, CD-ROM databases and software. These summer seminars not only permit faculty to become familiar with the new resources, they also enable faculty to think about how to utilize these resources in their classrooms.[27]

Another approach is to inform—delicately—the faculty of student's problems in using the library and in writing papers. Often faculty receive a finished product without being aware of the steps followed to produce it.

Documenting the results of a user-education program—comparing, for instance, the performance of students who receive library instruction with those who do not—can have a positive effect on faculty attitudes about library instruction programs. After all, "politics," as Patricia Breivik has said, not only concerns what a library does, but what people know about what it is doing. Being too busy doing library instruction to evaluate it in terms meaningful to faculty, administrators, board members, and legislators is tantamount to committing suicide in these days of tightening funds for education.[28]

Library instruction is labor-intensive. Campus administrators often find it difficult to understand why the library's personnel budget seems so swollen in comparison with the materials budget. It is essential, therefore that everyone who is influenced or influential be kept current about library instruction.

Another important political activity is to investigate how students view the instruction program. Students are likely to report their perceptions of its value to instructors. The success of the program may depend on their reactions.

THE INSTRUCTION PROGRAM

To those who attended college in the 1950s and 1960s, the term library instruction or bibliographic instruction may conjure up images of tedious library tours or irrelevant jargon-laden explanations of how to use the card catalog or the *Readers' Guide*. Both probably produced glazed eyes and inattention. Even today, college students are often presented a virtually useless introduction to the campus library through a unit of their freshman composition class on "bibliographic instruction." As described by Major Owens, a one weekend assignment requiring the "treasure hunt"-style pursuit of a set of standard questions via certain standard library tools is the total mandated bibliographic study for most of the nation's entering college classes. After that introduction, for all except a small percentage, the library becomes "a trysting place or the quietest place to study when cramming for an examination."[29]

One cause of Glazed Eye Syndrome is that while librarians think the intricacies of reference book use and library search are fascinating, students and faculty rarely share that enthusiasm. Another is that librarians'expectations concerning the amount of time and effort users will willingly commit to library activities are sometimes exaggerated. Conversely, of course, the expectations of library users concerning the amount of time and effort necessary to master use of indexes and develop facility in information-seeking processes may be equally unrealistic. Overkill is another source of frustration and student rejection. Librarians want to present *all* the information available. The average learner wants only the amount necessary to solve the problem or complete the project at hand.

A short explanation on library use during either first year student orientation or a unit in an introductory course is no substitute for real instruction. In addition, students will forget whatever is included in a library instruction lecture unless it is presented at a time when they need it and can link it to an assignment.

Arguing for a single method of instruction is a mistake. Although much progress has been made toward understanding how to create information-literate students, there is no single agreed-upon method of teaching library skills.

Most instruction librarians agree that it depends—on subject content, on the objectives of instruction, on the sophistication and motivation of learners, on the amount of time and facilities available, and on the instructors' own strengths and weaknesses.

Most instruction librarians also agree that user education must be integrated into the curriculum, and that interest and motivation are heightened by providing courses at the right time so that the instruction can resonate with the student's needs for information.

And finally, most agree with the contention that in order to be effective a library user education program must be designed to build on basic library use skills through a progressively sophisticated program tied to course curriculum at all levels, from first year to graduation and beyond. In order to plan cogent programs instruction librarians now study the organization of knowledge, patterns of research that underlie disciplines, and learning theory.

LEARNING THEORY, MOTIVATION, AND THE RESEARCH PROCESS

User instruction theorists have been investigating the relevance of learning theory and cognitive development as they try to understand how to shape instruction modules to produce meaningful library instruction. Jerome Bruner has asserted that successful learning is based on attention to four items: the structure of the body of knowledge to be taught, the sequence in which information is presented, the individual needs of the learner, and an understanding of the system of rewards and punishment which motivate students.[30]

Discipline Structure

Learning takes place when material presented is related to what the learner already knows because knowledge grows cumulatively. Critical thinking is always knowledge-based. Students must attain a sufficient store of information about a subject before they can think critically about it. This includes familiarity with a discipline's conventions and principles. Each discipline has its own research methodology, objects of study, and epistemological features. In the *Humanities*, for instance, research is generally an individual act. In *Science*, on the other hand, it is more often a collaborative effort. Humanists use retrospective as well as current material, while currency is emphasized in the sciences. Monographs, journal literature and archival materials are the resources of humanists. Scientists also use journals, but add to them proceedings. They also depend heavily on "invisible colleges," networks of peers doing similar work.[31]

Disciplines appear to share certain developmental stages of scholarly communication.

In their *pioneering* stages, they struggle for attention, recognition and converts. The bibliographic chain is characterized by informal communications such as newsletters, bulletins, papers at conferences, and polemical writings. A second stage, which has been labeled *elaboration and proliferation*, is distinguished by a struggle for scientific legitimacy and acceptance. In this period, the bibliographic chain becomes more standardized and includes directories, yearbooks, journals, texts, guides to subject literature, indexing and abstracting services, subject dictionaries, annual reviews and subject encyclopedias.

The *establishment* stage, where academic respectability has been achieved, includes in its bibliographic chain highly specialized publications, lists of research consultants, and research centers and institutes.[32]

Materials available to students will vary according to the stage of the discipline.

Other discipline-dependent facets of user instruction are topic selection and the nature of evidence, documentation and the use of citations (citations in the sciences demonstrate something different than they do in the humanities), evaluation of sources, and research strategy.

Sequence of Information

A number of cognitive development studies have indicated that abstract reasoning and reasoning by analogy are not common during the first two years[33] of college and may not even be attained by graduation. As a result, the expectation that instruction in the use of one reference source will be translated into the ability to use all similar tools, and that describing how knowledge is organized in a library can be converted into search strategies that fit any information need, is unrealistic. Certainly, initial library learning cannot hope to achieve these kinds of results. Presenting library instruction material that matches the student's cognitive stage of development holds greater promise of success than one which willy-nilly includes tools and tours.

Two psychologists, Jean Piaget and William G. Perry, have projected topologies of cognitive stages that bibliographic instructors find useful in planning and developing an appropriate sequence for presenting information. Piaget's scheme is a four-sequence progression through stages of cognitive growth. Only the last two relate to library instruction at the college level. These, Piaget termed *concrete operations*, the stage at which logical thought begins, and *formal operations*, when abstract reasoning occurs. The majority of students function at the stage of *concrete operations* or at a transition point between it and the *formal operations* stage. As a result, presumptions about students' abilities to employ substantial abstract reasoning should be lowered, and instruction planned accordingly.[34] Perry's model, also composed of four stages of learning behavior, specifically describes college students.

> *Dualism* [he says] prompts students to see the world as black or white, right or wrong. In this stage, they believe that right answers exist for everything and that an authority, usually their professor, knows the right answer. Diversity of opinion produces confusion for this student. Students in this stage may also think that all knowledge is known and if the library is approached properly there will be no dead ends in a search.
>
> *Multiplicity* causes students to question the assumption that absolute answers exist. They are easily confused, however, about different points of view and frequently base decisions on personal bias or emotion.
>
> *Relativism* produces students who do not see knowledge as absolute. Nonetheless, they continue to link objective evidence with personal bias. By this stage, students think analytically and can evaluate their own and others' ideas

and consider the qualifications of experts in light of possible opinions and biases.

Commitment to Relativism is the stage we hope students can achieve by graduation or before. At this point, they can analyze or synthesize information, use objective arguments, understand the qualifications and biases of experts and can understand that new evidence may require changes in points of view.[35]

Individual Student

While the above cognitive states describe development stages, students reach those conditions at different times. Learning theorists believe that individuals possess unique ways of deriving meaning from the environment and experiences. The way in which they learn has been influenced by family background, life experiences and personal goals, and by cognitive strengths and weaknesses. How people use symbols—words, numbers, senses—the cultural conditions which affect how they gain meaning from their surroundings, and how they think, all have importance in determining how they learn. "Academic research is, in essence, an intensely personal and subjective undertaking."[36]

Learners are motivated to learn what they are willing to learn when they are willing to learn it. As a result, not all methods work with all students. While librarians cannot design instruction to fit the individual learning behavior of each student, they need to remember that all human beings resonate, digest and integrate information differently. Providing choices in library instruction methodologies helps to mitigate to some extent the problem of individual learning. Programmed instruction may reach some students. Others may profit from paper-writing workshops and some may find point-of-use explanations of reference material most satisfactory.

Understanding Rewards, Punishments and Student Motivation

Unless they are offering a separate course, librarians lack the power of a grade to motivate students. Yet there are factors that impel students to learn which, properly understood, can be utilized by librarians. Among these are a desire on the part of students to succeed rather than fail, a need to be liked, and the wish to please those they respect. The importance attributed by the classroom instructor to a particular activity has a strong influence on how students perceive that activity. Research has indicated, for instance, that the value structure of students is such that many students would not really be concerned about the accuracy of information presented in a class paper if the instructor were not concerned.[37] A faculty member who considers library instruction important will communicate that esteem to students.

Another source of student motivation is the proximity of a goal. The closer its realization or the threat of not reaching it, the greater the motivation. Students are most receptive to library instruction when a research paper has been assigned. Insecurity and fear of independent action propels them to seek help. A good experience in response to a request for assistance induces students to continue to request aid on other occasions. It is well to bear in mind that most students are unnerved by the library. They may fear personal failure or wish to avoid appearing stupid and may well make an effort to distance themselves from such uncomfortable surroundings. Needless to say, librarian attitudes in response to student requests for information can help set a positive tone and create good information-seeking behavior patterns.

STRUCTURES AND FORMATS OF LIBRARY INSTRUCTION

A smorgasbord of user instruction structures and formats exist. Most libraries use one or more of the following methods: group tours, self-paced tours, classroom lectures, library lectures, credit courses, non-credit courses, labs, handouts, signage, displays, point of use information, AV productions, instructional aids, workbooks, programmed instruction, computer-assisted instruction, team-taught courses and term paper clinics, to mention a few. The most difficult task is deciding which will be most successful in reaching the greatest number of students in a *meaningful* way.

Orientation

Despite the problems described earlier in this chapter, if the college has an orientation period at the beginning of the academic year, the library should probably participate. Orientation, however, should not be confused with library instruction. It merely means introducing new users to the physical facility, and to the procedures and policies involved in using the library. All bibliographic instruction includes an orientation dimension, but the converse is not true. An orientation program should provide information about where different resources and services are located, point out the principal study areas and describe the process of obtaining help. Orientation may also be an appropriate time to distribute the library handbook, if there is one, and other printed instructions which students might find helpful in getting acquainted with library services. Orientation might take the form of a self-guided tour on tape or in a pamphlet, a traditional guided group tour, a slide or video-tape program available in the library, or a computer disc describing the library and its services. Most librarians contend that a self-guided walking tour of the library is more helpful and popular than the traditional group orientation tour, particularly if the route is well-marked and each desk or station has an explanation of the purposes and policies of that service.

Few librarians are satisfied with their efforts or the results produced by orientation. On the other hand, orientation can be useful because it provides an opportunity for librarians to demonstrate their concern and approachability. Orientation should not be directed only toward students. New faculty can profit from it, as well. Here, however, the method of choice is a one-on-one tour of the library by either the head of public services or the library director. Not only will it be helpful to the new faculty member, but it can serve as an effective public relations activity and can be used to build faculty support for bibliographic instruction as well as for other library programs.

Structures

The *structures* of library instruction most commonly practiced in academic libraries are course-related instruction, course integrated instruction, team teaching, separate credit courses, and library workshops.

The structure selected depends as much on faculty attitudes and preferences as it does on the library staff. Faculty provide the greatest impetus for student use of the library and for the program of library instruction. Relevant, and therefore successful, instruction occurs when faculty understand and support the aims of library instruction and are willing to engage in dialogue with librarians at the early stages of course planning.

Perhaps the most frequently chosen structure is course-related. Individual professors set aside time, usually a single class period, during which librarians lecture in a classroom, or give a tour while describing and displaying specific—usually subject-related—reference materials. In this situation, instruction librarians are challenged to present, in no more than 50 minutes, everything they think students might need to know to successfully retrieve information in that subject area.

This is particularly difficult if the instruction is attached to first-year seminars, basic writing courses, or other general education requirements. Too often library skills are taught in a vacuum without reference to their application. A good learning experience is need-driven and active. Without a research project, what is learned may be irrelevant and/or quickly forgotten.

A number of departments in colleges have included library instruction in a general research methods course or, alternately, a literature-of-the-field course, with librarians and faculty sometimes team-teaching or at least dividing the material to be presented.

Separate library instruction courses sound attractive to many librarians. They carry with them the power of the grade, are subject to the scrutiny of the curriculum committee, and therefore carry faculty approval. But few students are attracted to such a course. Even stand-alone workshops on the online catalog fail to draw library users in sufficient numbers to justify the expenditures of time, space and professional expertise.[38] Library instruction works best when it is discipline-related and applicable to work in progress.

Many librarians support a structure in which bibliographic instruction is mainstreamed, that is, appropriate materials and attitudes are integrated into all courses where they can reasonably be included. This requires that bibliographic instruction be directed, not towards students but faculty, who in turn teach the students.

Another course-related structure is directed toward developing research strategies. Faculty construct assignments around information in or through the library and join librarians in providing guidance on approaches to retrieving materials. Finally, students are turned loose to discover their own learning resources. This is similar to what Knapp tried at Monteith College. Evan Farber suggests further that libraries and faculty collaborate in developing alternatives to the term paper.

Students may be assigned, for instance, the preparation of an annotated bibliography or be given a practical assignment.[39]

Group instruction has limitations, as does one-on-one assistance at the reference desk. Term paper counseling, workshops or clinics followed by individualized tutorials, has emerged as a response to the restrictiveness of reference desk service and formal classroom instruction. Instruction in this case focuses on a real need rather than on something perceived as a need. Assistance automatically corresponds to the level of student development at a particular time.

What is important to remember is that with library use instruction, as with other skills, one-shot training is never enough. A good program includes sequentially planned instruction, progresses with the curriculum and is based on the student's cognitive abilities and levels.

Content of Instruction

There are as many opinions about what should be included in user instruction as there are user instruction librarians. There is simply too much content to be able to teach it effectively. Good user education integrates skills and methodology. Information literacy is not only knowing resources but knowing how to utilize them both in and out of the library.

In its initial stages, the thrust of bibliographic instruction is best approached as problem-solving. Students learn how to ask a question, how to determine whether it is answerable, how to learn whether it has been asked before, and how it may differ from similar ones which have been posed. Secondly, students are shown how to approach information. This might include an understanding of the research process, research strategy and knowledge of tools and resources. Third, students are taught about the nature of evidence, how to evaluate it, how to assess what is enough and how to determine the validity of a statement. A final component should consider documentation and the use of citations. The importance of contradictions, individual perceptions, points of view and analysis should be introduced when students seem able to handle ambiguity. At this point the library should be treated as evidence to be examined.[40] The ability to locate information, form opinions and make informed judgments prepares students for lifelong learning and produces independent and competent adults.

At a more advanced level, user instruction is discipline-oriented and students gain an awareness of information resources in their fields, the structure of the literature in that subject, and its research patterns and strategies. In addition, attention is given to evaluation of sources in light of the behavioral patterns in the discipline.

Formats of Instruction

Among the variety of formats of instruction are lectures, tours, workshops, self-instructional printed packages and workbooks, slide/tape materials, automated computer-assisted instruction, point of use, and printed materials.

The most basic format of library user instruction is appropriate signage. Notices, displays, and signs must be properly prepared and conspicuously hung. Handmade and poorly drawn materials will render the library even more confusing. Library user guides that describe the services and categories of materials available for public use require careful preparation, publication and dissemination. What the guides cover is a matter of subjective preference and the design of the instruction program. They may describe the scope of the collection, search strategy techniques, use of subject headings, titles and call numbers of representative or key reference sources, indexes and abstracts. They may include "How to Use an OPAC," "Checking out a Book," "Sources in Music" or "Using Government publications." No matter their content, what matters is the readability of the material presented. Library guides, handbooks, and other library information handouts are not easy to write, primarily because they attempt to describe information that is inherently complicated to explain. Unfortunately, these publications are often riddled with jargon and tend to be didactic.

Bibliographies on specific subjects, prepared in response to an observed need among students or to a faculty request, are a common format for library instruction. They may be passed out following a lecture, or kept for distribution at the reference desk. Printed materials are flexible and have multiple uses, but they can be time-consuming to prepare and there is always the risk that they will not be read, but will end up in the trash.

Pathfinders, another print handout, combine bibliographic instruction with methodology, usually within the context of a specific, fairly narrow subject. Pathfinders give students a search strategy that moves them from general sources such as encyclopedias to appropriate catalog headings to indexes. Pathfinders are commercially available, but can also be locally generated.

Point-of-use instruction appears in either print, audiovisual, or computer format and involves locating explanations of specific reference sources with the material itself. Reinforced learning is said to follow from simultaneously reading the instructions and using the tools.

Programmed instruction in which students can proceed at their own pace has become popular in recent years. Formats vary. Workbooks are common and there is increasing attention to computer-assisted instruction. The virtue of programmed instruction is that users can work their way through small segments or modules of information. It is particularly effective when the material to be learned is detailed and lends itself to being broken down into units.

Computer-Assisted Instruction (CAI), also known as Computer-Based Instruction (CBI) or Computer-Assisted Learning (CAL), presents opportunities in programmed instruction that no other format can offer. Among its benefits are interactivity, that is, it can provide immediate and appropriate feedback. CAI is flexible, can accommodate varying skill levels, and can be adapted to changing end-user requirements. It can be used any time the library is open, yet it is easily transportable, and can be made available at remote sites outside the library. CAI, on the other hand, is more expensive than other formats because it requires costly equipment and because preparing programs requires lengthy, time-consuming preparation since there are currently very few ready-made commercial packages available. Interactive video, too, has great potential as a format for user education. The major drawbacks again are its considerable cost and the lack of expertise among librarians in this new field.

SUMMARY

In the past twenty-five years, academic reference librarians have championed the cause of library instruction as a route to producing information literate students and providing them with life-long learning skills. This includes teaching students how to construct information search strategies and to locate, evaluate and effectively use information no matter where it appears. Good bibliographic instruction empowers students by giving them greater control of their lives.

Faculty may not accept the concept and may resist the appearance of librarians in classrooms. Librarians who teach need to incorporate learning theory and present students with a variety of well-designed options. Library administrators considering implementing a wide-ranging library instruction program have to plan carefully how to staff the reference department and maintain other services.

NOTES AND SUGGESTED READINGS

Notes

1. Helen R. Wheeler, *The Bibliographic Instruction Course Handbook* (Metuchen, NJ: Scarecrow Press, 1988), 2.

2. Richard Dougherty, "Stemming the Tide of Mediocrity: the Academic Library Response," in *Libraries and the Learning Society: Papers in Response to a Nation at Risk* (Chicago: American Library Association, 1984), 3-21; see also Dougherty, Richard, "Editorial," *Journal of Academic Librarianship* 10 (May 1984): 63.

3. Ernest Boyer, "Connectivity," in *Libraries and the Search for Academic Excellence* (Metuchen, NJ: Scarecrow Press, 1988), 7.

4. Summarized from James Kennedy, Jr., "Integrated Library Instruction," in *User Instruction in Academic Libraries*, comp. Larry Hardesty and others (Metuchen, NJ: Scarecrow Press, 1986), 232-3.

5. Material about the history of library instruction was gathered from Hardesty and others; Thomas Kirk, *Increasing the Teaching Role of Academic Librarians* (San Francisco: Jossey-Bass, 1984); Patricia Senn Breivik, *Planning the Library Instruction Program* (Chicago: American Library Association, 1982); Ann Roberts and Susan Blandy, *Library Instruction for Libraries* (Littleton, CO: Libraries Unlimited, 1989).

6. Kirk, 19.

7. *Ibid.*, 16.

8. Hardesty and others, 5.

9. *Ibid.*, 17.

10. *Ibid.*, 46.

11. *Ibid.*, 48.

12. Kirk, 21.

13. Patricia Knapp, "A Suggested Program of College Instruction in the Use of the Library," in Hardesty and others, 153.

14. Roberts and Blandy, 2.

15. *Ibid.*, 3.

16. Carla Stoffle and Cheryl Bernero, "Bibliographic Instruction Think Tank I: Looking Back and the Challenge for Think Tank II," in *Bibliographic Instruction: The Second Generation*, ed. Constance Mellon (Littleton, CO: Libraries Unlimited, 1987), 14.

17. Joanne Euster, "Technology and Instruction," in Mellon, 55.

18. Anita Schiller, "Reference Service: Instruction or Information," in Hardesty and others, 189.

19. *Ibid.*

20. Breivik, *Planning*, 4.

21. Benjamin Bloom and others, *Taxonomy of Educational Objectives* (New York: Longman, 1977).

22. Barbara Kwasnik, "Information Literacy: Concepts of Literacy in a Computer Age," in *Information Literacies for the 21st Century*, ed. Virgil Blake and Renee Tjoumas (Boston: G. K. Hall, 1990), 141-2.

23.   John   Cowley   and   Nancy   Hammond,   *Educating Information Users in Universities* (London: The British Library, 1987), 22.

24. Maureen Pastine and Bill Katz, ed. *Integrating Library Use Skills into the General Education Curriculum* (New York: Haworth Press, 1989), 19.

25. *Ibid.*, 18.

26. Stephen Stoan, "Research and Library Skills," *College and Research Libraries* 45 (March 1984):99.

27. Sherrie Bergman, "Course Transformation Support for Dana Faculty/Librarian Partnership Program at Wheaton College," Memo to Faculty (Norton, MA: 23 January 1991).

28. Breivik, *Planning*, 11-14.

29. Major Owens, "The Academic Library and Education for Leadership," in *Libraries and the Search for Academic Excellence*, ed.   Patricia Breivik and Robert Wedgeworth (Metuchen, NJ: Scarecrow Press, 1988), 14-15.

30. Mary Reichel and Mary Ann Raney, ed., *Conceptual Frameworks for Bibliographical Education* (Littleton, CO: Libraries Unlimited, 1987), XVIII.

31. Kirk, 40.

32. *Ibid.*, 39.

33. Bobbie Collins and others, "The Needs and Feelings of Beginning Researchers," in Mellon, 73.

34. Constance Mellon and Kathryn Pagles, "Bibliographic Instruction and Learning Theory," in Mellon, 138.

35. Sonia Bodi, "Critical Thinking and Bibliographic Instruction," *Journal of Academic Librarianship* 14 (July 1988): 150-153.

36. Sharon Rogers, "Science as Knowledge," in Mellon, 126.

37. Kirk, 57.

38. David King and Betsy Baker, "Human Aspects of Library Technology: Implications for Academic Library User Education," in Mellon, 97.

39. Kirk, 41.

40. Cowley and Hammond, 3.

Suggested Readings

Beaubien, Anne, Sharon Hogan and Mary George. *Learning the Library*. New York: R. R. Bowker, 1982.

Breivik, Patricia Senn. *Planning the Library Instruction Program*. Chicago: American Library Association, 1989.

Breivik, Patricia Senn and Robert Wedgeworth. *Libraries and the Search for Academic Excellence*. Metuchen, NJ: Scarecrow Press, 1988.

Cowley, John and Nancy Hammond. *Educating Information Users in Universities*. London: The British Library, 1987.

Hardesty, Larry and others. *User Instruction in Academic Libraries: A Century of Selected Readings*. Metuchen, NJ. Scarecrow Press, 1986.

Kirk, Thomas. *Increasing the Teaching Role of Academic Librarians*. San Francisco: Jossey-Bass, 1984.

Knapp, Patricia. *The Monteith College Library Experiment*. Metuchen, NJ: Scarecrow Press, 1966.

Mellon, Constance, ed. *Bibliographic Instruction: the Second Generation*. Littleton, CO: Libraries Unlimited, 1987.

Reichel, Mary and Mary Ann Raney, ed. *Conceptual Frameworks for Bibliographical Education*. Littleton, CO: Libraries Unlimited, 1987.

Roberts, Ann and Susan Blandy. *Library Instruction for Librarians*. Littleton, CO: Libraries Unlimited, 1989.

Wheeler, Helen R.. *The Bibliographic Instruction Course Handbook*. Metuchen, NJ: Scarecrow Press, 1988.

Chapter 13

CIRCULATION SERVICES

The final step in the process of making library materials available, once they have been acquired, cataloged, and identified as needed by a user, is circulation. The circulation function involves lending library materials and is based on answers to the following policy decisions:

— Who can borrow library materials?
— What materials will be lent?
— For how long may they be borrowed?
— What will happen if they are not returned?

It is easy to underestimate the importance of the circulation function. Many librarians complain that although systems of bibliographic access are improving, the systems of document delivery remain slow and cumbersome. Mechanisms have been developed that permit libraries to tell patrons when books or journals are due back, to recall particular items, or to determine if other libraries own particular books or journals. On the other hand, two or more weeks may elapse before the materials are placed in that patron's hand. Michael Buckland reminds us that a book at hand is used more than a book on the other side of the campus, let alone on another campus or in another state.[1]

The circulation staff performs a number of crucial but difficult functions in a college library. It must: rapidly and accurately issue, record and check on the return of several hundred items daily; administer the materials reserved as required reading by faculty; and maintain the efficiency of the materials supply service by keeping the stacks in good order, returning books promptly to the shelves and following up vigilantly on all requests for books that cannot be located by the user. The circulation staff, in consultation with the director or assistant director, generally creates and articulates circulation policies and keeps statistics of use. In addition, they have a major role to play in book conservation since materials that require replacement, binding, or repair are easily spotted at the circulation desk. They also must keep control of book loss, assist in guiding people to the locations and services in the library, and serve those using equipment such as photocopiers, CD-ROMs and microfilm reader-printers. In recent years, due to lengthened library hours, the circulation department has had the additional responsibility of general library supervision at times when other staff members are not on duty. This list does not cover all the routines and responsibilities of the circulation department staff, but it provides a rough description of its activities.

New students and faculty members often receive their first introduction to the library at the circulation desk. Failure at this point to provide fast, efficient and friendly assistance may have a damaging, sometimes permanent, effect on the image of the library. The circulation staff heavily influences the manner in which readers connect with materials. Success in carrying out its work requires understanding how the library functions, careful planning and organizing of duties and genuine concern on the part of the staff for the range of library constituents.

ORGANIZATION

The form of organization used in a circulation department is shaped by the size and nature of the student body; the size and composition of the library staff; the policies regarding open access, reserve books and the security of the collections; the physical arrangements for study and staff working quarters, and the nature of the college program itself, including its history and traditions.

If the college emphasizes independent study, and requires, for instance, a junior or senior paper, and the library has adequate carrel space, it will be helpful to place students in carrels near the subject collections where they are working. Assigning carrels generally falls within the jurisdiction of the circulation department. If teaching in the college is accomplished primarily through the use of textbooks or required paperbacks, there may be little need for an extensive reserve materials collections. Reserves, then, can probably be handled behind a circulation desk if extra bookstacks are provided to handle them. If the faculty assign a wide range of monographs, scholarly articles and other sources, much more extensive provision for reserve reading will be needed and will modify the organization system. If the circulation department is charged with maintaining copy machines, helping to load and unload microforms, servicing CD-ROM workstations and video playback machines, or teaching patrons how to accomplish these tasks—then equipment should be as near the circulation desk as is feasible. Often the circulation department is responsible for insuring the maintenance of the new book section, special book exhibits and the faculty publication shelf, if one exists.

In most small college libraries, the head of circulation is a senior support staff person with strengths in management, human relations and control over detail, and reports to the library director or the head of reader services. Circulation heads supervise staffs of many students and a few clerical employees. Some college libraries have combined reference and circulation areas into public service departments with a librarian as head. A few other libraries, experimenting with alternate arrangements based on automation, have included circulation in an operations department. The danger of creating too many bureaucratic layers between the head of circulation and the library director is that circulation staff will not see themselves as equal partners in the enterprise and will feel deprived of any say in how the library operates. While there must be communication and coordination through department heads to whom responsibility and authority have been delegated, directors cannot remain too aloof and remote or their best efforts will prove abortive. The pulse of the library is often revealed by students at the circulation desk as they give service to users.

STAFF: QUALIFICATIONS FOR CIRCULATION WORK

Conscientious, able circulation staff can find themselves fully occupied just trying to adjust to constantly shifting demands as various forces within the daily working situation affect their decisions. At the circulation desk, they are the interpreters of rules established for the sake of fair play for all users. Unfortunately, from many readers' point of view, no rational reasons explain these rules in the first place. Why shouldn't students be permitted to check books out for as long a borrowing period as faculty? Why shouldn't books be renewable by phone instead of having to be brought back to the library every two weeks, or month, or term? Why are faculty allowed keys so that they may use the library when other people are sleeping? Why are faculty denied access to the building when no staff are present? Why should high-school students be barred from the library when the college is seeking the best graduates from these schools? Why should high school students be allowed when they are not paying tuition? Not a day passes but the circulation staff is made conscious of these or similar problems. Indeed, it is a good week for the circulation department when their actions do not result in a complaint headlined in the student newspaper, or in the electronic version of a campus-wide suggestion box. The ability to explain sympathetically something difficult, and perhaps controversial, becomes a crucial skill. Ideal circulation staff members are never at a loss when it comes to explaining library regulations to students and faculty, particularly when they are mystified or have complaints. In daily work, circulation staff will be called upon to respond to high school students who have been assured by their principals that they are welcome to use the rare book room, seniors who complain that they cannot use their carrels because of the continued evening disturbances created by "underclass barbarians," professors in neighboring colleges who protest violently because they are ineligible for the privilege of "indefinite loan" which is accorded institutional faculty members, and alumni threatening reprisals if not assigned a research study.

The circulation head in a small college library is responsible for the greatest number of staff and for running a large and varied operation. Good administrative skills are required, among which are knowing how to delegate work and how to instruct assistants thoroughly and with patience. It is difficult to apportion unpopular work periods fairly among the staff, while covering the hours of service adequately and assuring that all of the department's routines are accomplished. Given the number of students working at the circulation desk, it is important to maintain close supervision. Being an effective head or member of the circulation department requires cheerfulness and stamina to survive a stressful daily routine. Circulation work involves handling a great deal of detail and, like technical services work, many records, and demands meticulousness, accuracy and orderliness. However, unlike technical services, circulation work must be performed in the face of constant interruption.

WORK AT THE CIRCULATION DESK

Circulation is one of the few library services where policies, procedures and rules have been developed, written down, and made available routinely to the public. In fact, without these rules, circulation librarians leave themselves open to severe problems. The most important underpinning of an effective set of circulation policies and procedures is a set of clearly defined objectives for the circulation department, framed within the larger context of the college library's aims and goals.

Who May Borrow Materials?

College libraries make loans to their faculty, students, and college employees and their families as a matter of course. Registration cards or staff cards are used as identification. Other persons may be given permission to use the facilities of the library within the building, with exceptions as mentioned later, but often restrictions are imposed on outsiders borrowing library materials, If library use within the building by persons not associated with the college becomes too heavy, or results in administrative problems that conflict with the service provided to students and faculty, it may be necessary to limit even reference use.

Alumni are encouraged to use the library and may generally borrow books, although some limitation may be placed on the number of books that can be taken home if the college collection is small and demand by students and faculty heavy. Identification is made by checking the borrower's name in the alumni directory, by alumni association card, or through the office of the alumni secretary.

As a rule visiting scholars and students from other institutions are allowed to use the college library for a limited period, at least, although they may be required to present a letter of introduction from the librarian of their college or university. Such use is often associated with holidays and intersession periods when students from the college have gone home. If there is a reciprocal cooperative agreement between libraries within a geographic area, or in a network, to permit inter-institutional library lending, that agreement must be honored. Library cards or a student's ID card are generally accepted by a cooperating member. For most consortia, the common agreement is that libraries who participate will supply the bread-and-butter needs of their own students and faculty and reserve reciprocal privileges for more specialized materials.

Requests for provision of services, particularly loans of materials, to persons not affiliated with the college, especially local residents, are often met with resistance on the part of college library workers. Taking care of the needs of local research workers can sometimes present vexing problems for the circulation staff. While the library is glad to help meet the legitimate demands of scholars, whether or not they are part of the college, it is extremely difficult to determine where to draw the line for outsiders. Rather than deny use to all members of the community outside the campus limits, some attempt should be made to identify those who have a special need to turn to the college library. In order to codify this use, each library must analyze its own institutional character and its larger geographic community.

Developing this policy and deciding how far a library can go in offering services to outsiders is not the exclusive task of the circulation department, it is a joint effort of all effected departments. Among librarians, it is a principle of reciprocal service that those in the community who are not associated with the college will first make use of other local library resources, such as the public library. Sometimes users are unfamiliar with the protocol and must be educated in how to gain entry to the system. If a local community member is writing a scholarly article or book, or preparing an address requiring the use of research materials unattainable elsewhere, college library services should probably be made available to them. Resident borrowers cards, issued for a fee, may help to eliminate casual or inappropriate use by non-college connected patrons. The cards permit users to borrow materials, ask reference questions and gain entry to interlibrary loan. Online searching services are generally not offered free to these users. Resident borrower card charges rarely cover the full costs of providing library services. However, the fees do permit a library to establish a policy regarding what services it will provide, for whom, and on what occasion.

High school students present special problems for the college library. They come to the college library because their school libraries are generally closed the moment school lets out, because the public library does not own needed research materials, because the college library is closer to home, or because the college library is a good place to socialize and be seen with college students. Whatever the reason, the problem becomes acute when substantial numbers of high school students attempt to use the college library. Unfamiliar with the larger library, they may make more demands on the staff, may displace college students at the reading tables during busy evening hours, or may be less responsible in their use of library materials, removing, misusing or. marking up books. They have often proved a disturbing or disruptive influence in the reading rooms, particularly when they are traveling in a group. While all of the aforementioned is true, no college librarian wants to bar all high school students from all use of the library. In communities with inadequate public and school libraries, a special window to the world of learning for ambitious, inquisitive high school students may be a college library. Some solution may be found in a referral procedure, whereby a high school or public librarian verifies a student's need to use the library. College libraries generally extend the courtesy of interlibrary loan to local high school libraries, which also helps to ameliorate the situation.

CIRCULATION POLICIES

Circulation policy in a college library should be governed by knowledge of the collection, of the patrons, and of use patterns. Frustration over not finding sufficient titles on the shelf must be balanced against limited, too short loan periods that also frustrate users. Automation and turnover in circulation help have resulted in college libraries utilizing fewer varieties of loan periods. Yet circulation librarians must be wary of substituting ease of operation for quality library service. Studies of procedures can guide program revision.[2]

Most college libraries have a handbook in which the regulations of the library on loan periods, renewals, overdue charges and the like are set forth. Some have separate student and faculty handbooks. Generally libraries lend all materials without restriction with the exception of reference books, certain government documents, periodicals, microforms, maps, music, other nonbook materials and associated equipment, reserve materials, and special collections, particularly those containing early imprints and manuscripts. New books may be displayed temporarily or circulated first to the requester. Not all campus borrowers may enjoy the same loan period privileges. Loan periods range from a minimum of two weeks or less, particularly for outsiders to a maximum of a term or more for faculty, unless the item is requested by another reader or for reserve. If in circulation, a book may be "recalled" and the patron requesting it notified when it becomes available. Whatever the period of circulation, libraries routinely retain the right to reclaim a book for use by another reader after it has been checked out for two weeks.

Faculty members are often granted special extended loan privileges, with the understanding that all material charged out will be returned or renewed at the end of a term, or at the end of the regular academic year. This privilege may not apply to new books, including fiction and popular nonfiction, although faculty sometimes are permitted to borrow materials denied to others—such as periodicals, reference books and audiovisuals—often only for a short period of time, say twenty-four hours or over a weekend.

Certain students, thesis writers, for instance, or those involved in independent research, may be granted extended loan periods or the privilege of charging material to a carrel or study in the stacks. In all instances of special extension privileges, it is understood that any specific title may be recalled for the use of another borrower at the end of two weeks, and that violation of carrel privileges or failure to respond to recall notices may result in the loss of extended privileges.

The brevity of many periodical articles, the frequency with which they are consulted when they are indexed in tools available in the reference department, and the availability of copying machines, has led most librarians to encourage their readers to use journal files in the library building. Some libraries circulate periodicals if users have special reasons for needing them outside the building, and still others make no distinction between periodicals and books, although they tend to limit the circulation of current, unbound volumes. Rules about periodical circulation are more often bent than those regarding other library materials because their use is harder to predict and define. An art student, for instance, may need to study illustrations in the studio, or a geology student compare rock drawings with actual specimens in the laboratory. Most faculty and students would like the library to liberalize journal circulation policies, but at the same time would be irate if the articles they needed were unavailable. Needless to say, it is easier to adopt a more liberal stance from a formerly conservative one. Unfortunately, the reverse is usually required and is far more difficult to impose. Having a single individual responsible for making decisions about exceptions helps to provide consistency in policy interpretation.

Renewals in college libraries range from no restriction, unless requested by another borrower, to one renewal or none.

Some libraries require renewals in person, others allow them to be effected by phone. Sheila Intner found that:

> The decision on whether to encourage or discourage renewals ought to be based on evidence of material use patterns, cost to administer, and similar facts. Instead, it seems to be an arbitrary choice made without any scientific foundation. No statements that limited collection size, heavy demand, or insufficient personnel to administer renewals are made to explain the stricter regulations, although it may be that any or all of these are the reasons behind them.[3]

Imposing fines and dealing with the failure of patrons to return books are among other duties of the circulation department. Fines are levied, not to increase the library's income, but to discourage the monopolization of books so that other readers may have a chance to use them also. Unfortunately, most users and probably most staff perceive overdue fines as punishment rather than incentive. Although some college libraries do not charge fines, and seem well satisfied with their handling of overdues, most colleges levy fees in order to impress upon students the need to return books promptly when they are due. Daily overdue fees range from 25 cents to $1.00. Overdues for reserve material are charged hourly, not by the day, and amounts are usually at least twice as high as for ordinary circulating materials. Many libraries offer substantial discounts if fines are paid in cash when materials are returned. For lost books the basic charge is normally the list price, plus a charge for ordering and preparing its replacement for library use. These can represent significant costs for an individual, given the current price of monographs. When fines are not paid, or materials not returned, most colleges threaten students with withholding grades, diplomas and transcripts. Some do not permit registration unless library bills have been settled. Others prefer to rely solely on persuasion, first the librarian's and if that fails, the more convincing influence of the dean. In the small college this is undoubtedly the best method; larger institutions may find it impractical. Library personnel and procedures are not infallible and mistakes occur. The possibility that material has been returned and escaped proper check-in procedures should not be discounted. Offers to double-check the shelves, or to make exceptions on certain occasions, are always in order.

Most college libraries do not charge faculty for overdue materials. However, the license taken by some faculty members often leads to friction between them and the library staff. Perhaps the most difficult and important job of the circulation department is to make users realize that returning materials in a timely fashion helps to insure quality library service for everyone. If faculty could be made aware of the extent to which abuse of current policies handicaps the library, their borrowing habits might improve. Some college libraries have persuaded their institutions to withhold faculty paychecks unless materials are returned. This seems unnecessary. Any official actions taken against faculty should be framed in the most diplomatic language, with every effort taken to avoid unpleasant confrontations. Faculty with materials in high demand, or faculty leaving the campus permanently or for an extended period of time, call for particular attention. If materials remain unreturned, further action by the library director or the dean may be required.

Circulation personnel, like other staff, sometimes appear to exhibit a we-they attitude toward faculty, an attitude exacerbated by faculty demands for special privileges. Almost everyone on the faculty is in favor of library regulations—but some consider that those restrictions should apply to others rather than to themselves. Librarians need to maintain an open mind in administering rules. If a professor is occasionally permitted to keep a journal out because of the nature of the research, or a student asks that the circulation desk contact the person who has checked out a certain book because it is needed immediately, those actions do not signify that the library has jettisoned all of its central policies to make an exception. Perhaps what is needed is more evidence that librarians can temper their regulations with consultation and common sense and that professors can listen as well as lecture. Ranganathan's famous third dictum to librarians was not "every book in its place on the shelf," but rather "every book its reader."[4] A broad and liberal interpretation of the rules furthers the library's objectives, provides better service to users and enables staff to use their best judgment for the good of the library and its community.

STATISTICS OF LIBRARY LOANS

The circulation department is responsible for keeping statistics of library loans. Those regularly kept should conform to the data requested by national statistical agencies, including those needed to complete the HEGIS (Higher Education General Information Survey) report. Of course, any special kind of statistic needed in the local situation should also be maintained. Generally, primary statistical data include the total number of items lent for home use and borrowed from reserve. The number lent for home use may be broken down by type of borrower—faculty, student by class and/or major, other, including college employees, alumni, and local community users. Circulation figures are often organized by Dewey or Library of Congress classes, as well as by format—audiovisual, periodical, and so on. Reserve book loans are categorized as overnight loans or one-, two-, or three-day loans, depending on the period established by the library. Libraries often keep a record of reserve book loans used within the building in order to provide some management information and comparative data for use from one year to another. If the library maintains carrel loans, these statistics may be itemized and included in the total. Statistics regarding interlibrary loans have become increasingly important. Libraries maintain data on the number of items borrowed and loaned, perhaps broken down further by type of material (book, periodical article, ERIC report, etc.). The information generated by ILL statistics is important for assessing the degree to which libraries are net lenders and net borrowers, as well as for use in collection development.

Interpreting and giving meaning to circulation statistics is difficult at best. They can represent the volume of business during a given year, and that volume can be compared with the business of other years. Too often, however, statistics of out-of-building circulation are used inter-institutionally in an attempt to compare libraries' effectiveness in reaching their constituencies. Teaching traditions, student attitudes and abilities, proximity to other libraries, the strength of the collection, geographic setting, loan periods themselves, and the rest of the ingredients that factor into the nature of a college library have an impact on library circulation. These variables are often ignored. Raw data are utilized to make unjustified claims. In addition, circulation statistics generally ignore the use of books and other materials inside the library building, thereby omitting a substantial area of library activity. Present in the library, but invisible in use statistics, are patrons who read current magazines, browse in the stacks, consult microfilm, use CD-ROMs and videos, and look up information in reference books. Compiling complete records of this kind of use is virtually impossible without allocating substantially more resources to keeping statistics than the results could possible justify; nor is it necessary.

A variety of short-term statistics gathering devices are available to the library to provide additional information on library use. Subject, author, and title fill-rates can be tracked during one week periods using patron questionnaires. The library can investigate how many persons use the building on an average day by sampling certain weeks during the academic year. Reserve collections can be studied to see which books placed on reserve are seldom used. Patterns of use by type of borrower can help determine collection development protocols. Shelving studies can be conducted to reveal in-house use of library materials. Chapter 20 describes many of these short-term statistics-gathering, evaluative methods. Statistics do not explain the uses to which library materials are put, but they often help administrators to support budgets, to improve services, or to explain the library's contribution to the college.

PROTECTION OF LIBRARY MATERIALS

The circulation department has primary responsibility for the security of the library's collection. College libraries are generally arranged so that the flow of traffic coming from the entrance and exiting the building is channeled past the circulation desk. In this way, materials may be easily returned, as well as circulated. Circulation staff are positioned to keep a watchful eye on what is being carried out of the library. Most libraries with fully open-access book collections have found it necessary to impose some method of checking the book bags and briefcases of readers leaving the library. Some have installed an electronic monitoring device to reduce losses. Others have added gates that permit egress only by action of an attendant.

The increase in theft of library books in recent years has been a major concern of some college libraries, particularly those in urban areas. On the other hand, some librarians detect a diminution of mutilation in periodicals due to the widespread acceptance and use of photocopying. There are those who place the blame for increased theft on our so-called permissive society, and it is true that many students do not regard removing books from the library as any more serious than illegal parking. Many faculty members and college officials do not appear to be concerned either, and it is rare to find the faculty- or student-sponsored honor code applying to the library. While librarians try to avoid making a moral issue of the problem, they are responsible as custodians of college property for taking every reasonable precaution to protect library material from vandalism and theft.[5]

Some librarians would like to think that their losses are not as bad as they are, and seem reluctant to talk about them. A more positive approach suggests, once again, the need to properly communicate and emphasize to the college community that the real sufferer in this matter is not the library, but the reader, both in loss of time and failure to be able to read assignments. Cooperation of faculty and college administration is most important and must be enlisted. Campaigns against theft are hard to mount. Penalties canot be imposed in the absence of hard evidence and threats of penalties do little to enhance the reputation of the library as a user friendly institution. Vigilance at the exit door probably represents the best defense. Some loss is inevitable. Some students assigned to inspect book bags for library materials shy away from requesting users, especially older users, to open their briefcases. Librarians bear responsibility for explaining students' hesitation to faculty and for encouraging them to display their book bags willingly for examination.

The circulation department is also in a strategic position to assist in the much neglected task of library book conservation. Circulation assistants can be taught to recognize books requiring repair or binding when they are returned to the circulation desk. While student and clerical staff cannot be final judges of whether a book should be conserved, replaced or simple discarded, a system can be established whereby damaged items, when returned, can be set aside after they have been checked in. A record of their whereabouts is made and the items are forwarded to the person in charge of conservation. Staff members handling reserve materials can scrutinize them at the end of a term when they are removed from reserve. If binding and repair are required, they can be expeditiously dispatched to the bindery in order to be available when once again needed. Circulation librarians who train student assistants to shelve books and "read" shelves (insure that books are in proper order by classification symbol) should also explain to them how to identify materials whose condition is poor and what procedures to follow in these situations. Attention should be drawn to proper shelving of large quartos and folios, the use and misuse of bookends, the importance of avoiding placement of heavy volumes on their fore-edges, and the need for loosening up crowded shelves in order to prevent damage when a book is pulled out. Promotional materials in the form of bookmarks can carry book preservation messages to users. Book shelvers should also keep an eye out for any sign of parasites—molds, silverfish, cockroaches, bookworms, and termites—and measures should be taken to prevent their spread. Temperature and humidity controls should be monitored frequently because these two factors are of the utmost importance in paper preservation, and circulation staff most frequently receive complaints about temperature and humidity.

CHARGING SYSTEMS

An efficient charging system, essential to a good circulation service, shows, first, what books are charged out to readers and where books are when they are not in their place on the shelf; and, second, when books charged out are due for return. Charging systems should permit libraries to know all material checked out to a single reader and provide librarians with the kind of management information they require for collection development and reporting.

By the end of this decade, if not sooner, virtually every college library will have an automated charging system, probably as a module of an integrated library system that includes, in addition, at least an OPAC (Online public access catalog) and acquisition and cataloging modules. With this system in place, libraries can retrieve machine-generated (that is, free from human errors in filing) circulation information, can check on the borrowing status of an item, learn if it should be on the shelf, or if it is charged out to someone, on order, or in process. Before the appearance of automated circulation systems, libraries could not track all of their materials all of the time. The shelf list, plus borrowing files, permitted a degree of inventory control, but the method was slow, cumbersome, labor intensive and subject to substantial error.

Automated circulation systems intensify the need to establish rules about who may use the library, which materials may be used, and for what length of time, and what the consequences of late or non-return of materials may be. The need for consistency in the face of automation has been responsible for the alteration of many circulation policies. Before a policy can be transferred to an automated system, it must be clearly articulated and unambiguous. Computers can only enforce rules, not interpret them.

In addition, automation brings new considerations about what constitutes invasion of privacy of borrowers. College libraries must insure, while collecting management information about borrowers—student level (first year, senior, and so on), major field; faculty by discipline; and the type of material being borrowed—that histories of individual borrowing behavior are not available. Most colleges program their systems to delete names of borrowers as soon as the materials they have charged out are returned.

Faculty members, suspicious of possible plagiarism, may ask to see student borrowing records. If they are non-existent—that is if they have been expunged from memory—there is no possibility of the library meeting these inquiries and a potentially unpleasant confrontation is avoided. On the other hand, an offer to help the faculty member search for possible origins of the suspect text may prove politically beneficial and satisfy the request.

A trace of whimsy accompanies Paul Metz's description of automated circulation system requirements:

> Above all, of course, a circulation system has to manage the circulation of materials. It has to marry patron and book temporarily, divorce them on the book's return and process a variety of 'engagements'...recall of books already checked out, holds for books that can't be found

or haven't yet cleared cataloging. It has to block the privileges of patrons who don't play by the rules and should automatically restore their privileges when they comply by returning their long overdue materials and/or settling their fines. It has to generate correspondence for overdue materials, usually keeping track of the number of notices sent so that the tone of successive letters will become more urgent.[6]

Properly designed automated systems can store, sort, select, search, and print large volumes of data. Two basic items of information are brought together in charging out a book: a bar code representing the borrower and a bar code representing the item to be borrowed. The former is affixed to an identification card retained by the borrower and the latter is attached to the item to be borrowed. The third element required to complete a circulation transaction is some indication of when the item must be returned to the library, usually a date due slip or transaction card. Based on this information, overdue notices are automatically generated, circulation statistics are compiled, and, most importantly, information about the current location of materials is easily accessible. Automated systems speed up charging, relieve the staff of monotonous routines and are more accurate than manual ones. As "wired campuses" become more common, and OPACs with circulation information are made available to faculty and students in their offices, users will place their own holds or reserves on library materials.

RESERVE BOOK SYSTEMS

Reserve book service is the term employed when books and other library materials assigned by the faculty in their classes are withdrawn from the open shelf collection and placed behind the circulation desk or in a separate area or reading room where they are made available on a restricted basis. These books, of course, are in heavy demand and the purpose of the procedure is to ensure that every student in the class has a fair chance to read the assignments. How a college library is viewed on a campus is often a function of how well it handles reserves. Indeed, two key elements which help to solidify a college library's reputation among students and faculty are the reserve system and the periodical collection, and the extent to which they are judged satisfactory.

Reserve books are usually of two kinds; those in heavy demand, charged out for two-hour periods during the day and for overnight; and those suggested for collateral reading and made available for a one- or three-day period. Fines levied for reserves are of sufficient magnitude to ensure the prompt return of materials so designated.

There are various methods of administering reserve books. The most common one is to place them behind the reserve desk, or the circulation desk if there is no separate reserve section, and to hand them out to students on request. Without adequate control, some books will be misplaced, some mutilated, and still others stolen. It is also necessary to allow students in some classes access to a considerable number of reserve books, and perhaps to magazine articles, pamphlets, and other types of library materials in a manner that gives them more freedom of access than the reserve book system permits. One arrangement that has proved satisfactory has been to maintain a small storage area for reserve books adjoining the main circulation desk. Here the reserve books are arranged by course on open shelves, but the exit, usually beside the circulation desk, is controlled by turnstile. This plan permits students to enter the reserve area and look over the books in a particular course, select what they need, and charge the material at the circulation desk for reading in the building. In large colleges with heavy enrollment it may be necessary to place all books on "closed reserve."

Many librarians, and some faculty members, have a low opinion of the value of reserve book reading and would like to see a college without a reserve shelf at all. President Henry Wriston of Brown and Lawrence Universities fought a life-long battle against the reserve system, contending that the most successful professors induced students to buy books and to read widely from the library collections. They required writing which included bibliographical work and had short or non-existent lists of books on reserve.[7] Studies have demonstrated that the percentage of reserve items that do not circulate rises sharply for lists longer than 20 items.[8] But neither the frustrating experience of trying to secure faculty cooperation in turning in reserve lists ahead of time nor the difficulty of insuring the return of reserve books when due should blind the librarian to the fact that this service touches the work of professors more closely than almost any other activity of the college library. The importance of the reserve collection will vary by college as well as by individual faculty member. The college whose faculty members emphasize textbook learning will view reserve materials as less important. Faculty at colleges that place a premium on student research will similarly put fewer books on reserve. The most prevalent form of college teaching today, however, combines lecture, text and reserve reading. In the face of that reality, librarians have no recourse but to design the best reserve system possible. One further use of the reserve collection is to insure that students who cannot afford to purchase a course's required texts will have them available in the library.

The care and handling of reserve book systems is difficult, at best, and requires great tact and diplomacy. Librarians find it embarrassing to have to report to some faculty members that the majority of books that were placed on reserve for their courses have never been used. In addition, it is difficult to explain that in order to provide wide access to users, all books are removed from reserve at the end of each term. Yet a librarian who does not take these actions becomes an accessory in the provision of a lesser education.

The major requirements for an effective reserve service are the following:

1. An efficient system for securing faculty reserve lists.
    Librarians complain bitterly about their inability to
    convince faculty to send reserve lists in a timely
    fashion. Yet some blame for the failure must rest on
    the library. College book stores are far more
    successful in obtaining lists of texts than are libraries.
    They send notices early, follow-up frequently, and
    make faculty aware of the consequences of not
    providing the necessary information. Librarians should
    insure that the same is done for reserves. Nonetheless,
    library staff may have to work overtime early in the
    semester to place requested materials on reserve
    because, despite pressures, some faculty will inevitably
    turn in their lists on the first day of classes.

2. A definite policy regarding duplicate copies of reserve
    books. Although formulas have been devised, none
    has proved entirely satisfactory.

3. Faculty cooperation in distinguishing on their reserve
    lists between books that are likely to be in heavy
    demand and those that can be placed on a less
    restrictive basis than the two-hour day and overnight
    loans.

4. Keeping the reserve shelves as free as possible of
    inactive books. Some professors place many more
    books on reserve than students will ever find time to
    read. Librarians who make frequent studies of reserve
    book use and keep the faculty informed of the results
    have a far better chance of persuading instructors to
    shorten their lists.

Books placed on reserve are, in effect, inaccessible to patrons
who require them for general use rather than to fulfill a course
assignment.

Reserve books, it should be emphasized, cannot be treated as a subordinate phase of college library service simply because most librarians are disenchanted with the system. If the library exists to serve the primary needs of instruction courses and if the instruction method requires the use of reserve books, then the library cannot escape its responsibility for complete cooperation and support. Periodic reviews of student and faculty satisfaction with the reserve system will keep it functional.

COPYRIGHT AND COPY SERVICE

The two technological developments that have had the greatest impact on libraries in the last several decides are the computer and the copy machine. It is hard to imagine a college library today without copy capability. Some wags have commented that contemporary college students have substituted copying documents for reading them. Certainly it is true that manual note-taking based on reading is fast becoming a lost art. Underlining, on copied documents, is now the preferred method of identifying important sections in text. For libraries, the ability to copy has generally helped to preserve material, has saved space, and has improved efficiency. For instance, loss has been diminished to some extent by students' ability to copy periodical articles when in the past the temptation to steal or mutilate the issue might have been irresistible. On the other hand, early copying machines were designed to handle single pages rather than books, and many volumes suffered broken spines when users attempted to insure that complete pages of text were reproduced. Fortunately, new copying machines are book-friendly and most material can be duplicated without damage to the binding. Many college libraries, however, have not yet had their older machines replaced.

The widespread use of copying machines engendered a full and sometimes acrimonious debate between publishers and librarians about copyright. For many years libraries have been operating under "fair use," a principle that was finally given statutory recognition in Public Law 94-553, the copyright law that went into effect on January 1, 1978. What this means is that educators and researchers are generally given the right to copy factual, educational, scientific or informational works for their own use. Creative, factional or entertainment works are less likely to come under the "fair use" exemption, as are items copied in greater numbers. The determination of "fair use" also depends on the degree of harm suffered by the copyright owner, whether the user should have purchased a copy or paid royalties, and how the material was used in succeeding works.

The following general rules dictate the procedures and extent to which copying is permissible in a college library.

1. Library photocopying services must display warning signs about copyright restrictions specified by the Register of Copyrights.

2. Library photocopying must be done without the intent of direct or indirect commercial advantage. This means that the library will not charge more for copies than is necessary to cover both the indirect and direct costs of making these copies. Equipment, utilities, supplies, postage, and labor costs attached to identifying, locating, and retrieving the material to be copied, making the copy, billing, record keeping and reshelving may all be included.

3. Libraries may make a single copy which becomes the property of the user providing the library has no indication that the copy will be used for any purpose but private study, scholarship or research.

4. Copying in substantial quantities reduces the market for a work. Therefore multiple copies are forbidden.[9]

There is no doubt that copyright has been seriously abused by the uninhibited photocopying of books and articles on coin-operated machines and other copying devices. While it is true that these abuses occur outside the monitoring capabilities of library staff, there is no excuse for librarians themselves to participate in violating "fair use."

Reserve collections are most vulnerable to copyright violation. "Fair Use" guidelines offer support here, as well. Creation of an anthology of readings by faculty, for instance, requires publisher permission, as does repeated use of a periodical article over several terms. Securing permissions is generally considered a faculty responsibility, although librarians, familiar with the rules, must alert faculty to them. Some libraries require faculty to sign a document attesting to their compliance with copyright restrictions.[10] The emergence of local computer networks has raised the question of how to encourage the development of electronic reserve collection and honor copyright and it appears that license fees will need to be negotiated.[11]

INTERLIBRARY LOAN SERVICE

Interlibrary loan came of age, or at least vastly matured, in most academic libraries during the last decade following the inauguration of the OCLC ILL subsystem in 1979, which permitted electronic verification, ordering, queueing and receipt notification. Five factors account for the growth of interlibrary loan: 1) availability of computer-based protocols, 2) development of national and regional electronic catalogs, 3) modification of the national code to permit ILL service to undergraduates, 4) acceptance of access rather than ownership as a secondary level goal in college libraries, and 5) improvements in delivery systems.

Activity levels have escalated and technological support increased, but staffing has not. The typical interlibrary loan office in a college library is still an adjunct of reference or circulation, with one support staff member and a few student workers. Only through a combination of technological power and staff productivity have college libraries been able to meet the increased demand for service.

Work in interlibrary loan divides naturally into that connected with loaning materials to other libraries and work associated with borrowing materials for patrons from other libraries. Requests coming to the library have already been verified by the borrowing library and searching them in the collection, packaging them and sending them out is relatively simple. Often, items reported to be in the collection are missing, fragile, or on reserve and therefore unavailable for loan. A request may be for articles in journals, necessitating that photocopies be made. Facsimile transmission and adequate staffing can facilitate responses to the borrowing library within hours of receipt of the request. At present the lack of extra staff in ILL means that facsimile transmission is reserved for rush items, or for service between members of local networks. Libraries with their complete holdings entered into OCLC or other bibliographic networks have experienced strong demand for older materials as well as for materials they own by virtue of their mission or location.

Many libraries honor requests from the libraries in their vicinity or local network without imposing any fees. Most college libraries are reluctant to impose fees other than reimbursement for the cost of processing the material, or for photocopying journal articles. These generally run ten cents a page with a one- or two-dollar minimum. Collecting fees takes staff time and this consideration, along with a general antipathy toward charging for library services, has held down the costs.

Records of each transaction are kept and reported on a monthly basis. Libraries that are net lenders, that is, libraries that loan more than they borrow, often exhibit conflicting attitudes about this status. While they are proud to be of service to other libraries, and they enjoy their reputation as strong libraries, there is concern that assistance may be rendered at the expense of regular users. Even when reimbursement for net lending activity is part of a regional agreement, payments never cover all the costs of interlibrary service, especially those associated with staffing.[12] Funds received are useful, however, in supplementing expenditures, supplies, postage, telephone and other miscellaneous expenses associated with interlibrary loan services.

Lending material is simpler than borrowing it and the job is usually relegated to student employees under supervision. One change in procedure resulting from widespread use of the OCLC subsystem is that requesting libraries now identify a string of libraries as their potential source of material, and list them in the order that requests will be placed with them. Each participating library is given four days to respond before the request moves to the next library on the list. Many libraries feel impelled to try to respond within twenty-four hours—one reason for the success of the subsystem as a cooperative venture. Larger libraries with higher levels of activity in lending and borrowing find it more difficult to reply quickly. Sometimes the requested material is located in branch libraries and must be locally retrieved before it can be sent out. Three days may elapse before an item is actually posted. Several more days may pass before the package arrives. The cycle would then have required ten to twelve days to complete. On the other hand, libraries within a region with a regularly scheduled courier van service often have request-to-delivery times of forty hours or less.

The process of borrowing materials begins with a request by faculty or students for an item not owned by the library. Staff determine whether requesters have time constraints and in what sources the citations appear. Too often students deliver strings of undigested references, gathered while searching in various electronic databases, and request that the described items be borrowed. The lists must be pared to materials that show the greatest promise of relevance. Time constraints become even more salient when considering the type of material to be borrowed. Requests for older materials in foreign languages, for instance, take longer to find. In those cases it is well to warn borrowers of potential delay. Citations are verified using OCLC, RLIN or print sources, and a group of potential lending libraries is established. Choices among lending libraries are based on proximity, participation in reciprocal borrowing agreements, lack of fees charged to users, the library's reputation for promptness, or simply item availability.

Borrowers request records are used to track the item, its return and assessment fees. Periodically, collection development officers study ILL records to determine whether certain types of materials are routinely sought, an indication that their purchases for the collection is probably warranted. ILL borrowing patterns are also examined to identify libraries with which it would be desirable to establish reciprocal borrowing agreements or deposit accounts to reduce paperwork.

ILL has grown as an activity, but it is not a substitute for collection development at the local level. Requests in certain subject areas identified as marginal to the library's purposes, but nonetheless deemed worthy of extensive service, are met through commercial document delivery services. Borrowing always involves a time delay, often unpredictable in its duration. Users cannot be certain that the material will be available when they need it or even whether it will be useful until they have it in their hands. Undergraduates feel these constraints most keenly. They, however, can often be satisfied with the substitution of other relevant materials in the collection. The distinctions between access and acquisition may gradually fade in users' minds with their increasing ability to use office terminals to request items and receive them through campus mail without knowing whether they are locally or externally owned.

Many local and state library networks formed in the past twenty years have made resource sharing their primary focus of activity. Despite rocky starts, excessive concern with hierarchical requesting patterns, and fear of collection raiding, most are now successful in meeting a high percentage of their interlibrary loan requests. The networks that have flourished best have a computerized bibliographical database that integrates OCLC, a relative absence of search request hierarchies, a method to compensate the largest net lenders and a good delivery system. With these elements in place, the question of participation in multi-type networks no longer troubles academic libraries. Indeed, academic libraries have found that they need the resources of other types of libraries to answer the information requests of their users.

Interlibrary loan is often administered by a support staff member, though policy changes as well as any decision about participation in one or more networks are ultimately made by librarians. As new access systems and other innovations are forged at the national level, staff at the local level need to know about them, as well as to be consulted about the local implementation of protocols and policies, and have their concerns and advice transmitted upward.

SUMMARY

Many users, especially students, judge library quality by the helpfulness of circulation staff and the reliability of their record keeping. Circulation staff are charged with the difficult and demanding task of enforcing library regulations about who may borrow which materials and for what purpose, and are constantly faced by patrons who believe their need is unique. Automation has brought order to circulation files, diminishing the opportunities for error, and has also permitted the generation of management information particularly useful in collection development work.

Reserve collections are of special concern to students and faculty who want these materials readily available. Circulation policies can be adjusted to improve the extent to which users find the materials they seek on the shelf, but even with improvements most libraries still impose fines for overdue materials and charge for replacement copies.

Interlibrary loan activities have mushroomed in recent years and show no signs of abating. Interlibrary loan is not a substitute for local ownership of materials needed frequently for users. Proximity, research has shown, is the strongest inducement to use library materials. The distinction between access and acquisition is gradually being effaced as users are increasingly able to request items on campus terminals and receive them through campus mail without knowing whether they are locally or externally owned.

NOTES AND SUGGESTED READINGS

Notes

1. Michael Buckland, "Library Materials: Paper, Microform, Database," *College and Research Libraries* 49 (March 1988): 117-118.

2. Pat Weaver-Meyere, Duncan Aldrich and Robert A. Seal, "Circulation Service Desk Operations: Costing and Management Data," *College and Research Libraries* 46 (September 1985): 418-431.

3. Sheila Intner, *Circulation Policy in Academic, Public and School Libraries* (Westport, CT: Greenwood Press, 1987), 59.

4. S. R. Ranganathan, *The Five Laws of Library Science* (Bombay: Asia Publishing House, 1931).

5. Terri L. Pedersen. "Theft and Mutilation of Library Materials," *College and Research Libraries* 51 (March 1990): 120-28; and Alan Jay Lincoln, "Reducing Personal Crimes," *Library and Archival Security* 10 (1990): 77-98.

6. Paul Metz, "Circulation Systems: The Tinker Toys of Library Automation," *Journal of Academic Librarianship* 13 (January 1988): 364d

7. Patricia Senn Breivik and E. Gordon Gee, *Information Literacy* (New York: American Council on Education, Macmillan, 1989), 32-33.

8. Patricia Senn Breivik and Robert Wedgeworth, *Libraries and the Search for Excellence* (Metuchen, NJ: Scarecrow Press, 1988), 28.

9. James Heller, "Copyright and Fee-Based Copying Services," *College and Research Libraries* 47 (January 1986): 29-30.

10. Bruce A. Shuman and Joseph J. Mika, "Copyright Issues: The Law and Library Interests," *Library and Archival Security* 10 (1990): 103-115.

11. Stuart Milligan, "Database of Scanned Reserve Readings," Electronic Communication on Public Access Systems Forum, March 14, 1991). PACS-L@CUHUPVM1.BITNET.

12. Charles B. Lowry. "Resource Sharing or Cost Shifting? The Unequal Burden of Cooperative Cataloging and ILL in Networks," *College and Research Libraries* 51 (January 1990): 11-19.

Suggested Readings

Boucher, Virginia. *Interlibrary Loan Practices Handbook.* Chicago: American Library Association, 1984.

Boucher, Virginia. "The Impact of OCLC on Interlibrary Loan in the United States," *Interlending and Document Supply* 15 (3), 1987.

Buckland, Michael. *Book Availability and the Library User.* NY: Pergamon, 1975.

Hammond, Carol Burroughs. "Kids, the Academic Library, and the Schools," *College and Research Libraries News* 50 (April 1989) 264-266.

Hubbard, William. *Stack Management: A Practical Guide to Shelving and Maintaining Library Collections.* Chicago: American Library Association, 1981.

Intner, Sheila. *Circulation Policy in Academic, Public and School Libraries.* Westport, CT: Greenwood Press, 1987.

Miller, Connie and Patricia Tegler. "An Analysis of Interlibrary Loan and Commercial Document Supply Performance," *Library Quarterly* 58 (October 1988) 352-66.

Strong, W. S. *The Copyright Book; a Practical Guide.* 3rd edition. MIT Press, 1990.

Trochim, Mary Kane. *Measuring the Circulation Use of a Small Academic Library Collection.* Washington. Office of Management Studies, Association of Research Libraries, 1985.

Chapter 14

INTERPRETATION AND OUTREACH

"Yes" or, at least, "I'll try" are the appropriate words for college librarians to use in answer to suggestions or requests from their constituents, contends Evan Farber, Director of the Earlham College Library.[1] This attitude, as undergirding for all college library endeavors, produces not only positive relationships, but leads to creative service patterns. A staff willing to listen and take action is the cornerstone of a library's efforts to interpret its services and reach out to its community.

The terms publicity, public relations and interpretation are sometimes used synonymously. Interpretation in this chapter describes an activity a little more sober than publicity, a little less pretentious than public relations. Applied to the field of college librarianship, it may be defined as the act or process of bringing information about the college to bear on library functions and policies, and the interpretation of library functions, policies and procedures to the public served by the college library.

In the course of buttressing the curriculum by supplying excellent materials, providing information for faculty research, developing competent staff, balancing budgets, even publicizing their programs, and performing their myriad other tasks, library directors and their staff must never lose sight of the evangelical dimension of their mission: to spread the word of the joys of reading and to celebrate the life of the mind. They do this through intellectual and cultural outreach, that is, by sponsoring cultural opportunities and promoting intellectual pursuits.

Activities intended to interpret the library or those designed to appeal to the intellect are in no way mutually exclusive. Nor, however, do they always coincide. In this chapter they are treated separately.

EXPLAINING THE LIBRARY

The functions of the college library are not fully understood by those who are responsible for its welfare at the top level or by those who use its services. Even less well understood are the activities performed by staff. Students often think a librarian is there to "check out books." The goal of interpretation is to communicate to each potential library user or user group those features of the library's program most pertinent to their interest.

Many library directors think about how best to promote their services, and some even allocate funds for that purpose. Fewer, however, understand the importance to library interpretation of their public presence, or that of their staff, on the campus. Consciously or unconsciously everyone connected with the library performs an interpretation function. Any carefully conceived interpretation program includes both personal contact between librarians and those with whom they must interact, and a program of planned distribution of written information about the library. The persons to whom the library must interpret its work are: 1) campus personnel, including college administrative officers, boards and committees, faculty and students, and 2) off-campus groups such as the local community, alumni, Friends of the Library and professional associations. Written information about the library is disseminated principally through annual reports, handbooks, college catalogs, local student and library newspapers, articles in college or professional periodicals, booklists, bulletin boards, signs and exhibits.

An average director works 45 hours a week at a minimum, 60 plus hours during peak times. Few librarians consciously allocate two to three hours of a normal week to activities outside the library. Yet many studies of effective directors indicate that those who devote a regular portion of their work time to cultivating and educating faculty and administrators in places other than the library are more likely to make a lasting impact on their institutions.[2]

Interpreting the needs of the library to administrators, faculty and students is crucial to their fulfillment. College presidents are busy people. They seldom use the library and usually hear about it only if is brilliantly or poorly managed. Convincing the president, therefore, to support the library's current and future needs requires determination and fortitude and depends, to some extent, on how well the library's track record has been communicated. Librarians are often reticent about proclaiming their successes and victories. Yet presidents must learn of them somehow. Some presidents appreciate receiving regular formal or informal reports; others prefer that their chief academic officer inform them of the library's ongoing needs. These latter are the same presidents who only involve themselves in library matters when questions of capital expenditures arise or when ceremonies calling for their presence occur. They may, in fact, be unreachable on a personal basis by library directors. In that case, a provost or other chief academic officer becomes the main focus of attempts to explain, interpret and promote the library.

Library directors who participate in campus-wide planning and development efforts have opportunities to tie the needs of the library to other campus projects, or at least to alert others to library needs. Whether and the extent to which librarians participate in faculty meetings varies on each campus and controls the degree to which faculty meetings represent a fitting place to discuss library concerns or promote library-sponsored events. Major changes in library policy are best presented in person to the faculty, but only after they have been shared with the relevant committees or individual faculty members and assurances have been received that these groups or individuals are prepared to publicly support proposed changes.

Most librarians find it necessary to communicate in writing with faculty once or twice a year. These memoranda or newsletters may contain explanations of new bibliographic instruction opportunities or new database searching services or other programs too important to relegate to the grapevine or chance visits by the faculty to the library.

Whereas the director bears chief responsibility for maintaining good working relations with the president, senior administrators and the faculty as a body, members of the library staff, including student assistants, are the library to students and must bear a substantial amount of responsibility for impressions this group gains of the library. Students meet the library as they would a person. Clearly, staff must welcome them warmly and with an attitude that conveys helpfulness and interest. There can be no room on a library staff for employees who cannot balance concern for library procedures with a sympathetic understanding of student or faculty behavior, or who have difficulty dealing with people whose backgrounds differ from their own. Conflicts and problems with patrons require delicate handling in order that mutually acceptable solutions may be reached with a minimum of rancor. Library staff know intimately how many errors the library can and does make. In view of this, it seems foolish to adopt a posture that suggests that the library is always right. Even when enforcing rules, staff must guard against permitting a natural concern for order and fairness to deteriorate into rigidity. How libraries view their users is made manifest not only in over-the-counter transactions, but in words and the tone used in written communications such as overdue notices, closed reserve procedures, and instructional signs.

Occasional audits taken to insure that the reality of daily library service coheres with descriptions of it appearing in promotional material, or with the library administration's understanding of how it is to be delivered, may produce surprising results. Problems emerge. If the same ones appear in the suggestion box, prompt attention is required. Opinion surveys about the library can also be used to learn how users feel about the services they are receiving. Although surveys find users generally satisfied, major problem areas can surface.

LIBRARY RELATIONS WITH OFF-CAMPUS GROUPS

Some off-campus groups that use the college library can become important supporters of the library. These include local residents, alumni, donors and Friends of the Library.

Most college libraries allow adult local residents to use the library, especially to browse or use the reference collection. Many will issue resident borrower cards at a modest fee permitting adult users the same library privileges as undergraduates. Under special circumstances students in local high schools will also be granted access, although they are not as well received as their adult counterparts. This is because of the tendency of high school students to come in groups and distract others and because their needs are often met equally well by the public and school libraries. What is important to remember in dealing with local residents is that town-gown relations are of concern to the college. Bad treatment exacerbates what is sometimes an already troubled relationship. Friendly, cooperative staff help to foster good feelings toward the college and the library among local residents.

Alumni

Contemporary college administrators have come to understand the wisdom of developing strong and supportive alumni and have advanced numerous programs designed to facilitate continued interaction with them. Libraries, too, have recognized the importance of keeping the college library in the minds of alumni, and have attempted to cement relationships in a number of ways. They have encouraged alumni to continue to use the college library. Many local alumni do indeed borrow materials long after they have graduated from the institution. Other alumni seek, information by mail because they are aware of special or unique materials or collections in the library or because they have established a beneficial relationship with a reference librarian. Occasionally library staff will contribute articles about the library or about books to the alumni magazine. Once in a while, they may develop a book list that will be sent directly to alumni, or appear in the magazine. Sometimes alumni magazines choose or can be prompted to highlight the library. Recent issues of the alumni magazines of the College of Wooster and Augustana College featured articles about alumni in information science professions and interviews with the library directors with students.[3]

Alumni are often generous and college libraries sometime benefit from their largesse, particularly when a library project has been singled out for attention by the development office. Alumni gifts may come in the form of major donations from members of a particular graduating class. Libraries have received major book collections, funds for computers, endowed chairs for library directors, or even library building additions from this source.

Friends of the Library

Some colleges have found it useful to form a Friends of the Library group. Organizations vary from campus to campus, but they are generally composed of a mix of faculty, alumni, trustees and local residents, all of whom share an interest in helping the library fulfill its educational and cultural mission. An association of library constituents often brings together a group of men and women who love books, reading and libraries and who are willing to help the college library by publicly proclaiming its virtues and by adding to its resources. Friends Groups have traditionally focused on generating financial support for the library's special collections, on the joys of book collecting as a hobby and on sponsoring formal programs, sometimes with visiting lecturers. Most are currently found in small, elite private liberal arts institutions and fit the above description. Some recently formed groups, however, follow a model closer in structure to Friends groups in public libraries, assuming a more active stance and engaging in a variety of fund raising activities to support the library. A decade of such activities by a dedicated group at Gustavus Adolphus College has enabled the college to establish an endowment that supports the entire book budget.[4]

It is essential to consult the college development office about whether to establish a Friends group, whether an endowment fund should be part of such an effort, how to set financial goals and how to levy membership fees or giving levels for different categories of benefactors. The potential for turf encroachment is high and care must be taken to coordinate all solicitations. Development office staff are most concerned about any weakening of the annual campaign which raises unrestricted funds for the college. However, experience at colleges with special library campaigns and annual funds indicates that the two types of fund-raising complement each other and stimulate additional giving.[5]

Friends groups are best formed when there is a strong demand for them by some influential collectors and donors in the community. They often provide funds for needed book purchases, directly contribute valuable books and collections, and donate funds for and sponsor cultural events such as lecture series or literary readings. Friends' organizations do not require elaborate machinery to be successful. Some have bylaws, but most dispense with formalities, although there are usually officers and an advisory council. The time demanded from the library to keep an organization active can sometimes seem excessive unless an alumni, a local resident, a trustee, or a retired professor is willing to take charge and accept responsibility for sending out notices, assuring that events occur, and keeping records. Some Friends groups generate interest by publishing an occasional bulletin or by producing a brochure describing the organization.

Successful Friends groups, such as those at Bryn Mawr, Franklin and Marshall, Smith, Amherst, Occidental, and Gustavus Adolphus Colleges for instance, have demonstrated that the time and effort devoted to them has been valuable. If a Friends organization seems to have outlived its usefulness or has degenerated, as they sometimes do, into a social club, it is probably better to usher it out of existence or simply let it lie dormant for a few years.

Other Library Friends

Many library supporters choose not to align themselves with Friends organizations, but they are nonetheless good friends. Faculty members who actively use the library for their own scholarship and teaching can and will, if asked, speak knowledgeably about library programs to the wider campus community. Trustees who are bibliophiles and understand the need to help fund the purchases of particular treasures for the library's special collections, or who are technological experts eager to support the library's funding request for an online system, can be counted on at budget time. In the same way that trustees and faculty are potential allies of the library, so, too, are college students. Student employees may become library advocates, as may other students who understand how they have profited from the library's services. A senior class may designate the library as recipient of its class gift. Not only is the gift itself welcome, but it can represent a stepping stone to future contributions.

Local residents who are active book collectors merit cultivation. While all private collections are not equally useful to the library, some may be of great value. A comprehensive set of publications by and about a given State, for instance, or the complete works of a noted American author may constitute an impressive addition to the library. A complete run of the *National Geographic* from 1945 to the present may not. But collectors of one kind of material can sometimes, because of their propensity to collect, be guided into gathering distinctive collections. Ideally, college librarians and benefactors collaborate on the definition of a desired collection and share responsibility for seeing it develop. Dr. and Mrs. Frederick Maser, for instance, support a Christina Rossetti collection at Bryn Mawr College and The Book of Common Prayer collection at Drew University, either by donating an item or by donating funds to the library to cover part or all of the cost of purchasing one.

Most college libraries have an established procedure for handling memorial gifts to the library in honor of a deceased faculty member or alumni. Large memorial bequests require particularly careful handling and obligate the library to respond with a number of suggestions of possible gifts to be purchased with the money. Small memorial donations may be used to purchase a specific book or group of books, to buy equipment, or may simply be placed in a fund to be spent at the librarian's discretion. Needless to say, all gifts require acknowledgment by the library director. A happier variation of this practice, one that has the long term potential to raise significant sums for library materials is the individual book endowment approach. At Davidson College in North Carolina and at Rollins College in Florida the libraries offer individuals the opportunity to donate, over a period of time, sufficient funds to ensure the ongoing purchase of a book or other form of library material every year or two. Individual and group donors establish funds to honor individuals on their birthdays, graduation, anniversary or retirement, or as memorials. In 1991, the endowment for one book was $350 at one college, $500 at the other, and the colleges had each raised over $800,000 in this manner. In an average year $10,000 is added to the fund. Development office staff manage the details of accepting and acknowledging the gifts, library staff may or may not keep records of donors linked to book titles, although increased use of integrated library systems does permit this kind of record keeping with less expenditure of staff time.

THE MEDIA OF INTERPRETATION

Media commonly used to interpret the library to its community are:

> Annual reports
> Handbooks
> College catalog
> Student newspaper
> Newsletters and booklists
> Exhibits and signs
> Campus networks

Most libraries will use all of these media at one time or another to describe and interpret themselves. With desk-top publishing, libraries now can (and should) make every document they generate look as though it has emerged directly from the college print shop.

Annual Reports

The annual report, while nominally prepared for the president and the board of trustees of the college, is generally widely distributed, both on and off campus, It serves to record the year's achievements and is an indication of what the librarian hopes to accomplish in the future. Most reports describe collection growth, reader services, staff, and library use, and include a brief summary that takes stock and suggests how the library may be improved. The best annual reports are written in a straightforward, factual manner without technical terminology or jargon. They honestly report both failures and successes and are accompanied by clear, understandable, simple statistical charts.

Annual reports in *public* libraries have taken some dramatic forms in recent years. Summaries of the year's activities appear on shopping bags, posters, calendars and postcards. College libraries, however, rarely experiment with format or even the graphic design of annual reports. As a result, while they do tell the story of a year in the life of a particular library, they fail to capture the excitement of college librarianship or to present the libraries' progress or priorities in a lively fashion.

Library Handbook

Library handbooks serve a dual, though related, purpose. They describe how to gain access to the library and its materials, thereby fulfilling a bibliographic instruction function. They also contain the library's rules and regulations, including hours, borrowing periods, fines, access to interlibrary loan, and data base searching stipulations. Some of this latter material also appears in the student handbook which is given to every incoming student. As is true with annual reports, handbooks must present and interpret the library in the best possible light. Here, too, hallmarks of successful handbooks are clear writing, good graphics, no jargon and an upbeat tone.

In the 1960s and '70s it became the practice to publish handbooks containing extensive information about the library, sometimes including lists of reference books, periodical indexes, bibliographies, and so on, as well as complete directions about how to use them. By the late '70s college libraries realized that the information they had presented in handbooks often became dated before the school year had finished or the supply in stock was depleted. Handbooks began to shrink in size and to contain only essential information. Auxiliary one page fliers, devoted to particular services such as "How to use an OPAC" or an "Index in CD-ROM Format" now prevail as ways to inform users. They can be changed as frequently as the material they describe changes.

A few college libraries publish faculty handbooks, though the practice is becoming increasingly rare. These contain the same material found in student handbooks, but differ in the inclusion of additional information of interest to faculty. A typical faculty library handbook might describe materials selection and acquisition procedures opportunities for faculty and student bibliographic instruction; or special aids to faculty research; major resources and special collections; and cooperative programs with other libraries, including resource sharing, reciprocal privileges, document delivery services and other means of gaining access to materials located off-campus. In the absence of a faculty library handbook, a packet for first-year faculty, containing information about basic library procedures—reserves and book ordering—can be assembled. A more ambitious package might list periodicals subscribed to in the faculty member's discipline, or names and numbers to call for certain types of questions.

College Catalog

Colleges use their catalogs not only as a contract with students but as a public relations device. Catalogs represent a major graphics effort, are often printed on glossy paper and are heavily illustrated. For students, the catalog is their first official college document and its contents, if read, can leave a lasting impression. Librarians who do not realize the new importance ascribed to college catalogs may be content to include a brief description of the library, without illustrations. Those who realize the catalog's potential as an interpretive tool will fight to make the portrait as full, lively and well placed as the editor will allow, and to have it accompanied by one or more pictures of the building, always with students in it. At a minimum, the extent of the library's collection is mentioned, as are its many services. If there is space, significant facts from the library's history can be included. The library should appear in the catalog's index in as many places as students are likely to look for it. For instance the Lawrence Pelletier Library at Allegheny College can be listed under "Library," "Pelletier Library," and "Lawrence Pelletier Library." Those that are called "Learning Centers" will be so listed, but appear under "Library" as well. All librarians should be listed, together with the faculty or as a separate academic group, depending on their status within the institution.

Student Newspaper

The library's relation to the student newspaper is both defensive and positive. From time to time, most college libraries become the target of student editorials. There seems to be a cycle to campus issues. In a year when students are complaining loudly and often about the quality of food served in the dining halls, the library may go unscathed. When the food improves, it may be the library's turn. Students frequently voice their dissatisfaction about crowded or noisy libraries, about the lack of popular reading material, about too few periodicals, about insufficient numbers of hours open, about discrimination in student and faculty loan periods, or about reserve room problems. When students' arguments have merit, they should be heeded and immediate steps taken to seek solutions to the problems. When students speak out of ignorance, correct information should be supplied. Sometimes the tone of a student editorial implies that the library does not care to build its collections, give service, be open evenings or have equipment in working order. These are perceptions the library must alter, perhaps by explaining budgetary constraints.

Libraries can negate some complaints by adopting a strategy whereby information that focuses a positive light on the library is regularly placed in all campus media, but in particular in the campus newspaper. Consider the following: Drew University's campus is known as the University in the Forest; when library staff began sending overdue notices by electronic mail, it was widely publicized as the library's "save a tree" campaign. Advertising library services, exhibits and programs, publicly answering concerns expressed by patrons in notes in the library's suggestion box or campus electronic discussion group file will indicate the library's good intentions. Such controversial decisions as the elimination of vending machines from the all-night study, for instance, will invariably provoke irate editorials or letters to the editor. These may be forestalled if a complete public explanation of why decisions were reached to take these actions is given prior to, not following, the time the new policy is implemented.

Getting acquainted with the student newspaper editors and reporters gives librarians a chance to redirect attention to the more positive aspects of the library. Welcoming student reporters who are writing feature articles on the library, according them sufficient interview time, even on short notice, rather than making it difficult for them to set up an appointment with the librarian, and permitting them to return if they still have questions are likely to result in a more favorable story. When there are newsworthy events in the library, the newspaper can be contacted and encouraged to write about them, or alternately, the library can supply article-length copy directly to the newspaper. Copies of all library publications should routinely be sent to the newspaper editor. It is well to remind newspaper staffers annually that the library maintains complete back files of the student newspaper. At Davidson College Library, large wall plaques honor all previous editors and student body presidents, and serve both as a source of college history and as subtle evidence of library-student leadership cooperation.

Newsletters and Booklists

Many college libraries publish newsletters, although often they appear irregularly or on an occasional basis. They can be an effective method of fostering public awareness about library services, staff, and programs and gifts. Typically, newsletters include a column by the director highlighting a new service or a recently hired staff member. Other articles may describe an advanced reference service or product, chronicle recent Friends of the Library activities, or report on a new collection or an addition to an old collection. Generally a member of the staff, often the library director, assumes responsibility for the publication and serves as its editor. Newsletters are used to best advantage during the years when a library is undergoing substantial changes that require explanation. It is better, however, to delay or suspend their publication when producing them becomes a chore or when there is little to report.

Acquisitions lists, or lists of new books, were once regularly issued by college libraries. Staff and time constraints have led to the abandonment of this practice. Faculty still want to know what books have been added to the library's collection in their own and related fields. Now, however, they must gain that information from the library's new book shelf or from an integrated, online system where this is available. Such a system, properly queried, will generate an acquisitions list by subject, or by year of publication or donor source, and may even include books on order.

Signs

The multiplicity of signs in any library gives library staff the opportunity to plan a coherent and attractive approach to presenting basic information. Range finder lettering, directories of collection locations, eating, drinking or smoking regulations, schedules of library hours, and closing procedures are common to all college libraries. Newer college libraries that benefited from the attention of a graphics designer during their building program stand in sharp contrast to older libraries with visually outdated and poorly coordinated signage systems. One way to begin improving signage is to ask an outsider to assess the helpfulness and appearance of building signs, and to note inconsistencies and poor designs. Another stimulus is to permit all handwritten signs to remain for 24 hours or less. Staff review of signage on a cyclical basis is necessary and sensitivity to the tone of messages is desirable. If local talent is not available, consider purchasing professional signs. Ohio State University Library's version of the standard "No Eating, Drinking" contains a hint of humor. It reads "Please do not eat, feed, devour, gulp." Georgia State's poster communicates whimsically the need for quiet by saying, "Quiet, Please, Silenzio."[6]

Campus Network

Electronic mail, voice mail, and cable TV distribution systems are becoming increasingly common in colleges. The campus network offers libraries a new array of tools useful in promoting and delivering library services. The new voice messages can be used to describe library hours. Versions of library guides can be developed. Electronic technologies permit fast and wide distribution of information at low cost. Unfortunately they lack the graphic appeal of print on paper. As a result they tend to complement, not supplant existing mediums.

Of course they require the same attention to the quality of communication as their predecessors.

Articles

A special event or a new service may prompt a library staff member to write an article describing it. Most often, the aim of such an endeavor is to garner recognition for the library effort or to share the experience with an audience likely to replicate it in their own institution.[7] Less frequently, articles are written to communicate to wider audiences, not simply to librarians.[8] Although there are articles about academic libraries in *Academe* and *Change* from time to time, thse are exceptions.[9] Articles have a place in the library's outreach program for each audience. It is unfortunate that the time for their creation is often crowded with the tasks associated with the completion of the major project that merits description. It is important, however, to maximize the available opportunity and write the article. Editorial assistance from the campus public relations office may also be available at such times.

INTELLECTUAL AND CULTURAL OUTREACH

The poet W.H. Auden once remarked that while he didn't think college was a wonderful place to learn to write, it was a wonderful place to learn to read.[10] Among today's college students, the practice of reading outside the narrow confines of the curriculum may have all but disappeared. Students read to pass an examination, write a term paper, prepare a report. For many the pleasure of reading for its own sake has yet to be experienced.[11] Yet reading is an essential attribute of culture. In a technological society, reading assures that the humane tradition will survive.

Many college librarians have willing accepted the challenge of promoting reading on their campuses, fully realizing that because of the classroom relationship faculty have the opportunity to be far more influential in stimulating students to read than they can ever hope to be. A faculty member who is a reader, who considers reading an important activity, creates an atmosphere in which students are increasingly brought to appreciate intellectual inquiry and exchange. Librarians do have a major role to play in piquing intellectual curiosity. They display new scholarship in new book sections; develop exhibits on relevant themes; purchase the latest fiction; and have browsing collections designed to stimulate interest. Some librarians act as catalysts to encourage the bookstore, a student group, and/or a department to bring to the campus authors who have written books of interest to college students or faculty. Others promote the exchange of paperback books among students by helping to set up racks in dorms and student centers.

Faculty appreciate receiving recognition for their scholarship and students are interested in what their professors have produced. The corpus of work can be collected and displayed or faculty members can be honored at receptions when they have published a new book. Libraries can sponsor readings of faculty works, particularly fiction and poetry, making sure that students are alerted and informed of the time and place. Exhibits which tell the story of how a faculty member developed an idea into a book honor the faculty member and educate students about the stages of publishing.

Featuring exhibits of books that faculty have found meaningful in their lives, or publishing a booklist or bookmark containing those titles, may generate student interest and serve as incentives for reading. So, too, may a summer or intercession reading list with titles selected by popular campus figures.

Other Cultural Contributions

Traditionally, the library has existed to collect, organize and disseminate information. Some activists now claim that the advent of electronic desk-top publishing and easy access to educational TV stations on cable TV have provided an opportunity for libraries to play a still greater role, that of producer of information and culture. For most college libraries, however, this goal is visionary, and librarians see the library, in the near future, at least, as primarily producing newsletters, exhibit catalogs, and library guides. However the library can initiate links to other campus · producers, generators and disseminators of culture, supplying information, publicizing their offerings and generally supporting their efforts. If a campus cable TV station that lists campus activities exists, a TV monitor displaying the schedule belongs in the library.

A few colleges have special funds for buying art, providing library-based cultural events and lectures, mounting special exhibits with accompanying catalogs, sponsoring contests for book collectors, and publishing a scholarly journal or attractive publications. Even libraries in reduced circumstances and with no recourse to special funds can promote cultural activities. The conceptualization of any program, whether well-funded or developed on a very modest budget that relies on voluntary or in-kind services, must begin with an understanding of the college library's current and potential place in the constellation that is campus cultural life.

College Library Exhibits

Libraries have traditionally mounted in-house exhibits. Displays are planned to mesh with campus events—Black History Month or college anniversary—to highlight a particular collection of materials. One exhibit may especially appeal to students, another attract an audience of senior faculty. Each exhibit, however, no matter its subject or particular appeal, can in some way exploit and call attention to library collections.

Planning and administration of an exhibit program is generally placed in the hands of a staff committee, often composed of volunteers, with one person responsible for coordinating the work. Designing and mounting exhibits is time-consuming and work-intensive, particularly at the outset. A scheduling system, including an exhibit calendar, helps to rationalize the process and permits individual faculty contemplating special programs to incorporate the exhibit space into their plan. It is desirable to form a calendar of exhibits at least six to ten months in advance and to continue displays for a period of a month or two. Exhibits must be visually attractive, so allocating start-up funds to purchase art supplies and equipment is a practical necessity.

Several years ago, Evan Farber began purchasing for the Earlham College Library the winning entry from the Senior Art Competition. These works are either shown in the library or made available to students on term loan. Not only does Farber purchase works of consistently good quality at reasonable prices (paintings average about $50), but there is added benefit in the good will this practice engenders among students and alumni.[11]

Lectures, Film Series and Other Cultural Events

Too often library programs, even when the topic relates to a particular department or activity, are planned in isolation. Joint sponsorship is not sought. Sometimes there is not even consultation. Good planning and a good topic, however, do not insure a large audience for a lecture. Librarians sometimes discover, to their chagrin, that the event has been scheduled at a time when other activities are occurring on campus. Lack of involvement of key relevant groups or insufficient publicity may lessen attendance. Not all events will or should attract large audiences. Libraries design programs to meet needs. A small group's needs are as important to the library as are those of larger ones. However, linking a library program with a campus-wide event, a Friends lecture or an Alumni weekend, for instance, may result in a wider audience. It is, in any case, inexcusable for librarians to be unaware of regularly scheduled and special upcoming occurrences on campus whether or not they wish to tie library programs to such events. Other contributions that librarians can make to campus cultural and intellectual life may be more subtle and less apparent. Film is a medium that attracts most college students. Librarians can sponsor, by themselves or in conjunction with a department or group, nightly film series. A library with fewer resources could establish a single weekly film night. Librarian attendance at campus lectures and concerts will be appreciated by the sponsors of these events, and their presence will be seen as support for departmental efforts. Lectures have the added benefit of familiarizing librarians with the discourse of a discipline. Discussing the lecture topic informally with one or more members of the sponsoring department keeps active the lines of communication between that department and the library. Concerts and films provide occasions for sharing mutual interests across departmental boundaries, opportunities to socialize, and to associate librarians with cultural pursuits.

SUMMARY

The outside world is often unfamiliar with what the college library is and what it would like to be. A rigorous program of interpretation will help to inform constituents about its programs, services and resources. Formal and informal channels of communication can be utilized to facilitate the process of interpretation and win friends who will subsequently be willing to aid in achieving the institution's goals. Friends of the Library and alumni are particular sources of strength and relations with these groups, as well as with other friends, should be nurtured.

College libraries play an important role in achieving a humane and cultured civilization. They do this by fostering positive attitudes toward reading and by supporting campus cultural endeavors.

In 1987, the English hymnist Brian Wren composed a hymn for the 10th anniversary of the Liturgical Studies Program at Drew University. It began with the verse

We are not alone. Earth names us: past and present, peoples near and far, family and friends and strangers show us who we are.

and finished with the verse,

Let us be a house of welcome, living stone upholding living stone, gladly showing all our neighbors we are not our own![12]

So, too, it is with college libraries which say yes.

NOTES AND SUGGESTED READINGS

Notes

1. Evan Farber, Earlham College. Interview by author, Caroline Coughlin, June 1984.

2. Joanne Euster, *The Academic Library Director, Management Activities and Effectiveness* (New York: Greenwood Press, 1987), passim.

3. Wooster: *A Quarterly Magazine for Alumni and Friends of the College* 103.1 (Fall 1988); and *Augustana College Magazine* 90 (Winter 1990).

4. Michael Haeuser, "What Friends Are For: Gaining Financial Independence," *Wilson Library Bulletin* 60 (May 1986): 25-27.

5. Elizabeth Brothers, "Putting the Fun in Fundraising" (Winter Park, FL: Rollins College, February 1991), photocopied.

6. Georgia State University Library, "Silence—in many languages." Poster. Atlanta, GA: Georgia State Library, 1980; and Ohio State University, "Please do not eat, gulp...." Poster. Columbus, OH: Friends of the Ohio State University Library, 1981.

7. Richard J. Kuhta, "The Scarlet Letter = A(utomation)," *College and Research Libraries News* 51 (June 1990): 540-543; Caroline M. Coughlin, "Innovation and Value Added Information Delivery," *College and Research Libraries News* 50 (December 1989): 1003-1006.

8. William Moffett, Guest Editorial, "Talking to Ourselves," *College and Research Libraries* 50 (November 1989): 609-610.

9. See "The Electronic Library," *Academe* 75 (July/August 1989): 8-30; and Patricia Senn Breivik, "Making the Most of Libraries," *Change* 19 (July/August 1987): 47.

10. W.H. Auden, as quoted in Lyle, G. *The Administration of the College Library*, 4th ed. (New York: H.W. Wilson Co., 1974): 123.

11. Farber, Interview.

12. Brian Wren "We Are Not Our Own," Hymn commissioned for the 10th anniversary of the Liturgical Studies Program, Drew University, Madison, N.J. 1988.

Suggested Readings

Butcher, Patricia Smith & Susan McCarthy Campbell. *College Library Newsletters*. Clip Note #13. Chicago: Association of College and Research Libraries, 1990.

Conroy, Barbara and Barbara Schindler Jones. *Improving Communication in the Library*. Phoenix, AZ: Oryx Press, 1986.

Ford, Sylverna. "The Library Newsletter: Is It for You." *College and Research Libraries News* 49 (November 1988): 678-682.

Ford, Vikki. "PR: The State of Public Relations in Academic Libraries." *College and Research Libraries* 46 (September 1985) 395-401.

Kies, Cosette N. *Marketing and Public Relations for Libraries*. Metuchen, NJ: Scarecrow Press, 1987.

Munch, Janet Butler. "College Library Friends Group in New York, New Jersey and Connecticut." *College and Research Libraries* 49 (September 1988) 442-447.

Oberembt, Kenneth. *Annual Reports for College Libraries*. Clip Note #12. Chicago: Association of College and Research Libraries, 1988.

Pollet, Dorothy and Peter C. Haskell. *Sign Systems for Libraries*. New York: R. R. Bowker, 1979.

Stevens, Norman D. *Communication Throughout Libraries*. Metuchen, NJ: Scarecrow Press, 1983.

Thompson, Ronelle. *Friends of College Libraries.* Clip Note #9. Chicago: Association of College and Research Libraries, 1987.

Wood, Elizabeth J. *Strategic Marketing for Libraries: A Handbook.* New York: Greenwood Press, 1988.

Chapter 15

THE LIBRARY DIRECTOR

In every library one person holds the title library director (or a variant thereof). This person is charged with managing the work of the library, helping to achieve the college's goals for the library, performing the duties of dean of the library faculty, overseeing collections of the college, and serving as an officer of the college with general oversight of the library. As titular leaders, library directors, like other heads of organizations, exercise power, authority and control. They plan, advise, make decisions and manage crises and conflict. This chapter discusses the forms of leadership library directors adopt as they seek to communicate their values and vision of excellent library service to college administrations and library staff and describes how a college goes about identifying, hiring, and evaluating directors. The day-to-day routine and ongoing tasks that directors perform appear in relevant chapters throughout the book.

PROTOTYPES AND PERSONALITIES

During her study of the activities and behaviors of academic library directors, Joanne Euster was able to isolate four main types. These she named: Energizers, Sustainers, Politicians and Retirees. Energizers she found are most closely associated with change in libraries; Retirees are content to rest on their laurels, while Sustainers and Politicians, respectively, concern themselves primarily with existing processes or with cultivating people.[1] Good directors combine characteristics of energizers, politicians and sustainers, but even the best director knows that it is possible to begin the day as a dedicated energizer and feel like a forced retiree at 6:00 p.m. that afternoon. In these situations, directors mix humility, humor, insight, dedication and intelligence to overcome the sometimes harsh realities of trying to effect and affect changes in the intimate environment that characterizes most college communities. What motivates directors to continue, and keeps the college library in need of their services, is their vision of what constitutes good library service and their steadfast intention to transform that vision into reality on the campus they serve. One director may produce the desired outcome by using political persuasion, another by employing systems theory, and still another by mobilizing staff.

VALUES AND VISION

Despite ambiguities about the definition of quality in academic libraries, all good directors recognize how collection development, technology, staff development, and public services, including the information literacy program, should obtain under ideal conditions. It is toward this optimum level of service delivery that library directors aspire and channel their energies. Successful directors clearly articulate their visions and provide plans of action to accomplish them in ways that convince other administrators, faculty and library staff of their rightness and achievability. Visions are always based on a deep understanding of the educational mission of the college. They are supplemented by familiarity with faculty and student strengths, and informed by the need to translate national concerns into local issues. A grasp of the nature and structure of academic disciplines offered by colleges lends depth to visions and enables directors to be active participants in the scholarly life of the community. It is as crucial for librarians to be cognizant of the intellectual arguments of the decade as it is for them to know how people learn or how to retrieve information. The ability to join the discourse earns librarians respect and respect leads to acceptance and support of librarians' visions.

Library directors are often called upon to share their ideas with constituents. Sometimes faculty are the audience; at other times remarks may be directed to trustees, administrators, Friends groups, students or potential donors. A carefully crafted and well-delivered message articulating options and potentials for the library's future helps to expand the listener's horizons and understanding of change, thereby enhancing the possibilities of realization of the director's vision for the library.

Unfortunately, vision is easy to lose in the course of day-to-day preoccupations and once lost, vision is difficult to recapture as events shift, personnel change and institutional goals alter. Without vision, directors run the risk of being manipulated into conceding staff positions, portions of the materials budget, or other elements of the program. Library directors can reinforce their visions by returning to the important texts of the library field, by keeping up with the new literature and, if time allows, by engaging in research.

Visions are influenced by context, and by the values brought to it. The value orientation of any director is forged in the crucible of personal and professional experience and guides the way he or she understands the ethical issues of importance in our society and applies them to the library. Broadened cultural horizons and a quest for knowledge lead successful directors to design programs that allow users to undertake research and enjoy knowledge for its own sake. Those with a narrow technical approach and limited imagination find the task more difficult. Librarians may hold alternate value orientations toward some issues. U.S. librarians, however, should accept and be committed to the precepts of the First Amendment to the US Constitution, the *Library Bill of Rights* and AAUP's stance on academic freedom. The basic assumptions of these documents serve as litmus tests to govern how controversies involving library materials, staff, policies and services are resolved.

Librarians thus accept as a tenet of faith the principle that all users must have equality of access and opportunity to use information without regard to differences in race, culture, ethnicity, economic status, education or sexual preference. They use these principles to develop operational definitions of access in a given situation.

Directors transmit to staff the belief that good libraries make a difference, that societies are better because librarians exist, and what it means to provide excellent library service in a pluralistic multi-cultural society.[2]

Career Patterns

Recent research into library career patterns, mentoring, leadership, and career paths of academic librarians and library directors has produced few surprises.[3] Proportionately more male librarians than female librarians become directors, although the number and percentage of women directors is increasing yearly; more male directors are external candidates, while more women accede to directorships as a result of internal promotions; there is little horizontal recruitment of library directors across types of libraries; many librarians who become directors have not previously served as directors; a majority of candidates do not have Ph.D.'s, but many have second Master's degrees; and, recently, affirmative action programs have been successful in enlarging the pool of minority and female applicants.

RECRUITMENT

Every college seeks the best possible candidate when it must replace its library director. Following a number of important procedures will ensure a good search and heighten prospects for a successful outcome.[4] The college's mission statement is reviewed by the chief academic policy officer or group early in the process. The library's mission and the role of the library director are then subjected to similar scrutiny prior to placing any advertisements or soliciting individual nominations for the position. General responsibilities considered most important need to be included in the position advertisement.

The best advertisements give a succinct description of duties and reporting relationships, list desired qualifications, and give some background flavor about the college. A well-written advertisement can be a recruiting device in itself. Basic information about salary ranges, deadline for applications and an indication of the college's commitment to affirmative action should also be included. Any campus initiatives relating to the library—a new building or the introduction of an integrated library system—that would influence desired qualifications are also mentioned. Colleges generally place advertisements in the *Chronicle of Higher Education* and *College and Research Library News* because most librarians in the job market consult these two publications. Some colleges also make use of the placement center at the ALA conference to list positions and hold preliminary interviews.

Wealthier colleges, colleges with clear and different missions, with very strong support for libraries and librarians or evidence of substantial new support, and those in more desirable locations may find that the number of applications they receive is substantially greater than most colleges can anticipate. When the response to advertisements or nominations does not produce a sufficiently large or strong applicant pool, or if a particular type of librarian is being sought, colleges can contact the regional accrediting association, one or more library schools, the offices of ACRL, the directors of libraries in comparable institutions or the heads of larger libraries in the region to solicit ideas on how to identify good candidates and request nominations for the position. Colleges need not limit their director's search to applicants with previous college library experience. Candidates who seek out college librarianship from other library work environments often bring relevant organizational experiences.

SELECTION

Because library directors have been compared in their range of responsibilities with provosts, library director search committees tend to be broad based and include influential faculty, one or more librarians, a senior administrator and in some colleges, library support staff and students as members. Decisions about which candidates to bring to campus for interviews are reached through consensus after careful review of applications, dossiers and references. The avenues of recruitment into college librarianship are not linear. Viewing qualifications of candidates as equivalent rather than absolute, therefore, lends flexibility to the process. Sending a full packet of information about the college and the library to each finalist ensures that candidates learn prior to their arrival on campus about issues of concern to the library. The committee can then assess and compare the approach taken by each potential director to the challenge of integrating the library into the life of the college.

Successful candidates convince campus leaders that their knowledge is broad and germane to the tasks at hand. They engender confidence in their ability to manage an operation larger than most others on that campus.

NEW DIRECTORS

Since many new directors come to their positions from lesser ranks, there is generally a settling-in period. If they come without management experience, opportunities for learning management skills are available through courses and ACRL and other continuing education programs. Typically these training programs address such topics as time- or financial management. However, those who are awarded college library director positions are often experienced middle managers and are therefore familiar with general management literature. They have probably attended management workshops and taken courses. But their knowledge of the specific concerns of a director—in particular, a new one—may be limited. Two ad hoc groups of experienced directors of liberal arts college libraries recently began advising new directors about strategies to follow and behaviors to adopt while in their first year in office. Their suggestions are summarized below.

1. Ask each staff member to list three objectives they have for the library and/or the new library director.

2. Seek out and/or accept every invitation to speak on campus, but limit your off-campus trips for the first few months to essential meetings.

3. Call and introduce yourself to directors of peer institution libraries and learn what their libraries are like by sharing data, visiting sites, and joining appropriate professional associations.

4. Request support to attend a well-recommended advanced management seminar within the first year or two of your tenure if you have never attended one.

5. Take the time to talk to retired members of the faculty and listen to their stories of the history of the campus.

6. Be prepared to request improvements to the library when you submit your first budget and be sure to develop good cost estimates for each improvement.

7. Have the staff go on a retreat and work on the tasks of team building, goal setting, and sorting out the objectives they offered individually.

8. Learn about curricular innovations of the past few years and seek out faculty who were active in these efforts to discover how the changes were made.

9. Find someone outside the library you can talk to candidly and on whom you can try out your ideas. This person should be wise, reasoned and discreet.

10. Learn which staff can be relied on for insight into library affairs, including personnel problems, but do not show favoritism.

11. Attend faculty meetings.

12. Read the last two self-study reports prepared by the college when it was evaluated for reaccreditation.

13. Attend campus events.

14. Learn the pattern of expenditures in each library department.

15. Develop a cluster of remarks which together articulate your vision for the library, and use these themes as you speak to groups or prepare reports.

16. Decide which programs the library does well and begin to brag about the library's strengths to the staff and the community.

17. Listen to all parties involved for at least three months before taking any actions affecting individuals or beloved programs.

18. After a few months, monitor your work patterns to determine the amount of time you are spending on various areas, for instance, personnel, budget, collection, faculty, planning. Set objectives and a timetable in each area.

19. Establish a personal calendar, coordinated with the college's schedule for such matters as budget presentations, salary recommendation and promotion request due dates in order to reserve sufficient time to complete each project before its deadline. Include also the completion dates for your personal list of objectives.

20. Plan for a vacation when you know the campus will be quieter than usual—and take it.

21. Thank people as you go along for their help and for their work.

22. If you have the opportunity to hire someone, hire the best person, pay the going rate or a bit more, and use any resulting discrepancy in library salaries overall to argue for upgrading other library salaries in the near future.

23. Use performance evaluation as a way to motivate staff.

24. Learn the employment history of current staff, including number of years worked, number of years until retirement, and also identify the positions with or without much turnover.

25. Pursue avocational interests by participating in campus activities; e.g., find a music group to play with or a racquet ball league to join as a way to meet people outside the library.

26. If three months have gone by and no one has invited you to lunch, take the initiative and set a luncheon date with the treasurer, directors of personnel, financial aid, development, alumni, and admissions, as well as the faculty chairpersons with larger interests in the library book budget. Tell them there is no agenda; you just want to learn more about the college and their responsibilities.

27. Try to establish one new program for one group within the first year of your directorship.

28. At the end of a year, request a formal performance evaluation, or, at a minimum, ask key individuals to tell you how they would evaluate your first year's effort.

29. Discuss with key faculty and administrators the history and current status of librarian involvement in classroom teaching and student advising on campus. Discuss findings with librarians.

30. Find out which faculty are actively doing research and interview them to see what additional help the library might offer to them.

31. Help untenured faculty and librarians develop a publication record by learning their interests and needs and offering encouragement, and if possible library support and mentoring.

32. Strengthen or begin staff development programs for librarians and support staff.

The most important recommendation offered by seasoned directors—implicit in all the other recommendations—was use your library and campus colleagues as mentors, friends, resources, stimulators, and sounding boards.[5]

WORK PATTERNS

Most directors find that their personal goals are directly related to those of the library. Harmony of goals fosters the provision of consistently good service, as successful fulfillment in one sphere indicates similar achievement in the others. Good service is further propelled by a pattern of collaboration, carefully set priorities and suitable allocations of time. A plan of action, amenable to modifications as exigencies occur, enables rational organization of tasks and brings to the surface incomplete or neglected activities.

Directors are forced to sift through a variety of demands on their time and attention in order to respond to those that are most important or pressing. Their desks are often cluttered with telephone messages, memoranda, letters, catalogs, minutes, grant applications, and so on. In responding to the pressures of the day, issues of greater moment are deferred. For instance, the continuing appearance of "Revise Collection Development Policy" on a list of "to be accomplished" tasks signals that the director's stated intention is at odds with his or her ability to produce a new document.

Lack of time or motivation may explain why it has yet to be completed. Perhaps the director's open door policy militates against sufficient opportunity for concentrated thought and writing. Too much energy may be expended in responding to mail, phone, and, now, electronic mail inquiries, which could be better handled with say, form letters or mastery of a new technology. Perhaps some work could be delegated to assistants. For instance, a committee might be asked to produce a draft of a revised collection development policy.

Effective directors continually review their activities to guarantee that the work of the organization is accomplished with dispatch, regularity, adequate documentation and within budget. They also define the domain of their activity broadly, devoting time to research and writing and to furthering the goals of professional associations that service college libraries. In this way they are assured a source of new ideas, some of which are immediately useful to the college, and others which simply keep the director abreast of new developments and challenges in library science.

LEADERSHIP OF STAFF

Confirming that librarians are planning, instructing, and evaluating work and not performing clerical tasks is one of the director's oversight responsibilities. Simultaneously assuring that support staff, including student staff, have opportunities to experience some of the real rewards of autonomy in their work, if only on a modest scale, is equally important. Staff deserve to be challenged and trained to use independent judgment and to share a sense of responsibility and ownership of the program. Good work experiences often form the basis for future career choices, and influence the delivery of service to the community.

RECRUITING NEW LIBRARIANS

The goals of college librarianship are not being met if employees or students are attracted to librarianship because they perceive the work to be safe from the turmoil of society, routine and non-demanding. If these beliefs are reinforced by the libraries they experience as students and workers, librarianship will suffer. Stimulating library directors benefit the library and the profession by making librarianship attractive to the best and the brightest undergraduates. Mentoring, and working with the college career center and with library schools to generate interest in and publicize the rewards of librarianship promote the recruitment of excellent candidates.

COLLEGE'S RESPONSIBILITY

College administrations sometimes hire library directors and assume their jobs are finished. There are additional obligations. College administrations are charged with verifying that their directors are adequately compensated, that is, paid a salary competitive with peer institutions and rewarded with increments that recognize effort and achievement. Recognition in other ways is also always welcome. A library director, requested to take on additional campus responsibilities on either an ad hoc or permanent basis, is generally pleased by the new challenge and flattered to be asked. Being invited to serve on search committees for a new dean, to help strengthen the academic computing center, to participate in campus-wide long range planning efforts, or to be part of an accreditation steering committee all reflect positive attitudes toward the library director.

PERFORMANCE EVALUATION

The performance of library directors, as of all other college employees—faculty, administrators and support staff—requires regular evaluation. The degree to which colleges currently appraise directors probably ranges from none to full. Some directors receive annual evaluation from the person to whom they report. Few surprises should result from these encounters. Directors anticipate them by collecting materials needed to update their vitae, and by summarizing in a page or two the year's accomplishments taking care to distinguish library accomplishments from personal ones in order to gauge the extent to which performance goals have been met. For example, a library may aim to be an online library by the year 1995. The director, of course, supports that goal. However, the directors's individual goal for 1990-91 may have been to create and have had accepted by the college administration a statement of need for an integrated system. Conversation between directors and evaluators will progress from accomplishments to new goals and to areas where improvement is desired and will do so quite naturally if both parties share a willingness to listen.

In institutions where assessments of library directors are not performed annually, contracts and evaluation cycles are often coordinated. A person holding a three-year contract can expect some evaluation procedure to occur at the end of the second year. To prepare for this event, library directors are advised to establish a file of accomplishments, and if possible, exchange views, no later than midway in the life of the contract, with the person to whom they report about their performance.

Some colleges have a five-year cycle for reviewing administrators at the level of library directors or deans. In this case, a special ad hoc committee is usually impaneled to perform the evaluation. It is composed of a few faculty members, one or two librarians, a library staff member, a college administrator from an office that interacts with the library, such as personnel or telecommunication, and perhaps, depending on the ethos of the campus, a student representative. Outside experts, peers from other institutions or individuals identified as knowledgeable about the director's work and the library field, may also be called in to meet with the committee at some point. Such an assessment is similar to a faculty tenure review process and directors prepare for it in much the same manner. They develop packets of information describing their work and the reception it has received. At the end of the process, typically, the contract is renewed and a key group has gained a greater understanding of the responsibilities of a library director.

Staff may be asked to evaluate a library director's performance. All managerial functions are appropriate fuel for staff assessments. They may consider, for instance, the director's willingness to delegate and give commensurate authority to others, the director's ability to act quickly and decisively when resolving problems, and the director's readiness to seek additional funding either through the budget process or in the form of gifts, or grants.[6] Staff assessment can shed a fresh and different light on director's performance. They should be heeded by directors as they assess their own contribution and by administrators as they endeavor to help directors improve their performance. Administrators sometimes shortsightedly resist evaluation from below, claiming that subordinates lack a sufficiently broad perspective to make a useful judgment.

TERMINATION OF A DIRECTOR

Largely unreported in the literature of college librarianship, but an issue that requires attention, is the question of when and how to terminate a library director. We know this is not a widespread problem because college library directors average more than nine years in office, one of the longest tenure periods reported for any category of academic administrators.[7] Directors generally serve under "continuous appointment understandings," with the expectation that, in the absence of other contingencies, they will retire at age sixty five or seventy. In some institutions the initial contract is for three years, with subsequent appointments either for five-year periods or on a continuing basis. Serious dissatisfaction with the performance of the library director requires immediate and firm handling. Directors are entitled to be notified, to have confidential reviews, to learn which areas are in need of improvement, and to be given a date for reconsideration of their efforts. Written documentation kept by the director and the administration provide verification and help guard against violations of due process. Some contracts contain provisions for severance pay or, in the event the library director has tenure, placement in a teaching department or another library position when a contract is revoked.

SUMMARY

College library directors have broad latitude to impose their visions and value systems on the institutions they lead and thereby to shape them into environments that foster and stimulate good teaching and learning. Sharing their vision with members of the user community and with staff helps gain acceptance for the library's program. Library directors have a special obligation to support field-wide library values and norms of behavior.

The search for a new library director necessitates casting a wide net to reach candidates who offer qualities that mesh with institutional needs. Newly appointed directors best learn about the college's mores and traditions from colleagues and associates both inside and out of the library. Library staff and the college administration have a right to expect a quality level of performance from the director and, in turn, the director has a right to expect ongoing evaluation as well as recognition when the job is well done.

NOTES AND SUGGESTED READINGS

Notes

1. Joanne Euster, *The Academic Library Director: Management Activities and Effectiveness* (New York: Greenwood Press, 1987), passim.

2. Cliff Glaviano and R. Errol Lam, "Academic Librarians and Affirmative Action: Approaching Cultural Diversity in the 1990's," *College and Research Libraries* 51 (November 1990):

513-512; Rick B. Forsman, "Incorporating Organizational Values into the Strategic Planning Process," *Journal of Academic Librarianship* 16 (July 1990): 151.

3. Terrence F. Mech, "Academic Library Director: A Managerial Role Profile," *College and Research Libraries* 51 (September 1990): 415-428; Barbara Moran, "Career Patterns of Academic Library Administrators," in *Building on the First Century: Proceedings of the Fifth National Conference of the Association of College and Research Libraries*, ed. Jan Fennell (Chicago: American Library Association, 1989).

4. Theodore Marchese, *The Search Committee Handbook. A Guide to Recruiting Administrators* (Washington, DC: American Association for Higher Education, 1988), passim; and Sharon Rogers and Ruth Person, *Recruiting the Academic Library Director: A Companion to the Search Committee Handbook* (Chicago, Association of College and Research Libraries, [1991] forthcoming), passim.

5. In 1987 William Moffett invited 62 library directors from selective liberal arts colleges to Oberlin College to discuss mutual concerns. The group has met annually since then, at various locations and is informally known as The Oberlin Group or the Obe Group. A tradition of these meetings is to give directors new to the group, and perhaps new to the position of director, the opportunity to ask questions of the directors present. Within ACRL, the College Library Section has a discussion group for directors of college libraries and it has a similar tradition of offering advice to new directors. The ideas represented in this section are a distillation of many different individuals' comments and advice as offered in these discussion groups.

6. Mike Simons and Anne Amaral, "Evaluating the Library Director," *College and Research Libraries News* 50 (May 1989): 360-63.

7. American Council on Education, "Table 116," in *Fact Book on Higher Education, 1989-90*, ed. Cecilia A. Ottinger (New York: American Council on Education and Macmillan, 1987), 182.

Suggested Readings

Albritton, Rosie L. and Thomas W. Shaughnessy. *Developing Leadership Skills: A Sourcebook for Librarians.* Englewood, CO: Libraries Unlimited, 1990.

Darling, John R. and E. Dale Cluff. "Social Style and the Art of Managing Up." *Journal of Academic Librarianship* 12 (January 1987): 350-55.

Engle, Michael O. "Librarianship as Calling: the Philosophy of College Librarianship." *Journal of Academic Librarianship* 12 (March 1986): 30-32.

Lee, Susan A. "Conflict and Ambiguity in the Role of the Academic Library Director." *College and Research Libraries* 38 (September 1977): 396-403.

Lee, Susan A. "A Modest Management Proposal." In William Miller and Stephen Rockwood, eds. *College Librarianship* (Metuchen, NJ: Scarecrow Press, 1981): 65-78.

Saunders, Laverna M. and Camille S. Clark. "Dean of Libraries, What's in a Title?" *College and Research Libraries News* 51 (September 1990): 697-701.

Schuman, Patricia Glass. "Women, Power and Libraries." In *Management Strategies for Libraries: A Basic Reader*. Edited by Beverly Lynch. New York: Neal-Schuman Publishers, 1985: 444-458; reprinted from *Library Journal* 109: (January 1984): 42-47.

Wilson, Patrick. *Public Knowledge, Private Ignorance: Toward a Library and Information Policy*. Westport, CT; Greenwood Press, 1977.

Woodsworth, Anne and Barbara von Wahlde, ed. *Leadership for Research Libraries: A Festschrift for Robert M. Hayes*. Metuchen, NJ: Scarecrow Press, 1988.

Chapter 16

HUMAN RESOURCES MANAGEMENT

Good library staffs bring libraries to life. Poorly trained and ineffectively motivated ones can severely damage a library's program. An exemplary human resources management program develops and accommodates excellent library employees and provides them with a sound program of personnel management, including unbiased position classifications, adequate compensation and benefits, recognition of merit, and a system that encourages job mobility and advancement. While human resources management is the currently preferred term to describe the larger field, in this chapter the term personnel is used to reflect library practices.

Traditionally, personnel management has been the province of the library director, who was the only one responsible for establishing the library's plan and setting major policies and procedures. It was anticipated that employees would passively accept assignments, working conditions and benefits. The emergence of a highly educated work force and new theories about management have led to increased participation and cooperation in generating individual and group goals and policies for institutions.

STAFF SIZE AND COMPOSITION

ACRL's *Standards for College Libraries* tie the number of staff to the annual rate of materials acquisition, the student population, and the overall size of the materials collection. The formula suggests that there be one librarian for each 5,000 books or book equivalents acquired each year, one librarian for each 500 FTE (full-time equivalent) students up to 10,000, as well as one librarian for each 100,000 books in the collection. For example a library with 400,000 books, purchasing 10,000 new ones annually, to meet the demands of 2,000 students, should have 10 professional employees.[1] The *Standards* do not suggest how staff is to be allocated between and among departments. Nor do they make distinctions between types of colleges or offer alternate formulas to control for differing needs. Additional staff, for instance, may be required by institutions with old, well-established special collections, or that maintain branch libraries, or 'that must answer to increased demand for materials generated by an extensive honors program.

The typical college library staff consists of librarians, support staff and student assistants. Attempts have been made to distinguish further among support staff and to utilize alternate classifications. Some libraries have "technical specialists." Others differentiate between exempt and non-exempt categories, that is, between employers who manage an area, supervise others and receive an annual salary, and employees paid on an hourly basis who are not managing others. No matter the nomenclature, however, the basic divisions remain—librarian, support staff and student assistant.

In general those called librarians are responsible for planning and developing new programs and for assigning the execution and maintenance of ongoing programs to others. Librarians and other professionals are expected to apply theory and leadership to the solutions of problems. Support staff are responsible for applying learned procedures to the solution of repetitive problems and for participating in the design of solutions for problems that emerge. A job classification system should provide guidelines to help clarify roles and distinguish between library tasks. Yet, blurring between professional and support tasks seems inevitable. In some libraries, for instance, distinctions between professionals and support staff are effaced when experienced employees who lack formal credentials head a periodicals, acquisitions, or circulation department. The traditional department that has five faculty members with Ph.D.'s and one secretary who is a high school graduate can be much clearer about the distinct roles assigned to faculty and support staff than can a library, particularly a library with a well-educated support staff. Another factor that makes library staffing more complex is that much of the clerical work in libraries requires special knowledge and is often more difficult and demanding than what is assigned to support staff in other parts of the college community.

Staffing patterns in the library are poorly understood by the rest of the campus. Users are unlikely to differentiate clerical from professional staff, bringing equal expectations to the person at the desk. Administrators are unlikely to distinguish between the demands made by library work on library assistants and the demands made on support staff in other parts of the campus.

Insufficient clerical assistance accounts for a substantial portion of the lack of distinction between professional and support staff and makes more understandable the campus confusion about the role of librarians. The ratio of clerical to librarian positions in academic libraries has hovered around two to one, despite strong recommendations from professional organizations that more clerical employees are needed, and that the ratio be closer to three to one. In 1985, a typical college had 10 librarians on the staff and 14 support staff, a substantial increase over 1970-71 when the comparable figures were 6.9 professionals and 9.4 support staff.[2] On the average, colleges also hire 30,000 hours of student help—the equivalent of 16 full-time employees—during a year. When student and clerical positions are combined, the total number of support staff employees reaches 30, and produces a ratio of support staff to librarians which is considerably closer to the ideal.

Ratios of professional to other library employees only reveal part of the staff story. The other important component is the amount spent for salaries, wages and benefits, in comparison with materials and other expenditures of the library. Recent formulas suggest that the ratio to describe the relationship between these categories should approximate 60:30:10.[3] Current practice is somewhat different. A recent study of quality liberal arts college libraries conducted by Richard Werking revealed that the average salary costs have claimed about 44% of the library budget, with materials at 38% and other operating expenses at 17.5%.[4] Raising the personnel budget of a library at the expense of materials is and will remain difficult. Despite the fact that professional staff cost ratios are substantially lower for the library than they are for the remainder of the institution, it is nonetheless uncomfortable for college administrators to witness growth in the personnel budget when they consider acquiring materials, not staff as the library's real objective. That ever-present tension mandates that library directors frame staff choices in terms that are understandable to administrators and causes them to link library programs with both staff and material costs rather than merely to categorize budgets into staff, materials and other expenditures.

PROFESSIONAL AND CLERICAL STAFF

Staff job descriptions are based on the range and complexity of tasks, the level of independent analysis required to perform them, and their impact on the work on others. Senior employees plan and execute programs, perform complex assignments, develop budgets, and supervise others. Beginning support staff, on the other hand, have limited spheres of activity, are closely supervised, and frequently assigned repetitive work. It is often true that employees after a time outperform their job descriptions and their compensation. Whenever possible, salary and grade levels are altered to match remuneration and recognition with staff members' contributions. Unfortunately, limited budgetary flexibility often necessitates reminding support staff that positions, not individuals are what are classified.

Filling vacancies for librarians presents an opportunity to review job descriptions and to strengthen the professional nature of the librarian position. In the past, much of the work assigned to librarians could have been performed by clerks, activities were restricted by tight desk schedules, and attention was focused on routine, unchallenging tasks. Involvement in planning and executing new programs was minimal. Yet these were the same people expected to carry the message about library programs to the faculty and student body.

Three possible outcomes resulted from the constraints placed on librarians in these environments. The first was that many librarians left the field for professions in which they could maximize their creative talents. The second was that librarians settled, sometimes very comfortably, into positions demanding too little from them. The third was that librarians struggled to do both kinds of work and experienced conflicts in time management and role definition.

Librarians who are products of earlier role definitions must now be helped to accept different functions for themselves and for their colleagues. Reluctance to change, born of years of habituation to lesser roles, is not unusual behavior. People become more concerned about job security than about individual growth or innovations. They find comfort in routine and are threatened by new methods. Gradually replacing outdated job descriptions with revised descriptions, couched of course within the framework of the library's transformed missions and goals, is an effective strategy for redirecting professional staff energies. A good text on personnel management in libraries, such as that by Creth and Duda, can be invaluable at times when general principles need to be explained and applied to a particular situation.[5] Scrutinizing tasks performed in a typical day or week appropriately begins the actual process of job redefinition.

Building on the talents of individual staff members is a practical necessity for college libraries with small staffs where all the required tasks can only be accomplished by assigning them to staff members who best can perform them, whatever their job description. Small staffs permit a large degree of autonomy, variety, innovation and flexibility to be applied to the construction of most jobs. Combining attention to individual strengths, with adherence to the principles of job design, performance evaluation, participative management and staff development, gives a library the best opportunity to develop a quality work environment. The "compleat" librarian, a relatively new concept, is expected to accept responsibilities in both public and technical services, to have a broader background and be willing to participate holistically in the entire library, rather than only in some of its parts. Similarly, libraries that develop mechanisms for staff in several departments to work together to accomplish certain tasks also utilize the "compleat" staff member model.

Contrary to notions of colleges as ivory towers, ivy-covered retreats from an uncivil world, today's campuses are fiercely competitive. Arguments are waged about virtually every aspect of academic life, and academics are good debaters. Skilled librarians learn how to mount strong cases, develop consensus, build coalitions and mobilize support on campus. Translating a larger vision into a plan of action for a new program, preparing the documentation, devising a tentative budget, and presenting it convincingly in a proper forum is one of the most challenging and rewarding tasks of a college librarian.

Among the other qualities of good librarians are honesty and personal integrity. Building trust for librarians on the campus and among the staff for each other is a step-by-step, time-consuming process. Without it, however, the library cannot hope to be effective.

LIBRARIANS' ROLES IN PERSONNEL MATTERS

Confidence in library managers is produced by their actions—willingness, for instance, to accept responsibility, to delegate authority, to reward efforts, to keep the staff informed and involved, and to participate in performance evaluations. Employees trust managers who are fair in their distribution of promotions and salary increases, who attend to the physical well-being of their staffs, who show appreciation for satisfactory performance and who are impartial in their criticisms.

Good managers have the obligation and responsibility to develop the talents of their staff. They permit ideas, not personalities, to dominate the discussion and always credit staff who shape the project. By encouraging participation, they promote a sense of group achievement, and replace needless competition between staff members with joint effort. Viewed from this perspective, it might be assumed that a successful manager's most significant accomplishment is to create a strong work environment in which each member of the group feels a sense of personal fulfillment and instrumentality in the group's output. Unfortunately, colleges are not altruistic organizations and a bottom-line mentality dominates the thinking of many college administrators. Nor is a strong work environment a permanent substitute for funds to undertake a project. While teamwork is desirable, administrators are as likely to measure success by evidence of an increase in financial resources as they are by an ability to do more with a static budget.

A library requires monitoring to ascertain that it is functioning properly, that individuals and departments are being provided with the information and resources needed to accomplish the work. Any administrative structure whether it is based on function—as in circulation, reference or cataloging, for instance—or form—media, periodicals, books, or type of user—develops differently depending on its staff. Together with library directors, middle managers are responsible for evaluating the effectiveness and efficiency of the organization and its parts. Radical transformations rarely result from these evaluations. Rather, modest incremental improvements in internal patterns of communication and procedures are instituted.

SUPERVISION

Good library managers recognize the importance of, for want of a better word, supervision. Supervision in this context refers not to close monitoring of employees' output, but to oversight and direction. Supervisors who identify with staff, encourage pride in accomplishment, and stimulate cooperation toward the common good contribute significantly to the effectiveness of the library and to staff morale. They supply clear definitions of individual staff responsibilities, give employees an opportunity to participate in all aspects of the library, and confer generous recognition for work accomplished. Mentoring, an activity whose importance has received increasing recognition over the past decade, is related to supervision. Librarians learn not only from texts and their own experience, but from the example of other librarians, role models. Experienced librarians accept the obligation to act in this capacity, to share with more recent entrants to the field their understanding of the profession, both in theory and practice. They offer assistance and guidance, pointing out opportunities and pitfalls; and encourage newer librarians, when they have reached the limits of their current positions, to develop their careers by providing them with greater responsibilities and by suggesting new avenues of challenge, either in-house or elsewhere.

ABILITY TO WORK WITH STUDENTS AND FACULTY

Managers are responsible for reminding staff that their primary mission is to develop services and collections that meet the information needs of the campus. Clearly, this means getting along with faculty, students and other library users. Among the less desirable characteristics of many library staff members is their attitude toward faculty and students. Library staff exchanges generally couched in terms of "we" and "they" may signal an unacceptable relationship.

Working with students who are not always behaviorally mature or intellectually sophisticated requires patience. Library faculty and staff, often less aware of the requirements of the educational program than their student assistants, tend to develop a defensive shell instead of reaching out to try to understand what students need. Expanding formal and informal structures of communication with students strengthens the library's ability to serve them. Participating in campus activities outside the library, perhaps serving as teachers or advisors to groups with whom they share an avocational interest encourages interaction without an intervening desk. Students who share in the life of the library, comment on policy, serve on the library committee, or are free to suggest materials feel a proprietary interest in the institution.

Some librarians, even those who enjoy students, tend to view faculty as burdens to be borne—a sentiment shared by many faculty members about librarians. This mutual lack of respect, a product of years of misunderstanding about the differences between desire for standardization of library services and a desire for faculty spontaneity and autonomy, is exacerbated by the inability of faculty to distinguish between librarians and support staff. One result is that faculty tend to see librarians as rule-bound and inflexible. A library staff that participates fully in the life of the campus meets faculty on neutral ground where they can interact without the accoutrements that accompany their trades, can begin to supplant distrust and disrespect with civility and credibility. Cordial relationships can foster creative problem-solving about library policies and faculty interests.

RECRUITMENT AND SELECTION OF THE STAFF

In the hierarchy of tasks that directors and managers must perform, no administrative duties may be more important than recruiting, hiring and developing appropriate personnel to staff the library. The first step is to formulate a clear and careful definition of the position to be filled, including salary, benefits and conditions of employment.

Among the characteristics sought in any potential employee are strong intellect, good sense of humor, ability to communicate, high energy level, and commitment to the goals of higher education. Most college libraries require the services of generalists and rarely demand excessive amounts of experience and specialization. However, any necessary specific knowledge and skills should be fully articulated in the position description. Bright graduates of library schools are often dissuaded from applying for positions because they call for extraordinary credentials. It is far better, in general, to risk trading specific competencies than potential excellence.[6]

Setting an appropriate salary for a position requires blending a sufficiently attractive stipend with a remuneration fair to those already on staff. At times, circumstances require that beginning librarians be hired at a somewhat higher than current rate, and that adjustments in the salaries of experienced staff be made later. Salary surveys are available for virtually all regions of the country, and within peer groupings of colleges. Knowledge of salary schedules in comparable institutions provides a basis for salary discussion and grounds for possible remediation. Placing advertisements in professional publications and library school placement offices and using the library grapevine assures wide-spread dissemination of the availability of the position. A broadly waged recruiting effort not only produces the best candidates but meets legal requirements as well. While it is not inappropriate to actively identify and seek out potential employees, care must be take to insure that this practice does not dominate the process. Both directly solicited and spontaneous applications merit equal consideration.

Affirmative action, in its best sense, can guide the successful recruitment of new employees in college libraries. It is not unusual for advertisements to contain phrases such as "the college is an equal opportunity employer and welcomes applications from minorities and women." Librarians should welcome strategies that encourage entry to the profession of any qualified applicant, regardless of racial or cultural background, rather than bemoan what they perceive to be rigid quotas or mandatory search procedures. The current composition of most library staffs in no way reflects the composition of the college community, much less the composition of the society at large.[7]

The process of hiring a professional librarian follows one of two models. Either the employee is hired by the director, in consultation with staff members and the college administration, or, following the collegial model, a search committee is formed and the decision is made by the library director and/or the college president, based on the recommendation of the committee. Committees may be composed of only librarians, or may also include faculty, staff and students, depending on the nature of the vacancy and its importance to the College.

The two to four applicants identified as the strongest candidates are usually invited to the campus to receive a comprehensive, fair, and careful interview that includes attention to skills that will be required in the job. These visits are financed by the college. Although helpful in identifying finalists, interviews at conferences or telephone interviews are less satisfactory for all concerned at the final stage. Campus visits typically include a tour of the campus, meetings with the director, department, search committee and staff. They are often scheduled to last one very full day, with an overnight stay dependent on transportation schedules.

Faculty being recruited for academic disciplines are usually asked to give a departmental or public lecture. Similarly, it is reasonable to require a potential library staff member to describe the resources they would utilize in solving a cataloging problem or preparing a library instruction session. Replicating real situations or seeking information about how each candidate would handle a similar problem enables the staff and director to compare the candidates' relative strengths and weaknesses.[8]

Written recommendations form part of the candidate's credentials packet, along with a current vita, and perhaps transcripts and, if there are any, publications. Verbal references, on occasion, are used to supplement written ones.

Final judgments are cumulative products of both tangible and intangible considerations, with evidence including information gained in interviews, recommendations and search committee judgments of the suitability of the candidate for the position and the institution. Too often the absence of an acceptable candidate causes libraries to settle for less, rather than following the better course of beginning the search anew. In the face of three equally, but differently qualified candidates, attention to affirmative action and each applicant's potential contribution to the library informs the decision about which one to hire.

WORK WITH CAMPUS PERSONNEL OFFICES

Neither policy formulation nor the record-keeping or other paperwork associated with personnel management need be onerous for the library if common sense prevails and the campus personnel department is permitted to assume its appropriate responsibilities. Essentially, the library must establish a set of files for each employee that includes a current job description, an up-to-date resume, any available evaluations, and other documents that relate to job performance. The campus personnel office maintains all other personnel records—vacations, sick leave, retirement benefits, wages, and so on.

The quality of the working relationship between the library and the personnel department will have an impact on the ability of the library director to secure better salaries, working conditions and benefits for the staff. Directors, and librarians who become knowledgeable about job evaluation systems, pay equity, changes in federal laws regarding pensions, and other personnel matters can confidently interact with those charged with administering the college's personnel policy.

Despite widespread attention to unionization in the 1970s, few college library staffs are unionized. Legal restrictions, union weakness, and suspicion and dislike of unions have slowed the movement in libraries. Their value is debated by library employees and ALA has been ambiguous in its attitude toward unions. Academic libraries have been particularly resistant to efforts to unionize.[9]

A further recent deterrent to unionization is uncertainty about whether library faculty are considered by the National Labor Relations Board (NLRB) to be subject to the "Yeshiva" decision. In 1980, by a vote of 5-4, the United States Supreme Court found faculty members to be part of management; that is they found that faculty play a significant role in operating the enterprise. The decision regarding librarians may hinge on whether they exercise authority on a regular or recurring basis.[10] Unionization of librarians or support staff occurs most frequently in publicly supported colleges in industrialized states or in larger institutions in states with permissive collective bargaining legislation. Directors who work in a unionized environment have an added obligation to understand the culture and structure of unions in higher education. William Weinberg warns that unless administrators accept the unions' continued presence on campuses, good working relations with them will be extremely difficult.[11]

Policy Formation

Librarians seek to work in an atmosphere that makes them feel they are significant and valuable members of the college's educational establishment. Personnel practices of the library can help to reinforce or negate a librarian's sense of worth. Clear, careful articulation of the library's personnel policies and practices suggests professional treatment. A library's policies are further legitimated if they represent the collective efforts of the professional staff who have struggled with the nuances and problems of creating fairness and equity. Codification, in the form of a published document laying out policies governing librarians' conditions of employment, provides further evidence of the importance attributed to library positions. When a campus personnel department agrees to allow a variation of its standards practice to accommodate the needs of the library, the agreement needs to be documented in memos to the file.

Policies that require definition are conditions for appointment, promotion, nonrenewal, and change of position. Institutions that offer librarians tenure as a faculty member generally adopt evaluation criteria similar to those used to assess teaching faculty and establish a program of peer review, although there may be variations in the criteria and the review process that address particular responsibilities of librarians. In institutions where faculty status is not granted, librarians need to develop and delineate in writing performance evaluation policies, and include a statement regarding peer review. Grievance procedures, if they exist, are spelled out and academic freedom rights explained. Policies regarding access to leaves, travel funds, and continuing education are included, as are statements regarding correlative expectations that librarians will engage in further training and participate in the scholarly and professional life of their field. The college personnel office is expected to provide written descriptions of benefit programs—retirement annuities, insurance, hospitalization, sick leave. If library support staff differ in status and benefits from clerical staff in other parts of the college, they should receive a similar document.

SALARIES

Salary being the major source of income for most librarians, an individual college library's ability to compete for high quality staff is influenced greatly by its salary schedule, its package of fringe benefits and how it compares in other aspects with similar institutions.

Library directors, working with personnel managers, bear responsibility for developing a systematic approach to salary administration and for establishing broad classes of positions reciprocally related to a salary schedule that undergoes continual review. The minimum objective of such an approach should be to offer librarians and other staff salaries competitive with similar libraries in the region, annual increases at least equal on a percentage basis with other campus salaries, and merit increases based on a continuing evaluation of each individual's work. In the absence of firm information about the remuneration of local faculty some data can be gathered using the annual salary survey conducted by AAUP and reported in *Academe* and the *Chronicle of Higher Education*.[12]

Library salary information is available from any number of sources. The American Library Association's Office for Research and Office for Library Personnel Resources publish one such survey, ARL another.[13] Some state library association offer salary guidelines and *Library Journal* lists starting salaries each year. Library directors at comparable institutions are generally willing to share basic information about salary ranges and classification systems.

Compensation includes more than salaries. Fringe benefits can represent as much 30% of a salary package. Library staff generally receive many of the same benefits as other members of the college community. Due to a recent change in federal law, institutions of higher education are now compelled, if they wish to offer a benefit, to offer the same benefits to similar categories of employees. As a result, tuition exchange programs or tuition benefits for offspring are now more accessible to all college employees, although different periods of service and waiting periods can be required to establish eligibility for different categories of employees groups. Similarly, colleges must offer equitable pension plans to all personnel.[14]

Library staffs are not typically highly paid. Salary considerations did not govern the choice most librarians made to join the profession. They chose the work for its importance, its inherent interest, or for a variety of other reasons, and accepted the trade-offs implicit in making their decision. Passivity, however, in the face of declining individual purchasing power when salaries do not even keep pace with inflation is inappropriate behavior. Library directors and librarians should inform themselves about the dimensions of faculty and staff compensation on their own campuses as well as nationally, in order to mobilize the best possible case for the adequate remuneration of all staff.

Information about salary practices in allied fields and remedial compensation strategies can provide library directors with ammunition to assist them in arguing for improved levels of support for library staff. Comparable worth, or pay equity, the concept that salaries of men and women in fields that are comparable should be roughly equivalent, has been helpful in raising salaries for librarians and library staff at some institution.[15]

Non-unionized library support staff depend on library administrators to secure for them the highest possible compensation. There are generally two types of support staff: library assistants and clerical workers. The first group tends to include college graduates whose education has not prepared them for a specific occupation. Their work may entail bibliographic searching, circulation desk supervision, or routine cataloging. The second group will have completed, at a minimum, a secondary school education. They will type, file, maintain records and do secretarial work. Clerical salaries on private college campuses are notoriously low and good clerks are hard to find; harder, in fact, than library assistants, who generally do not have the specific typing or accounting skills needed by business or industry. Many library positions actually require far less education than those who occupy them possess, but the attractions of a good work environment near home compensate these staff for the lower pay and lesser status, at least for the short term. Among this group can be found homemakers seeking part-time employment and faculty spouses, each group often composed of talented, capable people whose presence on the library staff adds to the competence and diversity of the institution. These staff members can serve to disseminate the library's story as they participate in the community's college's social life. On the other hand, faculty and administration spouses who become members of library staffs can affect the library negatively, particularly in situations where there is dissension between them and the library director or other librarians, or where there are matters under consideration that should not be discussed outside the library until an appropriate time.

The morale and enthusiasm of support staff must be maintained if the library is to be successful. A personnel program for this group takes into account salaries, appropriate classification levels, working conditions, flexible schedules, job enrichment, access to internal promotion and career opportunities for promising employees. Particularly discouraging is a pattern of compensating library support staff at a level lower than that paid to other non-credentialed members of the college community. Securing an appropriate level of salary for library assistants has been difficult because there are few commensurate positions on the campus. Academic computing centers serviced by technical specialists are one exception and may offer some basis for comparison with library support staff.

CONDITIONS OF WORK

Salary is an important factor in employee satisfaction and performance, but other conditions bear on staff members' attitudes toward work. Physical facilities, hours of work, vacations and other leave policies, health and retirement benefits, opportunities for accomplishment and advancement, and the quality of supervision, all contribute to employees' well-being and performance.

Physical Facilities

The absence of certain physical amenities will cause employees to express dissatisfaction or perhaps leave. Severely overcrowded work environments or noisy, dusty, dirty buildings with inadequate heating and ventilating systems may encourage widespread staff defections and high turnover. Sufficient lighting, proper equipment, adequate working space, bright and attractive quarters all promote good library morale. The link between employee satisfaction and good work environments is sufficient reason for the director, in conjunction with physical plant personnel, to develop a schedule of systematic maintenance and improvement of library staff work areas. A comfortable physical environment is a necessary condition of library employment. It is insufficient, however, in and of itself to motivate staff to do quality work. That is a product of good job design and supervision, recognition of work well done, and other factors that generate excellence in staff attitudes and behavior.

Working Hours

Librarians are expected to work between thirty-five and forty hours a week. Support staff share similar requirements. However, it is anticipated that librarians will complete their assignments no matter how much additional time is required. Support staff need only keep track of hours worked.

Some libraries insist that a librarian be on the premises at all times. This means that evening and weekend hours must be distributed among librarians. Other institutions depend on library assistants to supervise the non-traditional work hours.

As more and more librarians are expected to participate in the educational life of the institution and in the scholarly and professional work of their field, there has come a recognition that librarians on twelve-month contracts lack the kind of discretionary time available to their faculty counterparts. In order for librarians to function as expected, the institution must be flexible about its staff schedules. Granting time off, during periods when school is not in session, to read, think and write will help to revitalize overworked and perhaps under-challenged librarians. Other work arrangements—flex time, job sharing or ten-month schedules—can lead to greater productivity and more job satisfaction.

Vacations and Leaves

Although practices may vary among institutions, most librarians, and staff with over five years of service, receive between twenty and twenty-five days of paid vacation each year. Librarians on ten-month contracts are generally not eligible for a paid vacation. In addition, most library employees receive legal holidays. Support staff employees who are asked to work on legal holidays are given commensurate vacation at another time or may be paid a higher than usual hourly rate. Librarians are often accorded semester breaks as time off, although most libraries schedule at least one librarian to be available to meet the needs of faculty and students doing research.

It has become the goal, and to some extent the practice, for librarians to use spring breaks, winter vacations and other school holiday periods to research, write, and reflect on library matters of a less transitory nature. Staff, too, benefit from shorter library hours when class is not in session. While they must still work their requisite time, they are relieved of the burden of working evenings and weekends. Less busy times when school is still in session, inter-session term, for instance, or summer school, can be used to plan major library projects.

Institutions that accord faculty status to librarians often make access to sabbatical leaves available to them, as well. In most institutions sabbaticals are awarded on the basis of a project proposal that outlines a scholarly endeavor an applicant will pursue during leave time. Sabbaticals can range from three months to a year, and carry anywhere from half to full salary.

Most libraries offer staff a small number of personal leave days. Short term paid leaves are available to employees for personal reasons, jury duty, service, a death in the family and other emergency purposes. In addition, paid or unpaid leaves of up to one year can be granted in order for employees to pursue scholarly research, to further their education, or for parental and personal leaves. If the time period requested for the leave is a year or less, the library will generally hold the position secure. Leaves of longer duration may require negotiation. In these cases, employers generally reserve the right to fill the position if it is deemed necessary or appropriate.

Health Services

Medical, disability and life insurance, and sick leave are provided by most colleges, although specific features vary with each institution. The vast majority of colleges offer at least ten days of annual sick leave, and many permit employees to cumulate unused sick days and cash them in at retirement.

Institutional norms dictate whether sick leave may legitimately be used to care for relatives needing care—children, parents, and so on. Extended employee illnesses are often covered under worker's compensation funds, or other disability policies. Few college faculty are covered by sick leave policies. Generally, in cases of illness, they close ranks, cover the classes, and assume the responsibilities of sick colleagues who continue to receive full salary until they return to teaching or are placed on disability leave. Some librarians share this tradition. More usual, however, is the appointment model that includes a defined number of sick leave days.

Most colleges offer their employees free or low-cost life insurance. The amount available is usually tied to an employee's annual salary. Medical insurance, a standard and important benefit for full-time employees, can generally be augmented to include coverage for families by paying a premium above the basic cost. The high cost of medical insurance and the limited benefits available from many carriers have led a number of institutions to seek alternate methods of providing coverage. In some states, state law requires colleges to offer employees the option of securing traditional medical protection through agencies similar to Blue Cross/Blue Shield or through membership in health maintenance organizations. The extension of benefits to provide for dental work and vision care are most often found in publicly supported institutions, in those that have collective bargaining agreements, or in colleges with large endowments.

Child-care service, while neither strictly a health nor a work benefit, is becoming more widely available. Some colleges maintain child-care facilities for the children of employees. Others offer employees pre-tax salary deduction programs to cover some child care costs. Competition for a limited number of employees is as important a reason for establishing these programs as is the desire to see children well cared for in a time of increases in both the single parent family and the two parents in the work force phenomenon.

An experimental "cafeteria approach" to health benefits has been attempted at some colleges. Employees choose from a range of approved benefits those deemed most useful to them. For example, a married employee may wish to have dental coverage at the maximum level, but choose not to have basic medical care because it is available through a spouse's policy. The college contributes a predetermined amount of money, with employees providing any necessary supplement. The possibilities are extensive, but without knowledgeable staff, good counselors and acceptance of responsibility by individual employees for steering their own course, this approach may be an invitation to confusion.

Retirement benefits are a standard part of any employee package. Generally they supplement the U.S. Social Security Insurance Program, although some states have chosen not to participate in the federal system. Employees in state institutions often share in state-based retirement programs. While generous in coverage, these funds are not transportable to other locations when employees change positions. Vested funds, representing both the employee and employer contribution, plus interest, if they have accrued for a sufficient amount of time, are returned when an employee leaves state employment, and can then be rolled over into another retirement fund. Most private colleges and universities participate in TIAA-CREF, the Teachers Insurance and Annuity Association-College Retirement Equities Fund. Employers contribute a set amount of funds, as do employees, which are invested in one of several bond or stock funds as designated by the individual participant. Since TIAA is a common insurer for most academic organizations, the policies are transferable, thereby permitting professors and academic librarians to change institutions without loss of retirement benefits. For the few institutions with no coverage, or that do not extend their coverage to librarians, the American Library Association offers similar benefits through its insurance program for individuals.

APPOINTMENT, PROMOTION, TENURE AND NONRENEWAL OF LIBRARIANS

The philosophy governing appointment, promotion, and tenure of librarians is that the employing institution and the individual are engaged in an honest process, one utilizing standard criteria informed by the presentation of accurate information and unbiased appraisals. The process begins with the job description, a clear and consistent definition of expectations and responsibilities. It includes timetables for making judgments about continued employment that have been explained during the initial interview. Finally, written statements of the rights of each party in the process should be part of the contract or employment package.

Institutions that offer employees tenure often follow a schedule that includes several multi-year reappointment contracts, with a tenure decision during the sixth year. For institutions that do not offer tenure, the timetable is more varied. Some libraries offer continuing employment status following a one-year probationary period. Others institute a system of librarian peer review at the end of three years, or every fourth year, with a recommendation for continued employment following the review. Staff are frequently considered probationary employees for three months and then regular employees with annual renewal.

The termination of employees without adequate warning and sufficient opportunity to modify behavior identified as unsatisfactory is unacceptable practice. Following due process will insure that decisions are neither arbitrary or unfair. Staff members terminated for cause receive written notice to that effect. If termination follows a probationary period, the notice indicates the reason or reasons for dismissal. The library is legally and morally bound to permit appeals of dismissals. A grievance procedure, describing the steps a nonrenewed employee may take to contest a negative decision, must be in place and readily accessible.[16]

New librarians, in particular, have a right to expect constructive assistance from their peers and the library administration as they begin their careers. Annual performance appraisals are one way of informing new, as well as more experienced librarians, about their progress. They are equally valuable to staff. Performance appraisals incorporate both employee expectations about their jobs and institutional expectations for them. Assessing the degree to which they have been achieved and setting goals for the following year are agenda items for the annual review. The process is complicated and time-consuming, nerve-wracking and often confrontational. Properly conducted, however, it can prevent having to spend even more time, energy and emotion in discharging an employee whose performance is unsatisfactory but for whom there is no record of evaluation, or in searching for a replacement for a good employee who left feeling unrecognized. Performance appraisals provide an opportunity to challenge individuals with good work records to higher accomplishment, to restructure positions to take advantage of underutilized talents, to encourage employees to seek opportunities elsewhere if promotion to a higher position is unlikely, or, if necessary, to discourage employees who are perceived as unsuitable from continuing careers in academic librarianship. Written records of appraisals are signed by a supervisor and/or the director, and by the employee. When judgments vary between the appraiser and the appraised, employees are entitled to insert memoranda of disagreement in their files.

PROFESSIONAL DEVELOPMENT OF LIBRARIANS AND SUPPORT STAFF

Professionals in the field of adult education distinguish between continuing education and staff development. They see the former as the choice made by employees about which educational opportunities to pursue, and the latter as resulting from an employer's appraisal of the needs of the organization. In the first instance, employees judge what they require for career mobility, or to feel more competent. In the second, the library determines skills their staff members must acquire in order to keep up with the field and successfully accomplish their work. The library must insure that the reference staff, for instance, is capable of manipulating data on interactive information disks, or that administrators are exposed to the newest approaches to time management. Continuing education and staff development are not mutually exclusive endeavors, particularly in a college library environment where individual and group needs often coincide. For example, the librarian who enrolls in a computer course for personal reasons, but utilizes that knowledge when the library is debating which management information software package to acquire, satisfies both conditions.

Professional literature suggests that libraries devote up to 10% of their total personnel budgets on staff development.[17] A recent survey revealed, however, that for most college libraries the allocation remains at less than one per cent. The absence of expenditure does not always indicate that activities supporting staff training and enhancement are totally ignored. Supervision and mentoring, discussed above, are aspects of staff development. So, too, are access to sabbaticals and paid or even unpaid leaves for educational, professional or scholarly purposes.

Librarians working in small colleges suffer from a kind of intellectual and professional isolation, caused perhaps by the college's geographic location or alternately by the pressure of daily work; either may act as a deterrent to staff interaction with librarians at other institutions. Directors and staff alike require opportunities to alleviate this dissociation. Encouraging participation in association work is one method; supporting research and advanced study is another approach; helping staff develop workshops is yet another tactic. Finally, establishing a procedure to insure that staff will regularly read professional material guarantees that they will remain current with improvements and events in the field.

Orientation

The process of staff development begins on the day a staff member accepts a position. New employees have a right to expect a thorough orientation to the library and to the community. This includes acquainting them with general policies of the college and the library, the layout of the campus and the library building, and the operation of the particular department in which they will work. Introducing new employees, as soon as possible, to all staff members and explaining how each functions within the library discourages confusion. Optimally, the orientation schedule includes a period of time spent learning each phase of the library's operation. Knowing how the parts operate, how they interact with each other, and how they relate to the campus helps new employees understand their place in the college environment. The orientation period also represents the first and best opportunity to communicate with new staff members and socialize them to the values of the organization and its behavioral norms. Directors, for instance, who wish their librarians to assume an intentional stance toward library service will instill that concept in new staff members from the first day on, both by articulating its importance and by example.

College Courses

While the Association of College and Research Libraries (ACRL) considers a master's degree in library science to be terminal and sufficient for promotion into advanced professorial status or a library equivalent of that rank, this policy is often contradicted by campus practice. Many institutions require their librarians to acquire either a second master's degree or a Ph.D. in order to be promoted to the rank of assistant or associate librarian. Even in colleges where no written policy mandates education beyond the master's for librarians, informal norms and a desire for equal footing with teaching faculty create pressures to undertake advanced study. The director can help new librarians understand the benefits of further education and can design support mechanisms that enable them to pursue advanced degrees without damaging the ongoing work of the library. Advancement is by no means the sole or even most important reason for pursuit of further education. The library program is immeasurably enriched and strengthened by staff members who understand the structures of academic discipline and the nature of research, and can relate this knowledge to librarianship.

Support staff, too, require encouragement in their quest for further education. The availability of educational opportunity on the campus may for some have occasioned their decision to work at the library. Granting release time and flexibility in scheduling can act as an incentive to dedicated, capable employees to join the library staff at least for the period it takes to complete a degree. In addition, for the duration of their time in school they become, by default, spokespersons for the library and enhance and extend the ability of the library to present its message.

Staff Travel to Workshops and Professional Meetings

Funding travel for attending conferences, visiting other libraries to study procedures, and participating in workshops and institutes is part of the cost of maintaining continued excellence in library service. Although professional travel and staff development funds at most institutions are limited, each library will have some money available to support a few trips or attendance at several workshops. Library schools, professional organizations, state libraries, and network consortia all offer professional development opportunities for librarians to refurbish or hone old skills or to acquire new ones. The salutary effects of visits to other colleges, particularly those whose libraries are considered exemplary, can not be underestimated. Closer to home, staff retreats, lasting from a few hours to perhaps two days and held in a campus location other than the library, can stimulate fresh thinking about old problems, or enthusiasm for new ventures. Brainstorming and other problem-solving techniques facilitate the development of consensus and build group cohesiveness. A brown-bag lunch in the library with a featured speaker from an academic department or an administrative office in the college is simple to arrange, may be politically wise, and can provide a useful learning experience.

Attendance at local, state and national library association meetings and active participation in organizational work encourage useful cross-participation and broaden staff horizons. Librarians, like other professionals, have a need to confer, to compare notes, consult and share experiences. Most libraries may have insufficient funds available to defray completely the expenses of full participation in outside professional local events. Even-handed treatment of staff is best assured by guidelines which equitably distribute limited resources. Among the criteria considered when making decisions about allocating travel funds are whether staff are members in the organization whose conference they wish to attend, whether they hold an office, have committee responsibilities, are presenting a paper or participating in a panel. Some academic libraries choose to apportion the limited travel funds equally among their librarians, with the choice of professional activity left to the recipient. While libraries may, by necessity, offer scant financial support to those traveling to meetings, they can accord recognition of the value of participation by permitting attendance on library time. However limited funds are, some of them should be earmarked for activities that benefit the whole staff.

ETHICAL RELATIONS OF LIBRARIANS

Professions, as distinct from occupations or trades, are characterized by formal training in a field whose core is a cognitive body of knowledge, the development of skills relating to this knowledge, and an institutional framework controlling the application of those skills. A code of ethics that defines the relationship between the individual or group and the society, and to each other, is an integral part of a profession's social ethos. Two important American Library Association documents form the ethical base from which all librarians operate: the *Code of Ethics* and the *Library Bill of Rights*. The first focuses on the responsibilities of librarians to each other and to the agencies in which they are employed.[18] The other stresses the rights of library users to receive information from all points of view, and the obligation of librarians to supply it.[19]

Librarians have a responsibility to be honest stewards of the resources entrusted to their care, to be fair in their dealings with all individuals, employees, co-workers and library users, to speak out in support of the rights of individuals to access to information, and to insure the confidentiality of library circulation records. Most college librarians will not have to contend, as did *Columbia University* and many others, with requests from the FBI to search circulation records to determine whether any alleged spies have checked out materials. On the other hand, college libraries are regularly asked by faculty and students to reveal who has borrowed a particular book. While less common, it is not unusual for faculty to request circulation librarians to allow them to see the borrowing records of a particular student in order to help identify plagiarized materials. A decision about whether to purchase a controversial item should be based on merit and need, not pressure from a campus faction.

Attempts to censor college library materials must be met with resistance, and principles of academic freedom vigorously defended. Librarians participating in discussions of social issues have a duty to distinguish between their social responsibilities as citizens and their social responsibilities as librarians.

Care must be taken not to permit an "ends justifies the means" attitude to prevail when setting policies and determining goals. The need to retrench, for instance, requires honest and realistic appraisal of priorities. Collection development decisions should be based on objective criteria, not coercion by aggressive faculty. Attaching undue importance to numbers of library holdings leads to dubious methods of counting, to abandonment of book selection principles, or to inadequate weeding. Over-infatuation with library statistics of all kinds brings with it the danger of emphasizing quantity rather than quality of performance.

Ethical conduct in personnel matters requires librarians to judge employees fairly and not let professional rivalries or personal bias intrude on decisions. Librarians must not permit the needs of the library to impede an employee's progress. Promotions should be granted even when this may mean a temporary loss of sufficient personnel for a particular department. Similarly, requests for professional references should be met honestly and be reliable, objective and free from bias. With the opening of personnel files, letters of reference have grown more generous and thus, less reliable. It is tempting to wax eloquent about the few good virtues of an inadequate staff member whose presence on the staff is a constant irritant. Needless to say, such a response is unethical.

The nature of the college's responsibility to the librarian in matters of appointment, promotion or tenure have been discussed earlier in the chapter. Librarians, too, have responsibilities to the library and the institution. Except when circumstances are intolerable, librarians have an obligation to remain in a position long enough to have achieved definite results before considering a move. Training on any job is expensive, and benefits to the employer do not begin to accrue for some time after a new employee has joined the staff. While the time period may vary with the position and the institution, two years is considered a minimum. Common courtesy calls for librarians actively considering another position to discuss their plans with the director. When a true decision to leave has been made, librarians owe their directors at least two or three months before departure, and if possible should arrange to have their leave-taking coincide with the end of the semester.

Just as college librarians accept the responsibility to behave in an ethical manner toward their community, the community has the same obligation to behave ethically toward its librarians. Library directors must often protect staff from attacks, particularly by faculty requesting special privileges. Defending the rights of the library and its employees in these situations can be difficult and unpleasant, and may require appeal to the highest authorities in the college. Library employees have a right to expect this level of loyalty and support from their directors.

SUMMARY

Without competent staff, a good library collection languishes and the college loses the benefit of its investment. The goal of human resources management, the term currently used to describe personnel work, is to make certain that all employees are treated fairly and that they remain motivated to perform good work. Libraries are among the civilizing institutions in our society and their treatment of employees should reflect that orientation.

Managers review job descriptions, help establish classifications for positions, evaluate performance, offer adequate compensation and working conditions and make commitments to provide for ongoing development of the staff. Librarians have a right to loyalty, support and ethical behavior from the library and college administration.

NOTES AND SUGGESTED READINGS

Notes

1. "Standards for College Libraries," *College and Research Libraries News* 47 (March 1986): 194.

2. Association of College and Research Libraries, *Library Statistics of Colleges and Universities, 1985: National Summaries, State Summaries, Institutional Tables* (Chicago: ACRL, 1987). Data on 3,000 academic libraries from 1985 HEGIS study.

3. Patricia Senn Breivik and E. Gordon Gee, *Information Literacy: Revolution in the Library* (New York: American Council on Education and Macmillan, 1989), 112.

4. Richard Hume Werking, "Collection Growth and Expenditures in Academic Libraries: A Preliminary Inquiry," *College and Research Libraries* 52 (January 1991): 8.

5. Sheila Creth and Frederika Duda, *Personnel Administration in Libraries*, 2nd ed. (New York: Neal Schuman, 1989).

6. June Lester, "Education for Librarianship, a Report Card," *American Libraries* 21 (June 1990): 580 +.

7. Office for Library Personnel Resources, American Library Association. *Academic and Public Librarians Data by Race, Ethnicity, and Sex, 1986.* (Chicago: American Library Association, 1986). Also summarized in *Library Personnel News* 5 (January/February 1991): 5.

8. Association of College and Research Libraries, "Guidelines and Procedures for the Screening and Appointment

of Academic Librarians," *College and Research Libraries News* 38 (September 1977): 231-233; American Library Association. Office for Library Personnel Resources, *Hiring Library Staff* (Topics in Personnel, No. 8 (Chicago: American Library Association, 1986); Gregory Pogue, "The Academic Search Process: A Candidate's View," *Black Issues in Higher Education* 7 (28 February 1991): 7.

9. James M. Kusack. *Unions for Academic Library Support Staff.* (Westport CT: Greenwood, 1986) 24.

10. Ronald Gilardii, "The Representational Right of Academic Librarians: Their Status as Managerial Employees and/or Supervisors under the NLRB," *College and Research Libraries* 51 (January 1990): 40.

11. William M. Weinberg, "Collective Bargaining and Librarians," in *Recurring Library Issues: A Reader*, ed. Caroline M. Coughlin (Metuchen, NJ: Scarecrow Press, 1979), 362-378.

12. "Annual Report on the Economic Status of the Profession, 1990-91," *Academe* 7 (March/April, 1990) 9-90 and *Chronicle of Higher Education* 38 (April 1990) 1+.

13. Mary Jo Lynch, Margaret Myers and Jeniece Guy, *ALA Survey of Librarian Salaries, 1990* (Chicago: American Library Association, 1990).

14. TIAA-CREF, *Getting Your Plan in Shape* (New York: TIAA-CREF, 1988) and TIAA-CREF, Keeping Your Plan in Shape (New York: TIAA-CREF, forthcoming [1991]); and *Benefits Plan Counselor*, 1980-date, a newsletter published by TIAA-CREF.

15. Carolyn Kenady, *Pay Equity: An Action Manual for Library Workers* (Chicago: American Library Association, 1989) and American Library Association. Office for Library Personnel Resources, *Pay Equity Issues and Strategies (Topics in Personnel,* 9) (Chicago: Office for Library Personnel Resources, American Library Association, 1986).

16. Elaine S. Fox, "Employer Checklist for Determining Just Cause Discharge," *Library Personnel News* 4 (Spring 1990): 24.

17. Charles Martell and Richard Dougherty as quoted in Jana Varlejs, "Cost Models for Staff Development in Academic Libraries," *Journal of Academic Librarianship* 12 (January 1987): 360.

18. Lee W. Finks, "Librarianship Needs a New Code of Ethics," *American Libraries* 22 (January 1991): 86.

19. American Library Association. *Intellectual Freedom Manual.* 3d. ed. (Chicago: American Library Association, 1989): 14.

Suggested Readings

American Library Association, Office for Library Personnel Resources. *Managing Employee Performance.* Topics in Personnel, No. 11. Chicago: American Library Association, 1988.

American Library Association, Office for Library Personnel Resources. *Writing Library Job Descriptions.* Topics in Personnel, 7. Chicago: American Library Association, 1984.

American Library Association, Committee on the Status of Women in Librarianship. *Equality in Librarianship: A Guide to Sex Discrimination Laws*. 2nd ed. Chicago: American Library Association, 1990.

Association of College and Research Libraries. *Academic Status: Statements and Resources*, compiled by the Academic Status Committee. Chicago: Association of College and Research Libraries, 1988.

Creth, Sheila D. *Effective On-The-Job Training: Developing Library Human Resources*. Chicago: American Library Association, 1986.

Getz, Malcolm. "Fringe Benefits." *The Bottom Line* 3:2 (1989): 39-42

Heim, Kathleen M. and William E. Moen. *Occupational Entry: Library and Information Science Students' Attitudes, Demographics and Aspirations Survey*. Chicago: Office for Library Personnel Resources, American Library Association, 1989. Also summarized in *American Libraries* 19 (November 1988): 858-60.

Jenkins, Barbara Williams. *Performance Appraisal in Academic Libraries*. CLIP Note #12. Chicago: Association of College and Research Libraries, 1990.

Library Personnel News, 1987-date. Office for Library Personnel Resources, American Library Association.

Lipow, Anne, ed. *Staff Development in Libraries Bibliography*. Chicago: Library Administration and Management Association, American Library Association, 1989.

Oberg, Larry. "Paraprofessionals: Shaping the New Reality." Guest editorial. *College and Research Libraries* 52:1 (January 1991) 3-4.

White, Herbert S. *Library Personnel Management.* White Plains: Knowledge Industry Publications, Inc., 1985.

Chapter 17

STUDENT ASSISTANTS

College and university libraries, unlike other types of libraries, hire a great number of student employees and rely on them to accomplish work that is done elsewhere by permanent support staff. In sheer numbers, student assistants comprise the majority of personnel in most libraries. Unfortunately, given an average work week of seven hours, an average tenure of two years, lack of previous work experience and relative immaturity in meeting responsibilities outside of the classroom, they rarely are fully integrated into the library's program.

OPPORTUNITIES AND LIMITATIONS

Student assistants are capable of and render useful service to the library in a variety of ways. Not only do they perform routine tasks such as shelving books, checking out materials, filing, and typing, but they also provide exceptionally good access to the student body. By using student assistants properly, staff can gain better understanding of student needs for library service and in turn can transmit information about the library back to students. At the same time, student assistants acquire good work experience, become more effective students through their association with library procedures and materials, and are exposed to career possibilities in librarianship. Successful cultivation and exploitation of this mutually beneficial relationship depends, in part, on how carefully the library selects and trains student assistants, as well as investigating mechanisms to improve their productivity and job satisfaction. Contrary to initial impressions, that may not be as easy, or as practical, as it first appears. Cost-benefit ratio scales tip heavily toward the expense side when student assistants are so numerous and require so much attention that they overwhelm the staff with supervisory duties.

The sheer number of student employees required by a library to meet its service schedule, combined with the exigencies of student behavior, dictates that regular staff will be continually engaged in training new students. Students think, justifiably, that school work must take precedence over a library obligation if they are to achieve their education in a timely fashion. As a result, they frequently fail to work their full complement of hours, particularly during examination times. Often mercurial, students change jobs on short notice, usually because of opportunities to better their pay or improve their schedules. Some immature students take unanticipated holidays, oversleep, or simply don't meet their assigned schedules. Others, limited by their work-study package to a specific number of hours, sometimes find they have reached their allowable amount by mid-semester and must immediately stop working.

On the benefit side, students are willing to work evenings, weekends and odd times, permitting the library to extend hours beyond what could be offered using only permanent staff. Student assistants enable the library both to be more flexible in scheduling than is possible using only full-time help and to insure that sufficient staff is available when the library is busy. Generally bright and quick to learn, student employees know and comprehend curricular requirements far better than do regular staff, are often more familiar with computers and other new technology, and certainly understand better and have easier relations with their peers. Finally, students bring a questioning attitude to their work, regularly challenging established patterns of thinking and operating.

The advantages to students of working in the college library should not be under-estimated. Student assistants quickly become well acquainted with the library, acquire familiarity with a great variety of books merely by handling and shelving them, overcome the bewilderment experienced by most freshmen when they first confront a large college collection, and learn that there is more to a library than the reserve book room.

WORK ASSIGNMENTS

Meshing imperfect work schedules of students, who must remain students first and employees second, with the needs and the goals of the library presents a challenge. The demonology of library staffing places students at the bottom of the heap and bestows on them the least desirable jobs. Keith Cottam argues that students have the potential to be excellent library employees if the permanent library staff will develop proper roles for them.

Students should be given significant tasks in their library experience, work which provides them with responsibilities commensurate with their abilities and is capable of promoting critical analysis and decision making. They can be successfully given direct contact with the public through information desks and other service points, they can plan and coordinate many different types of projects and programs, they can supervise fellow students, they can work with communications through such things as staff bulletins and committee meetings, they can do creative work with displays and they can compile bibliographies.[1]

What at first glance may seem a visionary and inflated notion of what students can accomplish in the library becomes more realistic in light of the realization that they already perform much of the work Cottam describes. They have steady, direct contact with the public at the circulation desk. Many students staff the information desk as aides to reference librarians. More experienced student assistants function as supervisors to newer employees. The problem, however, is not that students lack the ability to perform more challenging work, but that permanent staff may have neither the time nor the inclination to assist them in doing it. Libraries are chronically understaffed and much of the work is repetitive and unchallenging. It seems only natural that the least desirable tasks be assigned to those employees who work short shifts and limited hours, and to save the more interesting work for permanent employees. A good mix of skilled and unskilled work assignments, sufficient variety, socializing and responsibility will keep students from becoming bored.

CLASSIFICATION AND COMPENSATION

The new professionalism in many college student aid and employment offices has led to the development of systems of classification for student jobs. The systems mimic regular job classification schedules, but generally identify only three grades of student employees, rather than the ten or twelve categories that ordinarily appear in a more comprehensive employee system.

Grade One jobs are generally repetitive in nature and require substantial training and supervision. No previous experience or particular set of skills is required from the employee.

Grade Two jobs call for limited use of independent judgment and knowledge of various systems and procedures.

Grade Three jobs may involve supervision of other students, use of specialized knowledge and substantial independent judgment.

All student library jobs are amenable to analysis using this division and all libraries have jobs at each level that can be offered to students.[2] Some students prefer to see their employment as incidental to their school work and do not seek to advance beyond mastery of basic tasks. This is an acceptable choice, one that should be respected if the student's work is satisfactory. Students who wish to progress, who have proven their competence and shown initiative, can be provided with additional challenges and responsibilities, and moved up the classification ladder. Proceeding in this manner may help to diminish the turnover rate among student employees. Pay scales that reflect the increased responsibility required at each level may act as a further incentive for students to return to the library rather than seek other employment.

Unfortunately, libraries often play little or no part in setting salaries for student employees. Wage policy is generally established for the entire college, and libraries must act accordingly. The library can assure, however, that their student assistants are not paid less than students in positions of comparable responsibility in other parts of the campus. Every effort should be made to provide a small increase in wages to students at the end of a certain period of service. Even a token amount may encourage a good assistant to remain with the library. As one of the larger employers of students, it is also appropriate for the library administration to be involved in or to stimulate the creation of campus-wide task forces on the subject of student employees.

Students employed in college libraries are compensated with funds allocated in the library budget for hourly wage work, from scholarships or from grants-in-aid, sometimes referred to as work-study or bursary grants. A student employment budget that allocates both work study and hourly categories is preferable to one that permits payment only from aid packages. Some colleges mandate that work-study students be given priority in employment. Others allow experienced students—those who have worked before for the library—to be hired first, but demand that preferential status be given students on aid when filling subsequent jobs. Students are chosen on fitness for the position, not need, but the two are not mutually exclusive.

HIRING, ORIENTATION AND TRAINING

A single library staff member, one who communicates well, can recognize student potential for accepting responsibility, and can match the needs of library departments with the talents of assistants, is generally delegated responsibility for selecting, and hiring students and giving them their assignments. Applicants are asked to complete a form containing essential information: name, home and local address, local telephone number, college status, social security number, amount of the work-study allocation, if pertinent, and how many hours of work are desired. An upper limit in the number of hours students can work in campus jobs is imposed by most colleges. Conversely, libraries restrict hiring to those students willing to work a minimum of five hours per week. Application forms for students should be designed with sufficient space to list previous employment on and off campus as well as information about volunteer experience or special skills. Libraries receiving an insufficient number of applications to meet needs must actively recruit students by sending letters to selected groups—all first-year students, for instance, or other targeted groups—or by attending an all-campus work fair. The most effective recruiting is through current student assistants.

A brief interview is used to ascertain students' qualifications, explore possible work assignments, explain basic responsibilities of the position, describe the wage scale and learn the hours that the student has available for work. Needless duplication in staffing can be avoided if this information is acquired prior to hiring. Successful applicants are offered a position in writing, and acknowledge acceptance of it by signing an employment contract. Among the provisions in a typical contract is the statement that students are responsible to work their assigned hours, or, if unable to work, that they notify their supervisor in advance. Failure to do so may carry a penalty—perhaps being scheduled in an undesirable time slot, or being assigned a less interesting task. Repeated failure should produce more serious consequences.

Students who receive clear, consistent and complete instructions at the outset about their responsibilities and tasks become far better and more dependable workers. Orientation for students, in addition to meeting the staff, includes introduction to the library goals and objectives, to its rules and regulations, and to its procedures. It also involves careful training in specific work routines. Also, students must be reminded that they are involved in real work, rather than a recreational situation, and that there are behavioral expectations, including appropriate demeanor and conscientious attention to work.

Students learn quickly, but often incompletely. The impatience of youth sometimes results in partial understanding of a job. Frequent checks of their work, therefore, are essential, particularly at the outset. Students are formally evaluated after a probationary period. A simple rating checklist enables librarians to identify absenteeism, attitude, industry and the quality of work, and to take action based on the record. Acceptable performance needs to be recognized and praised, and unsatisfactory work clearly specified. If students do not adequately meet the demands of the job, they must be warned, and later reevaluated and dismissed if their work shows no improvement.

Students like to feel they are welcome on the staff. They enjoy being included in staff-wide social gatherings (especially ones with homemade food) and other library events. Recognition ceremonies for graduating student assistants acknowledge all students indirectly and help to cement relations.

Library staff who care and who listen to students can begin to serve as their mentors vocationally, academically, and in other ways. Teaching faculty on college campuses report great satisfaction from helping to shape young minds. Library faculty and staff deserve no less from their work with student employees.

When students terminate their library employment, a permanent record of their work history and performance is placed in their files. A document describing duties assigned and containing an overall evaluation of the employee's efforts, as well as length of service and reason for leaving, provides ample information on which to base a recommendation. For many students, their position at the library represents their total work experience. Students should be informed that they may use the library director or a particular staff member as a reference when applying for a position, and made to understand that their work performance will be the basis of a recommendation.

Students as Potential Librarians

Many current librarians had their first library work experience in college. Some report that they were attracted to the field because of the pleasure of working on interesting projects with dedicated and creative librarians. It is also unfortunately true that others have found the field a safe harbor as a result of work with kind, steady, unchallenging library workers. An experimental project of the Council on Library Resources (CLR) at Yale University Library offers specialized, rigorous internships in management to a select group of undergraduates as a recruitment device. The concept seems worthy of emulation elsewhere. A student provided with a challenging and exciting experience gains deep understanding of the issues facing college librarianship, can share those perceptions with others, and represents a possibility for attracting talent to the field.

SUMMARY

Hiring, training and making good use of a flock of new employees each year is a challenge to any supervisor. It is an even greater challenge when the employees are not full-time, have had little or no previous work experience and perhaps, due to inexperience, lack a strong orientation to work. College libraries are different from their counterparts in other parts of the profession in the reliance they must place on undergraduate students. Students can, however, make excellent contributions to the library both in their work and as conduits through which information is channeled from and to the library. Appreciation of good performance should include raises, recognition, increased responsibility and, at graduation, a good reference placed in the student's file.

NOTES AND SUGGESTED READINGS

Notes

1. Keith M. Cottam, "Student Employees in Academic Libraries," *College and Research Libraries* 31 (July 1970): 247.

2. Michael D. Kathman and Jane McGurn Katham, *Managing Student Workers in College Libraries*, CLIP Note No. 7 (Chicago, Association of College and Research Libraries, 1986) 15-26.

Suggested Readings

Fuller, F. Jay. "Evaluating Student Assistants as Library Employees." *College and Research Libraries News* 51 (January 1990): 11-13.

White, Emilie.   "Student Assistants in Academic Libraries: from Reluctance to Reliance."   *Journal of Academic Librarianship* 11 (May 1985): 93-97.

Woodward, Beth S. "The Effectiveness of an Information Desk Staffed by Graduate Students and Nonprofessionals." *College and Research Libraries* 50 (July 1989): 455-67.

See also Chapter 4, Astin and others.

Chapter 18

BUSINESS AND FINANCIAL AFFAIRS

The business and financial affairs of the college are entrusted to a number of individuals, each of whom is ultimately responsible to the president. The typical college has a treasurer, a comptroller and a business manager who report to the president, either directly or through a vice president for administration. The treasurer, with advice from the comptroller, sets financial policy, controls the flow of money in and out of the college, and establishes proper accounting procedure. The business officer disburses and collects money for services that the college provides, among other activities, orders supplies, prepares the payroll and collects tuition fees. In smaller colleges, personnel services and the bookstore operation may also be the responsibility of the business officer. Larger colleges with sufficient staff may subdivide financial tasks still further and maintain separate departments to handle accounts payable, accounts receivable, purchasing and inventory, investments, personnel, and perhaps budget monitoring.

Although financial officers must oversee and ensure the fiscal integrity of an institution, their duties will probably not include judging the merit of a particular budget request, or granting it final approval. This duty belongs to the chief academic officer, although in many colleges a select group of faculty review budgets in terms of their relationship to campus priorities. Academic deans provide leadership about budget priorities; treasurers document the college's financial state. Based, then, on information about previous and current income and expenditures, the combined group sets future budgets. Relationships with both faculty and administrators who work on the budget are important to the library. The director must provide them with pertinent and clear information in a timely fashion. A director who has earned a reputation for competence and reliability among members of the finance group will place the library in an advantageous position when decisions must be reached.

Business offices and finance committees require different kinds of information. A review of the budget cycle—development, implementation and evaluation—should clarify the director's tasks, types of information required, and schedule for action. At any given time, budget events may overlap. Budgets are developed one full year in advance of implementation, during a period when money is being spent for a budget that was approved the previous year. Through the course of a year, librarians may be required to create, in addition to an annual budget, project budgets for capital expenditures or for grant applications. Winning sound financial backing for a library requires the successful performance of two important tasks. The first is to establish rational and mutually satisfying procedures to deal with campus officers who handle the library's financial affairs. The second is to develop cost-effective, convincing and defensible budgets which include adequate resources to support the short- and long-term goals of the library.

Among characteristic transactions among librarians and business managers and controllers are: placing purchase orders, paying bills, checking monthly business office ledgers and reports against library financial records to guard against budget overruns, determining insurance inventories and coverage, inventorying equipment, paying staff salaries and benefits, transferring funds from one budget category to another, and collecting any fines charged against student accounts. A satisfactory relationship with these officers depends on applying common sense and courtesy as well as on sound business practices. The business office will expect the library staff responsible for working with it to maintain adequate records for the library, to adhere to common practice with respect to deadlines, and authorizations, and to handle carefully direct expenditures of funds. Personal relations between library staff and business office personnel will help to smooth out the small but regular snags which occur in any organization dealing with a multiplicity of small pieces of paper. In addition, library financial procedures developed over a period of time should be documented to help avert disagreements and to avoid problems when there is staff turnover.

SOURCES OF INCOME

There are three main sources of library funds. The principal source is an appropriation from the current operating budget of the college. The other two sources are grants and gifts. Adequate allocations for colleges depend most heavily on the general availability of funds. Presidents and budget committees have only a small amount of discretionary money to allocate each year. The smaller the budget of the entire college, the smaller the budget of its parts, including the library. The second crucial element in securing funds for the library is the ability of the library director to convince the decision makers of the soundness of the library's projected budget.

The period of rapid financial expansion that characterized higher education in the 1960s and 1970s has ended and been replaced in most colleges by a need for budget tightening. This may include imposing cutbacks, reallocating resources, or simply managing in a steady-state environment. Actual dollars dedicated to the tasks of higher education have continued to increase. However, the combined effects of years of high inflation and an increase in the number of programs competing for a share of the available dollars have resulted in shortfalls for academic libraries. Their budgets have often lagged behind the pace of inflation, particularly that part allocated to book and periodical acquisition. In some colleges there have also been periods of retrenchment as enrollments have declined or state governments have withdrawn support in the face of weakened economies. Some colleges have been forced to make across-the-board reductions mid-year in the budget cycle, or when preparing the following year's budget. The strong private liberal arts colleges have suffered least, and their libraries are less likely to have retrogressed during this difficult financial period. But accountability now reigns even in those institutions, and all budget requests for new services and collections must be justified and vigorously defended.

One salutary by-product of the decline in funding is that libraries, along with other parts of the academic community, have begun to pay stricter attention to issues of financial planning, cost benefits, alternate budget models and budget presentation. The need to make choices has had serious consequences for some excellent academic programs. Often the library is among those that has suffered from these decisions. A few institutions have chosen, as did Trinity College in Texas, to place major emphasis on the rapid development of outstanding library collections in preference to other undertakings.

Most privately-controlled colleges have endowment funds specifically designed for the library. In older, well-established institutions these funds may be substantial, but most colleges receive only a small income from endowments or, as a matter of fact, from any alternate income sources.[1] Funds from endowments are usually designated to be used to purchase books. The fortunate library is also permitted to use endowment income to pay for the processing of materials purchased with endowment funds. Memorial funds in honor of a distinguished faculty member, a college officer, an alumnus, student, or friend are often made part of the library's endowment, rather than used immediately to make a purchase. The larger the endowment, the more useful it is to the library. If fewer subject or other restrictions are imposed the value of the gift is similarly enhanced. Development offices generally work closely with the library director to attract endowment gifts and to help establish guidelines for their use. Most college libraries set a minimum size of $5,000 for a named endowment, but the amount varies with the general fortunes of the library.

Grants

Grants from foundations are another potential source of non-appropriated income. Both local and national foundations are often willing to support library building programs, library automation efforts, or the establishment of collections to support one or more newer areas of the curriculum. A local foundation that agrees to fund a new professor and program in Near Eastern Studies may also be willing to consider granting the library seed money to build the collection in that area. The articulate, visible library director will have convinced development officers that library materials are needed to support any new program, so that as grants are being developed a sum is included for the purchase of materials. National foundations such as the Pew Charitable Trusts or the Kresge Foundation may identify certain library needs as target areas for their funds. Librarians are expected to gather information documenting need that development officers can use to shape a proposal, and to give informed briefings to foundation officials who make campus visits. Foundation giving is an important source of support, particularly for private colleges.   Alert directors maintain an interest in foundations which regularly grant funds to college libraries. The activities of major foundations that support libraries can be located in the *Bowker Annual*, annual reports of foundations and the *Foundation Directory*.

A number of state and federal agencies fund library-related programs.   The purposes of grants administered by these agencies are generally tied to national and state educational goals and can range from increasing retention rates of minority students to wiring the campus for newer technologies. Governmental agencies establish sets of procedures to follow when making application for grants. Often complicated, they almost always entail a substantial amount of paperwork. Before embarking on the application process, it is well to insure that the central program being promoted in the grants is one that supports the mission of the library and that there is a fit between the college's agenda and the guidelines of the funding body. Preliminary conversations with the staff of the grant agency prior to application may save needless effort.

Small grant applications, ones that require little preparation and make limited demands on staff time, are not a problem. Grants entailing major investments of time and effort in preparation, and mandating excessive commitments for implementation, are only sought when their goals fit well with those of the library. All libraries desire the support that comes from external funding agencies but caution should be taken to avoid any unanticipated and deleterious side effects.[2]

Gifts

Increased pressure to look beyond routine channels for library funds has caused librarians to view with mounting favor gifts from personal libraries. Practically all libraries receive gifts of books from members of the faculty, alumni and friends of the college. Unfortunately, the great majority of items are of little value or use. Nonetheless, all individual gifts should be acknowledged by the director and accepted with the understanding that the gift policy of the library will guide the disposition of the item. If the donor has requested an appraisal of the collection, assistance should be offered to the extent that the law permits. The wisest course is to maintain a list of independent appraisers who will assess the value of the gift. Donors appreciate their names being placed on a bookplate. Large or valuable collections may merit the design of a special bookplate. The library must retain the right to decide on the disposition of a gift. Items useful today may become inappropriate over time and lack of control over their ultimate disposal may result in stacks full of useless material. Some gifts should be discouraged at the start. In these cases, a frank but tactful discussion with the donor, in which the librarian stresses the costs of processing items and the need to develop collections that support the curriculum, may help to ameliorate any potential slight.

THE BUDGET AND EDUCATION AND GENERAL EXPENDITURES

Standards for College Libraries recommends that a minimum of six per cent of the Educational and General Expenditures portion of the college budget be allocated to libraries. In the most selective colleges, the figure often exceeds—sometimes by several percentage points—the recommended minimum. In 1985 the median Education and General Expenditures for libraries was 4% in publicly supported bachelor degree granting institutions of higher education and 3% in private bachelor degree granting institutions. Only 25% of these publicly supported and 15% of the private ones reach 5% for their libraries in Education and General Expenditures. The 95th percentile for public bachelor degree-granting institutions is 8% and for private, 6%.[3] In the 1983-84 budget year, 82 billion dollars were expended on higher education, with 1.46 billion (2.8%) disbursed by academic libraries in the public sectors and 77 billion (2.6%) spent by those in private colleges and universities.[4] These dollar figures, while impressive in the aggregate, offer little solace to library directors faced with the difficult task of increasing the library's share of the education budget by even as little as one-tenth of one per cent. Proportions allocated to various college library services do not change easily. Indeed, over time the library may have seen its share diminish in the face of more pressing campus needs such as the development of a technological infrastructure or the strengthening of the admissions or development offices. Given the campus competition for available funds, library budget documents represent the most important short-term planning statements of the library. In most cases, they are also viewed as opportunities for political persuasion.

The budget is an estimate of the amount of money the library will require during the coming year or biennium in order to carry out its program. It is difficult exercise at best, but if the budget must be drawn up several years in advance of disbursement, as some state colleges require, the task of estimating financial need for specific programs is even more arduous. The director will have to remind college financial officers and others that the budget is an *estimate* of what will be required to purchase books, equipment, and staff, and that changes within categories between the time of the budget's creation and its execution may be necessary. No two college library directors will prepare the same budget. Variations result from differing college missions, the history of the library, college practices with respect to charge backs for physical plant and other services, and the budget development guidelines of the college.

BASICS IN BUDGET MAKING

Library directors have primary responsibility for preparing the library budget. Prior to its submission, they will have consulted with library staff, especially department heads, and held discussions with the library committee and the dean. The final document, however, and decisions about how much to request and for what are the responsibilities of the library director. Librarians are fortunate when they work in an institution where the cycle of budget request, budget approval and budget implementation permits them sufficient lead time to recruit new staff or design appropriate procedures after the request for new funds has been granted.

Previous year's budgets and expenditure statements form part of the data base necessary to compile a new budget. Typically, forms distributed by colleges for budgets are arranged by line item, with such categories as personnel, fringe benefits, supplies, equipment and materials called out in a predictable order and identified by codes unique to the college library and accompanied by a blank to accommodate the requested amount. Some institutions provide a two-column approach to budget requests, with the first representing a minimal request and the second, a desired one. In certain categories, the previous year's expenditures will predict the minimum amounts necessary for the following year. If, for instance, the postage budget was overspent because the cost of mailing first-class materials rose during the budget year, an increased amount must be built into the following year's budget. Similarly, an expectation of a price rise in the cost of membership for a regional bibliographical utility will be reflected in the proposed budget. Once the non-negotiable items are identified, then attention is turned to identifying budget categories where changes are desirable or at least negotiable. Even apparently fixed cost items may have some variability, and these should be considered as well. For example, the number of hours the library is open is subject to increase or decrease. Imposing a change in either direction will require more or fewer dollars to pay staff for service.

The assumption underlying all budget discussions is that the library serves a public good, and is, in effect, the best and most cost-effective agency to provide information options for the entire community. Ann Prentice suggests that the social contract which affirms these assumptions may not be as firmly or securely established on college campuses as librarians believe it to be. Reasserting its centrality may become increasingly important in the future as more alternative, often private, information agencies develop.[5] The argument made by faculty, that their departments rather than the library should conduct and therefore be allocated funds for end-user on-line searching, illustrates how real is the potential for shift in the campus social contract about the appropriate location for information access and retrieval.

Because of the possible dangers of privatization, librarians must be certain that each budget category has sufficient funds to support a sound program of library service, one which will deter college administrations from hiring outside suppliers. Aggressive action may be necessary and librarians may be forced to argue vigorously, not only for continued funding at high levels of the basic program but also for support of new, expensive services.

Zero-based budgeting, the expectation that all programs both new and ongoing must justify their value on an annual basis, is rarely imposed today in college environments. Instead, new programs are expected to be fully described and costed out, and possible savings from other parts of the budget allocated to them. This approach represents a modified version of program budgeting. The library's standard programs are those of acquiring materials, organizing them for use, and disseminating and interpreting them through activities of circulation, administration, reference and bibliographic instruction. Linking these functional areas of the library to the changing goals of the college is equally important to budget preparation, even if the documentation is abbreviated.

Creating retrenchment budgets has been painful for librarians. On the other hand, it has permitted staffs and directors to come to grips with the necessity of making choices among programs, choices which perforce have been analyzed in terms of costs and benefits and placed in the context of alternatives. Cost-benefit studies that translate services into economic terms can indicate the degree to which such enterprises as interlibrary loan or processing a monograph are worth the investment.[6]

The final set of commonly agreed priorities, usually a mix of ongoing and new programs, becomes the budget. No matter the method used to develop a budget, it is almost always translated into traditional line categories of staffing, supplies and materials.

New curricular thrusts of the college, for instance, will find echoes in the library's budget. A library may seek funds to enlarge the periodical collection in order to meet recently increased needs of students in a newer program area. Too often, administrators bypass the library when instituting new courses, and needs for material may go unrecognized until a faculty member learns a new subject well enough to be aware of its scholarly output. Alternatively, the acquisitions of library resources may be deferred until the program has gained acceptance on the campus and generated sufficient student enrollment to insure its long-term viability. In either case, by year two or three of a new program, sufficient evidence of its staying power and its material requirements should be available to make a case that will gain support.

The argument for funds to offer students and faculty free online searching can also find its base in the college's mission. Estimates of use and cost, as well as a description of the nature of the service and a review of its current availability compared with similar institutions, will be required.

A sagging book budget, one that has suffered from excessive inflation over the past decade and received insufficient support in previous budgets because only a four per cent rate of inflation was factored, ill serves a college's ability to provide for the information needs of its students. This can be demonstrated by providing actual inflation figures for books and periodicals, and by buttressing the arguments with accounts of the number of books *not* bought in a particular discipline.

Obviously, all these projections assume growth. When growth is impossible, and the program descriptions must address the issue of declining support, the choices are more difficult. It is never wise to propose cuts that cannot be implemented, and it is always appropriate to describe the impact of cuts in terms meaningful to faculty and students. If possible, divide the proposed cut into segments. If a 50% cut is required, first reduce service by 25% and then by an additional 33%. One campus asks budget managers to begin their proposed budgets at 95%, and identify what programs this would eliminate. So successful is this exercise in revealing possible change and substitution that managers often find the proposed cuts remaining and new programs instituted when the budget is rebuilt to 100% or beyond.

The requirements for budget presentation will differ from campus to campus. A fortunate director is given the opportunity to present the budget in person to a review group. In colleges where faculty participate in budget determination, they will form part of the team to be educated and convinced. The director's goal for the budget presentation is to demonstrate how essential the library is to the academic program. A clear, well-documented description, with time allowed for a question and discussion period, furthers the effort. All too often the budget goes directly to the dean, and the decision is unilateral, or solely an administrative one. While the text of the final budget document may include comparative data about support given to libraries of similar institutions, the soundest approach to justifying the budget estimates is careful description and analysis of the library's own activities and needs. Whether the presentation is made to a committee or a single administrator, the need for copious attention to detail and justification remains essential.

The same principles of budgeting apply whether the document in preparation is a routine annual budget or a capital one designed to support a major effort—an integrated library system or a remodeling project, for instance. The request document must be linked to the goals of the college, should outline the program elements, estimate their respective costs, offer a timetable for implementation and describe the impact that a positive or a negative decision will have.

Budgets, as plans of action, should retain flexibility. For instance, the quality of microform service may be improved by buying a particular machine or by transferring some documents to microfiche from microfilm. Though one solution has been substituted for another in the middle of a calendar year, the spirit of the budget allocation has nonetheless been fulfilled. On the other hand, money designated for the improvement of microformatted services should not be spent on an entirely different program without returning to the budget authority to request permission to transfer funds. Directors must be especially cautious about shifting allocated funds from one large category to another—from, say, materials lines to staff lines. On many campuses, however, directors do have the authority to move money around within certain categories without outside approval. In addition, it is acceptable for them to recommend transfers as they become necessary or desirable. For example, money presently in the budget for a part-time circulation clerk may, if the position becomes vacant, be reallocated to the microforms room and used to hire staff to service machines—a currently more pressing need and therefore a better use of the funds. Requests should be made to the appropriate office to arrange this transfer.

DISTRIBUTION OF THE BUDGET

The principal parts of the library budget are salaries, materials and other operating expenses. While recommendations vary about the proper percentages to allot to each of these categories, a 60-30-10 breakdown—60% staff, 30% materials and 10% other—has frequently been suggested. The proportions deviate from institution to institution, based, in part, on current financial exigencies, past history, and book endowment funds. Institutions, for instance, that have suffered recent layoffs may find a larger proportion of their budgets invested in materials;

those that have not curtailed staff, but must retrench or control costs, may spend proportionately less for materials. A recent study of library expenditures by Richard Werking revealed that the proportion of most college library budgets allocated to staff and other expenses has enlarged over time, and that the increase has been at the expense of materials. The trend appears to be irreversible and may be responsible for the heightened importance accorded to funding *access* to materials, and for articulating that need in budget allocations that make it possible to deliver documents to patrons in a timely fashion.

Within the materials budget, further decisions about allocation ratios—between, for instance, monographs and periodicals—are necessary. While some libraries spend two-thirds or more of their budgets on serials, the median during the past ten years has fluctuated between 45% and 57%.[7] A college that does not use formula budgeting for the materials budget may find it fruitful to develop alternate ways to describe the relationships among expenditures for staff, materials and operating expenses. One approach is to cluster costs into categories of use by program. A discussion of allocation formulas that can be applied to the materials budget is found in Chapter 8.

Librarians are often reluctant to spend college funds to support their own professional endeavors, be it subscriptions to professional journals, money for continuing education workshops, or travel to professional meetings. It is a shortsighted policy that ultimately harms both librarians and the institution. Librarians who mask travel funds under other categories, use their own money, or decide not to make the expenditure do a disservice to the profession. In the words of the ancient philosopher Hillel, "If I am not for myself, who will be? And if not now, when?"

OTHER FINANCIAL CONCERNS

In addition to developing and monitoring the annual budget, and creating other budget documents or related cost-benefit studies, the library administration is responsible for maintaining additional fiscal records.

Insurance

For insurance purposes, an up-to-date inventory and evaluation of the books and other materials, catalog records and equipment is necessary. Fire and extended coverage insurance is maintained by most colleges for all buildings and their contents, generally on a blanket form with a 90% co-insurance clause. Most college librarians, however, consider this insurance inadequate for their libraries because it improperly values the contents of the buildings.

A variety of methods are available for estimating how much insurance is needed to properly cover a library's contents. Three elements are generally combined, no matter the method: one covers the bulk of the collection, based on an average per volume cost plus acquisition and accession fees; the second coverage is specific and usually applied to one kind of property—rare books, original paintings, and the like, which may have to be listed and evaluated individually; the third element covers the contents of the catalog, the cabinets or computers and the terminals themselves. The determination of the value of resources included by the blanket policy allows for some variation from the average insurable rate for very expensive books—art books, for instance—bound journals and microforms, and also for depreciation and appreciation of varying types of materials. The rate of obsolescence within disciplines varies and must be accounted for in the insurance estimate. In certain subjects, the older the publication the greater its value. In others, age decreases its usefulness. A document listing the size of collections according to classification, using the shelf list to estimate the number of items within a category, accompanied by an average cost of replacement for each discipline, should be maintained and can be used as the library's evaluation of the cost of its materials. If the policies are written on a co-insurance basis, it is important that the values of the various types of materials be reviewed every three or four years to assure that the coverage remains adequate.[8]

Library Bookkeeping

The fundamental purpose of library bookkeeping is to keep expenditures and encumbrances within the budget. Some other important use of these records are 1) to aid in the preparation of the next budget; 2) to plan for the prudent expenditure of the present budget; 3) to assist the teaching departments as they expend their allocated funds; and, 4) to serve as a planning tool.

In virtually all colleges, the major accounting responsibility for library funds, as for all other college funds, resides in the office of the comptroller. Most libraries receive from this office monthly records of expenditures and balances for various budget categories. If the library has endowment book funds in addition to the college appropriation, they are generally listed separately and an accounting of each fund is provided. The monthly recapitulation of the library's total transactions may be accompanied by a summary of percentages spent and remaining in various categories for the year to date to facilitate a comparison between anticipated revenues and expenditures and figures for the preceding year. Vigilant monitoring of these reports insure that the flow of funds is progressing at an acceptable rate. To ignore monthly financial summaries is to imperil the library's fiscal well-being.

Salary and Wages Records

Under normal circumstances, salaries of the library staff will remain constant from month to month. When there are variations, however—vacancies in position for an extended period, unpaid leaves of absence, sick leaves covered by workmen's compensation, replacement salaries that differ from budgeted ones—they must be noted and explained. During a year with many staffing changes, this can become complicated and difficult. Keeping track of redeployed funds when temporary, rather than permanent employees have been used to fill vacancies, or when money saved in one department has been allocated to paying for a one-time project—for example, bar-coding books for automation—is essential.

Library hourly and student employees are usually required to complete time sheets indicating the hours worked and have them signed by their supervisors. While originals of these records are forwarded to the business office for payment, the library should maintain copies of them to settle any disputes that may arise between an individual and the business office or to explain any discrepancies between the monthly financial statements and the library's records. When inconsistencies appear, accurate records quickly dissipate the potential for misunderstanding between agencies.

Automating financial records both in the library and in the business office has facilitated reporting capabilities and eliminated some errors. Problems, however, continue to occur and dual record keeping is still mandatory. Both the business office and the library are staffed by people, and people make mistakes. Remembering that all humans are fallible helps to ensure that the relationships between the library and the business office will remain cordial in the face of the occasional need to rectify mistakes.

Material Purchase Records

The college "budget activity sheets" furnish a monthly record of payments to book dealers, with subtotals indicating the outlays for the month, those for the year to date, and the balance remaining in the various book funds. These data are insufficient for library purposes, however, where a deeper level of specificity is required. Libraries must be aware of funds spent by various departments; they must track their encumbrances—orders sent to vendors that eventually become invoices and paid bills; they must monitor standing order accounts where material is sent automatically when published, rather than at periodic frequencies or in response to orders. Instituting procedures for record keeping is the responsibility of the head of acquisitions or collection development in larger libraries, or of the director in smaller ones. Many of the newer automated approaches to acquisitions work offer subsystems which facilitate record keeping. Unfortunately these systems are still imperfect and most libraries continue to maintain manually created back-up records. Keeping track of material purchases is not only time-consuming, but often tedious. The drudgery, however, can be offset by a smooth-running, well-oiled operation and by the pleasure of being first to see the new books before other staff or library users!

Miscellaneous Income, Petty Cash and Revolving Funds

In general, petty cash accounts are handled in two ways. Some libraries turn fine and replacement monies directly into petty cash. In other libraries, the petty cash fund is established by a cash payment from the treasurer's office. In this case, fines and other collectible income are turned over to the college, either as general income or as income credited to one or more library accounts earmarked for specific uses. Establishing a petty cash fund with the treasurer's office is preferable to handling both receipt and disbursement of local income exclusively within the director's office. If the first method, income from fines, is employed, a separate account book for all transactions should be kept. The second method requires drawing funds from the library's miscellaneous account housed in the treasurer's office to supply the petty cash fund. As small purchases using this money are made, vouchers indicating the item acquired and its cost, as well as receipts for it, are deposited in a petty cash box. When the funds have been depleted, records are presented to the business office and the library is presented with an amount equal to the total disbursements.

Revolving funds formed from income from fines, photocopy service fees and book sales are sometimes used to support particular programs—book replacements or purchase and maintenance of photoduplication equipment. In some colleges, these accounts must cohere with the library's budget year. More typically, colleges permit these funds to be carried from year to year as revolving accounts. Revolving accounts have additional sources and uses in college libraries. Some institutions utilize them to hold funds received from other agencies for contract services; others employ them to keep track of gifts of money to purchase books. Revolving accounts are often created to hold grant monies until a particular date, usually for the six months following the termination of the grant-related activity, after which the account is closed. Some colleges permit income from library-related programs to be placed into library accounts that are most needy at a given point in the budget year. This practice results in an imbalance between projected and actual expenditures, but it permits the director to bolster parts of the budget that may have suffered most from excessive inflation.

The records described above are not the only ones that libraries are obligated to form or expected to keep. Nor is it suggested that the procedures that have been outlined are the best or only means of building budgets or keeping such records. Colleges are complex institutions. Unique and peculiar patterns of organization characterize many of them. A library director will determine which records and budget planning documents are required to operate an effective and efficient library. Accommodations may be necessary in order to make the library conform with local practice, but these can be negotiated as long as they are based on a vision of what constitutes good library financial management.

SUMMARY

The financial responsibility of the library director can be described as a stewardship carrying the obligation to use the college's current resources in a manner that protects its investment in the future. The college is the major source of library funds, although external sources of support are of increasing interest and potential importance. Grants should be sought primarily when the grant agencies' goals are in keeping with the needs of the library. The business and financial offices of the college develop policies and procedures that relate to the disbursement of library funds, and it is crucial that relations between the library and those offices be cordial and harmonious.

The library budget is built according to guidelines established by the college and represents a short-term plan of action and argument for the library's program. Once the budget has been approved it will be translated into a line item budget and expenditures monitored monthly.

NOTES AND SUGGESTED READINGS

Notes

1.   Mary Jo Lynch, *Alternative Sources of Revenues for Academic Libraries*. *Chicago*: American Library Association, forthcoming [1991].

2.   Alice Gertzog, "Gathering Grants—Financial Boom or Bust?" *The Bottom Line*. Charter Issue [1986].

3. John Minter. *Statistical Norms for Colleges and University Libraries*. Boulder CO: John Minter Assoc., 1987 (derived from United States Department of Education 1985 Survey of Academic Libraries, known as HEGIS survey). The 2d edition covering the 1988 Survey of Academic Libraries was announced as available in April 1991.

4. American Council on Education, *1987-88 Handbook on Higher Education* (New York: Walter de Gruyter, 1987): 11.

5. Ann Prentice, *Financial Planning for Libraries* (Metuchen, NJ: Scarecrow Press, 1983): 3-52.

6. Carl Vinson "Cost Finding: A Step by Step Guide," *The Bottom Line* 2:3 (1988) 15-19.

7. Richard Hume Werking, "Collection Growth and Expenditures in Academic Libraries, A Preliminary Inquiry," *College and Research Libraries* 52 (January 1991): 20.

8. Gerald E. Myers, *Insurance Manual for Libraries*. (Chicago: American Library Association, 1977); and *Security for Libraries*, ed. by Marvina Brand (Chicago: American Library Association, 1984).

Suggested Readings

Boss, Richard. *Grant Money and How to Get It*. New York: R. R. Bowker, 1980.

Bottom Line 1987-date. NY: Neal Schuman.

"Faculty and the Budget." Special Issue. *Academe* 75 (November/December 1989: 9-33.

Hoenack, Stephen and Eileen L. Collins, eds. *The Economics of American Universities: Management, Operations and Fiscal Environment*. Albany, NY: State University of New York Press, 1990.

Martin, Murray. *Budgetary Controls in Academic Libraries*. Greenwood, CT: JAI Press, 1978.

_____. "Budgets in Smaller Academic Libraries." In The Smaller Academic Library. ed. Gerald McCabe. Westport, CT: Greenwood Press, 1988: 105-126.

Morris, John. *The Library Disaster Preparedness Handbook*. Chicago: American Library Association, 1986. This book could also be listed in Chapters 10, 16, 19, etc., since no one area is immune to disaster.

Newman, George Charles. "Budgetary Trends in Small Private Liberal Arts College Libraries." In *College Librarianship*, ed. William Miller and Stephen Rockwood. Metuchen, NJ: Scarecrow Press, 1981.

Spyers-Duran, Peter and Thomas Mann, Jr. *Financing Information Services: Problems, Changing Approaches and New Opportunities for Academic and Research Libraries*. Westport, CT: Greenwood Press, 1985.

Tellefsen, Thomas E. *Improving College Management: An Integrated Systems Approach*. San Francisco: Jossey-Bass, 1990.

Ungarelli, Donald "Are Our Libraries Safe from Losses?" *Library and Archival Security* 10 (1990) 55-58.

See Also Chapter 5, Peterson.

Chapter 19

THE LIBRARY BUILDING AND EQUIPMENT

Library buildings make statements about themselves. The location of the library, the kind of architecture employed, the interior design, colors, furniture, all reflect the values of those who build, furnish or refurbish and care for them. Library services, as we have reiterated throughout this book, are and should be products of their context, should translate, for instance, the curriculum into a program. In the same way, the library building is determined by the institution, its history, geography, student body, faculty and its traditions.

Prior to World War II, library buildings were conceived as monuments to their precious contents, books. They were "fixed form" structures, incapable of modification, where the security of the bound volume was stressed over the time and energy required from users and staff as they grappled with the problem of gaining access to the materials. In the post-war period, library planners came to realize the inability of monumental

513

structures to address contemporary realities, the most important of which was change. Simultaneously, modular building design, emphasizing flexibility, adaptability, and a new concern for function over form, became the prevailing mode of construction in gymnasia, supermarkets, parking garages and other buildings requiring flexibility. Librarians were quick to adapt the concept of modular buildings to their needs. With a modular approach they were able to create interchangeable space, to utilize open floorplans, and to cluster permanently enclosed building elements at the outer edges so that interior space could be altered when necessary. Load-bearing floors were not limited to predetermined stack areas, but were spread throughout the building. Lighting and air conditioning were also made uniform so that patrons and staff could be located anywhere. Users became the focal point. Library design was placed on a more scientific footing, with attention to ergonomics (the effects of environment on human productivity), proxemics (the perception of social and personal space), and environmental factors.

Unfortunately, the new attention to functional considerations required aesthetic sacrifices. A dull sameness began to characterize (and still does) modular buildings despite frequent efforts, as David Kaser says, to "dress up the box" by adding atria, courtyards, reader terraces, landscaping and increased use of glass. Fickle fashion is as common in library architecture as it is in other areas of human endeavor. "In fact," says Kaser, "for a time following the opening of Atlanta's Hyatt Regency Hotel, resplendent with a cavernous atrium, libraries, like bagels, seemingly all came with holes in the middle."[1]

The search for a more harmonious relationship between attractiveness and utility continues, always tempered by cost considerations. The ability to deliver to users, wherever they may be, information generated by the new technology may augur the reappearance of fixed-form monumental buildings to house texts which have been made superfluous by alternate means of conveying information, in other words, to act as museums.

Alternatively, the new technology may permit libraries to become centers of intellectual activity where teachers and students can engage in scholarly pursuits, because technical services will occupy less space or be moved elsewhere. Whichever prediction is more accurate, there is no doubt that technology will produce changed relationships between activities and their patterns of use, and drastically alter how libraries look and are functionally arranged. As libraries become "smart buildings," or, as they are sometimes called, "intelligent buildings," sophisticated technology is used to provide computer-controlled card entrance and egress, computer-controlled environmental management, sophisticated data reception using both dedicated lines and microwave transmitters. Electric power and dataline outlets are everywhere because "smart buildings" make different demands on wiring, lighting, acoustics, environmental controls and furniture. Until there is more certainty about "smart buildings" and their contents, libraries must continue to be constructed with maximum flexibility.[2]

Today, constructing a new academic library building, or renovating, or adding to an old one is a very expensive undertaking. It is therefore essential that the process of planning and equipping the library should be done efficiently and economically. Because of skyrocketing costs, fewer and fewer academic libraries are being built. The building boom of the late 1960s and early 1970s has given way to a more modest number of new constructions and renovations. In the five-year period from 1967 to 1971, 445 academic libraries were built. The next five years saw the erection of 202 new college and university libraries. From 1977 to 1981, there were 143 new buildings, and from 1982 to 1986 the figure had fallen to 133.[3] The end of the academic building boom coincided with cutbacks caused by shrinking academic enrollments and financial problems. In addition, inflation during the intervening period resulted in the cost per foot of a college library rising from $26.08 in 1970-71 to $150.00 in 1990. New libraries that ranged in cost from $1 to $2 million dollars during the late 1960s now average $6 to $8 million or more. Construction of a new library building today means a very substantial investment for the college, one that does not stop with the completed structure. A new building always means higher maintenance and greater expenditures arising from increased use, demands for longer hours, and a larger structure. Operating costs may escalate more than 200 per cent over those associated with the old building. These exigencies are not mentioned to discourage anyone planning a new building, but rather to drive home the importance of great care in such planning in order to see the maximum return expressed in functional, comfortable and attractive library quarters.

TO BUILD OR ENLARGE

Needs Assessment

Although there may be a variety of reasons why a college community finds an existing library building less functional—changing patterns of use, for instance, or new building standards—the most urgent cause is generally inadequate size, with growth in the collections as the key pressure point. Diminished capacity to house new acquisitions is never a sudden event, but is the result of incremental growth. The time to begin thinking about the problem and developing documentation demonstrating the projected inadequacy of the current building is several years before the need is urgent. Many librarians report that decisions to act are not made until several years after space problems are acute.

Librarians who find their library buildings unsatisfactory and have garnered campus support for some form of action have four courses of action open to them. First, they can renovate the existing structure; second, they can build an addition and remodel; third, they can occupy and convert to their needs an existing structure originally designed for another purpose; or, finally, they can erect a totally new building. While librarians

may be convinced that their problems will best be solved by a
new structure, because of the high costs of a new building, or
perhaps because older members of the faculty and alumni are
very attached to the existing library, or because of other campus
financial exigencies, the question of whether it is feasible to
renovate or enlarge an existing building is often raised. Each
institution must arrive at its own solution. At this point, the
library staff's obligation is to insure that the decision is based on
adequate consideration of all the factors involved. The best
approach to providing sufficient information on which to make
a judgment is to undertake a needs assessment. A needs
assessment has two elements: what is required, and what exists.
The comparison between the two should reveal whether a new
library is called for, or whether one of the other options can be
adopted.

NEEDS ASSESSMENT TEAM

The first step in any needs assessment is to organize a needs
assessment team. This may be an expanded library committee,
or what will later become the building committee. The
importance of this group is confirmed by appointing to it
respected representatives from the college administration,
faculty, and student body, a building consultant, if there is one,
and, of course, the library director. Appointing members with
varied backgrounds, from different academic disciplines, and
with diverse types of expertise enhances the team's usefulness.
As users of the library, faculty and students are, more often than
not, unfamiliar with or indifferent to the details of its technical
services operations and will require careful coaching and
orientation about them. Placing a library-minded trustee on the
committee can help facilitate communications with the board of
trustees about the library's needs and influence their willingness
to provide financial support to the project. While the committee
should be representative, there is a danger of it growing too
large. On the other hand, since those serving on the committee

become advocates of the program, limiting numbers also limits vocal support.

It is the job of the needs assessment team to review library goals, evaluate existing conditions, examine alternatives to a new building, determine objectives for the new space, decide its space requirements and prepare a document for presentation to the administration, trustees, and other community members. The components of a needs assessment statement include collections, in all formats, reader facilities, library staffing, and the capacity of existing building space to accommodate change and projected growth. Much of the work of the needs assessment team must be repeated from a somewhat different perspective by the planning team. This is one compelling reason to have the same team function in both capacities. For instance, the needs assessment group will consider what changes, if any, are projected for academic programs and whether it is anticipated that the size of the population to be served will change. The answers to both of these questions will have some impact on whether additional library space is required. The planning committee will use the information to help write the building program, described below.

The needs assessment documents objectives for the library and user services and should explain the library and its organization, within the context of the existing structure. It should, therefore, describe the collection and new technology, and consider the scope and nature of the need for flexibility, in light of expected changes and how the old building is to be used. For instance, the three following statements might appear:

The building must be organized and designed so that it is user-oriented;

The library must collect, house and service all materials needed by users;

New space must accommodate technology.

Specific objectives regarding collection growth, services, reader accommodations will be developed for the building program.

A number of factors determine whether to remodel, renovate or build anew. Among them are obsolescence, inefficiency, disruption of service, and other uses for the present building.

Obsolescence

Will remodeling and enlarging the present library merely perpetuate a structure which, for library purposes, is now obsolete? Libraries generally grow at a rate of 4-5% annually, doubling the size of the collection in 16 to 17 years. Even libraries aiming for "steady-state" collections, ones that assumes little or no growth, find themselves experiencing at least 2-3% increase annually, doubling their holdings in 25-40 years.[4] Is there enough shelf space to house that kind of growth?

What is the relationship of print and nonprint resources as they pertain to space needs? While it is true that information can be housed in far smaller packages than books, currently the equipment required to use those packages is space consuming. A videocassette does not occupy any more shelf-space than a book, but a VCR, a monitor, and a dark area with appropriate seating are necessary for its use. In yet another example, CD-ROMs use far less shelf room than bulky indexes, but provision must be made for the microcomputer and terminal, the space for thesauri and other user manuals, and adequate seating—no small space expenditure.

Is there a multi-tier stack breaking the stack and reading areas squarely off from each other? Can handicapped students be properly served? Is the building so badly cut up with small room areas that it is impossible to secure open reading and book space without gutting the inside? Does the library meet current library standards? If not, can it expand to provide seating for at least 30% of its student body? Is there enough shelf space to house sufficient volumes to meet standards? If money is invested in remodeling and enlargement, how long will it be before the administration and board of trustees will again be faced with the problem of seeking funds for another addition or a new building?

Adequacy is not difficult to measure once objectives have been determined. Standards and texts will, cookbook style, describe the ingredients and how to combine them. Translating quantities into shelf and floor space, for instance, is simply a matter of turning amounts into equivalencies. An average of ten volumes per square foot and six volumes per linear foot is generally assumed.[5] Dividing the amount of space by the number of volumes indicates how close a library is to capacity. Stacks are considered to be full when they are at 86% of capacity.[6]

Can the library accommodate the new technology? Is there room for the widespread installation of computers? Is there sufficient wiring or can additional capacity be provided? Is the building one that meets present-day building code standards, handicap access and stable environmental controls for collections.

The following seven approaches are suggested as methods of coping with space shortages if no new building or addition to an old one is contemplated. Unfortunately, most are merely stopgap or short-range solutions.

— Weeding the collection. The traditional path to controlling growth and creating space is to embark on an intensive weeding program. In libraries where weeding is an on-going activity, the benefits may be minimal. Also, too much weeding may produce an inadequate, unacceptable collection, one which does not meet standards. In any case, weeding is a finger-in-the-dike activity, useful only in the short term.

— Stack reformation. Physically altering the bookstack into a reformed pattern is an expensive solution, andthe gain in additional shelving may be modest, compared with the cost.

— Storage of lesser-used materials. This, too, produces only a short-range, transitional solution, one which is probably antithetical to a college library's aims and goals, and not recommended except as a last resort.

— Compact shelving. Mechanized shelving can hold twice the number of books in the same space. The equipment is expensive to install, maintain and service, particularly if it is frequently used. Strong floors are required to accommodate additional weights and the tracks on which the shelving slides have to be laid.

— Converting to microforms. Microforms require much less shelf space, but the equipment to use them does not. In addition, they can be expensive, people tend to dislike the format, and conversion of older periodicals is not justified by the use they receive.

— Geography. Some libraries gain space by cooperating with other libraries if they are in the same geographic area and users have access to them. The feasibility of this course is probably limited to libraries located in cities and depends on careful planning and arrangements.

— Existing building. Internal adjustments can sometimes create more space without extensive construction or remodeling. Internal walls can be dismantled. Non-library activities can be transferred to other locations. Aisles can be narrowed. Operational relationships can be altered and staff work space reduced.[7]

Inefficiency

Are there fundamental errors in the design of the building which will critically handicap efficient service in an enlargement? Do access and exit points cut across reading areas? Do monumental rotundas and stairways limit the use of valuable book and study space? Are the book stack levels and main building floors constructed at different levels so that it is difficult to move freely from one to another or to transport books from one place to another? Are the ceilings so high that it is impossible to provide adequate artificial lighting without either installing an expensive false ceiling or using table lamps? Is the present building so designed that it is impossible to provide a central reference service?

Disruption of Service

Remodeling and enlargement will seriously disrupt service in the present structure and will damage books unless temporary quarters can be found during the renovation or addition construction—a period likely to exceed one year if the work is extensive. Can temporary quarters be provided? Is the college willing to deprive the students of any substantial opportunity to use the library for one or two years of their college life, or can the work be scheduled to cause a minimum of disruption?

Other Uses of the Present Building

Can the present building be used more efficiently for something other than a library? This question requires careful study. Perhaps it should be worded, "Can the present library, if remodeled, be used more effectively and economically for other than library purposes?" At first there is bound to be strong opposition from the administration and faculty to using the present library for any other purpose. But once the decision is made to build a new library and abandon the old, it is equally certain that half a dozen different departments will be clamoring for space in the relinquished one.

Inevitably, the cost of a new building will be raised as one of the issues, if not *the* issue, in reaching a decision. A new building will cost more initially, but in the course of time, if well planned, it will prove to be a sound investment. Keyes Metcalf says: "A good new building, it should be taken for granted, can be far more useful and satisfactory than the old one ever was, for there have been great advances during the recent years in the art and science of library planning. In addition to space for books, therefore, a new building promises better accommodations and service for readers and staff."[8]

The needs assessment presentation should include findings, use some detail as documentation, but avoid clutter. Most importantly, it should be endorsed by all members of the committee, either with their signatures on the document or on an accompanying letter of transmittal.

PLANNING THE NEW LIBRARY BUILDING

If the decision is "go" on a new library building, the first steps are to organize a planning committee, select an architect and reach a collective judgment on the important administrative and educational questions which have to be settled before a formal program can be written, or a suitable site chosen.

The Planning Committee

Building a library on a college campus is not only expensive; it is a momentous undertaking that, properly publicized, will generate excitement and enthusiasm among all segments of the community. Libraries have a residue of good will, and with a little effort the proprietary interest that most faculty will feel toward the library can be translated into a broad base of support. A committee on the proposed library building, by whatever name it is known, is an absolute necessity. While it is desirable that the same people serve on the planning and the needs assessment committees, strong political reasons may militate against their playing both roles. When a new planning committee must be established, the makeup of its membership should be similar to that of the needs assessment committee and reflect equally all of the campus constituencies.

It cannot be stressed too strongly that the library director should take the lead in informing the planning committee of new developments in library building and equipment. Nor can it be stressed strongly enough that this requires careful preparation before any meeting is held. Directors without experience sometimes tend to minimize the amount of effort required to build a new building or to participate in a major renovation. For the life of the project, it may be almost all-consuming, causing other activities to be placed on hold. In the beginning, key members of the staff must familiarize themselves with recent professional literature on buildings and equipment. In addition they may want to borrow dedication brochures and written programs and plans from other libraries. Manufacturers' and dealers' catalogs about shelving, mechanical equipment, exhibit cases, lighting, movable partitions, tables, chairs and so on will all prove useful. All of these will provide librarians with sufficient information on which to base extensive wish lists which will later be negotiated down to meet available funds.

A packet of materials is prepared for study by the library planning committee and is supplemented by visits to successful new library buildings where first-hand observation can clarify points not easily understood. The director may find it convenient to draw up a checklist of items for committee members to consult during site visits. For instance, visits may serve to demonstrate to committee members and help them understand the necessity of locating copying equipment in proximity to where it will be most heavily used, but where it can also be easily serviced by a staff member. The committee can also learn about the importance of attention to detail and about mistakes in planning that have been made at institutions elsewhere. Visits to other campuses at this stage may also help to stretch the imagination of all involved and deflect any tendency to define library service narrowly and only in terms of their current library facilities.

THE BUILDING CONSULTANT

Most college library directors who undertake to build a new library consider hiring a building consultant mandatory, for a variety of reasons. They may need outside support to stand up to influential professors and/or administrators, and sometimes even architects. They also may require expert advice on new developments, say, in technology. Consultants, by virtue of their experience, can save library staff time, avoid problems and protect staff morale. In short, the tyranny of expertise can work in a library's favor. Hiring an outside consultant often has the effect of securing a library advocate, a known authority, who commands respect and whose word carries credence. Richard Boss contends that any project which will cost over $50,000, or which is intended to meet the needs of the library for a period of at least five years, requires a building consultant.[9]

Building consultants are generally hired for one of three purposes. 1) As "critics," only briefly involved with the project and usually at milestones in the process. This might include the needs assessment statement, the building program, the schematic or design drawings, and the specifications; 2) As "full consultants," totally involved from start to finish. This kind of advisor sits on the needs assessment and planning committees, goes on site visits, and writes reports; 3) As "mediators," more involved than the critics, but less so than full consultants. They pay frequent visits as the work progresses, and review and advise at all stages.[10]

Applications from consultants are generated by nominations or in response to advertisements in professional publications. Librarians can be asked to recommend consultants with whom they have recently worked successfully, and those named can then be invited to apply. Applicants are asked to describe how they view their role and what services they provide. Alternately, they can be required to respond to a Request for Proposal (RFP) that outlines the project's problems, constraints, time schedule, and expectations for consultant participation. When the field has been narrowed to a few candidates, interviews for this sensitive position must be conducted. Hiring only from resumes and recommendations is a dangerous practice, since the relationship between the consultant and library director is crucial to the success of the project. Judgments, in addition to subjective feelings, should be based on evidence of the consultants' knowledge and experience, persuasiveness, sensitivity to the political environment, good writing skills, commitment and responsibility. It is desirable to have both the president and financial vice president approve the final choice since it is hoped that the consultant's advice will prevail when financial arguments are used in an attempt to limit the building program. All skills being equal, a consultant who lives nearer to the college may provide better service and more flexibility at less costthan one located at a distance.

THE ARCHITECT AND THE LIBRARIAN

A great deal has been written about the selection of an architect, about the interaction between the architect and the librarian, and about potential problems in the relationship. What seems important to stress is that librarians and architects can, and frequently do, work well together, despite reports to the contrary. When problems emerge, they are often generated by the conflicting goals that each may have for a new building. Architects look at completed buildings as products of good design, as aesthetically appealing, attractive combinations of stone and mortar. Librarians, on the other hand, want structures that accommodate patrons comfortably, that allow control over collections, that address security problems. Is it possible for a library building to be both beautiful and functional? Perhaps no, perhaps yes. The challenge is a creative one and the tension is present in each building program.

Librarians and architects must try to develop a non-adversarial relationship which implies mutual respect and an attempt to understand the end product each desires. Over forty years ago MIT's Dean Burchard summarized what he considered the proper attitude. His expectations should still prevail: "The architect and the librarian should approach each other with mutual respect, should welcome conflict if it springs from honest conviction, and should collaborate and not compete. Neither should try to dominate the other."[11] Only in an atmosphere of mutual respect will an architect regard the librarian as a professional colleague rather than an intruder.

Librarians, and committees, sometimes select architects on the basis of their reputations, rather than for more objective reasons. There are a number of steps that can be taken to ascertain whether the architects who are being considered will do. Have they built a college library before, and if so, when and where? While experience in building a college library is not essential, it is certainly desirable. If the architect has built other libraries, the librarian and other available members of the planning team can visit those buildings to determine how successfully they have worked out and can interview their directors about the process. It is important to learn whether the architect and the firm have been easy to work with and about other aspects of their history or behavior. Do they flout program requirements? What else have they built? Does the firm have a reputation for integrity? Do they seem to exhibit any of the seven deadly characteristics of unacceptable architects:

Pride:	are they willing to bend?
Arrogance:	can their decision be questioned?
Ignorance:	are they well grounded in basics?
Myopia:	are they sufficiently sensitive to changes to accommodate them in their designs?

Waste: have previous projects been characterized by cost
          overruns?
Procrastination: do they make decisions in a sufficiently timely
          fashion to permit ordering furniture, carpeting and
          other accessories without expensive delay.
Sloth: is their work marked by chaos and disorganization?[12]

Another important question to pose is whether there are
engineering services associated with the architect, or, if not,
what consulting firms are used for this purpose. It is essential
that the firm responsible for engineering services be first-class.
One other matter that should be checked at the outset is the
relationship between the architect and the interior designer. The
interior designer is the one who helps to select carpets,
upholstery, drapes, paint colors and the like. Architectural firms
sometimes have designers on their staffs. If they do not, it is
important to locate one who can get along well with the architect
and, of course, the client, share a vision of what the building
should be, and plan accurately to insure that it can be
implemented. Too often, architects patronize interior designers,
and interior designers belittle architects, and the library suffers.

After all the questions have been investigated, answers
compared and considered, and the list winnowed, what should
influence most strongly the final selection of the architect is the
preference, subjectively determined, of the library director.
Following these steps will help to avoid the twin hazards of
library buildings:

Expensive structures that are delightful to behold and win
awards from the American Institute of Architects and
ALA—but do not quite function as libraries; and

Inexpensive buildings that are workmanlike, mundane and
functional—but dreary to use on a daily basis.[13]

Sometimes a college needs preliminary or schematic plans to mount a capital funds drive before the final arrangements are made for planning and financing a new building. For funding purposes, most architects will develop a schematic plan and elevation, rendering a model with an approximate cost estimate, for a set sum or a percentage of their total services fee if they are chosen later as the architects for the building. Two other practical considerations relating to the architect's services may be mentioned. The campus may have an ongoing relationship with an architectural firm and expect the library to use it, as well. Unless the choice is completely circumscribed, however, the process of selecting an architect as described above produces far better results. The second consideration relates to the choice between an outside firm and a local one. Assuming equal qualifications, the local architect offers the advantages of easy, more frequent and more economical consultation. In addition, a local architect who feels pride in the community and region may work that much harder. On the other hand, architects are marked by certain styles that characterize their work. To hire a local architect may be tantamount to purchasing a certain type of building.

Administrative and Educational Problems

After a building committee has been formed, its first task is to try to arrive at some collective opinion about a number of administrative and educational matters. The kinds of administrative and educational problems the planning committee will be called upon to discuss are suggested by the following questions:

1. How many students are to be accommodated in the new library?

2. What is the best available site for the building?

3. What is the college policy regarding the provision of audio-visual aids and other mechanical teaching devices? That is, will they be handled separately by departments or will there be a centralized audiovisual service for all departments, and will it be in the library?

4. Will existing departmental collections be absorbed in the new library building?

5. How will the building accommodate new technology?

6. Will the library share its quarters with other activities?

What a campus needs may determine what goes into a new building. One university combined a student center with the library because it desperately needed the former, but could only raise money for the latter. Politics, as the saying goes, often makes strange bedfellows. College libraries have found themselves sharing buildings with any number of college services and/or academic departments, including TV production studios and college bookstores. Most recently, many colleges have combined libraries and academic computing centers. Sometimes the two activities learn to cooperate. More often, however, the two exist under the same roof, but remain very separate in their operations. One important caveat about sharing space should be mentioned. Libraries housed in shared spaces sometimes come up short. They are likely to occupy the major portion of a building and often feel impelled to concede space or technological capabilities in order to keep peace and harmony.

The committee will also have to have some idea about how much the building will cost and whether the amount is acceptable to the institution. Costs are based on a general idea of how big the building needs to be, the price of projected construction, expenses for equipping, furnishing, and landscaping the building as well as architect's and consultant's fees. While the librarians' wish list may include all that is desirable in a new building, the building program should be realistic and based on what has been budgeted for the library. A planning committee cannot hope to resolve all problems for the life of the building, but it must do its best to reduce the incidence of irreversible mistakes.

For some reason faculty members and college administrators are frequently unwilling or unable to make judgments about the questions raised above. Unless the building committee crystallizes its thinking, there is real danger that the architect and the librarian will reach an impasse because of a lack of clear-cut direction, or else the architect may go ahead and design the program of activities without appropriate information.

These are some of the questions about which the planning committee will have to deliberate and reach a decision. They should refer to the college's planning and developmental documents—a master or long-range plan, for instance—if they exist, as well as to the library's planning materials, including of course, mission, goals and objectives statements. Important as these decisions are, it seems well to remember that they represent collective judgments and are not immutable. Planning decisions are always matters of opinion and related to budget. It is impossible to know in advance what a library will be like in twenty-five years, or even, perhaps, fifteen. The planning committee must therefore keep as many options open as possible.

Site

Several factors deserve extensive consideration when deciding where to locate a building. If the site is close to other academic buildings, its use by students between class periods will be increased. On the other hand, once the student leaves the residence hall it does not matter whether the library is two or three buildings away so long as the distance is not too far. Accordingly, assuming the site is spacious, a central location in relation to the greatest concentration of academic buildings is preferable to one further removed but nearer to the student residence halls. The siting of a library may symbolize the esteem it is accorded on that campus. If a library is considered the heart of the college, its anatomical importance should be reflected in its location. To shunt a library to the periphery of a campus, is to make a statement about its relative status and position. Examining sites from the point of view of potential neighbors and traffic patterns is also necessary before deciding where to place the library.

The orientation of the building is of consequence, too. A site that enables the long axis of the building to face north and south is favored over one that faces east and west; glass exposure east and west often creates the need for louvers, overhangs, blinds and more air conditioning to overcome the discomfort of the sun streaming in through windows.

A good site must afford vehicle access for library deliveries of books, materials and equipment, as well as space for staff parking, especially at night, and for visitor parking. The extent to which parking for students must be provided will vary depending on whether the college is residential or has a very large commuting enrollment, although many residential schools have recently experienced a large increase in the number of on-campus student-owned vehicles. Many other site considerations which have little to do with library functions nonetheless matter a great deal. Will the chosen site require removing an existing building; tearing up a great many water, gas and electrical lines; or cutting down beloved trees? Is the site so far removed that it will be very costly to bring utility lines up to it? Does it require expensive excavation in order to get a basement floor (bedrock) or to expand the building without interfering with other buildings? Finally, is the site hospitable, aesthetically, to the design of the new building?

THE BUILDING PROGRAM

When the building committee has reached a decision on both the objectives of the proposed new library and the administrative and educational problems involved—and only then—the librarian is ready to write a program that intelligently sets forth the requirements the architect will be asked to resolve. This statement "...specifies the purposes, functions and operations which the building will serve. It provides useful data on the people, materials and equipment to be housed, and describes the library's views of the essential relationship of component functions and operations."[14] Good libraries are designed from the inside out.

Library planning is fundamentally a problem-solving activity and the written program is an important step in that process. It should be inclusive, but compactly written. After all, not everything can be covered. In addition, many compromises will be required in the course of reaching solutions. The needs assessment team may have visited new libraries as part of its deliberations, but visits in conjunction with the new building program are also recommended because they have different objectives. Some librarians advise looking at recently constructed academic libraries buildings before writing the building program. Others, and we are among this latter group, suggest writing first, and looking later, unless the visit is designed to enlarge the horizons of administrators and trustees who are yet unconvinced of the need for a new building. Visits after the program has been articulated serve to sharpen the focus of inquiries and insure that all aspects of the project have been given attention.

Every library building, no matter its size and function, is unique and should be approached from that standpoint. The purpose of the program is to crystallize thinking about a particular library building and to set forth priorities for it.

Scope of the Program

The program itself may be properly developed in two principal parts: a brief discussion of each of the general conditions which the library staff expects the architect to be aware of in the structural planning of the building; and a description of the detailed requirements of the purpose, space and location of each of the areas in the building. The general conditions will include a statement of the overall capacities required for books and readers—the former in terms of the numbers of sections of shelving needed rather than in number of volumes, and the latter in terms of the number of seats of various types to be provided. In addition, the document will state what is to be emphasized in the way of performance standards for lighting, air conditioning, spatial relationships, noise reduction, and similar matters. The description of the detailed requirements of purpose, space and location may be likened to a written walk through a finished building, pointing out the activity in each area and the special furniture it requires. Many librarians recommend giving an estimate of the square floor area of each space or room, but others prefer not to freeze the plan in this way before the architect puts pencil to paper.

A systems approach to the building program is desirable, with relationships and interactions between departments carefully delineated. Each area should be described in terms of what happens there, how many people are involved, what kinds of space are needed, and other special requirements which will affect arrangements. The architect can only work out appropriate spaces if the building program and the library director have clearly communicated the functions and activities the building is to house. On the other hand, the architect is not merely a technician. The college's money should hire more than that. Architects are not only responsible for translating librarians' programs into adequate buildings, on time and on cost, but are also charged with providing them with designs that surprise and delight and are recognized as "good" when they are received.

Estimating Capacity Requirements

The problem of estimating future reader capacity, staff working quarters or materials stock is a genuine one for the library director, particularly in light of the rapidity with which change occurs and of the uncertainties about new technology. Nearly all academic libraries built before the sixties, and many since then, have outgrown their capacity in one or more of these areas far too soon. Changes in enrollments, curriculum, and equipment make planning very tricky. Most colleges cannot afford to rebuild a library for, at the very least, twenty-five years and therefore must make an estimate which is as near right the first time as possible. There is no magic formula for calculating reader capacity, but librarians generally recommend between 25 and 40 per cent of the projected upper limit of enrollment. The *Standards for College Libraries* suggest that one-third of the student body of a residential liberal arts college should be accommodated at any given time. For many institutions where there is heavy library use built into the curriculum, that figure represents far too little seating. Philip Leighton and David Weber say that a quality residential liberal arts college in a rural area or small town should be able to seat 50 to 60% of its students at a given time.[15] Commuter colleges in urban areas, on the other hand, may require seating for no more than 20%. A standard of at least 25 square feet per reader station is usually applied but technological considerations may necessitate a recalculation of the square feet requirements.

Recognizing that the proportion of space required for staff is small in contrast with that required for collections and readers may help ensure that personnel are adequately housed. Library staff quarters are often congested and become inadequate long before other parts of the library. Although it is contrary to current library practice, we believe that all professional staff members should have their own offices. It is rare on a college campus for a faculty member not to be provided with an office, the same should hold true for professional library staff. An average of 150[16] to 175 square feet per staff member is probably sufficient.[17]   The average includes 300 square feet for the shipping and receiving clerk and 100 square feet for the clerical assistant in the reference department. While some contend that technology will reduce the number of staff members, the space required for an automated work station will be somewhat larger than for its manual predecessor. Some suggest that an additional 20 square feet should be added to a secretary's work station where use of a microcomputer or word-processing terminal is involved.[18]

College library collections, on average, are no longer doubling every thirteen to twenty-seven years, but they are nonetheless continuing to increase in size. For mature libraries, the net annualincrease is predicted to be closer to two per cent, because libraries can rely more heavily on online sources and interlibrary loan for lesser used materials.[19]   However, national averages do not reveal the history nor predict the future of a particular library. Probably the best librarians can do is to study their institution's annual acquisition rate for the past ten years, and—taking into account annual withdrawals and the library's financial prospects in the immediate years ahead—arrive at what seems a reasonable acquisition rate for the next decade. If this figure is projected for twenty-five years, using as a base the anticipated number of volumes, or volume equivalents, held at the time the library is likely to occupy the new building, and adding 10 to 20 per cent for the increase in book gifts which will come with a new building, the resulting total should not be too far afield. This total in volumes and volume equivalents can then be translated into sections of shelving. The figure of 125 volumes per section for the college library is considered sound, but some experienced librarians build in an extra margin of safety by using the formula proposed by R. W. Henderson in

1934 and known as the cubook formula, which calls for a calculation of 100 volumes to the section.[20]

It is impossible to describe in detail everything that requires articulation in the written building program, but the following areas have frequently been allocated inadequate square footage in new buildings and should receive careful consideration in the document:

staff working quarters

work space behind a circulation desk

space for receiving and sending out library material

sorting area with shelving for preliminary examination of gift collections

supply closet spaces, both central and in the individual staff offices or working areas

photo duplication services

library instruction quarters

faculty reading rooms

reserve reading areas

special collections

rest rooms

other library areas for which no department assumes responsibility, such as exhibit space, new book display areas, all-night studies places, stairwells, coat rooms, drinking fountains, janitorial services, etc.

When the written program is completed, it is important that representatives of all parties on the campus have an opportunity to review and criticize it. Such modifications as may be suggested by faculty, library staff, students or administrators should be discussed by the library planning committee and incorporated into the program if they prove useful. The final draft of the program should be approved by the college administration before it is turned over to the architect. Changes made after this date bring up the cost of the project and are to be made sparingly and with a firm understanding of who is authorized to do so on behalf of the library. Clarity about the rights and responsibilities of the library director and the head of the physical plant vis a vis the construction company is also needed.

Flexibility

The new technology has impact on the library both as a service and a resource. For instance, the installation of an OPAC requires rethinking about the use to which that primary public space where libraries have traditionally provided information about their holdings can now be put. Nature, as we know, abhors a vacuum, and without careful planning that space may be seized by an inappropriate activity. Significant changes will be necessary in the configuration and operation of reading areas, the reference area, and other service points. Technology is attended by different requirements in sizes and shapes of work stations for staff and in carrels for students. Bob Cormack says if technology creates "questions and heightens feelings of uncertainty, don't feel lonesome—you have a lot of company. The best you can do is read the literature, seek advice and be flexible."[21]

Flexibility has been axiomatic to those planning library buildings during the last two decades and it is probably more crucial today than it has ever been, in order to avoid the straitjacket of a permanent structure that renders change difficult or impossible. New technology is not the only arena in which change can be predicted to occur. By the time a new building is ready, an innovative theory of administration may have been introduced that will influence the library's organization. New faculty may enter the scene with ideas different from those of their predecessors. The department chair who lobbied for a separate education library housed in the education building may have been replaced by one who wants the collection transferred to the main library for pedagogical and faculty office space reasons. Curriculum changes will have substantial impact on the library facility. The holder of the newly established endowed professorship in Women's Studies feels that the subject needs greater visibility and campaigns for a separate collection near a seminar room. The building committee is sympathetic to the appeal and allocates it space. Two years later, the faculty of that department feel that mainstreaming the Women's Studies collection would be more beneficial. Making provision for specific goals in the original plan does not eliminate the possibility of other goals emerging later.

To meet changing patterns in organization and service requirements, the one indispensable characteristic a library building must have is flexibility—flexibility in design, in structure, in mechanical facilities and lighting and in furnishing. A library building may be looked upon merely as the expression of the librarian's technical ability and of the architect's aesthetic achievement. It may also be judged by whether or not it offers a helpful solution to the problem of growth in education. If library walls could speak, they would expose the efforts of generations of librarians to make their libraries more responsive to the changing needs of higher education. Flexible libraries have been called "forgiving." Among the physical characteristics that render a structure "forgiving" are:

modularity—based on the concept that with the exception of columns placed at regular intervals, the fixed elements in a building are kept to a minimum and are carefully located to have little effect on flexibility;

load-bearing capacity, spread throughout the building;

walls which are demountable unless required for privacy and acoustic control;

windows that are placed or treated with architectural overhangs, baffles or tinted glazing to control the amount of light because of increasing use of computer terminals and video screens.

floors that have been carpeted in all public and staff areas as a means of acoustical control; and

ceilings which have been made acoustically absorbent.[22]

Flexibility is essential in the mechanical and electrical systems as well as in the design and structural aspects of the building plan. The need to provide adequate and flexible access to power and communication lines is critical. Believing that the library is a vital element in the "wired campus" means that lines must be available to faculty and administration offices as well as to dormitories and homes. Transmission lines that enable communication to and from great distances are also needed. In-house electrical requirements are staggering. For instance, Philip Leighton and David Weber maintain that the average staff work position needs at a bare minimum four electrical power outlets, which are quickly exhausted by a terminal, modem, monitor, printer, desk lamp, electric pencil sharpener, fan, calculator, clock, electric eraser and so on. Modular furniture now comes with its own outlets—permitting libraries to devise work space tailored to each job's requirement and arranged in any configuration and changed as needed. Students, too, need electrical outlets as personal computers are increasingly used for taking notes and gaining access to collections.

SPECIAL PROBLEMS IN LIBRARY PLANNING

A high proportion of seating in today's college library—65 to 75 per cent—is made up of individual tables or carrels. This percentage has grown steadily over the past three decades, although it has leveled off, if not slightly diminished, as our understanding of the sociology of seating arrangements has increased. Most people, though not all, prefer a semi-isolated space which gives them a sense of privacy. On the other hand, isolation for some is quite unwelcome. A proper balance in types of seating as well as in its arrangement in reading rooms and stacks is desirable.

The ability to offer library instruction in the library, particularly in a seminar room adjoining the reference collection where materials may be brought together for discussion purposes, contributes to the effectiveness of the bibliographic instruction program. This room can be used, on other occasions, for poetry readings, book discussion lunches or other public events.

Providing some separate quarters for faculty in the library is both politically wise and pedagogically sound. Faculty use libraries differently from undergraduates and their space requirements also differ. Small faculty reading rooms are less appropriate than faculty studies or cubicles. In addition, however, a small social area for the use of faculty may be worth consideration. A number of libraries hold coffee hours for faculty on a weekly basis; others have a small faculty lounge where faculty can eat their lunch or take a break without leaving the library.

Noise control, particularly where a seminar or meeting room adjoins a study area, is a matter of great importance. Patrons often complain when staff talk animatedly and loudly in areas lacking adequate sound-absorbing materials. Some degree of noise is inevitable. Reading rooms are often in a constant state of movement. College libraries as both social and intellectual centers witness constant traffic and a buzz of conversation, paper shuffling, chair rearrangement, coughing and other sounds. The building plan should consider placing activities in which there is heavy traffic away from reading areas. Circulation and reference desks, the reference collection and current periodicals are busy and noisy areas and should be placed as far from general reading areas as possible. In addition, carpeting brings peace and quiet and should be widely used throughout the library. Carpeting may lower the cost of maintenance, particularly if it is the best grade, has a tight weave and a looped pile. Many librarians prefer carpet tile to rolled carpet because the tiles can be replaced in areas of heavy traffic.

Opinions and recommendations on lighting continue to elicit controversy. Energy concerns have led to a general reduction in lighting levels and attempts have been made to vary the amount of lighting in different areas of the library based on the tasks to be performed in each. Glare-free overhead lighting at a level of 50 foot-candles in the reading room is more than adequate. Some even contend that 35 foot-candles, if properly placed, may be sufficient. On the other hand 5 to 10 foot-candles in inactive stacks and microform areas is as much as is needed. Stacks should have individual switching as an energy saving mechanism as well as to guard against deterioration of materials caused by constant light. Lighting for staff areas must be based on the tasks to be performed. Work stations with terminals, for instance, are particularly susceptible to glare. Temperature and humidity are major considerations. Libraries should be kept at a constant temperature, 65-70 degrees Fahrenheit and 45 to 55% humidity, but computer rooms may require separate heating, ventilation and air conditioning (HVAC) systems. Cooler temperatures may be needed in other areas, too, such as rare books, manuscripts and audio-visual collections.

The degree to which various security systems are necessary depends to a great extent on the particular institution. All college libraries require emergency exits, fire controls and fire and police call systems. Most librarians now prefer to have a public address system for emergencies as well as for notifying patrons of closing time. The need for book detection systems and for equipment alarms is more discretionary, and dependent on the environment. A college in a community where vandalism is high will add security measures that might be unnecessary in schools located elsewhere. Where the security of readers in the stacks is a matter of concern, the building should be designed so that as many areas of the stacks as possible are in the sight of and can be supervised by library personnel.

The building should be planned to take advantage of those items that may reduce maintenance and operations costs. Improperly placed janitor's closets, difficult to clean windows and lighting fixtures, window shades and draperies that require constant opening and closing, or that shred, poorly designed rest rooms, and vulnerable surfaces which have not been specially treated are all wasteful and unnecessary.

INTERIOR DESIGN AND FURNITURE

When the major problems of space relationships, projection of book and reader capacities, air conditioning, lighting, and sound control have been thrashed out, it may seem that the time to relax has finally arrived. Unfortunately, the job is still incomplete. The formidable tasks of planning floor layout and furnishing individual areas remain to be accomplished. In this segment of the enterprise heavy staff participation is even more crucial than it has been previously. Consider, for example, how intimately the librarian must understand the binding and mending process in order to design properly an area that will answer its space and equipment requirements. There is the question of where the space should be located, its relationship to shipping and receiving, its proximity to a service elevator, the need for long, counter-height work space with cabinets above and shelves below, and the accessibility of a laundry-type sink and a large supplies closet.

Similarly the reference department must take into account how its readers and staff will use every type of material. They must consider which materials require special furniture and equipment, for example, maps, periodical indexes, CD-ROMs. Every phase of library operation from an OPAC to interlibrary loan, to library instruction, demands the same kind of careful study and thorough understanding. Areas requiring even greater attention are those new to a library or those which will be shared by several departments. Ergonomic issues of technology require that attention be paid to avoiding terminals with screen glare which cause staff eye problems, or furniture with insufficient work surfaces which cause staff muscle strain, neck pain or poor posture. Errors will occur despite constant attention to detail on the architect's part. Librarians must make every effort to avoid those that result from failure to secure full participation and information from all members of the library staff.

The interior design and selection of furniture may be handled by the architect or by a design firm. Only in cases of extreme economic necessity should librarians undertake to do the interior design themselves, and then only in consultation with any campus expertise that can be discovered. Most librarians prefer the architectural firm to complete the task because the interior may be seen as an extension of the work of planning the structure itself. Who should know better what percentage of the overall cost to allocate to interior design and furnishings? Who has reason to be more concerned about the quality of the interior than the architect who designed the building? Why should the librarian who has worked successfully with the architect be obliged to begin all over again with a new set of outside experts? These are persuasive arguments, and the proof is that most colleges accept them and provide in some degree for the architect to take charge or to participate in the planning of the interior decor and the selection of furniture. On the other hand, if the architect has no interior designer on staff, it may be well for the architect or the library to hire an outside firm to do this part of the work. In either case, there should be early involvement with the architectural plan. Interior designers are generally responsible for the overall color scheme, how to match color furnishings (woods, metal end panels, upholstery covers) with wall and floor colors to give unity to the building. They also make choices about wall surfaces, selection of carpets and movable furnishings, and advise librarians about signage. Purchasing standard library furniture is almost always preferable to embarking on a program of custom design.

PLANNING FOR HANDICAPPED USERS

As a result of the Rehabilitation Act of 1973, which made discrimination on the basis of handicaps illegal, colleges are now enrolling increasing numbers of students who are confined to wheelchairs, are blind, deaf, or otherwise impaired. Bearing in mind that the goal is to make a handicapped user as independent as possible, each campus makes choices about the extent to which it is prepared to meet the needs of handicapped students based on its current population and its financial status. Planning a new building, or renovating an old one, affords the opportunity to create an environment that is accessible to the handicapped. At a minimum, entrance and access to the library's main services can be provided. The following conditions are easily met in a new building:

Convenient parking with designated spots for disabled users located close to curb ramps between the library and the parking area;

At least one library entrance at ground level with doors wide enough to accommodate a wheelchair and light enough to allow easy entry, unless equipped with an automatic opener and closer;

An elevator, if the library has more than a single story;

Hallways and public areas wide enough for wheelchair passage;

Stacks and study carrels, OPAC terminals, water fountains, toilets, and pay phones designed for accessibility;

Bold, clear signage for those with low vision. Raised letters are often added to permit tactile sign reading. Hearing-impaired persons also profit from good signage and detailed maps.

Libraries can also help handicapped persons by providing special equipment for them. Kurzweil Reading Machines, with their optical scanning face, will read any book to a student. Used primarily by non-sighted people, the machines also benefit dyslexics and those who are visually impaired. Saltus readers hold rolls of printed text and automatically advance or rewind paper at a continuous rate. Libraries may want to build teletype phone systems into their technology plans. These TTYs translate letter images over the phone. Hearing-impaired students can use them from their dorm rooms and hook into various places on the campus, even the reference desk.

Accommodating handicapped students is not a simple matter and it may not be economically feasible to provide everything. For instance, in order to be accessible to a user confined to a wheelchair, book stacks require a minimum aisle width of four feet. Without that consideration, three feet between bookshelves would more than suffice. Widening aisles by one foot can effectively ‑reduce stack capacity by 23%. A collection of 100,000 volumes with appropriate handicapped aisle distances could have held 123,000 volumes if the shelves were three rather than four feet apart. Even if the aisles are of requisite width, patrons in wheelchairs may still not be able to reach upper and lower shelves, but this loss of shelving capacity is not common. Purchasing special equipment remains expensive. As of this writing, Kurzweil Reading Machines cost close to $20,000. As with all other building issues planning for handicap access takes foresight, flexibility and clarity about goals.

SUMMARY

Planning for a new library building requires the collaboration of a building committee, the library director, the architect and library staff, as well as a broad base of community support. The library director is probably the best person to prepare the written program, although one who is inexperienced in planning a building may find it advantageous to bring in a building consultant at this early stage. The architect will first cover the canvas like a painter, visualizing and interpreting in preliminary drawings the general requirements. Later revisions will result in reassembling and rearranging the requirements so that the final assortment will fit into an integrated and harmonious product and meet budgets. When the preliminary drawings are complete and approved, the architect proceeds to prepare working drawings, including structural, mechanical, elevational and electrical ones. Eventually there will be diagrams of the layout for furniture and equipment, telephones, carpeting, water fountains, shelving, and the like. During all these stages, the library director, assisted by others, must study the plans and revisions with great care and thoroughness. Too often campus personnel, including the library director, fail to monitor adequately the work of architects or to insist that the program be actualized as written. The distinguished architect Ralph Adams Cram is reported to have insisted in his office work that "nothing is unimportant" in dealing with cathedral and college design. It is a point worth remembering in college library planning.

NOTES AND SUGGESTED READINGS

Notes

1. David Kaser, "Twenty Five Years of Academic Library Building Planning," *College and Research Libraries* 45 (June 1984): 273.

2. Philip Leighton and David Weber, "The Influence of Computer Technology on Academic Library Buildings," in *Academic Librarianship: Past, Present and Future*, ed. John Richardson, Jr. and Jinnie Y. Davis (Englewood, CO: Libraries Unlimited, 1989), 26.

3.   Nancy McAdams, "Trends in Academic Library Facilities," *Library Trends* 36 (Fall 1987), 287-88.

4.   Keyes D. Metcalf, *Planning Academic and Research Library Buildings,* 2d ed. by Philip D. Leighton and David C. Weber.   (Chicago: American Library Association, 1986), XVIII.

5.   Lester K. Smith, ed., *Planning Library Buildings: From Decision to Design.*   Papers from a Library Administration and Management Association Buildings and Equipment Section Preconference at the 1984 American Library Association Conference, Dallas, TX.   (Chicago: American Library Association, 1986), 11.

6.   Bob Cormack, "Needs Assessment for Academic Libraries," in Smith, *ibid.*, 10.

7.   *Ibid.*, 16-21.

8.   Keyes D. Metcalf, "When Bookstacks Overflow," *Harvard Library Bulletin* 8 (Spring 1964):205.

9.   Richard W. Boss, *Information Technologies and Space Planning for Libraries and Information Centers* (Boston: G.K. Hall, 1987), 102.

10.   Margaret Beckman, "The Library Building Consultant and the Library Planning Team," in Smith, 59-62.

11.   John E. Burchard and others, *Planning the University Library Building* (Princeton, NJ: Princeton University Press, 1949), 126.

12.   Eric Rockwell, "The Seven Deadly Sins of Architects," *American Libraries* 20 (April 1989):307, 341-2.

13. Elaine Cohen, "Talking to Architects," *American Libraries* 20 (April 1989): 299.

14. George Snowball. "The Building Program-Generalities," in Smith, 71-81.

15. Metcalf, *Planning*, 98.

16. *Ibid.*, 224.

17. Boss, 90.

18. Metcalf, *Planning*, 225.

19. *Ibid.*, XVIII.

20. R. W. Henderson, "The Cubook," *Library Journal* 59 (November 15, 1934):865-868.

21. Cormack, in Smith, 16.

22. Summarized from Novak, Gloria, "Toward a Forgiving Building: Technical Issues Relevant to New and Existing Libraries," *Library Hi Tech* 5 (Winter 1987): 94-99.

Suggested Readings

Boss, Richard. *Information Technologies and Space Planning for Libraries*. Boston: G. K. Hall, 1987.

Cohen, Aaron and Elaine Cohen. *Designing and Space Planning for Librarians*. New York: R. R. Bowker, 1979.

Edwards, Heather. *University Library Building Planning*. Metuchen, NJ: Scarecrow Press, 1990.

Fraley, Ruth A. and Carol Lee Anderson. *Library Space Planning*. New York: Neal-Schuman, 1985.

Holt, Raymond. *Planning Library Buildings and Facilities*. Metuchen, NJ: Scarecrow Press, 1989.

Kaser, David. "Twenty-Five Years of Academic Library Building Planning." *College and Research Libraries* **45** (June 1984): 268-281.

Metcalf, Keyes. *Planning Academic and Research Library buildings*. 2d ed. by Philip D. Leighton and David C. Weber. Chicago: American Library Association, 1986.

Metz, T. John. "Getting from Here to There: Keeping an Academic Library in Operation during Construction/ Renovation." *Advances in Library Administration and Organization* 5 (1986): 207-19.

Richardson, John and Jinnie Y. Davis, eds. *Academic Librarianship, Past, Present and Future*. Englewood, CO: Libraries Unlimited, 1989.

Smith, Lester, E., ed. *Planning Library Buildings: From Decision to Design*. Papers from a Library Administration and Management Association Buildings and Equipment Section Preconference at the 1984 ALA Conference, Dallas, TX. Chicago: ALA, 1986.

Chapter 20

EVALUATION OF LIBRARY SERVICES

Library evaluation, difficult at best, is made more so because of the elusiveness of the concept "goodness" when used to describe libraries. Even "adequacy" is hard to pin down. Part of the problem stems from the number of ways in which we use the term "goodness." We speak, for instance, about the capability of a library to collect material that meets an articulated need. Or we describe that library's ability to make the information accessible and available so that it can be used. Two kinds of goodness are contained in the above descriptions. One refers to quality and the other to value. In other words, we may ask, How good is a library? (quality) and/or What good does a library do? (value).[1] A comprehensive collection of materials on the subject of Alaskan kinship systems would undoubtedly contain information needed by a student writing a term paper on the subject. All things being equal, the system is capable of meeting the student's needs. On the other hand, if the student has trouble reading at the level at which most of the books are written, then the holdings are of no value to him.

Difficult as it is, however, to judge "goodness" in either of these characteristics, quality or value, evaluation is nonetheless necessary to any library. It enables librarians to make appropriate decisions particularly about the allocation of resources, to report accurately and in depth to administrators and funding bodies, to demonstrate responsibility and accountability for activities, to diagnose problems in a particular area, to compare programs and activities with like institutions, and to document efforts for the historic record and for longitudinal analysis. Evaluating the effectiveness of a service simply means assessing how well the service meets the demand or needs of the community to be served. At any given time, some library program and/or service should be undergoing scrutiny. But systematic evaluation should never be taken lightly. It is difficult, time-consuming and fraught with dangers that, unless avoided, may harm a library.

What should be evaluated? Everything is appropriate to evaluation and, further, a method can be found to evaluate anything. However, simply data-snooping without focus or clarity of intent produces muddy results. Before embarking on any evaluation, the following important questions must be confronted: what information is required, by whom, and for what purpose? In this way the decision can be made to evaluate at the appropriate level and to select the method best suited to securing the wanted information. Most evaluations do not *require* the use of computers; however, the ability of computers to process large amounts of information and generate reports rapidly makes using them attractive when there are quantities of data to be manipulated.

Libraries seeking to evaluate various parts of their operations and programs would do well to consult F. W. Lancaster's *If You Want to Evaluate Your Library*, and Nancy Van House's *Performance Measures for Academic Libraries*.[2] Manuals for evaluating specific activities such as reference service or the collection are included when the evaluative considerations for each are discussed.

TYPES OF EVALUATION

The most useful library evaluation assesses the degree to which a library staff meets the goals and objectives that it has set for the library, based on its understanding of the needs of its parent institution and its users; in other words how a library has performed within its own staff's expectations and aspirations as measured by pre-chosen performance indicators.

In recent years, evaluation in librarianship has moved toward judging effectiveness in terms of the success of users in securing what they are seeking. Performance evaluations always involve: 1) an indication of what constitutes effectiveness or success for the services, the person or the institution to be evaluated; 2) formulated criteria or objectives; 3) criteria translated into measures; 4) data collected using the measures that have been established; and 5) results compared with the definition of effectiveness.[3] Step 6 is synonymous with step 1 and marks the beginning of a new cycle.

Mary Cronin has suggested applying the following five step performance measurement process to an academic library program:

1) consider possible kinds of measurement based on available or easily collected data;
2) describe user expectations;
3) establish local standards of service;
4) formulate objectives; and, finally,
5) evaluate, or compare the outcome with established standards and user expectations.[4]

A description of a projected performance evaluation of an interlibrary loan service might look like this:

1) Possible kinds of measurement:
   number of requests from library users
   number of requests sent
   number of requests received
   % of requests successful
   time between date of request and date sent
   time between date sent and date received
   average turnaround time

2) User expectations based on interview with students, faculty and administrators:
   most (over 80%) of my requests should be filled within three weeks

3) Standards:
   past library performance has had a success rate of 85% with an average turnaround time of 24 days; turnaround at other local libraries has been between two and four weeks
   staff determines that an 85% success rate with two-three week turnaround time will be the standard for excellent interlibrary loan service

4) Objectives:
   long range: to improve access to materials not available in the library collection

   short-term: to fill 50% of interlibrary loan requests after two weeks, 85% after three weeks

   individual: to verify and send 60% of all borrowing requests after one week, and 90% after two weeks.

5) Evaluation:
   measure the % of requests filled within the specified time.[5]

The problem, of course, with undertaking an evaluation of the kind described above is that it requires generous commitments of time and staff. For this reason, and sometimes because of fear of the unknown, librarians often opt for less demanding forms of evaluation.

The most frequent type of assessments undertaken by college librarians are counting and comparing inputs. Inputs are such items as the level of support for the library, the number of questions asked of the reference staff, the number of users, number of materials circulated, size of staff, acquisition rates, hours of service, size of building and periodical holdings. These inputs can then be compared across institutions, or longitudinally for the same institution. Unfortunately, inputs do not correlate reliably with the effectiveness of a program.[6] Outputs, on the other hand, measure use. They look at such variables as circulation per capita or circulation per volume owned, reference questions per capita, and so on. In other words, they report services delivered and uses made of the library.

There are caveats to observe when using output measures:

1) Conditions can be manipulated to improve performance on a measure, but not necessarily result in better service.

2) There are no "good" or "bad" scores except as they compare with institutional or service goals.

3) Output measures reflect user success, not simply library performance.[7]

Unfortunately, even with output measures we are still likely to base judgments about quality and effectiveness only on quantitative results, some of which are immutable, no matter how diligent our attempts to influence and better them. In the absence of qualitative assessment, there is no information about whether students are using library books as doorstops and little insight into whether a reference question has really been addressed or whether the response reflects a librarian's misperception of what the question might have been.

Evaluations can be internal or external, administered by members of the institution or done by others. Some happen automatically. At budget time, for instance, committees review programs. An allocation, while reflecting many factors, probably indicates, at least to some extent, the satisfaction or attitudes of decision-makers about the library. Accrediting associations generally ask individual colleges to prepare a self-study that gives as complete a picture as possible of the institution before an accreditation visit. In this situation, the library is usually a component of the self-study and later is reviewed and inspected by the visiting team.

There are other occasions on which the library engages in self-study. Self-study should always precede or be the firm foundation for planning efforts so that the plan finally adopted is based upon a clear sense of a library's strengths and weaknesses. Self-study is often undertaken as a response to a specific, perceived problem, perhaps a space shortage, high staff turnover, or apparent user dissatisfaction. Evaluation is never simply "self," however. If it is to be of use, there must be input from every affected segment of the campus.

A number of aids are available to libraries wishing to undertake a full or partial self-study. The Association of Research Libraries Office of Management Studies has a useful package for mid-sized academic libraries called The Academic Library Development Program.[8] Librarians may also want to consult Herbert Kells' *Self Study Processes*.[9]

In recent years, many colleges and universities have embarked on regularly scheduled, periodic evaluations of their academic departments. Libraries, particularly in institutions where they are not considered departments, are generally and unfortunately excluded from the evaluation schedule. The appraisal of the library by an outside expert independent of any accrediting or professional group is usually associated with a particular project—automating services or constructing a new building—or is the result of unhappiness on the part of the library or the college community. Whatever the motivation for calling in an outside consultant, the appraisal should be viewed as an opportunity rather than a threat, and should use the consultant's presence to generate recommendations and suggestions that will enhance the library's position.

STANDARDS

After decades of struggling to devise standards and measures that could be used to evaluate college libraries, most librarians now acknowledge that absolute criteria, universally applicable, are not only nonexistent, but are probably undesirable. Standards, in fact, are not scientifically arrived at quantities or qualities describing excellence, but rather represent minimal norms, based on the statistical means of large numbers of libraries. How a library compares to those norms depends on tradition, wealth, the student body, library leadership, geography and all of those contextual and environmental elements we have been stressing throughout this book. Standards, misunderstood, can work to the detriment of a college library. An unenlightened administration, for instance, may find justification to reduce a library's budget because its collection or number of staff members exceeds standards. On the other hand, standards do function to establish a bottom point in a library's offerings to a community—building, staff, materials or services—beneath which libraries may not fall, lest they be judged inadequate in comparison with other institutions, or—perhaps worse—by an accrediting association. In some cases standards do provide the incentive for libraries to develop and grow.

The Middle States Association, one of the regional secondary and higher education accrediting units, has historically stressed a qualitative approach to standards and bases its evaluation on the articulated mission and goals of the college under accreditation review. The library section of the *Characteristics of Excellence in Higher Education; Standards for Accreditation* has six paragraphs devoted specifically to the college library. The first one reads:

> A library/learning center is of paramount importance to the educational program and to the research of students and faculty. The types and variety of books and other materials depend on the nature of the institution; therefore collection development must relate realistically to the institution's educational mission, goals, curricula, size, complexity and degree levels; and the diversity of its teaching, learning and research requirements. The centrality of a library/learning resource center to the educational mission of an institution deserves more than rhetoric and must be supported by more than lip service. An active and continuous program of bibliographical instruction is essential to realize this goal.[10]

The final section on bibliographic instruction has recently been appended and provides concrete evidence of the increasing importance ascribed to this activity.

A revised version of the Association of College and Research Libraries *Standards for College Libraries*, a copy of which appears as the Appendix to this book, was published in March of 1986. The decision to continue to provide quantitative standards was based on the results of a study undertaken by Ray Carpenter which revealed that a large percentage of college libraries fail to meet minimum standards in terms of collection size, staff or budget, and these libraries, in particular, find tangible numbers useful.[11]

ACRL *Standards* treat eight topics: objectives, collections, organization of materials, staff, services, facilities, administration and budget. For each a standard is given, and commentary appended. As described in earlier chapters, the standards about collections, staff and buildings include formulas and procedures for self-grading.

College administrators and accrediting agencies are wary of approaches that present rigid standards which can be manipulated, considering them simultaneously overly subjective and overly dogmatic. Directors should employ them sparingly and with caution.

Making Comparisons

Performance and output measures stress the importance of a library meeting its own goals. On the other hand, being informed about national, local and regional trends, and what peer institutions are doing provides ammunition for budget presentations, reports, grant proposals and other uses.

The U.S. Department of Education's National Center for Educational Statistics biennially collects data on libraries through its Integrated Postsecondary Education Data System (IPEDS) and organizes the data by level of highest degree awarded. The data for 1988 were published in August of 1990.[12]

Many helpful statistical reports are generated using the IPEDS data. The Center for Planning Information at Tufts University and the National Data Service for Higher Education in Boulder, Colorado both reformat the basic data into peer groupings. The non-ARL doctoral granting institutions, known as ACRL University Libraries, also issue statistical information every other year in non IPEDS years through ACRL. This compilation is modeled on the annual Association of Research Libraries survey.[13]

The Associated Colleges of the Midwest and the Great Lakes College Consortium produce annual compilations of library data for members of the groups, as do other regional associations in the Pacific Northwest and the South. A mix of public and private institutions are covered in each region.

PROCEDURES FOR EVALUATION

The procedures that have been developed for evaluating various aspects of college libraries are treated here under seven headings: 1) administration, 2) materials collections, 3) staff, 4) finance, 5) physical plant, 6) technical processes, and 7) public services, which is divided into reference, bibliographic instruction, and use.

Administration

Evaluating library administration means considering how well the library is meeting its purposes generally. It entails examining formal and informal governance and organizational characteristics and assessing the degree to which they enable the library to fulfill its purpose. For instance, does the reporting mechanism insure that the channels of communication between the library and the college administration and between the library and the college faculty are open and clear, without intervening "noise" caused by mixed signals? Is the person to whom the library director reports at an appropriate level within the institution and does this person command respect from peers and faculty? Does the director have an opportunity to participate in faculty committees, particularly those whose business touches the library closely? Does the library committee have a carefully defined role and a clear-cut statement of its duties? Is the library director given sufficient authority and responsibility for major matters of library policy?

In assessing the internal administration, it is important to determine whether the work has been organized in a way that insures maximum productivity. Does the director set and meet goals? Is the staff involved in decision-making? Are positions clearly defined? Is the library staffed with well-trained personnel? Are there appropriate levels of responsibility and authority? Is the structure amenable to change? Does the organization provide mechanisms for problem-solving? Is there frequent formal communication with staff?

Any evaluation of administration should also look at the informal mechanisms that play a role in how the library functions. Relationships, ritual events and other societal patterns have an important impact on the way things happen in the library. The "grapevine," for instance, is an important communication mechanism for transmitting attitudes and values. Examining its path, participants, and messages is one aspect of understanding organizational behavior.

Among the most exciting uses of automation has been the development of management information systems which permit administrators to work on the "what if" questions, those which utilize varying input data to test outcomes. What impact, for instance, will closing down a department library have on the available shelf space in the main library? Modeling of this sort requires large volumes of operational data. With the development of comprehensive models of the library, it is possible to manipulate variables, produce paper outputs of various scenarios and never have to disturb current operations.

Staff

ACRL *Standards* suggest that college libraries should have one professional librarians for each 500 FTE students up to 10,000 and that the support staff shall be no less than 65% of the total library staff. Quality of staff, however, is more difficult to measure, but is a far better predictor of library effectiveness.

Chapter 16 has described the ways in which employees should be evaluated. Performance appraisals based on pre-established objectives, rather than ones which consider traits, would seem to produce the most valuable results. The director's performance, too, should be regularly evaluated, both from above and below, as well as by classroom faculty. Peer assessment based on the perceptions of other library directors, either within the state or at similar institutions, should also be sought. Comprehensive reviews which relate the director's performance to library outcome, provide information that can be used to enhance effectiveness.

The lack of staff turnover, or an excess of it, the number and qualifications of applicants for positions, staff attainment of higher positions—either internally or in other workplaces—are all key indicators of the attractiveness of the library as a workplace and reflect the extent to which it is competitive with other institutions. If beginning salaries have not kept pace with comparable colleges, then recruitment will be more difficult. If the library is unable to offer faculty status or equivalent ranks, then it may be unable to offer quality in its library instruction programs. If sabbaticals are not part of an employment package, then scholars may be reluctant to join the staff. If the library cannot afford to hire staff members who possess advanced training or expertise in some aspect of college librarianship, then these specialties may remain unavailable in that library.

Finance

There are no absolute standards to apply in measuring the adequacy of a library's financial support, because the amount of money needed depends on the goals of the particular college and the extent and quality of service needed to support those goals. While placing a dollar value on the way a reference librarian shows a student how to use a certain major bibliographical tool is difficult, there have been recent attempts to determine the cost-effectiveness of various library services. Cost-effectiveness analyses consider the costs associated with particular levels of effectiveness. Cost-effectiveness can be determined by holding effectiveness goals constant and measuring costs against them to determine the most advisable level of expenditure. For instance, a reference department may consider that it performs adequately by answering 80% of the questions addressed to it. However, it may feel that its expenditures for that reference service are too high. In order to lower the cost, a decision is made to discontinue some of its reference materials because they receive little or no use. If the department's ability to respond to questions is unchanged, the library has improved its cost-effectiveness ratio while maintaining its desired level of service. Cost effectiveness determinations are far easier to make about single services than they are about the institution as a whole where cost effectiveness deals with the best allocation of resources.[14] The danger here is that reallocation may cause improvement in some services and deterioration in others.

Several formulas have been developed to measure the adequacy of the library budget. The simplest and in many ways the best for college library purposes is the ACRL standard that recommends that the library receive a minimum of 6% of the general and educational budget of the college.[15] It has been criticized as insufficient, inflexible, unrealistic for many, outdated, and simplistic; it is all of these things, but it still represents a bottom line number and therefore has merit. In some cases establishing a minimum percentage of the instructional budget may be more meaningful.

Some librarians have sought to place their allocations on a student per capita basis. The per capita library cost is simple and easy to understand, but it carries with it the danger that in times of falling enrollments the library may have serious financial reverses. Any budget based on enrollment must build in factors such as higher rates of support for honors and graduate students, as well as periodic review of the base ratio to control for the rising costs of materials and of living.

Formulas all have their weaknesses. In the last analysis the library budget will be determined by what the faculty think they must have in the way of library materials and what the library director and the administration regards as a rock bottom figure for processing and making these materials available for use.

Most commonly, in evaluating and justifying the library budget, college librarians keep careful records of expenditures from year to year, compare the growth over a period of years, and compare the library's progress against the financial progress

of other libraries of comparable size and programs.   New
programs, of course, can only be reported in terms of budget
estimates and anticipated benefits.

Physical Plant

In judging the building and equipment, consideration should
be given to the adequacy of book and seating capacity, how well
the arrangement of books and readers encourages the use of
library materials, how well the climate controls and building
maintenance program protect the collections, the space and
convenience of the staff working quarters, the comfort and
variety of furnishings, the flexibility of the building plan to allow
for rearrangement and expansion, and such important physical
conditions as good lighting, ventilation, and noise control.   In
addition, the state of the building, how well it is maintained and
the relative shabbiness of its interior decoration should be
examined.   If not already in effect, a plan for regularly
scheduled improvements and replacements should be adopted.

TECHNICAL PROCESSES

The procedures for ordering, cataloging, and classifying both
printed materials and nonprint media should be considered in
evaluating the library.   The evaluator must confirm that sound
management principles are being applied, that there is a
reasonable division between clerical and professional duties, that
users have adequate bibliographic access to microforms and
nonprint media, and that the various steps in the technical
processes are being carried out in an economical and efficient
manner.   Technical processes are more amenable to quantitative
measurement than are many other parts of the library.   It is
possible to evaluate, for instance, the efficiency of technical
services using time and cost factors.   The cost of purchasing an
item, cataloging it and preparing it for the shelf can be
determined.   In addition, how long it takes to do any one of

those processes is calculable. Data can be gathered by observation or by logs, and costs computed from invoices, overhead estimates and staff salaries. Comparisons can be made from employee to employee, or with like institutions, or by type of material and performance goals established.

Staff tenure is an important factor in the efficiency and economy of processing services. If staffing has remained relatively constant in size for a number of years, an increase in the number of titles cataloged may indicate improved conditions of work assignment and procedures or a reduced labor turnover in the staff. On the other hand, a decline in titles cataloged and classified may reveal the library's difficulty in retaining qualified staff at its present salary levels, or in motivating those who remain to work at a satisfactory pace.

Routine inspection of books on the shelves reveals whether staff is alert to those requiring mending, binding, or other preservation techniques. Journals in the current periodical area too are checked to determine if they are regularly collected and bound promptly. In binding, the question of quality is a primary concern, but speed in getting material back to the shelves after the volumes are returned from the bindery is also important.

EVALUATION OF REFERENCE SERVICE

Evaluation of reference services has had a checkered career. Librarians have traditionally collected input data about the reference department. They have counted the number of personnel, examined their duties, described their organization and staffing patterns, and their educational and experiential backgrounds. They have also counted and described the reference collection and assessed the quality of the materials.

Analysis of reference questions has focused on enumeration and classification. Reports have been made about the number of questions posed, and to a lesser extent, the number which have been answered correctly. Various categorizations of these questions have been applied, the most common of which is the one which describes the ease or difficulty of answering them. Time spent in finding an answer has usually played a role in how the categories are established. Some variation of a tripartite categorization such as Directional, Ready Reference, and Search has been employed to distinguish between types of questions. While of some use, the categorization is only as precise as those who share an understanding of its meaning. Dan, for instance, may classify a question about the former name of Namibia as a Search question, while Carol may consider it Ready Reference because she knows it to be South West Africa without ever having to consult a Historical Atlas.

Librarians have used four approaches to determine the quality of a reference transaction. They themselves have judged the process to be successful (self-reported); the patron has reported satisfaction (user feedback); proper reference procedures have been followed (peers or supervisors have judged it to be so); the information supplied is true (usually based on manufactured questions and objective testing). Each of these approaches has a corresponding problem: the librarian may be wrong; the patron may have low expectations and accept bad answers or reject good ones; a shortcut may lead to the best results; and test questions may not represent a true load.[16]

More recently, so-called unobtrusive methods have been employed to evaluate reference service. An unobtrusive study is one in which the object being studied is not aware of the researcher. True unobtrusive measures would be those in which there was no interaction between the researcher and those being studied. For instance, counting the wear on tile marks in a bathroom to determine the pattern of use would be genuinely unobtrusive. Unobtrusive studies of reference service have used manufactured questions, submitted in a way that permits researchers to be treated as "real" users with "real" questions. While not genuinely unobtrusive, these simulations have produced results that seem to suggest an answer accuracy rate of 50-60%. Libraries richer in reference material had somewhat better rates of response and accuracy.[17]

One important aspect of reference service evaluation that has recently been investigated is the availability of staff, or what is sometimes called the nuisance factor of how long a patron must wait for reference assistance.

EVALUATION OF THE COLLECTION

Library collections have been subjected to the most substantial evaluation over the years. When a library is called "good," people generally refer to the depth and breadth of its collections. But the measure of a collection's "goodness" is elusive and there is no agreement on how to judge its excellence. The traditional forms of collection assessment have been quantitative and qualitative. The newer measures have looked at collection use.

The *Standards for College Libraries* with regard to collections have already been described and appear in the Appendix. It should be emphasized, once again, that they are minimum requirements, rather than desirable or optimal levels. While number of volumes held does not indicate quality of a collection, some studies have found that there is a positive correlation between size of the library and quality of the institution.[18] Many librarians have found it useful to compare their holdings and their acquisition rates with peer institutions.

Another avenue to evaluating a collection is to have the collection assessed by an expert in the field—sometimes called the "impressionistic" approach. The expert can be an outside consultant or a member of the faculty. Choosing the latter has an added benefit of solid library support. People who are asked to use their expertise in assisting a respected institution to better itself are much more likely to remain committed to that institution. An additional benefit is that an expert can look at the totality of the collection, rather than make only an item-by-item assessment. The major drawback to this method is that scholars/experts are likely to have a bias that prevents an objective appraisal, and an in-house expert may have been responsible for building the collection in the first place.

Yet another method of evaluating a collection is to use lists or so-called standard bibliographies within a field. There are virtues and problems in this method, as well. In the absence of local expertise, these lists describe what is considered "best," and a library can assess its holdings against the "best." The bad news is that what is "best" for some is "useless" for others. However, there is no doubt that evaluation using bibliographies can help to identify existing gaps in the collection.

Computer-based systems provide libraries with information about collection use which was virtually unattainable manually. Information can be collected and tabulated about language, country of origin, publication date, subject (using classification), format, and type of materials being used in the library. Systems can be programmed to monitor, analyze, and project growth and to help plan for future collection development. Decisions about preservation, storage and weeding can then be reached less subjectively or intuitively. Computers also render the kind of evaluation that must be made for cooperative acquisitions and resource sharing relatively easy to accomplish.

USE AND USER STUDIES

College libraries have traditionally kept statistics of use which include home use of materials categorized by those loaned to students, those loaned to faculty and those loaned to others. In addition, reserve use, loans to carrels, and interlibrary loans and photocopies have been carefully tracked. Consistently maintained, reported and interpreted, these statistics—incomplete as they are—have some value. They represent the volume of business during a given year, and that volume can be compared with circulation of previous years, as well as with libraries elsewhere. Librarians must chose carefully those libraries with which they will be compared. In order for the comparison to be valid, the colleges must be similar in student enrollment and curriculum pattern, be about the same size and, most important, keep like statistics with common definitions of variables such as the length of circulation period and the types of users.

Circulation statistics are of limited use as a basis for evaluating a library. They are insufficiently detailed and, further, they do not measure in-house library use—particularly browsing, a frequent activity in the college library. Materials used within the library are probably similar in kind to those which are borrowed. Incorporating their numbers escalates use statistics many-fold. On the other hand, a definition of use which involved usefulness might negate the inclusion of many titles which are examined in-house but never borrowed.

Resource-sharing activities, particularly interlibrary loan and consortia arrangements, are evaluated both as a measure of the effectiveness of cooperation and as an indication of an individual college library's holdings. A library may assume that it should be meeting 85-90% of its interlibrary loan requests. Other interlibrary loan data available at most libraries can be used to evaluate fill rate, delivery speed, transactions per request (the number of sources contacted before an item is located), labor hours per request and total cost per request. In addition to efficiency, consortium membership can be judged from the perspective of savings resulting from non-purchase of materials covered by cooperative collection development agreements.

Computer-based systems also make possible, for the first time, an accurate detailed picture of library users and non-users and of the use made of discrete parts of the collection. The categories of patrons who are borrowing what types of materials is readily accessible through automated management information systems.

Quantitative studies of library use have identified three patterns which have appeared so frequently that they are now referred to as laws: scattering, decay, and inertia. All are manifestations of the law of diminishing returns and all are useful concepts in library evaluation.

Scattering refers to the use of periodical materials from title to title across a subject. Some materials are used more heavily than others and it is necessary to understand the variations in use of library materials in order to plan what needs to be available to users. Citation analysis, library usage records, and "best" lists have all been useful in determining scattering. S. C. Bradford counted the number of references to each periodical title carrying material about applied geophysics and the literature of automation. Through this method he identified and ranked the most productive periodicals. A diminishing number of references were contributed by successively less productive periodicals. This became known as "Bradford's Law of Scattering."[19] *Decay* is most easily understood as lessened use over time. Studies have consistently demonstrated that use declines with age,[20] although demand varies widely by subject. The final pattern has been referred to as *inertia*, and describes the decline in library use due to the relative effort required to utilize it. The greater the distance one is from library, for instance, the greater the effort required to use it. Considerations of "least effort" account for much of library use and non-use.

Use studies have also focused on weeding decisions, but thus far rules that have been developed for making determinations about retaining, storing, or discarding materials have either been simplistic (based on date of publication) and thereby relatively ineffective, or expensive to administer and therefore, while relatively effective, uneconomic. Overlap studies, not only of one library's holdings compared with those of another's, but also of indexing and abstracting services covering the literature in various areas, have also received attention.

User surveys, based on questionnaires or interviews which tap behavior in and attitudes towards the library are less frequently administered now than they were at one time. Their usefulness depends on the attitudes and cooperation of the students and faculty who choose to complete the questionnaire or agree to be interviewed. And their results are likely to be skewed by the population that consents to participate. Another limitation is that those being surveyed generally want to praise the library, rather than condemn it. As a result, librarians who take at face value the results of such a survey develop a false security which may be at odds with how the community really views the library. In spite of the limitations of questionnaires and interviews, the results can prove helpful in revealing the uses made of library materials, what materials students find most important in connection with their studies, what general reading they do in journals and new books, what success they have in finding material they need, and what suggestions they have for improving library service. It also affords a clue as to the satisfaction and dissatisfaction which students feel toward the conditions of study in the library, the problems they have in using the catalog, and the successes and failures of the reference department. A word of caution. Those planning to undertake a user survey should probably consult a specialist in survey design and data gathering techniques while preparing their instrument.

Studies of when—that is at what time, on which day, and in what month—libraries and/or their departments are used should help to determine at which hours to open or close the library, how many staff and at what level should be available, whether weekend hours are advisable and, if so, at which times on Saturday and/or Sunday to make the library available. Limitations imposed by current practice must be considered when study findings are presented. For instance, a college library that closes on Sunday morning cannot track use during those hours.

The Materials Availability Study

In the mid-1970s, Saracevic, Shaw and Kantor sought to identify the reasons why students seeking materials at the Sears Library at Case-Western University were successful less than 50% of the time.[21] In the process of analyzing data, they developed a sequential branching matrix that permitted them to

measure the library's effectiveness at a number of points along
the use continuum. Their study was limited to "known-item
searches," that is, where the material was sought by author and
title, rather than by subject. First, the researchers looked at
whether the library had acquired the item being sought. If it had
not acquired the book, nothing else mattered. Second, they
investigated whether the book being sought was in circulation.
If so, the hunt would cease. The third task, based on the
assumption that the book was "in," was to ascertain whether it
was properly shelved, that is, not stolen, out of order, or at the
bindery. The final step, if all the previous steps had been taken,
was to determine whether user error accounted for failure to
secure the material. At completion, the branching diagram
looked like this.

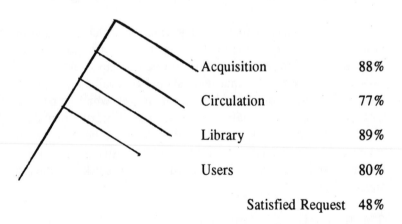

Acquisition	88%
Circulation	77%
Library	89%
Users	80%
Satisfied Request	48%

Figure 13: Outcomes of Requests for Books From a Library

The percentages represent the degree of success achieved by the user. In other words, 88% of the materials sought had been purchased by the library; 77% of those which had been acquired were in circulation; 89% of those which had been acquired and were not in circulation were in their proper place on the shelf; and 80% of those which had been acquired were not in circulation, were in their proper place on the shelf, and could not be located due to user error. In short, 48% of the initial user searches were successfully completed. Based on this information, the searchers decided to limit the loan period from a semester to four weeks and to study for impact of that action. When they examined user satisfaction two years later, they found a substantial increase in success (8%). Below is a comparison of the results of the two studies, the one taken in 1972, the other in 1974.

	1972 Semester Loan Policy	1974 Four-Week Policy
Acquisition	88%	91%
Circulation	77%	87%
Library	89%	86%
Users	80%	82%
Satisfaction Level	48%	56%

Figure 14

Measures of Performance for the Sears Library, Case Western Reserve University, From the Outcomes of Requests for Books During the Surveys in 1972 and 1974

The differences between the Acquisition, Library, and Users percentages from one study period to the next are not considered statistically significant, that is, they are probably due to chance. The 10% improvement in the circulation percentages, however, has probably been produced by intervention, that is, by changing the loan period. Based on their initial findings, the researchers attention should next turn to user error. They may decide to institute an orientation program, provide better signage or other library education measures.

This study has been presented in some detail, not to advocate shortened loan periods, or even a particular method of studying or evaluating library activity, but to illustrate the potentially beneficial effects of examining and assessing how and how well the library is being utilized.

LIBRARY INSTRUCTION

Many approaches to evaluating bibliographic instruction programs are being developed and tested, particularly as objectives and methods of instruction change. The objective of the evaluation will help to determine which of the following approaches is apt to produce the most useful information.

Library skills tests, locally developed or standardized ones, are often administered at the beginning of a BI program to develop data about baseline student knowledge, or at the end to determine the extent that instruction has been successful in familiarizing students with library services and procedures.

Performance measures have been utilized to determine the extent to which user behavior has been changed. Approaches to measuring performance have taken the form of simulated experiences, reports by students, and analyses by librarians of completed products, as well as by observation of behavior.

Another method of library instruction evaluation might include tapping student opinion and attitudes toward instruction. This can be done informally in conversation or through a formal survey. As mentioned above, survey research is more difficult than it appears. A hastily conceived, poorly constructed question instrument will produce inadequate or invalid information. Decisions have to be made as to whether to administer an open-ended or structured survey. And if the latter, whether to include only "Yes/No" questions or whether to develop a more sensitive attitude scale. The real dangers in evaluating library instruction are that in an attempt to prove the effectiveness of the service, in order to justify their work to administrators or funding agencies, librarians neglect the steps necessary to systematically test results.[22] Using ACRL's *Evaluating Bibliographic Instruction* will help bibliographic instruction librarians gather the information useful to evaluation.[23]

SUMMARY

Research into procedures, policies, personnel and other aspects of college library service has produced a variety of methods to evaluate and judge how we are doing and whether we are doing what we should be. Jane Robbins and Douglas Zweizig named their manual on library evaluation, *Are We There Yet?*[24] to indicate that evaluation should be a process of checking on a regular basis how much progress a library has made towards a stated goal. The importance of systematic evaluation cannot be underestimated. Nor, however, should instinct and educated guesswork. Experienced librarians develop a sixth sense about their institutions. Eyeballing a shelf of books often produces instantaneous knowledge about the degree to which particular information and a subject literature are being utilized. While intuition is never a substitute for formal evaluation, instinct can act as a warning signal and an indication that the time has arrived to initiate a more rigorous examination.

It may be, as Russell Shank contended, that human nature makes one inquisitive so that counting things and arraying the tally in various displays comes with the genes.[25] But data are not information. They must still be analyzed and interpreted and put to use.

NOTES AND SUGGESTED READINGS

Notes

1. R. M. Orr, "Measuring the Goodness of Library Services: A General Framework for Considering Quantitative Measures," *Journal of Documentation* 29 (September, 1973): 315-32; Michael Buckland, *Library Services in Theory and Context* (New York: Pergamon Press, 1983): 194-95.

2. F. W. Lancaster, *If You Want to Evaluate Your Library*. (Champaign, IL: University of Illinois Press, 1988); Nancy Van House, Beth Ward and Charles McClure, *Measuring Academic Library Performance* (Chicago: American Library Association, 1990).

3. Van House, *ibid*.

4. Mary J. Cronin, Performance Measurement for Public Services in Academic and Research Libraries, Occasional Paper #9 (Washington, DC: Office of Management Studies, Association of Research Libraries, February 1985).

5. *Ibid.*

6. *Ibid.*, 7

7. Van House.

8. Duane Webster, *Library Management Review and Analyses Program: A Handbook for Guiding Change and Improvement in Research Library Management* (Washington, DC: Association of Research Libraries, 1973); Grady Morein et al., *Planning Process for Small Academic Libraries: An Assisted Self-Study Manual* (Washington, DC: Association of Research Libraries, 1980); see also Grady Morein et al., "The

Academic Library Development Program," *College and Research Libraries* 38 (January 1977): 37-45.

9.   Herbert Kells, *Self Study Processes* (New York: MacMillan, 1988).

10.   Middle States Association of Colleges and Schools, Commission on Higher Education, *Characteristics of Excellence in Higher Education: Standards for Accreditation* (Philadelphia, PA: Middle States Association of Colleges and Schools, 1988): 34-35.

11.   Ray Carpenter, "A Comparative Analysis in Terms of the ACRL Standards," *College and Research Libraries* 42 (January 1981): 7-18.

12.   National Data Service for Higher Education, *1988 Academic Library Survey Response: Survey by U.S. Department of Education, National Center for Educational Statistics* (Boulder, CO: National Data Service for Higher Education, 1990). Vol. 1, Public Institutions. Vol. 2, Private Institutions.

13.   Tufts University, Higher Education Data Sharing Consortium [HEDS], *IPEDS* [Integrated Post-Secondary Education Data System] *Academic Libraries* 1990, Report 90-13 [Private Institutions] (Medford, MA: Tufts University, 1990); John Minter Associates, *Statistical Norms for Colleges and University Libraries*, 2d ed. Derived from U.S. Department of Education 1988 Survey of Academic Libraries (Boulder, CO: John Minter Associates, 1990); Association of College and Research Libraries, *ACRL University LIbrary Statistics 1988-89* (Chicago: Association of College and Research Libraries, 1990.)

14. Lancaster, 15.

15. Association of College and Research Libraries, "Standards for College Libraries," *College and Research Libraries* 47 (March 1986): 189-200.

16. Paul Kantor, "Quantitative Evaluation of the Reference Process," *RQ* 21 (Fall 1981): 43-52.

17. M. J. Myers and J. M. Jirjees, *The Accuracy of Telephone References/Information Services in Academic Libraries* (Metuchen, NJ: Scarecrow Press, 1983); C. R. McClure and P. Hernon, *Improving the Quality of Reference Service for Government Publications* (Chicago: American Library Association, 1983).

18. Lancaster, 20.

19. S. C. Bradford, *Documentation* (London: Crosby Lockwood, 1948).

20. H. H. Fussler and J. L. Simon. *Patterns in the Use of Books in Large Research Libraries* (Chicago: University of Chicago Press, 1969).

21. T. Saracevic, W. M. Shaw and Paul Kantor, "Causes and Dynamics of User Frustration in an Academic Library," *College and Research Libraries* 38 (January 1977): 7-18.

22. Mary George, "Instructional Services," in *Academic Libraries: Research Perspectives*, ed. Mary Jo Lynch and Arthur Young (Chicago: American Library Association, 1990): 120.

23. Association of College and Research Libraries, Bibliographic Instruction Section, *Evaluating Bibliographic Instruction: A Handbook* (Chicago: American Library Association, 1983).

24. Jane Robbins and Douglas Zweizig, *Are We There Yet? Evaluating Library Collections, Reference Services, Programs and Personnel* (Madison: School of Library and Information Studies, University of Wisconsin, 1988).

25. Russell Shank, in *Library Automation as a Source of Management Information*, ed. Wilfred Lancaster (Champaign, IL: Graduate School of Library and Information Science, University of Illinois, 1982): 2.

Suggested Readings

Association of College and Research Libraries, Bibliographic Instruction Section. *Evaluating Bibliographic Instruction: A Handbook*. Chicago: American Library Association, 1983.

Cronin, Mary J. *Performance Measurement for Public Services in Academic and Research Libraries*. Occasional Paper 9. Washington, DC: Office of management Studies, Association of Research Libraries, 1985.

Hall, Blaine H. *Collection Assessment Manual for College and University Libraries.* Phoenix: Oryx, 1985.

Hernon, Peter. *Statistics for Library Decision Making*. Norwood, NJ: Ablex, 1989.

Jackson, Gregory. "Evaluating Learning Technologies." *Journal of Higher Education* 61 (May/June 1990): 294-311.

Kantor, Paul B. *Objective Performance Measures for Academic and Research Libraries*. Washington, DC: Association of Research Libraries, 1984.

Lancaster, F. W. *If You Want to Evaluate Your Library....* Champaign, IL. University of Illinois, 1988.

Lynch, Mary Jo and Arthur Young. *Academic Libraries: Research Perspectives*. ACRL Publications in Librarianship, 47. Chicago: American Library Association, 1990.

McClure, Charles. *Information for Academic Library Decision Making*. Westport, CT: Greenwood Press, 1980.

Robbins, Jane and Douglas Zweizig. *Are We There Yet? Evaluating Library Collections, Reference Services, Programs and Personnel*. Madison, WI: School of Library and Information Studies, University of Wisconsin, 1988.

Van House, Nancy, Beth T. Weil and Charles McClure. *Measuring Academic Library Performance*. Chicago: American Library Association, 1990.

Young, Peter R. "U.S. Library Statistics." *Library Administration and Management*. 3 (Fall 1989): 170-175.

Appendix

Standards for college libraries, 1986

Prepared by the College Library Standards Committee
Jacquelyn M. Morris, Chair

The final version approved by the ACRL Board of Directors.

The Standards for College Libraries were first prepared by a committee of ACRL, approved in 1959, and revised in 1975. This new revision was prepared by ACRL's Ad Hoc College Library Standards Committee. Members are Jacquelyn M. Morris, University of the Pacific (chair); B. Anne Commerton, State University of New York at Oswego; Brian D. Rogers, Connecticut College; Louise S. Sherby, Columbia University; David B. Walch, California Polytechnic State University; and Barbara Williams-Jenkins, South Carolina State College.

Foreword

These Standards were approved as policy by the ACRL Board of Directors at the ALA Midwinter Meeting in Chicago on January 19, 1986. They supersede the 1985 draft Standards published in *C&RL News*, May 1985, and the 1975 Standards published in *C&RL News*, October 1975.

The Ad Hoc Committee was appointed in 1982 to examine the 1975 Standards with particular attention to the following areas:

a. Non-print collections and services;

b. Collections (Formula A), Staff (Formula B), and Budget (% of Education & General);

c. Networking and cooperative associations;

and to recommend revisions which would bring them up to date and make them more generally useful.

The Committee studied each standard in terms of the charge and reviewed several recent studies on the subject of Standards, including:

Larry Hardesty and Stella Bentley, *The Use and Effectiveness of the 1975 Standards for College Libraries: A Survey of College Library Directors* (1981).

Ray L. Carpenter, "College Libraries: A Comparative Analysis in Terms of the ACRL Standards," *College & Research Libraries* 42 (January 1981):7–18.

"An Evaluative Checklist for Reviewing a College Library Program, Based on the 1975 Standards for College Libraries," *C&RL News*, November 1979, pp. 305–16.

The Committee also published a call for comments on the 1975 Standards (*C&RL News*, December 1983) and held hearings at the 1984 ALA Midwinter Meeting and the 1985 ALA Annual Conference.

One of the primary issues with which the Committee has dealt is the effect of new technology on the Standards. While no one predicts the immediate demise of books as we know them, one cannot ignore the multiplicity of formats in which information appears. For example, will the emerging body of online reference tools eventually make it possible for libraries to provide comparable or improved service with smaller book collections?

Access to the major bibliographic utilities is another issue related to technology and libraries. In an information-rich society, does lack of access to these utilities have a detrimental effect on the scholarly programs college libraries are attempting to support? How should the Standards address this lack of concern?

A similar related issue centers on resource sharing and networking. Through access to the emerging "National Database" (defined as the totality of OCLC, RLIN, WLN, and LC) we have greatly increased our knowledge of other libraries' collections. Online identification and location of needed material has shortened the retrieval time. Electronic mail will have a similar impact on resource sharing. Since even the largest libraries find it difficult to collect comprehensively, resource sharing has become an increasingly common fact of life. The 1975 Standards placed a very high value on browsability and immediate access to materials, whereas resource sharing is somewhat contradictory to this concept. On the other hand, cooperative agreements allow for exposure and access to vastly more extensive resources than was hitherto possible.

The Committee discussed extensively the topic of performance measures. While the library directors surveyed and reported in the Hardesty-Bentley article stressed the need for performance measures in the College Library Standards, the Committee concluded that providing them *at this point* is beyond the scope of its charge. Obviously, however, this is a concept whose time has come: the ACRL Ad Hoc Committee on Performance Measures for Academic Libraries, chaired by Virginia Tiefel, has received a five-year appointment which gives some indication of the complexity of the task. The library profession should monitor and support the work of this ad hoc committee.

Some sentiment has been expressed for standards with less emphasis on quantitative measures, patterned after the more abstract "Standards for University Libraries" (*C&RL News*, April 1979, pp. 101–10). While there are certain advantages to standards written in this way, the vast majority of those expressing opinions to the Committee supported the quantitative measurements provided for in the College Library Standards. Most who expressed this view cited Carpenter's findings, noting that a very large percentage of college libraries fail to meet minimum standards in terms of collection size, staff size or budget. Consequently, prescribed goals continue to be regarded by librarians as an important component of the Standards.

While many statements have been modified in these Standards, certain important points should be noted. For example, while the 1975 Standards addressed collection size, they did not address serial subscriptions, on which it is not unusual now for a library to spend half or more of its annual materials budget. Each Standard has been reviewed in light of library technology, networking, and resource sharing, and audiovisual materials. The inclusion of these aspects of libraries has been addressed in Standard 2, Collections; Standard 3, Organization of Material; Standard 6, Facilities; and Standard 8, Budget.

Introduction to the standards

Libraries have long been considered an integral

and essential part of the educational programs offered by colleges. Their role has included collecting the records of civilization and documentation of scientific pursuit. An equally important role is to offer various programs to teach or assist users in the retrieval or interpretation of these records and documents. These information resources are essential for members of the higher education community to pursue their academic programs successfully. Total fulfillment of these roles is, however, an ideal goal which continues to be sought and is yet to be attained. Expectations as to the degree of success in achieving this goal vary from institution to institution, and it is this diversity of expectations that prompts the library profession to offer standards for college libraries.

The Standards seek to describe a realistic set of conditions which, if met, will provide a college library program of good quality. Every attempt has been made to synthesize and articulate the library profession's expertise and views of the factors contributing to the adequacy of a library's budget, resources, facilities, and staffing, and the effectiveness of its services, administration, and organization.

These Standards are intended to apply to libraries supporting academic programs at the bachelor's and master's degree levels. They may be applied to libraries at universities which grant a small number of doctoral degrees, say, fewer than ten per year. They are not designed for use in two-year colleges, larger universities, or independent professional schools.*

The eight sections of the 1975 College Library Standards have been retained, and include:

1. Objectives
2. Collections
3. Organization of Materials
4. Staff
5. Services
6. Facilities
7. Administration
8. Budget

Each standard is followed by commentary intended to amplify its intent and assist in its implementation.

Whenever appropriate, the terminology and definitions in the ANSI Z39.7 Standards published in 1983 have been used.

Standard 1:
Objectives

1 *The college library shall develop an explicit*

---

*Specifically these Standards address themselves to institutions defined by the Carnegie Commission on Higher Education as Liberal Arts Colleges I and II and Comprehensive Universities and Colleges I and II. See the revised edition of *A Classification of Institutions of Higher Education* Berkeley, Calif.: The Council, 1976.

statement of its objectives in accord with the goals and purposes of the college.

Commentary

The administration and faculty of every college have a responsibility to examine the educational program from time to time in light of the goals and purposes of the institution. Librarians share this responsibility by seeking ways to provide collections and services which support those goals and purposes. Successful fulfillment of this shared responsibility can best be attained when a clear and explicit statement of library objectives is prepared and promulgated so that all members of the college community can understand and evaluate the appropriateness and effectiveness of the library program.

1.1 The development of library objectives shall be the responsibility of the library staff, in consultation with members of the teaching faculty, administrative officers, and students.

Commentary

The articulation of library objectives is an obligation of the librarians, with the assistance of the support staff. In developing these objectives the library should seek in a formal or structured way the advice and guidance of its primary users, the faculty and students, and of the college administration, in particular those officers responsible for academic programs and policies.

1.2 The statement of library objectives shall be reviewed periodically and revised as necessary.

Commentary

In reviewing the objectives of the library, careful attention should be paid to ongoing advances in the theory and practice of librarianship. Similarly, changes occurring within the education program of the parent institution should be reflected in a timely way in the program of the library.

Standard 2:
The collections

2 The library's collections shall comprise all types of recorded information, including print materials in all formats, audiovisual materials, sound recordings, materials used with computers, graphics, and three-dimensional materials.

Commentary

Recorded knowledge and literary or artistic works appear in a wide range of formats. Books represent extended reports of scholarly investigation, compilations of findings, and summaries prepared for instructional purposes. The journal communicates more recent information and is particularly important to the science disciplines. Reports in machine-readable form are an even faster means of research communication. Government documents transmit information generated by or at the behest of official agencies, and newspapers record daily activities throughout the world.

Many kinds of communication take place primarily, or exclusively, through such media as films, slide-tapes, sound recordings, and videotapes. Microforms are used to compact many kinds of information for preservation and storage. Recorded information also exists in the form of manuscripts, archives, databases, and computer software packages. Each medium of communication transmits information in unique ways, and each tends to complement the others.

The inherent unity of recorded information and its importance to all academic departments of an institution require that most, if not all, of this information be selected, organized and made available for use by the library of that institution. In this way the institution's information resources can best be articulated and balanced for the benefit of all users.

2.1 The library shall provide as promptly as possible a high percentage of the materials needed by its users.

Commentary

While it is important that a library have in its collection the quantity of materials called for in Formula A, its resources ought to be augmented whenever appropriate with external collections and services. A library that meets part of its responsibilities in this way must ensure that such activities do not weaken a continuing commitment to develop its own holdings. There is no substitute for a strong, immediately accessible collection. Moreover, once a collection has attained the size called for by this formula, its usefulness will soon diminish if new materials are not acquired at an annual gross growth rate of from two to five percent. Libraries with collections which are significantly below the size recommended in Formula A should maintain the 5% growth rate until they can claim a grade of A (see Standard 2.2). Those that meet or exceed the criteria for a grade of A may find it unrealistic or unnecessary to sustain a 5% growth rate.

The proper development of a collection includes concern for quality as well as quantity. A collection may be said to have quality for its purposes only to the degree that it possesses a portion of the bibliography of each discipline taught, appropriate in quantity both to the level at which each is taught and to the number of students and faculty members who use it. While it is possible to have quantity without quality, it is not possible to have quality with quantity defined in relation to the characteristics of the institution. No easily applicable criteria have yet been developed, however, for measuring quality in library collections.

The best way to preserve or improve quality in a college library collection is to adhere to rigorous standards of discrimination in the selection of materials to be added, whether as purchases or gifts. The collection should contain a substantial portion of the titles listed in standard bibliographies for the curricular areas of the institution and for supporting general fields of knowledge. Subject lists for college libraries have been prepared by several learned associations, while general bibliographies such as *Books for College Libraries* are especially useful for identifying important retrospective titles. A majority of the appropriate, current publications reviewed in scholarly journals and in reviewing media such as *Choice* or *Library Journal* should be acquired. Careful attention should also be given to standard works of reference and to bibliographical tools which describe the broad range of information sources.

Institutional needs for periodical holdings vary so widely that a generally applicable formula cannot be used, but in general it is good practice for a library to own any title that is needed more than six times per year. Several good lists have been prepared of periodical titles appropriate or necessary for college collections. Katz's *Magazines for Libraries* describes 6,500 titles, of which approximately ten percent may be regarded as essential to a broad liberal arts program for undergraduates. To this estimate must be added as many titles as are deemed necessary by the teaching faculty and librarians to provide requisite depth and diversity of holdings. It may not be necessary to subscribe to certain less frequently used titles if they are available at another library nearby, or if needed articles may be quickly procured through a reliable delivery system or by electronic means.

The library collection should be continually evaluated against standard bibliographies and evolving institutional requirements for purposes both of adding new titles and identifying for withdrawal those titles which have outlived their usefulness. No title should be retained for which a clear purpose is not evident in terms of academic programs or extra-curricular enrichment.

Although the scope and content of the collection is ultimately the responsibility of the library staff, this responsibility can be best fulfilled by developing clear selection policies in cooperation with the teaching faculty. Moreover, the teaching faculty should be encouraged to participate in the selection of new titles for the collection.

2.2 The amount of print material to be provided by the library shall be determined by a formula (see Formula A) which takes into account the nature and extent of the academic program of the institution, its enrollment, and the size of the teaching faculty. Moreover, audiovisual holdings and annual resource sharing transactions should be added to this volume count in assessing the extent to which a library succeeds in making materials available to its users.

Commentary

A. PRINT RESOURCES

A strong core collection of print materials, augmented by specific allowences for enrollment, faculty size, and curricular offerings, is an indispensable requirement for the library of any college. The degree to which a library meets this requirement may be calculated with Formula A.

B. AUDIOVISUAL RESOURCES

The range, extent and configuration of nonprint resources and services in college libraries varies widely according to institutional needs and characteristics. Although audiovisual materials may constitute an important and sometimes sizable part of a library collection, it is neither appropriate nor possible to establish a generally applicable prescriptive formula for calculating the number of such items which should be available.

FORMULA A—

1. Basic collection	85,000 vols.
2. Allowance per FTE faculty member	100 vols.
3. Allowance per FTE student	15 vols.
4. Allowance per undergraduate major or minor field*	350 vols.
5. Allowance per master's field,when no higher degree is offered in the field*	6,000 vols.
6. Allowance per master's field, when a high degree is offered in the field*	3,000 vols.
7. Allowance per 6th year specialist degree field*	6,000 vols.
8. Allowance per doctoral field*	25,000 vols.

A "volume" is defined as a physical unit of a work which has been printed or otherwise reproduced, typewritten, or handwritten, contained in one binding or portfolio, hardbound or paperbound, which has been catalogued, classified, or otherwise prepared for use. Microform holdings should be converted to volume-equivalents, whether by actual count or by an averaging formula which considers each reel of microfilm, or ten pieces of any other microform, as one volume-equivalent.

*For example of List of Fields, see Gerald S. Malitz, *A Classification of Instructional Programs.* Washington, D.C.: National Center for Education Statistics, 1981.

Audiovisual holdings may be counted as bibliographic unit equivalents and this number should be added to that for print volumes and volume-equivalents in measuring a library's collection against Formula A. These materials include videocassettes, films, and videodisks (1 item = 1 BUE), sound recordings, filmstrips, loops, slide-tape sets, graphic materials including maps, and computer software packages (1 item = 1 BUE); and slides (50 slides = 1 BUE). If some or all of this material is housed in an administratively separate media center or audiovisual facility, it may be included in the grade determination if properly organized for use and readily accessible to the college community.

C. RESOURCE SHARING

The extent of resource sharing through formal cooperative arrangements among libraries should be recognized in any assessment of the ability of a library to supply its users with needed materials. Annual statistics of resource sharing should be added to print and audiovisual holdings for purposes of grade determination, as follows:

1. Number of books or other items borrowed through ILL channels or from other sources, including film and videocassette rental agencies.

2. Number of items borrowed from a nearby library with which a formal resource sharing arrangement is in effect.

D. DETERMINATION OF GRADE

The degree to which a library provides its users with materials is graded by comparing the combined total of holdings (volumes, volume-equivalents, and bibliographic unit equivalents) and resource sharing transactions with the results of the Formula A calculation. Libraries which can provide 90 to 100 percent of as many volumes as are called for in Section A, augmenting that volume count with figures from Section C, shall be graded A in terms of library resources. From 75 to 89 percent shall be graded B; 60 to 74 percent shall be graded C; and 50 to 59 percent shall be graded D.

Standard 3:
Organization of materials

3 *Library collections shall be organized by nationally approved conventions and arranged for efficient retrieval at time of need.*

Commentary
The acquisition of library materials comprises only part of the task of providing access to them. Collections should be indexed and arranged systematically to assure efficient identification and retrieval.

3.1 *There shall be a union catalog of the library's holdings that permits identification of items, re-gardless of format or location, by author, title, and subject.*

Commentary
The union catalog should be comprehensive and provide bibliographic access to materials in all formats owned by the library. This can best be accomplished through the development of a catalog with items entered in accord with established national or international bibliographical conventions, such as rules for entry, descriptive cataloging, filing, classification, and subject headings.

Opportunities of several kinds exist for the cooperative development of the library's catalog. These include the use of cataloging information produced by the Library of Congress and the various bibliographic utilities. It may also include the compilation by a number of libraries of a shared catalog. Catalogs should be subject to continual editing to keep them abreast of modern terminology and contemporary practice.

3.1.1 *The catalog shall be in a format that can be consulted by a number of users concurrently.*

Commentary
A public catalog in any format can satisfy this Standard if it is so arranged that the library's users normally encounter no delay in gaining access to it. While this is rarely a problem with the card catalog, the implementation of a microform, book, or online catalog requires that a sufficient number of copies (or terminals) be available to minimize delay in access at times of heavy demand.

3.1.2 *In addition to the union catalog there shall also be requisite subordinate files to provide bibliographic control and access to all library materials.*

Commentary
Proper organization of the collections requires the maintenance of a number of subordinate files, such as authority files and shelf lists, and of complementary catalogs, such as serial holdings records. Information contained in these files should also be available to library users. In addition, the content of library materials such as journals, documents, and microforms should be made accessible through indexes in printed or computer-based format.

3.2 *Library materials shall be arranged to provide maximum accessibility to all users. Certain categories of materials may be segregated by form for convenience.*

Commentary
Materials should be arranged so that related information can be easily consulted. Some materials such as rarities, manuscripts, or archives, may be segregated for purposes of security and preservation. Materials in exceptionally active use, reference works, and assigned readings, may be kept separate as reference and reserve collections to facilitate access to them. Audiovisual materials,

maps, and microforms, are examples of resources that may be awkward to integrate physically because of form and may need to be segregated from the main collection. Fragmentation of the collections should be avoided wherever possible, however, with the bulk of the collections shelved by subject in open stack areas to permit and encourage browsing.

3.3 Materials placed in storage facilities shall be readily accessible to users.

Commentary

Many libraries or groups of libraries have developed storage facilities for low-use materials such as sets or backruns of journals. These facilities may be situated on campus or in remote locations. The materials housed in these facilities should be easily identifiable and readily available for use in a timely fashion. If direct user access is not possible, a rapid retrieval system should be provided.

Standard 4:
Staff

4 The staff shall be of adequate size and quality to meet the library's needs for services, programs, and collection organization.

Commentary

The college library shall need a staff composed of qualified librarians, skilled support personnel, and part-time assistants to carry out its stated objectives.

4.1 Librarians, including the director, shall have a graduate degree from an ALA accredited program, shall be responsible for duties of a professional nature, and shall participate in library and other professional associations.

Commentary

The librarian has acquired through education in a graduate school of library and information science an understanding of the principles and theories of selection, acquisition, organization, interpretation and administration of library resources. It should be noted, that the MLS is regarded as a terminal professional degree by ALA and ACRL. Moreover, developments in computer and infor-

mation technology have had a major impact on librarianship requiring further that librarians be well informed in this developing area.

Librarians shall be assigned responsibilities which are appropriate to their education and experience and which encourage the ongoing development of professional competencies. Participation in library and other professional associations on and off campus is also necessary to further personal development.

4.2 Librarians shall be organized as a separate academic unit such as a department or a school. They shall administer themselves in accord with ACRL "Standards for Faculty Status for College and University Librarians" and institutional policies and guidelines.

Commentary

Librarians comprise the faculty of the library and should organize, administer, and govern themselves accordingly. The status, responsibilities, perquisites and governance of the library faculty shall be fully recognized and supported by the parent institution.

4.3 The number of librarians required shall be determined by a formula (see Formula B) and shall further take into consideration the goals and services of the library, programs, degrees offered, institutional enrollment, size of faculty and staff, and auxiliary programs.

Commentary

Formula B is based on enrollment, collection size, and growth of the collection. Other factors to be considered in determining staff size are services and programs, degrees offered, size of the faculty and staff, and auxiliary programs. Examples of services and programs include reference and information services, bibliographic instruction, computer-based services, collection development, and collection organization. In addition, auxiliary programs, *e.g.*, extension, community, and continuing education, as well as size and configuration of facilities and hours of service, are factors to be considered for staff size.

4.4 The support staff and part-time assistants

FORMULA B—

Enrollment, collection size and growth of collection determine the number of librarians required by the college and shall be computed as follows (to be calculated cumulatively):

For each 500, or fraction thereof, FTE students up to 10,000	1 librarian
For each 1,000, or fraction thereof, FTE students above 10,000	1 librarian
For each 100,000 volumes, or fraction thereof, in the collection	1 librarian
For each 5,000 volumes, or fraction thereof, added per year	1 librarian

Libraries which provide 90–100 percent of these formula requirements can, when they are supported by sufficient other staff members, consider themselves at the A level in terms of staff size; those that provide 75–89 percent of these requirements may rate themselves as B; those with 60–74 percent of requirements qualify for a C; and those with 50–59 percent of requirements warrant a D.

shall be assigned responsibilities appropriate to their qualifications, training, experience and capabilities. The support staff shall be no less than 65% of the total library staff, not including student assistants.

Commentary

Full-time and part-time support staff carry out a wide variety of paraprofessional, technical, and clerical responsibilities. A productive working relationship between the librarians and the support staff is an essential ingredient in the successful operation of the library. In addition student assistants provide meaningful support in accomplishing many library tasks.

4.5 Library policies and procedures concerning staff shall be in accord with institutional guidelines and sound personnel management.

Commentary

The staff represents one of the library's most important assets in support of the instructional program of the college. Its management must be based upon sound, contemporary practices and procedures consistent with the goals and purposes of the institution, including the following:

1. Recruitment methods should be based upon a careful definition of positions to be filled and objective evaluation of credentials and qualifications.

2. Written procedures should be developed in accordance with ACRL and institutional guidelines, and followed in matters of appointment, promotion, tenure, dismissal and appeal.

3. Every staff member should be informed in writing as to the scope of his/her responsibilities.

4. Rates of pay and benefits of library staff should be equivalent to other positions on campus requiring comparable backgrounds.

5. There should be a structured program for orientation and training of new staff members, and career development should be provided for all staff.

6. Supervisory staff should be selected on the basis of job knowledge, experience and human relations skills.

7. Procedures should be maintained for periodic review of staff performance and for recognition of achievement.

For references, the following documents may be consulted: "Guidelines and Procedures for the Screening and Appointment of Academic Librarians," *C&RL News*, September 1977, pp. 231–33; "Model Statement of Criteria and Procedures for Appointment, Promotion in Academic Rank, and Tenure for College and University Librarians," *C&RL News*, September and October 1973, pp. 192-95, 243–47; "Statement on the Terminal Professional Degree for Academic Librarians," Chicago: ACRL, 1975.

Standard 5:
Service

5 The library shall establish and maintain a range and quality of services that will promote the academic program of the institution and encourage optimal library use.

Commentary

The primary purpose of college library service is to promote and support the academic program of the parent institution. Services should be developed for and made available to all members of the academic community, including the handicapped and non-traditional students. The successful fulfillment of this purpose will require that librarians work closely with classroom faculty to gain from them a clear understanding of their educational

---

SUPPLEMENTARY STAFFING FACTORS TO BE CONSIDERED

Organizational and Institutional

The individual library's organization and institutional factors also influence its staffing needs. Additional factors to be considered are as follows:

Library	*Institutional*
Services and Programs	Degrees Offered
Size and Configuration	Size of Faculty and Staff
of Facilities	Auxiliary Programs
Hours of Service	
Examples of Services and Programs	*Examples of Institutional Factors*
Reference and Information	Undergraduate Programs
Bibliographic Instruction	Graduate Programs
Computer Based Services	Research
Collection Development	Community
Collection Organization	Continuing Education
Archives	
Audiovisual Services	

objectives and teaching methods and to communicate to them an understanding of the services and resources which the library can offer. While research skills and ease of access to materials will both serve to encourage library use, the primary motivation for students to use the library originates with the instructional methods used in the classroom. Thus, close cooperation between librarians and classroom instructors is essential. Such cooperation must be a planned and structured activity and requires that librarians participate in the academic planning councils of the institution. They should assist teaching faculty in appraising the actual and potential library resources available, work closely with them in developing library services to support their instructional activities, and keep them informed of library capabilities.

5.1 *The library shall provide information and instruction to the user through a variety of techniques to meet differing needs. These shall include, but not be limited to, a variety of professional reference services, and bibliographic instruction programs designed to teach users how to take full advantage of the resources available to them.*

Commentary

A fundamental responsibility of a college library is to provide instruction in the most effective and efficient use of its materials. Bibliographic instruction and orientation may be given at many levels of sophistication and may use a variety of methods and materials, including course-related instruction, separate courses (with or without credit), and group or individualized instruction.

Of equal importance is traditional reference service wherein individual users are guided by librarians in their appraisal of the range and extent of the library resources available to them for learning and research. Professional services are optimally available all hours the library is open. Use patterns should be studied to determine those times when the absence of professional assistance would be least detrimental. The third major form of information service is the delivery of information itself. Although obviously inappropriate in the case of student searches, which are purposeful segments of classroom assignments, the actual delivery of information—as distinct from guidance to it—is a reasonable library service in almost all other conceivable situations.

Many of the services suggested in this commentary can be provided or enhanced by access to computerized forms of information retrieval. In fact many information sources are available only in computerized format, and every effort should be made to provide access to them. Services may be provided in person or by other measures such as videocassette, computer slide tape, or other appropriately prepared programs.

5.2 *Library materials of all types and formats that can be used outside the library shall be circu-*

lated to qualified users under equitable policies without jeopardizing their preservation or availability to others.

Commentary

Circulation of library materials should be determined by local conditions which will include size of the collections, the number of copies, and the extent of the user community. Every effort should be made to circulate materials of all formats that can be used outside the library without undue risk to their preservation. Circulation should be for as long a period as is reasonable without jeopardizing access to materials by other qualified users. This overall goal may prompt some institutions to establish variant or unique loan periods for different titles or classes of titles. Whatever loan policy is used, however, it should be equitably and uniformly administered to all qualified categories of users. The accessibility of materials can also be extended through provision of inexpensive means of photocopying within the laws regarding copyright.

5.2.1 *The quality of the collections shall be enhanced through the use of interlibrary loan and other cooperative agreements.*

Commentary

Local resources should be extended through reciprocal agreements for interlibrary loan according to the ALA codes. Access to materials should be by the most efficient and rapid method possible, incorporating such means as delivery services and electronic mail in addition to, or in place of, traditional forms of delivery. First consideration must always go to the primary users, but strong consideration should be given to fostering the sharing of resources.

5.2.2 *Cooperative programs, other than traditional interlibrary loan, shall be encouraged for the purpose of extending and increasing services and resources.*

Commentary

The rapid growth of information sources, the availability of a myriad of automation services, and the development of other technologies such as laser beam, videodiscs, microcomputer systems, etc., make new demands on budgets. Cooperation with other institutions, and particularly with multi-type library organizations, often becomes a necessity. It must be recognized that this does not only involve receiving but demands a willingness to give or share on the part of each library. This may mean a commitment of time, money, and personnel, but it is necessary if it is the only way to provide up-to-date services to users. Careful weighing of costs and benefits must be undertaken before such agreements are put into effect.

5.3 *The hours of access to the library shall be consistent with reasonable demand.*

Commentary

The number of hours per week that library services should be available will vary, depending upon such factors as whether the college is in an urban or rural setting, teaching methods used, conditions in the dormitories, and whether the student body is primarily resident or commuting. In any case, library scheduling should be responsive to reasonable local need. In some institutions users may need access to study facilities and to the collections, in whole or in part, during more hours of the week than they require the personal services of librarians. However, during the normal hours of operation the users deserve competent, professional service. The high value of the library's collections, associated materials, and equipment, etc., dictates that a responsible individual be in control at all times. The public's need for access to librarians may range upward to one hundred hours per week, whereas around-the-clock access to the library's collection and/or facilities may in some cases be warranted.

5.4 *Where academic programs are offered at off-campus sites, library services shall be provided in accord with ACRL's "Guidelines for Extended Campus Library Services."*

Commentary
Special library problems exist for colleges that provide off-campus instructional programs. Students in such programs must be provided with library services in accord with ACRL's "Guidelines for Extended Campus Library Services." These guidelines suggest that such services be financed on a regular basis, that a librarian be specifically charged with the delivery of such services, that the library implications of such programs be considered before program approval, and that courses so taught encourage library use. Services should be designed to meet the different information and bibliographic needs of these users.

Standard 6:
Facilities

6 *The library building shall provide secure and adequate housing for its collections, and ample well-planned space for users and staff and for the provision of services and programs.*

Commentary
Successful library service presupposes an adequate library building. Although the type of building will depend upon the character and purposes of the institution, it should in all cases be functional, providing secure facilities for accommodating the

---

FORMULA C—

The size of the college library building shall be calculated on the basis of a formula which takes into consideration the size of the student body, the size of the staff and its space requirements, and the number of volumes in the collections. To the result of this calculation must be added such space as may be required to house and service nonprint materials and microforms, to provide bibliographic instruction to groups, and to accommodate equipment and services associated with various forms of library technology.

a. *Space for users.* The seating requirement for the library of a college where less than fifty percent of the FTE enrollment resides on campus shall be one for each five students. That for the library of a typical residential college shall be one for each four FTE students. Each study station shall be assumed to require 25 to 35 square feet of floor space, depending upon its function.

b. *Space for books.* The space allocated for books shall be adequate to accommodate a convenient and orderly distribution of the collection according to the classification system(s) in use, and should include space for growth. Gross space requirements may be estimated according to the following formula.

	Square Feet/Volume
For the first 150,000 volumes	0.10
For the next 150,000 volumes	0.09
For the next 300,000 volumes	0.08
For holdings above 600,000 volumes	0.07

c. *Space for staff.* Space required for staff offices, service and work areas, catalogs, files, and equipment, shall be approximately one-eighth of the sum of the space needed for books and users as calculated under a) and b) above.

This formula indicates the net assignable area required by a library if it is to fulfill its mission with maximum effectiveness. "Net assignable area" is the sum of all areas (measured in square feet) on all floors of a building, assignable to, or useful for, library functions or purposes. (For an explanation of this definition see *The Measurement and Comparison of Physical Facilities for Libraries*, American Library Association, 1970.)

Libraries which provide 90 to 100% of the net assignable area called for by the formula shall be graded A in terms of space; 75–89% shall be graded B; 60–74% shall be graded C; and 50–59% shall be graded D.

---

library's resources, sufficient space for their administration and maintenance, and comfortable reading and study areas for users. A new library building should represent a coordinated planning effort involving the library director and staff, the college administration, and the architect, with the director responsible for the preparation of the building program.

The needs of handicapped persons should receive special attention and should be provided for in compliance with the Architectural Barriers Act of 1968 (Public Law 90-480) and the Rehabilitation Act of 1973, Section 504 (Public Law 93-516) and their amendments.

Particular consideration must be given to any present or future requirements for equipment associated with automated systems or other applications of library technology. Among these might be provision for new wiring, cabling, special climate control and maximum flexibility in the use of space. Consideration should also be given to load-bearing requirements for compact shelving and the housing of mixed formats including microforms.

6.1 *The size of the library building shall be determined by a formula (see Formula C) which takes into account the enrollment of the college, the extent and nature of its collections, and the size of its staff.*

6.2 *In designing or managing a library building, the functionality of floor plan and the use of space shall be the paramount concern.*

Commentary
The quality of a building is measured by such characteristics as the utility and comfort of its study and office areas, the design and durability of its furniture and equipment, the functional interrelationships of its service and work areas, and the ease and economy with which it can be operated and used.

6.3 *Except in certain circumstances, the college library's collections and services shall be administered within a single structure.*

Commentary
Decentralized library facilities in a college have some virtues, and they present some difficulties. Primary among their virtues is their convenience to the offices or laboratories of some members of the teaching faculty. Primary among their weaknesses is the resulting fragmentation of the unity of knowledge, the relative isolation of a branch library from most users, potential problems of staffing and security, and the cost of maintaining certain duplicative services or functions. When decentralized library facilities are being considered, these costs and benefits must be carefully compared. In general, experience has shown that decentralized library facilities may not be in the best academic or economic interest of a college.

Standard 7:
Administration

Matters pertaining to college library administration are treated in the several other Standards. Matters of personnel administration, for example, are discussed under Standard 4, and fiscal administration under Standard 8. Some important aspects of library management, however, must be considered apart from the other Standards.

7 *The college library shall be administered in a manner which permits and encourages the fullest and most effective use of available library resources.*

Commentary
The function of a library administrator is to direct and coordinate the components of the library—its staff, services, collections, buildings and external relations—so that each contributes effectively and imaginatively to the mission of the library.

7.1 *The statutory or legal foundation for the library's activities shall be recognized in writing.*

Commentary
In order for the library to function effectively, there must first be an articulated understanding within the college as to the statutory or legal basis under which the library operates. This may be a college bylaw, a trustee minute, or a public law which shows the responsibility and flow of authority under which the library is empowered to act.

7.2 *The library director shall be an officer of the college and shall report to the president or the chief academic officer of the institution.*

Commentary
For the closest coordination of library activities with the instructional program, the library director should report either to the president or the chief officer in charge of the academic affairs of the institution.

7.2.1 *The responsibilities and authority of the library director and procedures for appointment shall be defined in writing.*

Commentary
There should be a document defining the responsibility and authority vested in the office of the library director. This document may also be statutorily based and should spell out, in addition to the scope and nature of the director's duties and powers, the procedures for appointment.

7.3 *There shall be a standing advisory committee comprised of students and members of the teaching faculty which shall serve as a channel of formal communication between the library and its user community.*

Commentary
This committee—of which the library director

should be an ex officio member—should be used to convey both an awareness to the library of its users' concerns, perceptions and needs, and an understanding to users of the library's objectives and capabilities. The charge to the committee should be specific and in writing.

7.4 *The library shall maintain written policies and procedures manuals covering internal library governance and operational activities.*

Commentary
Written policies and procedures manuals are required for good management, uniformity, and consistency of action. They also aid in training staff and contribute to public understanding.

7.4.1. *The library shall maintain a systematic and continuous program for evaluating its performance, for informing the community of its accomplishments, and for identifying needed improvements.*

Commentary
The library director, in conjunction with the staff, should develop a program for evaluating the library's performance. Objectives developed in accordance with the goals of the institution should play a major part in this evaluation program. Statistics should be maintained for use in reports, to demonstrate trends, and in performance evaluation. In addition, the library director and staff members should seek the assistance of its standing library advisory committee and other representatives of the community it serves.

7.5 *The library shall be administered in accord with the spirit of the ALA "Library Bill of Rights."*

Commentary
College libraries should be impervious to the pressures or efforts of any special interest groups or individuals to shape their collections and services. This principle, first postulated by the American Library Association in 1939 as the "Library Bill of Rights," (amended 1948, 1961, 1967 and 1980 by the ALA Council) should govern the administration of every college library and be given the full protection of the parent institution.

Standard 8:
Budget

8 *The library director shall have the responsibility for preparing, defending, and administering the library budget in accord with agreed upon objectives.*

Commentary
The library budget is a function of program planning and defines the library's objectives in fiscal terms. The objectives formulated under Standard 1 should constitute the base upon which the library's budget is developed.

8.1 *The library's appropriation shall be six percent of the total institutional budget for educa-*tional and general purposes.

Commentary
The degree to which the college is able to fund the library in accord with institutional objectives is reflected in the relationship of the library appropriation to the total educational and general budget of the college. It is recommended that library budgets, exclusive of capital costs and the costs of physical maintenance, not fall below six percent of the college's total educational and general expenditures if it is to sustain the range of library programs required by the institution and meet appropriate institutional objectives. This percentage should be greater if the library is attempting to overcome past deficiencies, or to meet the needs of new academic programs. The 6% figure is intended to include support for separately established professional libraries, providing the budget for those schools is incorporated into that of the University.

Factors which should be considered in formulating a library's budget requirements are the following:

1. The scope, nature and level of the college curriculum;

2. Instructional methods used, especially as they relate to independent study;

3. The adequacy of existing collections and the publishing rate in fields pertinent to the curriculum;

4. The size, or anticipated size, of the student body and teaching faculty;

5. The adequacy and availability of other library resources;

6. The range of services offered by the library, for example, the number of service points maintained, the number of hours per week that service is provided, the level of bibliographic instruction, online services, etc.;

7. The extent of automation of operations and services, with attendant costs;

8. The extent to which the library already meets the College Library Standards.

8.1.1 *The library's appropriation shall be augmented above the six percent level depending upon the extent to which it bears responsibility for acquiring, processing, and servicing audiovisual materials and microcomputer resources.*

Commentary
It is difficult for an academic library that has not traditionally been purchasing microcomputer and audiovisual materials to accommodate such purchases without some budgetary increase. The level of expenditure depends upon whether or not the institution has an audiovisual center separate from the library that acquires and maintains both audiovisual materials and hardware as well as a computer center that absorbs all costs related to microcomputer resources, even those included in the library.

8.2 *The library director shall have sole authority to apportion funds and initiate expenditures within the library budget and in accord with institutional policy.*

Commentary

Procedures for the preparation and defense of budget estimates, policies on budget approval, and regulation concerning accounting and expenditures vary from one institution to another. The library director must know and conform to local procedure. Sound practices of planning and control require that the director have sole responsibility and authority for allocation—and within college policy, the reallocation—of the library budget and the initiation of expenditures against it. Depending upon local factors, between 35% and 45% of the library's budget is normally allocated to acquisition of resources, and between 50% and 60% is expended for personnel.

8.3 *The library shall maintain internal accounts for approving its invoices for payment, monitoring its encumbrances, and evaluating the flow of its expenditures.*

Commentary

Periodic reports are necessary and provide an accurate account of the funds allocated to the library. They should be current and made accessible for fiscal accountability.

Other works cited

American Library Association, Ad Hoc Committee on the Physical Facilities of Libraries. *Measurement and Comparison of Physical Facilities for Libraries.* Chicago: ALA, 1970.

"[ACRL] Guidelines and Procedures for the Screening and Appointment of Academic Librarians." *C&RL News,* September 1977, pp. 231–33.

"[ACRL] Guidelines for Extended Campus Library Services." *C&RL News,* March 1982, pp. 86–88.

"[ACRL] Model Statement of Criteria and Procedures for Appointment, Promotion in Academic Rank, and Tenure for College and University Librarians." *C&RL News,* September and October 1973, pp. 192–95, 243–47.

"[ACRL] Standards for Faculty Status for College and University Librarians." *C&RL News,* May 1974, pp. 112-13.

"[ACRL] Statement on the Terminal Professional Degree for Academic Librarians." Chicago: ALA/ACRL, 1975.

"Library Bill of Rights" (ALA Policy Manual, Section 53.1). In the *ALA Handbook of Organization 1984/85.* Chicago: ALA, 1984, pp. 217–18.

Library Education and Personnel Utilization: A Statement of Policy. Adopted by ALA Council. Chicago: ALA/OLPR, 1970.

[RASD/IFLA] *Interlibrary Loan Codes, 1980; International Lending Principles and Guidelines 1978.* Chicago: ALA, 1982.

INDEX

593

ABOUT THE AUTHORS

CAROLINE M. COUGHLIN (A.B., Mercy College; M.Ln., Emory University; Ph.D., Rutgers University) is the Director of the Library and Associate Professor of Research and Bibliography at Drew University, Madison, New Jersey. She has taught at the library schools of Emory University, Rutgers University, the University of Alabama, and Simmons College. Dr. Coughlin is active in national and regional library associations and has been elected Member-at-Large, ALA Council; Director (for Associate Members), Center for Research Libraries Board; and President, College and University Section, New Jersey Library Association. In 1988 she was named a Senior Fellow, Graduate School of Library and Information Science, the University of California at Los Angeles. She regularly serves on accreditation visiting teams for the Middle States Association, on evaluation panels judging federal grant applications, and as a consultant in human resources management. She has published several articles in professional journals and edited a book of readings, Recurring Library Issues (Scarecrow, 1979).

ALICE GERTZOG is a graduate of Antioch College. She earned her MLS from Catholic University of Washington and Ph.D. from Rutgers University. Dr. Gertzog has been a librarian at the University of North Carolina, Yale University, and New Haven College. In addition, she has worked in special and public libraries, has been a library consultant, and has taught at the Rutgers University School of Communication, Information, and Library Studies. Her Case Studies in College Library Administration (Scarecrow, 1992) was designed to be used in conjunction with this present volume.